HIDDEN H
Historical A
of the Overseas Chinese

Compiled and Edited by
Priscilla Wegars

Baywood Monographs in Archaeology Series
Series Editor: Robert L. Schuyler

Baywood Publishing Company, Inc.
AMITYVILLE, NEW YORK

Library of Congress Catalog Card Number: 91-37295
ISBN: 0-89503-091-8 (Paper)
ISBN: 0-89503-095-0 (Cloth)

Library of Congress Cataloging-in-Publication Data

Hidden heritage : historical archaeology of the overseas Chinese /
    compiled and edited by Priscilla Wegars.
         p.   cm. – – (Baywood monographs in archaeology series)
    Includes bibliographical references and index.
    ISBN 0-89503-095-0 (Cloth). – – ISBN 0-89503-091-8 (Paper)
    1. Chinese Americans– –Antiquities. 2. Chinese Americans–
–Industries. 3. Chinese– –New Zealand– –Antiquities. I. Wegars,
Priscilla. II. Series.
E184.C5H54 1993
973'.04951– –dc20   91-37295
                                               CIP

Acknowledgments

I would like to thank people who have helped, directly or indirectly, in the preparation of this volume. First of all, Roderick ("Rick") Sprague, Director, Alfred W. Bowers Laboratory of Anthropology, University of Idaho, has been a staunch supporter of the Asian American Comparative Collection (AACC) since its beginning. He is particularly valued for his ability to tolerate the AACC's precarious financial condition. Sharon Pettichord's unique contributions to a lively office setting are worthy of mention, as is Mary Butler's cheerful willingness to photocopy yet another manuscript. Thanks also to Jing S. Liu and Cong Zhang for providing translations of Chinese characters and transliterations into Pinyin romanization where these were not furnished by the individual authors, and to Michal Pierce for assistance with the index. Special thanks to all concerned for their cooperation in this endeavor.

Jerry Wylie made the initial suggestion that these papers be made into a book. The late Norman Cohen, as President of Baywood Publishing Company, convinced me to proceed, and his successor, Stuart Cohen, saw the project to completion; their confidence and encouragement was and is very much appreciated. The final product benefitted greatly from helpful suggestions provided by the anonymous reviewers, and by "voices of experience" Robert L. Schuyler and Roberta S. Greenwood. Thanks also to Judith Liu, Ruthanne Lum McCunn, and Judy Yung for their comments on the appropriateness of the chosen title. I am very grateful to Paula Cohen and Bobbi Olszewski of S. L. Edco for their valuable contributions during production, and to Terry Abraham for his moral support. Finally, publication was assisted by a much appreciated grant from the University of Idaho's John Calhoun Smith Memorial Fund.

P. Wegars

Chapter 1

I am pleased to acknowledge the financial support of the Lounsbery Fund for Predoctoral Research in Anthropology of the American Museum of Natural History; the John Calhoun Smith Memorial Fund of the University of Idaho; the Department of American Civilization, University of Pennsylvania; and the Alfred

W. Bowers Laboratory of Anthropology, University of Idaho. Robert Spencer, Clearwater County Historical Society, provided invaluable support in working with the various documents and in sharing his vast knowledge of the local history. I also want to thank Julia Longenecker, Roderick Sprague, and Priscilla Wegars for their assistance with this study.

D. C. Stapp

Chapter 2

Preparation of this manuscript could never have been completed without the support and assistance from my wife Carla. Carla completed much of the typing, editing, and formatting of the draft and final documents. She was also understanding of the many weekends and evenings spent in preparing the manuscript.

Steve Wright's efforts in completing several of the illustrations are greatly appreciated.

I also would like to thank Priscilla Wegars for her continuing enthusiasm and commitment to the study of Chinese archaeology. Her longstanding support of the management of those cultural resources along the Lower Salmon River eventually led to the development of this chapter.

D. A. Sisson

Chapter 3

Without the support, commitment, and patience of Jerry Wylie and Priscilla Wegars, I may have never had the opportunity to write "Idaho's Chinese Mountain Gardens." Cheryl Helmers, who graciously shared information she had gathered through years of research, deserves a special thanks.

Thanks go to Ruthanne Lum McCunn, Neville Ritchie, Richard Thomas Wright, and David Sisson for their time, personal interests, and valuable perspectives. My friends and artists Colleen LeClair and James A. Amell provided talent for the sketches used in this and an earlier version of this paper respectively. Herb McDowell, long-time resident of Warren, donated valuable historic photos and information.

To the late Harry Vaux of Warren, who shared imported beer and rare information on the Warren Chinese with a motley group of archaeologists, we'll miss you. And thanks to a very special couple, Tim and Ruth Williams. Ruth filled (and continues to do so) our spirits with humor and love and our stomachs with the "best dern sourdough pancakes in the Salmon River Mountains." Tim, an old miner with a heart of gold, an intimate friend of the last Chinese residents of "Warrens," contributed significantly to helping "give the Chinese their deserving place in Idaho history."

To all people of the Warren Mining District (living and gone): We've spent countless hours gathered on a front porch, huddled around a wood stove, or leaning against a horse corral, sharing and passing on the legends and legacies of our unique Salmon River mountain heritage. Thank you for sharing your knowledge and experiences, and may our future generations pass on the legacy.

A very special loving thanks to my wife Judy who spent countless hours helping me in the field and on the research for this manuscript. Also, I extend loving thanks to my mother, father, sister, brother, friends, and all other Forest volunteers who directly or indirectly contributed to "Idaho's Chinese Mountain Gardens."

J. M. Fee

Chapter 4

The archaeological excavations mentioned in this chapter were supported by the National Endowment for the Humanities; the National Geographic Society; the John Calhoun Smith Memorial Fund of the University of Idaho; and the Alfred W. Bowers Laboratory of Anthropology, University of Idaho. We also thank John Miller, Karl Roenke, Robert Schuyler, Ralph Space, Bob Spencer, Roderick Sprague, and Priscilla Wegars for their assistance and support.

J. G. Longenecker and D. C. Stapp

Chapter 5

We appreciate the Department of Community and Human Development, City of El Paso, for their support. Special mention is given to Henry Neil, Deborah G. Hamlyn, Craig Thompson, and Gordon Cook. Their patience and commitment to the projects were unwavering. The opportunity to direct these projects derived from the support and encouragement of a number of scholars. Special thanks are given to Fred Plog, Steadman Upham, and David Batcho. Roberta Greenwood, a recognized leader in the field of overseas Chinese archaeology, freely gave her time and advice as consultant to the El Paso projects. Finally, the crew chiefs, field excavators, lab personnel, and other staff who worked on the projects, through summer heat and winter snow, are appreciated.

E. Staski

Chapter 6

We would like to thank Dr. Sucheng Chan (University of California, Santa Cruz), Ms. Teresa Chow, Dr. Liu Yu-zun (Asian American Studies Center, University of California, Los Angeles), Ms. Wei-chi Poon (Head Librarian, Asian American Studies Library, University of California, Berkeley), and Mrs. Annie Wong (Center for Chinese Study, University of California, Berkeley), for suggestions and comments about these records and translation problems. Jane Allen (Bishop Museum, Honolulu, Hawaii) provided housing in the Berkeley area during the translation period, which was greatly appreciated. We also are grateful for the research suggestions and editorial assistance of Dr. Peter D. Schulz and Betty

Rivers (California Department of Parks and Recreation). Dr. Glenn Farris and Jeanette Schulz (California Department of Parks and Recreation), and Susan Harless (The High Desert Museum, Bend, Oregon), brought information about other collections of Chinese business records to our attention. Communications with Paul G. Chace, Jay Frierman, Roberta S. Greenwood, Dr. Karen Ito, Chuck Hibbs, John M. Liu, Harvey Steele, Alison Stenger, and Priscilla Wegars have been sources of encouragement and constructive comments on various aspects of work reported here.

This research has been discussed previously at the Third Annual Ethnology at Home Conference, California State University, Sacramento, November 5, 1983; The Society for California Archaeology Annual Meeting, Salinas, March 31, 1984; and the Society for Historical Archaeology Annual Meeting, Sacramento, January 9, 1986.

R. A. Sando and D. L. Felton

Chapter 7

Thanks to Priscilla Wegars for her enormous patience. I thank Peter Schulz, Richard Reynolds, Mary Praetzellis, Stanley Olsen, Julia Longenecker, and James Ayres for commenting on the manuscript. All the mammalian data used in this report are available on disk. Send your request along with two IBM formatted $5^{1}/_{4}$ (or one $3^{1}/_{2}$) inch floppy disks in a disk mailer (be sure to include a return label and return postage) to the author at George C. Page Museum, 5801 Wilshire Blvd., Los Angeles, California 90036. The data were recorded using the database Reflex (Borland, Inc.), but can be exported in other formats. Request the database format you want: Reflex, Lotus (1-2-3), dBase, or Wordstar. An ASCII text file with notes, abbreviations, and so on, will be included on one disk.

Sacramento: Thanks to Adrian and Mary Praetzellis of Sonoma State University for the opportunity to work on the IJ56 fauna (Gust, 1982). The original data were reanalyzed for this chapter.

Woodland: Larry Felton of the California State Department of Parks and Recreation brought this fauna to my attention and provided information about the site. The original faunal work was done under contract to the State of California and published by them (Gust, 1984). The original data were reworked for this chapter.

Tucson: Stanley Olsen of the University of Arizona kindly provided access to the TUR fauna, his comparative collection, and working space during my stay in Tucson. John Olsen guided me to useful research materials in the UA collections and arranged for me to meet with previous TUR researchers. James E. Ayres, director of the TUR project, helped enormously by sharing his knowledge of the excavations. Camm Swift of the Los Angeles County Museum of Natural History assisted me in identifying most of the fish bone. Peter Schulz of the California Department of Parks and Recreation also identified some fish bone. The bird identifications were provided by Alan Ferg from work done while a student at the University of Arizona.

Ventura: Roberta Greenwood tracked down the bone from the Ventura Chinese features, arranged the loan, and provided a great deal of information. The data were collected while I was employed by the California Department of Parks and Recreation under Title II Grant No. 78002142 of the Public Works Employment Act of 1976. The fish bone was identified by Kenneth Gobalet and the bird bone by Dwight Simons.

Lovelock: Amy Dansie of the Nevada State Museum generously provided me with her original data on Wells One and Two. This allowed me to spend the short time available in recording butchering information. As a result, the data on the major skeletal elements of cow and pig are my work and the remainder is Ms. Dansie's. Don Tuohy of the Nevada State Museum provided access to the Lovelock fauna, as well as working space. The avifaunal remains were identified by Dwight Simons.

S. M. Gust

Chapter 8

Many people have been involved in the archaeological and historical research involving the Warrendale Cannery and the Chinese cannery workers. The late Ivan J. Donaldson, a retired fisheries biologist, had devoted many years to the history of fishing on the Columbia River and graciously made his extensive collection of notes, records, historical photographs, and personal memories available for incorporation into this research project. Mr. Donaldson also assisted in the tracking down of knowledgeable informants who shared their memories of the early days of steamboat travel, fishing, and canneries on the Lower Columbia. Mr. Charles Coe, having lived in several Chinese bunkhouses throughout the region, provided insights into the living conditions of the Chinese cannery workers.

Several local archaeologists and members of the Oregon Archaeological Society assisted with the field and laboratory work. James S. White provided a boat and organized a team of volunteer divers to do the underwater explorations. Jo A. Reese and Daniel D. Sullivan helped with the organization and execution of the field and laboratory work, and both continued on with their own research projects at the Warrendale Cannery. Daniel Sullivan photographed the artifacts, Bonnie J. Mills produced Figure 38, and Priscilla Wegars provided valuable comments on earlier drafts of this paper and on other aspects of the Warrendale research project in general. Several anonymous reviewers also provided helpful editorial suggestions and comments on the draft. I appreciate the field and laboratory assistance, the shared memories and insights, and the moral support from the many individuals who have been a part of this project. I hope this chapter will provide them with a token of my appreciation for their help.

J. L. Fagan

Chapter 9

This chapter is a much-revised version of a paper presented at the 37th Annual Northwest Anthropological Conference, Spokane, Washington in March 1984, and again at the 19th Annual Meeting of the Society for Historical Archaeology, Sacramento, California in January, 1986. I am especially grateful to Judy Yung for her suggestions for its improvement; any errors which remain are, of course, my own. Thanks also to Ruthanne Lum McCunn, Connie Chou, and Wei Du for their observations on combs and other artifacts, and to those people who called relevant references to my attention. I also appreciate the help of Boots Otto, who donated a Chinese earring to the Asian American Comparative Collection; Dora Mih, who translated a medicine bottle label; and Vyolet Chu, who allowed me to photograph her family heirlooms. Julia Costello, John Fagan, Charles R. Knowles, Verna McConnell, and Roderick Sprague shared useful artifact information with me, Roberta Greenwood sent articles on her Los Angeles Metro Rail excavations, and Mary Anne Davis and Sr. M. Catherine Manderfeld provided information on Polly Bemis' possessions. The National Endowment for the Humanities' Travel to Collections program partially funded a visit to the San Francisco Bay Area which gave me the opportunity to see some of the artifacts mentioned, and an American Fellowship from the American Association of University Women Educational Foundation assisted with the revision of another version of this chapter as part of my dissertation. All the artifacts discussed are documented on Asian Artifact Inventory Forms in the Asian American Comparative Collection, Laboratory of Anthropology, University of Idaho.

P. Wegars

Chapter 10

John Eldredge generously allowed us to study and photograph his extensive and well-documented collection of opium smoking paraphernalia. Without his assistance it would have been difficult to conduct this study. Other materials were made available by William Geer, Don Reed, John Edwards, Ken Smith, Rich Filke, Max Davis, and Mr. and Mrs. Poe. Opium smoking paraphernalia from the Riverside Chinatown was provided by Clark Brott, and portions of our earlier research for this chapter were used in the Riverside report by Wylie and Higgins (1987). Translations of Chinese inscriptions were provide by Tammy Tsai and Fred Mueller. Priscilla Wegars located and provided may of the historical references listed in her 1985 bibliography of opium. She also reviewed several drafts of this chapter, improving them considerably in the process. Published and unpublished information was provided by Neville Ritchie, Paul Chace, and Peter Schultz. We thank you all.

J. Wylie and R. E. Fike

Chapter 11

The data on which this chapter is based are derived from cooperation with three outstanding chemists employed by the United States Customs Service. They are Fred Davis of San Francisco, Carson Watts of Savannah, and Paul Doemeny of Los Angeles. Without their assistance, and that of Dr. Steven Fike, Director of the San Francisco Customs Laboratory, the agency would not have allocated time and funds for what is essentially basic research. I would also like to express my gratitude to my colleagues at the Ceramics Analysis Laboratory, particularly Dr. Dan Scheans and Herb Beals, for encouragement at very early stages of our composition analysis project. Many others, including Alison Stenger, Charles Hibbs, Jr., Dan Sullivan, Blaine Schmeer, Carol Steele, Jim King, and Dave Palmrose, have provided insights at various stages of the research.

H. Steele

Chapter 12

The finalization of this chapter would not have been possible without a significant amount of assistance from Priscilla Wegars. Two other individuals provided critical input; microscopists Fred Davis and Geoffrey Hodson. This chapter is the result of the combined efforts of the Ceramics Analysis Laboratory at Portland State University, the Laboratory of Anthropology at the University of Idaho, the United States Customs Laboratory in San Francisco, and the Environmental Sciences Section of Intel.

A. Stenger

Chapter 13

My thanks to the many students who assisted me in the excavations mentioned in this paper.

N. A. Ritchie

Table of Contents

Part One: Rural Contexts

Part Two: Urban Contexts

List of Figures

Chapter 1

Chapter 2

Chapter 3

Chapter 4

Chapter 5

Chapter 6

Chapter 7

Chapter 8

Chapter 9

Chapter 10

Chapter 12

Chapter 13

Chapter 14

List of Tables

Chapter 1

Chapter 2

Chapter 3

Chapter 4

Chapter 5

Chapter 6

Chapter 7

Chapter 9

Chapter 10

Chapter 11

Chapter 12

Chapter 13

Introduction

The Chinese have been venturing forth from China for many hundreds of years. During the 19th century in particular, adverse conditions there combined with opportunities for work elsewhere, and thousands of Chinese, chiefly men, left their homes and families to seek their fortunes elsewhere. Most hoped to accumulate enough money to return, eventually, to their homeland, giving rise to the pervasive stereotype that the Chinese were merely "sojourners," a term that is seldom applied to other ethnic groups for whom it was also true, such as Greeks and Italians.

Not all the Chinese could or did return to China; many died in foreign lands. Those who wished to remain abroad were often victimized by anti-Chinese exclusion laws that, in general, also forbade the immigration of most wives and families.

While the history and experiences of the Chinese outside of China during the late 19th and early 20th centuries have been examined by scholars for some time, it is only in recent years that the field of Asian American Studies has become established. Within this discipline, writers of both Asian and non-Asian descent are producing comprehensive, well-researched works that attack and demolish traditional anti-Chinese attitudes and stereotypes. These are either general, comparative, publications (e.g., Daniels, 1988; Takaki, 1989) or treat more specific topics, such as Chinese exclusion (Chan, 1991), Chinese women (Yung, 1986, 1990), or Chinese in particular regions, occupations, or towns (e.g., Lydon, 1985; Chan, 1986; Minnick, 1988).

Concurrent with this research has been the study of expatriate Chinese from an historical archaeological standpoint. Locations where Chinese people once lived and worked abroad are, today, archaeological sites that can yield structural information, artifacts, food remains, and other details enhancing knowledge and interpretation of the Chinese experience outside of China and supplementing the historical record as found in such primary sources as census records, maps, city and county archives, early newspapers, and other documents.

Reports and conference papers on Chinese historical archaeology began to appear in the mid- to late 1960s. In 1980 Baywood Publishing Company issued *Archaeological Perspectives on Ethnicity in America: Afro-American and Asian American Culture History,* edited by Robert L. Schuyler (Schuyler, 1980), as the first volume in its *Baywood Monographs in Archaeology* series. Four of the articles in that book dealt with Chinese topics, and an Asian American archaeological bibliography contained thirty-seven entries.

The ensuing decade has seen a tremendous increase in overseas Chinese archaeological studies. By "overseas Chinese" we mean people from mainland China who emigrated to other places such as the United States, Canada, Peru, Mexico, the Caribbean, Australia, New Zealand, and Southeast Asia. Many, perhaps hundreds, of Chinese sites have been recorded during cultural resource management studies by private firms and government agencies. These sites include, for example, urban "Chinatowns" and rural mining claims, work camps for railroad and other construction activities, terraced fruit and vegetable gardens, salmon canneries and shrimp camps, laundries, stores, cook shacks, cemeteries, and temples.

Because of planned development in a particular area it has been necessary to conduct archaeological excavations of some Chinese sites before they are destroyed by construction; others have been the focus of research excavations, particularly field schools. This work has produced much new information, resulting in numerous published and unpublished reports, theses, and dissertations. An annotated bibliography of overseas Chinese history and archaeology appeared in 1984 (Ehrenreich et al., 1984) and another is in preparation (Asian Comparative Collection *Newsletter,* 1991:2); reviews of the archaeological literature have also appeared (e.g., LaLande, 1981:63-70; Tordoff and Seldner, 1986:I, 1-4–1-6; Praetzellis and Praetzellis, 1990:9-12, 15; Stapp, 1990:7-9). The bibliographies in the present volume, while extensive, represent only a fraction of the work that has been done in the field of overseas Chinese archaeology.

Many of the newer materials have progressed well beyond the simple descriptive levels of earlier reports. More recent work has focused both on the development and testing of theories, against which the data can be evaluated, and on refinement of artifact analyses, including trade networks, standardization of terminology, and typological studies of Chinese artifacts.

In spite of all this effort, until now no single publication existed that brought together the research being done by a number of people on a variety of different archaeological sites in various locations. While reports on individual sites are published from time to time, they are, of course, limited in scope to the particular type of site discussed. They tend to be even more limited in their distribution, since often the contracting agency does not produce copies for sale; when copies can be purchased, they are frequently very expensive.

The need for the present volume was first addressed at the Society for Historical Archaeology's 16th Annual Meeting in Denver, Colorado, in January 1983. While papers on overseas Chinese archaeology had been included at previous SHA conferences, the Denver meeting was the first to have enough papers for a half-day symposium. Entitled "Chinese Historical Archaeology: Studies in Adaptation and Cultural Stability," it contained twelve reports emphasizing various aspects of overseas Chinese sites, artifacts, and mining techniques. Although the participants discussed publishing the papers from that symposium, no publication then resulted. However, several of the presentations given then have been rewritten and updated for inclusion here.

The Overseas Chinese Research Group, formed under the auspices of the Society for Historical Archaeology, began about the same time to formulate a research design and pose research questions relevant to the study of the overseas Chinese in this country and elsewhere. A comparative collection of Chinese artifacts, together with slides and bibliographical references, was established in the Alfred W. Bowers Laboratory of Anthropology at the University of Idaho several years ago. Now known as the Asian American Comparative Collection (AACC), in tribute to its broadened emphasis, this repository assists researchers with site and artifact identification. Because the AACC has no secure source of funding, the contributors to the present volume have generously agreed to donate their royalties towards its support.

REFERENCES CITED

ASIAN COMPARATIVE COLLECTION *NEWSLETTER*
1991   Bibliography of Overseas Chinese Archaeology, Asian Comparative Collection *Newsletter, 8*:1, p. 2, March.

CHAN, SUCHENG
1986   *This Bittersweet Soil: The Chinese in California Agriculture, 1860-1910,* University of California Press, Berkeley.

CHAN, SUCHENG (ed).
1991   *Entry Denied: Exclustion and the Chinese Community in America, 1882-1943,* Temple University Press, Philadelphia.

DANIELS, ROGER
1988   *Asian America: Chinese and Japanese in the United States since 1850,* University of Washington Press, Seattle.

EHRENREICH, DIXIE L., PRISCILLA WEGARS, JONATHAN HORN, and KAREN E. SMITH
1984   An Annotated Bibliography of Overseas Chinese History and Archaeology, *Northwest Anthropological Research Notes, 18*:2, pp. 125-211, Fall.

LaLANDE, JEFFREY M.
1981   Sojourners in the Oregon Siskiyous: Adaptation and Acculturation of the Chinese Miners in the Applegate Valley, California, ca. 1855-1900, Master's thesis, Oregon State University, Corvallis.

LYDON, SANDY
1985   *Chinese Gold: The Chinese in the Monterey Bay Region,* Capitola Book Co., Capitola, California.

MINNICK, SYLVIA SUN
    1988   *Samfow: The San Joaquin Chinese Legacy.* Panorama West Publishing,
            Fresno.
PRAETZELLIS, MARY and ADRIAN PRAETZELLIS
    1990   *Archaeological and Historical Studies at the San Fong Chong Laundry, 814
            I Street, Sacramento, California,* Anthropological Studies Center, Sonoma
            State University, Rohnert Park, California.
SCHUYLER, ROBERT L. (ed.)
    1980   *Archaeological Perspectives on Ethnicity in America: Afro-American and
            Asian American Culture History.* Baywood Publishing Company, Amityville,
            New York.
STAPP, DARBY C.
    1990   The Historic Ethnography of a Chinese Mining Community in Idaho, Ph.D.
            dissertation, University of Pennsylvania, Philadelphia.
TAKAKI, RONALD
    1989   *Strangers from a Different Shore: A History of Asian Americans,* Penguin,
            New York.
TORDOFF, JUDITH D. and DANA McGOWAN SELDNER
    1986   *Cottonwood Creek Project, Shasta and Tehama Counties, California: Exca-
            vation at Thirteen Historic Sites in the Cottonwood Mining District,* 2 vols,
            The Hornet Foundation of California State University, Sacramento and
            Theodoratus Cultural Research, Fair Oaks, California.
YUNG, JUDY
    1986   *Chinese Women of America: A Pictorial History,* University of Washington
            Press, Seattle.
    1990   Unbinding the Feet, Unbinding their Lives: Social Change for Chinese
            Women in San Francisco, 1902-1945, Ph.D. dissertation, University of
            California, Berkeley.

PART ONE
Rural Contexts

Significant numbers of Chinese began arriving in the United States in the early 1850s in response to gold discoveries in California. As work opportunities opened up elsewhere, the Chinese gradually migrated to other locations in the western United States and Canada. Idaho is a particularly fruitful location for examining overseas Chinese in rural contexts, because many such areas there, to which the Chinese ventured, are still very remote and often remain undisturbed. The results of archaeological and historical investigations in that state thus provide a standard to which work on rural sites elsewhere can be compared.

Because the Chinese worked in remote areas one might think that there would be no documentary records of them, in contrast to what might be expected from urban locations. A long-term archaeological and historical research project focusing on the Idaho mining camp of Pierce City has, however, recovered a wealth and variety of information in archival sources regarding the Chinese there. Darby C. Stapp discusses how he has used the Pierce Mining District records, county records, federal census data, contemporary newspapers, and oral-historical information to produce an historic ethnography of the Pierce City inhabitants. Pierce City's population characteristics, economic systems, household composition, and wealth distribution are examples of the kinds of information the documentary sources have yielded, which eventually, together with the archaeological evidence, will provide a full and complete picture of the Pierce City Chinese inhabitants over time.

Historic Chinese mining activity also took place along the Lower Salmon River in central Idaho. Because this wild and scenic part of the state is at present almost inaccessible except to river rafters, a number of stone structures and rockshelters built by Chinese miners have survived virtually intact. David M. Sisson compares general building characteristics in China with the archaeological evidence for Chinese sites both on the Lower Salmon River and elsewhere, such as New Zealand, Australia, Texas, Nevada, Oregon, and California. The types and purposes of the Lower Salmon River structures, as well as the similarities and differences in their observed architecture, are particularly important because of the rarity of such well-preserved sites elsewhere in the West.

Although the area along the South Fork of Idaho's Salmon River is even more remote, Chinese garden terraces of commercial capacity were carved out of the slopes of the rugged canyons there, in what is now the Payette National Forest. While Chinese horticulture was practiced on a large scale in the West, the terraced gardens that were created in many places are now so overgrown that they are often simply no longer recognized. Idaho's Chinese terraced gardens, recently featured in a National Public Radio special report, were developed to serve the Warren Mining District, and are so far the most extensive known outside of Asia. Jeffrey M. Fee's chapter focuses on the identification of garden terraces, gardening methods, typical crops grown, and marketing of the produce, together with architectural descriptions of the Chinese structures found in association with the gardens.

Other rural Chinese "foodways" are explored by Julia G. Longenecker and Darby C. Stapp in their chapter on the faunal remains from a Chinese mining camp. Documentary accounts have provided details of historic meat systems, including kinds of meat and their supply networks, consumer characteristics, and Chinese meat processing technology, particularly butchering methods and tools. This information is integrated with data obtained through analysis of faunal assemblages from two Chinese mining sites.

CHAPTER 1

The Documentary Record of an Overseas Chinese Mining Camp

Darby C. Stapp

A long-term anthropological program focusing on an historic gold mining community in north-central Idaho began in 1983 (Stapp and Longenecker, 1984; Stapp, 1990). The community under study, known as Pierce City, Idaho (Figure 1), had a large subpopulation of Chinese inhabitants for over fifty years. Investigations during the initial stage of research centered on the documentary record in order to place Pierce City in the proper context of western settlement and to assist in the interpretation of the archaeological record. In this chapter, the documentary database, which includes federal census schedules, county and mining district records, and contemporary newspaper accounts, is used to describe the formation and evolution of the Pierce Chinese community.

Pierce City, which was one of several north-central Idaho mining camps, was selected for study because of its 1) long-term association with Chinese gold miners, 2) location along the northern fringe of overseas Chinese North America, and 3) rich combination of archaeological and documentary data. These three reasons give the Pierce data considerable significance to the study of the overseas Chinese because in order to understand overseas Chinese macro-society, we must have knowledge of the various micro-societies. For example, we need to know how Chinese society was structured in the major cities, in the railroad construction camps, the mining camps, the canneries, the fishing villages, and other areas where the overseas Chinese lived. Further, we need to know how groups were structured in the peripheral areas of overseas Chinese America, as well as in the core area. And finally, we need to know how different segments of the overseas Chinese society changed during the first century of their American experience.

Figure 1. Map of the northwestern United States showing the location of the Pierce area (drawn by author).

From an analytical standpoint, the Pierce study has additional significance to overseas Chinese research because of the rich primary documents that are included in the database. The Pierce mining records appear to be among the few near-complete collections which document Chinese involvement in a mining district; the records are certainly among the first records to be analyzed and described (Stapp, 1987). The county records, apparently equally as rare, also provide considerable insight into Chinese interactions within the community. When combined with federal census data, rich archaeological resources, and oral historical data, the Pierce database provides views of overseas Chinese society that have escaped researchers heretofore. For this reason, the Pierce data have the potential to stimulate current thinking about the overseas Chinese and should prompt other researchers to collect and examine the documentary record of other communities.

HISTORICAL OVERVIEW

The 1860 discovery of gold-bearing alluvial deposits in the Clearwater Mountains led to the gold rush of 1861 and the formation of the Pierce Mining District. Euroamerican miners spread out over a 40-square-mile area in search of gold, while merchants set up shop nearby, creating the mining towns of Pierce City and Oro Fino City. Settlement also occurred in the adjacent grasslands, where ranches and overnight stops were located, and along the Clearwater River, where the ferry and Indian farms were located.

While every Idaho and Pacific Northwest history book mentions the 1860 discovery of gold on Oro Fino Creek and the subsequent gold rush in 1861, few say more. For example, Rodman Paul, eminent historian of the West, gave what has become the common impression of the history of the Pierce locality, stating (Paul, 1974:138):

> Camps like Orofino [Oro Fino (1861-1867) was located 2 miles from Pierce City] sprang into existence in 1861, only to be hastily abandoned within the year when news arrived of gold in the Salmon River mines, farther to the south.

In actuality, placer mines in the Pierce Mining District (also occasionally referred to as the Oro Fino Mining District) continued to produce significant quantities of gold for another thirty years (Wells, 1963:6):

> Relegated to a position of secondary importance by the Salmon River excitement, Pierce and Oro Fino City nevertheless remained productive during a quiet, unspectacular 1862 mining season. Several hundred miners continued to work each summer for the next few seasons, and with ample water they made a steady production. The September census showed a population in 1863 of 525 for the area and, although the County Assessor

estimated that 500 miners were active at the beginning of June 1864, the fall census showed only 336 men remaining there in mid-September. Chinese miners commenced to purchase claims around Pierce in 1864, and by 1866 they pretty much had taken over what the Euroamericans regarded as a worked-out district. Chinese activity continued there for years; although the Chinese did not require so high a daily yield to keep up interest in mining, they gradually made a substantial production themselves. The Oro Fino mines may not have matched the expectations of E. D. Pierce [discoverer of the Oro Fino mines], but they were extensive, and they employed miners many years.

Today, the Chinese are gone, but Pierce City is still there; the rich timber resource granted the town another few generations of life.

THE DATA

During the initial stage of this study, secondary sources were used to identify the primary documentary sources. The analysis of the primary documents began with those records that were deemed to have the greatest validity and reliability; this judgment was based on how close the document was, both in time and space, to the actual event. The advantage of this approach is that documents that have greater uncertainty associated with them can be evaluated as they are encountered. Using this strategy, the primary documents from Pierce were analyzed in the following order:

1. Federal census data;
2. Pierce Mining District records;
3. Shoshone County records;
4. Contemporary newspapers from Lewiston and Boise; and
5. Oral historical reports.

Federal Census Records

Microfilms of the original federal census schedules from the Pierce locality were obtained for 1870, 1880, 1900, and 1910 (U.S. Bureau of the Census 1870, 1880; 1900; 1910). The records from 1890 were destroyed in a fire and hence only the aggregate data were available, as was the case for 1920 and 1930, for which the complete schedules have not been released. The information recorded by each federal census taker differed slightly from decade to decade. Items consistently recorded included name, age, sex, profession, place of birth, color/race, and household. Other items of interest to this study which were recorded irregularly included value of personal property and real estate (1870), relationship to head of household (1880 through 1910), and years in the United States (1900). It is clear from studying the census schedules for the Pierce locality that the census taker did a thorough job (or at least he wanted it to appear so); the information is also, for the most part, extremely legible.

Pierce Mining District Records

The first item of business for the miners after gold was discovered and placer claims were staked was to write a set of laws to govern the behavior of those mining in the Pierce Mining District. The district encompassed the drainages to the east, north, and west of Pierce City and all claims and sales of mining rights were recorded by the district recorder or his assistant; for many years, each seller was confirmed by the Justice of the Peace. An analysis of the Pierce Mining District documents (Stapp, 1987) indicated that the records are largely complete, but that all of the transactions were not recorded. For example, there were cases of a mine being sold where there was no record of the seller having claimed or purchased the mineral rights.

The records are in bound books, and all books referred to in the records have been located. Included in the bound documents were the laws of the district; the recordings of mining claims; bills of sale for claims, mines, and water ditches; mining claim renewals; water rights; and mortgages. Also included in the mining records were sales of businesses and town properties. Thus, there appears to be some overlap between the mining records and the Shoshone County records. An example of a typical mining document from Pierce is shown below (Pierce Mining Records 1861-1890, Book C:187):

> Know all men by these presents that we R. L. Yantes & Co of Pierce City County of Shoshone and Territory of Idaho Hereby grant bargin and sell set over and give possession to Sam Low & Co of the Aforesaid Town County and Territory All my right Tytle and interest in the following discribed property to wit Five Mining claims, more or less, on the Oro Fino Creek about three miles below Pierce City in the Above mentioned County and Territory for the consideration of one hundred dollars to me cash in hand payed the receipt of which is hereby acknowledged. In witness where of I hereby Affix my hand and seal the 17th day of April A.D. 1867

> Witness Tho Hudson R.L. Yantes & Co

> Recorded July 16th John B. Lauck, Rec
> 1867

Shoshone County Records

Many of the records pertaining to the Chinese in the Pierce locality relate to the operation of Shoshone County, which was formed in response to the rapid population growth created by the 1860 gold discovery on Oro Fino Creek. Shoshone County was originally part of Washington Territory, but due to the great population growth of the mining regions, a new territory, Idaho, was created in 1864. Except for Moose City (1867-1871), a small mining community located approximately 70 miles east of Pierce, virtually all of the Euroamericans in Shoshone County lived in the Pierce locality until the Coeur d'Alene discoveries of the early

1880s. For this reason, virtually all of the county records prior to the early 1880s pertain to events at Pierce. The bulk of these records remained in Pierce City after the county seat was moved from Pierce to Murray, and many of these records exist today.

The records of Shoshone County fall into three broad groups: political, economic, and legal. The political records include voting lists, election returns, and the minutes of the county supervisors' meetings. The economic records pertain to the financial dealings of the county. These include records related to revenue enhancement (annual assessments, polling taxes, hospital taxes, foreign miners' tax) and expenditures (bills to the county for county services such as building and maintaining roads, capturing and holding criminals, and taking care of indigents). The legal documents consist primarily of court petitions and power of attorney declarations.

The completeness of the pre-1884 collection is difficult to determine because most of the documents relate to irregular events. While there are no major temporal gaps in the pre-1884 records, it is clear that the collection is more haphazard than not; it is best characterized as bits and pieces of the business of Shoshone County. Few records have been located relating to the period after the county seat moved to Murray in 1884. Thus, the Shoshone County documents must, for the most part, be treated as any incomplete database would be: carefully.

Contemporary Newspapers

The majority of contemporary newspaper articles, and those with the highest validity, were printed in the *Idaho Signal* (Lewiston), the *Lewiston Teller*, and the *Tri-Weekly Statesman* (Boise). Most of the newspaper entries were in the form of weekly or seasonal news updates; other entries related to specific events. The newspaper data are generally not amenable to quantification, but do provide some of the richest qualitative data available for study. The authors of nearly all the articles or items are identified and were either current on former residents of the Pierce locality.

Oral Historical Reports

Several high quality documents are oral historical in nature. These include an autobiography (Goulder, 1909), a biographical interview (Boyd, 1924), and personal recollections (Space, 1957). Also included in this category is the material pertaining to the Pierce locality that was collected by Trull (1946). Trull collected most of the Pierce information from a "pioneer" named P. T. Lomax, who first appeared in the mining documents in 1882.

PIERCE CHINESE POPULATION CHARACTERISTICS

Population Size

Following the initial rush to Pierce, the Chinese were excluded from working in the district, as was common in western mining camps, by Section 19 of the Pierce Mining District Mining Laws, which stated (Pierce Mining Records 1861-1890, Book D:300):

> That the Resolution as passed by a prior meeting in regard to the complete exclusion of the Chinese and Asiatic races and the South Pacific Ocean Islanders from these mines be confirmed.

Within a few years, most Euroamericans lost interest in the Pierce mines and those who remained were forced to reconsider the issue of Chinese exclusion out of economic necessity. On October 18, 1864, the mining laws were amended to read "All citizens or Foriengers [sic] who pay a County license may hold claims" (Pierce Mining Records 1861-1890, Book D:301).

Although the mining district did not allow the owning of claims by the Chinese until October, 1864, the mining records indicate that one Chinese individual, Ah Cow, purchased a claim for $150 in July, 1864 with the stipulation that if he was not permitted to mine, his money would be returned (Pierce Mining Records 1861-1890, Book D:157). Ah Cow may have been a lead man for a large Chinese mining company, sent to a district to negotiate with the Euroamerican miners and explain the economic advantages of permitting the Chinese into the district. Supporting this contention is the record of an Ah Cow in the 1870 federal census, whose profession was listed as "Chinese Agent." If these documents refer to the same individual, then Ah Cow was sixteen years old in 1864, assuming that the census was correct in listing him as twenty-two years old in 1870. Interestingly, Ah Cow bought his claim from a "Kanacker" (Hawaiian Islander), who, according to the same law that excluded the Chinese, should also have been excluded from the mining district.

Bills of sale from the Pierce Mining District records indicate that it was not until 1866 that significant numbers of Chinese began purchasing placer mines from the Euroamericans (Table 1). Why it took over a year for the Chinese to get to Pierce is not known; perhaps there was a shortage of laborers available to come to Pierce. By the end of 1866, however, there was a labor force of 700 to 800 Chinese in Pierce working the mines (*Daily Oregonian*, 1866), most of whom were probably working in the twenty-six mining operations purchased by the Chinese from 1864 to 1866. Judging from the increase in bills of sale in 1867 (Table 1), the number of Chinese probably increased that year. We know little about where the first Pierce Chinese miners came from; presumably most left other mining regions in California and Nevada to come to Pierce.

Table 1. Chinese Mining Purchases between 1864 and 1890[a]

Year	Number	$	Year	Number	$
1864	2	200	1878	8	3295
1865	2	1300	1879	14	10425
1866	22	16375	1880	4	570
1867	52	42418	1881	7	2550
1868	23	5865	1882	12	19082
1869	30	9860	1883	5	739
1870	32	10282	1884	10	881
1871	18	6715	1885	10	770
1872	11	2553	1886	10	1370
1873	14	1733	1887	8	2005
1874	11	955	1888	14	1018
1875	16	3451	1889	7	530
1876	10	2450	1890	—	——
1877	7	1080	Totals	359	148,472

[a]Based on bills of sale in the Pierce Mining Records (1861-1890).

If the 700 to 800 population estimate is reliable, the Chinese population in Pierce peaked during the late 1860s and steadily dropped thereafter (Table 2). It must, of course, be remembered that the population figures presented in Table 2 are from the federal census records, which may not have included all those who lived in the locality; the Chinese avoided at least some authorities, as documented in the following recollection (Boyd, 1924:259):

> During the years 1868-69 I was deputy sheriff of Shoshone County. . . . One of my duties was to collect the mining tax from the local Chinamen. . . . At that time there were a good many of these yellow men in the various mining camps and a monthly tax of $5.00 a head was levied on them by the Territory. The collector, myself, got 20 per cent of this and in annoyance the task was well worth this return. Often when the Orientals saw the collector coming they would run into the woods or other hiding places and I had to round them up and force them to pay. Sometimes they would claim that they did not have the money and I marched them in pig tail file down the trail to the store where they would borrow the required sum from the store keeper. It usually took me one week of each month to collect the Chinese tax.

After 1892, some of the Chinese would have had good reason to avoid the census taker. The 1892 Geary Act required all Chinese in America to obtain certificates of residence. Many Chinese from the mining regions of Idaho refused to comply and were arrested when found.

Table 2. Chinese Population in the Pierce City Locality[a]

Year	Chinese[b]	Population[c] (percent)	Miners[d] (percent)	Women[e] (percent)
1870	461	78	91	2
1880	296	75	86	2
1890	201	84	NA	NA
1900	73	26	88	5
1910	19	5	89	0
1920	8	1	NA	0
1930	2	<1	NA	0

[a]All population figures from U.S. Bureau of the Census records (1870; 1880; 1897; 1900; 1910; 1922; 1931).
[b]Number of Chinese recorded by census taker.
[c]Percent of Chinese population in Pierce locality.
[d]Percent of Chinese population identified as miners.
[e]Percent of Chinese population identified as female.
NA = information not available.

The primary factor in the Chinese population decline during the 1870s and 1880s was undoubtedly the declining gold reserves. A major population decline also occurred around 1890, as reported in the following newspaper account (French, 1891):

> . . . in the Fall of 1889 Judge Willis Sweet's decision, to the effect that a Chinaman could not legally hold mining ground, fell like a thunderbolt among them. Half of them left the country; and white men located on their ground. At present many of the Chinese continue to work and hold their ground by paying white men a suitable salary to live upon and hold the property.

Since the 1890 census was taken during the summer of 1890, French's article indicates that the population prior to the legal decision was between 300 and 400. If so this would mean that the Chinese population during the 1880s grew, or at least was stable; this stability would have been in contrast to most Idaho communities where the Chinese population decreased, largely because of anti-Chinese agitation. It may be that the isolated mining regions offered a haven to the Chinese during this decade of increased hostility toward the Idaho Chinese by other Idahoans.

Sex and Age

The Pierce Chinese population was dominated by males (Table 2), as was all of overseas Chinese America. The percentage of women was less than 2 percent in

1870 and 1880, and, excluding children, was less than 3 percent in 1900. No Chinese women were reported in the Pierce locality after 1900.

The small percentage of Chinese women was largely responsible for the great increase in the average age of the Chinese men in Pierce between 1870 and 1910 because it limited the number of offspring. In 1870 the average (mean) male age in Pierce was 30.7 years; this was six years younger than the mean age of Euroamericans. Many of the Chinese were teenagers and several were over sixty years of age. By 1880, the average age of male Chinese had increased to 35.4 years. If there had not been a steady influx of young Chinese men from China to North America throughout the 1870s, the age increase would have been closer to ten years. By 1900, the average age (excluding children) had increased to 52.6, an increase of nearly eighteen years over a twenty-year period. This was surely due to the sudden decrease in Chinese immigration which resulted from the Chinese Exclusion Acts of 1882 and 1892. In 1910, the average age was sixty-three years.

Chinese Names

The names of the Chinese in Pierce were extracted from the federal census records (1870, 1880, 1900). With the exception of variations in spelling, the census taker appears to have made a serious attempt to record the names of all individuals. Unfortunately, the names from the census do not always correlate with the names from other documents. A particularly disturbing example is found in the records from 1880, when both census and assessment records are available (Table 3). While some of the incongruity could be due to multiple professions or changes that occurred between the time the census was recorded and the assessments were made, most is probably due to the problems associated with recording Chinese names. These problems, discussed by Louie (1985-86: 7-10), include spelling problems, name shortening, and failure to record family names.

Even though there are problems associated with Chinese names found in census records, an analysis of the Pierce names was conducted to document the common names recorded. Since the overseas Chinese appear to have formed social units based upon surname, dialect, and place of origin, the spatial patterning of certain names may relate to the distribution of particular Chinese groups in North America, and possibly within a community. This is speculative because, according to Louie (1985-86:8), monosyllabic names prefixed by "Ah" (the pattern in most Pierce names) were only given names.

To conduct the analysis, similar sounding names (e.g., Sin and Cin) were combined and counted; a name was counted regardless of its relative position. If the assumptions made are valid, the data indicate that there was a change in the frequency of certain names recorded in Pierce between 1870 and 1880 (Table 4). The most significant name change was in the name "Sam," which increased from

Table 3. Examples of Chinese Names from the 1880 Federal Census
and Shoshone County Assessment Records

Assessment Records[a]		1880 Census[b]	
Name	Property[c]	Name	Profession
Ah Gong	Merchandise	Goo Gong	Huckster
Too Shong	Merchandise	Ah Shin	Keeps store
Hong Yune	Merchandise	Ah Bone	Retail grocer
Quong Gee Long	Merchandise	Quang Lung	Keeps store
Ah Hing	Merchandise	Lip Key	Huckster
		Ah Kow	Keeps store
		Some You	Store clerk
		Ah Cong	Store clerk
Ah Allen	Blacksmith shop	Lam Yong	Blacksmith
Ah Hang	Blacksmith shop	Ah Youk	Blacksmith
Ah Sing	Garden		
Ah Yen	Garden	Ah Yen	Gambler
Ah Yee	Garden	Ah Yeng	Doctor
Ah Chom	Hogs		
Jimmy Fee	House	Ah Sam	Barber
Tong Lee	House	Tung Lee	Keeps gambling house
Sing Lee	House		
Ah Sam	House	Ah Sam	Keeps wash house
		Ah Coy	Keeps gambling house
		Ah See	Keeps gambling house

[a]Information extracted from the Shoshone County Assessment Records, 1880 (Shoshone County Records, 1861-1884).
[b]U.S. Bureau of the Census (1880).
[c]Principal property on which the individual was taxed.

four to twelve during a period when all other major names decreased in frequency. It is tempting to speculate that this suggests a movement of a particular group of overseas Chinese into Pierce between 1870 and 1880. Then again, it could reflect the use of the American name Sam, although the virtual absence of other American names attached to Chinese men suggests that this is not the case. This analysis was hampered by the lack of similar descriptions of Chinese populations in 19th-century America. As similar analyses from different communities are produced, the significance of Chinese names in America will become clearer.

Table 4. Frequency of Chinese Names Recorded in Pierce
in 1870 and 1880[a]

1870		1880	
Name	Number	Name	Number
Sing	18 (1)	Sing	12 (1)
Chung	17 (3)	Sam	12 (3)
Lee	16 (10)	Chung	11
You	15 (1)	Lee	9 (2)
Wing	12 (1)	Tung	9 (3)
Jim	11 (2)	You	9
Wan	9 (5)	Chee	7 (3)
Cow	8 (1)	See	7 (5)
Fook	6 (2)	King	6
Teung	6 (2)	Wan	6
Toy	6 (1)	Cow	5
		Foo	5 (1)
		Wah	5

[a]Names were obtained from the U.S. Bureau of the Census (1870; 1880). "Number" identifies the total times a name was found in any part of a person's name; number in parentheses indicates the number of times the name was found as a "first" or "second" name and not as a "last" name. Most names cited here were preceded by the prefix "Ah," which was a custom of central and south China (Louie, 1985-86:8). No attempt was made to differentiate female from male names. Only the most common names are listed here.

PIERCE CHINESE OCCUPATIONS

The economy of 19th-century Pierce was based upon placer gold. Not surprisingly, the overwhelming majority of Pierce Chinese were placer gold miners (Tables 2 and 5); other Chinese moved to Pierce to supply the miners with various goods and services (Table 5). Several changes in the nature of the Chinese professions deserve comment. One change was the increase in laborers from zero to eleven between 1870 and 1880. While this could indicate an increase in social differentiation, it was more likely due to changes in reporting methods (i.e., laborers were probably reported as miners by the 1870 census taker). Another change was in the number of Chinese retail merchants between 1870 and 1880. In 1870 there was one merchant, one clerk, and one trader; in 1880, there were three storekeepers, two hucksters (peddlers), two clerks, and one retail grocer. This increase in retailers is especially interesting when one considers that the population had decreased 35 percent between 1870 and 1880.

Table 5. Occupations of Chinese in the Pierce Locality[a]

Profession	1870	1880	1900	1910
Gold miner	420	254	64	16
Laborer	—	11	—	—
Merchant	1	—	—	—
Huckster	—	2	—	—
Keeps store	—	3	—	—
Saloon keeper	—	—	1	—
Trader	1	—	—	—
Clerk	1	2	—	—
Retail grocer	—	1	1	—
Gardener	3	—	—	—
Blacksmith	3	2	—	1
Hotel keeper	1	—	—	—
Hotel waiter	1	—	—	—
Hotel cook	3	—	—	—
Cook	—	7	—	1
Servant	—	3	—	—
Laundryman	1	1	—	—
Gambler	14	1	—	—
Keeps gambling house	—	3	—	—
Brothel keeper	1	—	—	—
Prostitute	8	—	—	—
Keeping house	—	4	—	—
Barber	1	1	—	—
Doctor	1	1	—	—
Chinese agent	1	—	—	—
Totals	461	296	66	18

[a]Data extracted from the U.S. Bureau of the Census (1870; 1880; 1900).

A third change was the decrease in the number of gamblers. While much of this decline was doubtless due to the 35 percent decrease in Chinese population, the 71 percent decrease in gamblers suggests an additional cause. Related to this issue is the decrease of prostitutes from eight in 1870 to zero in 1880. Even if all four of the Chinese women in Pierce in 1880 were prostitutes (all were listed as "keeping house"), the 50 percent decrease was still greater than the 36 percent decrease in Chinese population.

Finally, there was an increase in Chinese cooks and servants between 1870 and 1880; this was due principally to the hiring of Chinese by Euroamericans. Why this happened after 1870 is not fully understood, but it was apparently due to a

combination of economic factors on the part of the Chinese (i.e., need for employment) and social factors on the part of the Euroamericans (reduction in racial
prejudice). An increase in racial prejudice after 1880 may explain why there were
no cooks and servants working for Euroamerican households in Pierce in 1900. By
1900, the only Chinese non-miners were a saloon keeper, who actually ran a
saloon for Euroamericans, and a retail grocer. The lack of service-oriented professionals was most likely due to the population size (sixty-four Chinese).

PIERCE CHINESE HOUSEHOLDS

The majority of information pertaining to the level of the household comes from
the federal census records. Household data were extracted from the records to
answer two central questions. First, to what extent did Chinese and Euroamericans
live in the same household? And second, did the size of the Chinese households
change over time?

Chinese/Euroamerican Households

The number of households with Euroamerican and Chinese individuals
increased from zero in 1870 to fourteen in 1880. The fourteen mixed households
consisted of the following:

- Seven households had several Euroamericans and one Chinese "cook,"
  "servant," or "laborer."
- One household, designated as a hotel, had several Euroamerican boarders and
  two Chinese cooks.
- One household had two Euroamericans and one Chinese woman, listed as
  "keeping house."
- Five households were composed of several Chinese "miners" or "laborers"
  and one or two Euroamerican miners.

In 1900 there were no households recorded with both Euroamerican and Chinese
members.

The numerous Chinese/Euroamerican households documented in 1880 combined with an absence of such households in 1870 and 1900 may have been a
common pattern throughout Idaho, if not the West; we will have to wait until more
comprehensive census studies have been conducted. The pattern certainly suggests that Chinese/Euroamerican relations were, if not good, at least marked by
tolerance on the part of the Euroamericans. The Chinese motive was likely
economic. The occurrence of Chinese cooks and servants in Euroamerican
households likely decreased rapidly during the mid-1880s, when acts of violence
and feelings of resentment swept the West.

Size of Chinese Households

The census data indicate that the size of Chinese households changed significantly between 1870 and 1880, and again between 1880 and 1900 (Figure 2). In 1870, the average household was composed of 3.7 individuals; by 1880, this had increased to 5.9 individuals, an increase of over 50 percent. Interestingly, during this same time period, the average Euroamerican household nearly doubled in size, increasing from 2.0 individuals to 3.7 individuals. These increases suggest that the forces which led to the household size increase may have transcended ethnic boundaries. ("Household" is interpreted as the number of occupants living at a locus, not necessarily the number living in a structure.)

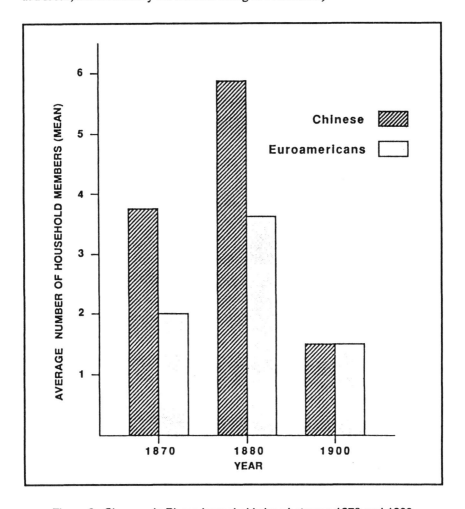

Figure 2. Changes in Pierce household sizes between 1870 and 1900.

One possible explanation for the household size increase between 1870 and 1880 relates to mining technology. Since no major new gold discoveries were made around Pierce during the 1870s, we know that there was less gold available to miners in 1880 than there was in 1870. Typically, as reserves are depleted in a mining region, miners who wish to remain in a location are forced to work in areas which are less productive; to do this economically, they must often adjust their technologies accordingly. Thus, it is possible that the 1880 miners adopted mining strategies which increased the number of men needed at a mine, hence the increase in household size. However, when mining and non-mining households were compared, it became clear that factors other than technology must have been responsible, as non-mining households increased in size similarly to the mining households.

Economic factors may have played a role. We know that the period between 1870 and 1880 was not a period of economic boom or even stability, but rather decline. The gold deposits were being worked out, the population was decreasing, and the national economic trends were not much better. Under conditions such as these, individuals often will band together to reduce living costs. Thus, the economic motive might explain the increase in household size.

Between 1880 and 1900, Euroamerican and Chinese household size decreased significantly (to 1.6 for both the Chinese and the Euroamericans). This increase was likely due to a combination of social and technological factors. By 1900, miners in Pierce were generally mining by themselves; they were referred to as "gopher miners" because they would search for small pockets of placer ground which had been missed by the earlier miners (Ralph Space, 1983:personal communication). The level of technology required to mine the pockets was low, often simply requiring the use of a rocker, hence working individually was the most economical method. Many of the miners lived alone in Pierce City. Since this is generally not the most economical way to live, this pattern may have been due to some social factors related to their age, bachelor status, or profession.

DISTRIBUTION OF WEALTH IN PIERCE

The collection of Pierce documents contains numerous references to the dollar values of property and merchandise. Since many of the documents identify the property held by individuals, it is possible to analyze the distribution of wealth between the Euroamericans and the Chinese in the Pierce locality, and within the Chinese community itself. This section begins with a diachronic comparison of the total property assessed to the Euroamericans and Chinese. An analysis of the total value of merchandise owned by both groups is then presented, followed by an analysis of the transfer of mining and town properties from the Euroamericans to the Chinese. The section concludes with a description of the distribution of wealth within the Pierce Chinese community.

Assessable Property in the Pierce Locality

Shoshone County annual assessment records provide insight into the personal property of the Pierce residents. The most common items assessed were real estate, equipment (non-mining), merchandise, notes, livestock, watches, and dogs. All personal property was obviously not assessed, as evidenced by the fact that less than 10 percent of the population had any assessable property. Miners were apparently a group that received special treatment as the only items owned by miners that were taxed were water ditches. Especially perplexing are the rare occurrences of assessments filed on cash, gold dust, and "households." Either most individuals simply did not have any of these items, which seems doubtful, or there was a minimum value below which no assessment could be made. Still, the property which was assessed does reflect the relative distribution of wealth in the Pierce locality and it is useful to examine this distribution in greater detail.

Although the Chinese outnumbered the Euroamericans in Pierce by the late 1860s, they never did surpass the Euroamericans in assessable wealth during the period for which we have records (1863-1884). As shown in Figure 3, the Chinese value of property rose during the 1870s, especially in proportion to the Euroamerican value. The fact that the assessable value of Chinese property quadrupled during a period when the Chinese population fell 37 percent is particularly interesting.

Assessment records indicate that most of the increase in Chinese assessable property during the 1870s was due to an increase in merchandise (Table 6). Since population was decreasing during this period, either the amount of money being spent by the Chinese miners for merchandise increased, or there was a change in the trade network which supplied the goods to the Chinese miners. For example, the Chinese might have begun purchasing more merchandise because of physical forces (e.g., liquor and opium addiction), psychological forces (e.g., depression brought on by deculturation), or cultural forces (e.g., acculturation—Euroamerican miners were reputed to be spendthrifts, while the overseas Chinese were purported to be frugal; over time they may have become more extravagant).

Concerning the change in trade network scenario, two possibilities could account for a network change. During the early period, goods might have been shipped directly to mining companies via teamsters, excluding the middleman or merchant; this property would not have been assessed in Shoshone County. Later, the trade network was altered and the merchandise came directly to the merchants, who then distributed it to the miners. Alternatively, it may be that the early Chinese purchased non-Chinese items directly from the Euroamerican merchants and that later the Chinese merchants added non-Chinese goods to their inventories, which increased the dollar value of their total inventory.

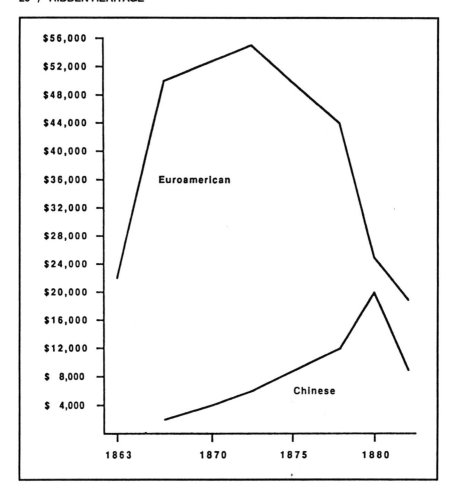

Figure 3. Assessed value of Chinese and Euroamerican property
between 1863 and 1884.

Property Transfer

Additional insight into the distribution of wealth can be gleaned from the records that document property ownership transfers. For the Pierce locality this includes the transfer of placer mines and town lots with buildings. As was shown in Table 1, the majority of claims were sold to the Chinese during the late 1860s. The placer mines included from one to many claims, and occasionally water rights, equipment, and supplies.

Because the descriptions of the mines are terse, it is impossible to identify comparable mines to determine whether or not the Chinese were paying higher

Table 6. Pierce Merchandisers and the Value of Their Merchandise[a]

Year	Total Merchandise	Chinese Merchandise	Chinese Percentage
1868	$17,500	$900	5
1873	$18,340	$940	5
1878	$11,250	$5,750	51
1880	$11,100	$7,600	69
1882	$9,875	$5,075	51

[a]Dollar amounts represent the sum of assessed merchandise for years shown as identified in the Shoshone County Annual Assessment Records (Shoshone County Records, 1861-1884).

prices for placer mines than were the Euroamericans. The following evidence suggests that the prices were similar. There are many cases of a Euroamerican purchasing his partners' interests in a particular mine, and soon thereafter selling the entire mine to the Chinese at the same valuation. Although the prices paid to the partners could have been contrived for this purpose, this was probably not the case; the Chinese were good miners and certainly knew the value of a claim. While the average cost of a mine sold to the Chinese was higher than mines purchased by Euroamericans (Table 7), this was generally due to the fact that the Euroamericans were purchasing mines adjacent to properties which they already owned in order to create larger packages which they could then sell to the Chinese.

The mining records also document a lag between the period when the Chinese purchased most of the mining properties and when they began purchasing town properties (Tables 1 and 7). We know from the 1870 census, however, that there were Chinese merchants and other Chinese who provided services located in Pierce City; presumably they were renting buildings prior to the early 1870s. The increase in Chinese ownership of town properties may somehow be related to the increase in Chinese merchandise. This possibility is developed further in the final section of this chapter.

Chinese Economic Differentiation

A considerable degree of economic differentiation existed within the Pierce Chinese community. The 1870 census schedules provide more information regarding each individual than do the assessment records, which only list the individual's name. The assessed values for each individual's personal property and real estate are shown in Table 8. This record is also advantageous because it identifies the number of individuals that did not have any assessable property:

Table 7. Sales of Mining and Town Properties in the Pierce Locality, 1864 to 1890[a]

	Average Mine Price[b]		Chinese Town Purchases[c]			
	Euro-americans	Chinese	From Euroamericans		From Chinese	
Year	($)	($)	(#)	($)	(#)	($)
1864	56	100	—	—	—	—
1865	103	650	—	—	—	—
1866	528	744	—	—	—	—
1867	288	815	2	35	—	—
1868	143	255	—	—	—	—
1869	195	328	—	—	—	—
1870	402	321	—	—	—	—
1871	198	373	1	60	—	—
1872	141	232	1	120	2	410
1873	123	124	1	200	—	—
1874	154	87	1	100	1	280
1875	104	215	2	175	1	30
1876	242	245	—	—	1	300
1877	1264	154	1	300	1	300
1878	70	412	2	300	1	NA
1879	5	745	—	—	—	—
1880	108	143	—	—	1	150
1881	50	364	—	—	—	—
1882	289	1590	—	—	2	270
1883	1250	147	—	—	1	30
1884	108	88	1	100	1	90
1885	—	77	—	—	1	210
1886	13	137	1	50	1	100
1887	6	251	—	—	—	—
1888	68	73	—	—	—	—
1889	450	76	—	—	—	—
1890	50	—	—	—	—	—
Totals	247	414	13	1440	14	2170

[a]Compiled from bills of sale (Pierce Mining Records, 1861-1890).
[b]Includes all bills of sale involving mining claims.
[c]Divided into Chinese purchases from Euroamericans and purchases from Chinese.

Table 8. Value of Personal Property and Real Estate in 1870[a]

Dwelling Number	Name	Profession	Real Estate	Personal Property	Size of Household
23	Ah Cain	Gold miner	—	100	5
33	Ah Hinn	Gold miner	—	250	5
40	Ah Foong	Gold miner	150	—	3
41	Ah Chee	Gold miner	—	100	3
76	Ding Chung	Clerk	—	300	1
77	Ah Tom Ah	Gold miner	—	800	6
114	King Chin	Gold miner	500	770	3
187	Ah Sam	Merchant	—	2000	1
189	Ah Wong	Blacksmith	400	300	2
195	Yow Wy	Prostitute	—	200	3
205	Ah Hen	Doctor	—	700	3
206	Ah Cooey	Trader	—	500	1
210	Lee Sing	Brothel keeper	—	200	2
212	Ah Ung	Blacksmith	—	100	1
213	Ah Lye	Gardener	150	—	2
213	Ah Fou	Gardener	150	—	2

[a]Information from the U.S. Bureau of the Census (1870).

455 (97% of the population). This contrasts with the Euroamerican population, 70 percent of which had no assessable property.

The major sources for quantitative data related to economic differentiation are the annual property assessments, which provide the description and value of each individual's personal property and real estate. Again, only certain items apparently could be taxed, because the majority of individuals, mostly miners, were not taxed on anything. The assessment records also fail to identify the individual's occupation, though in some cases (e.g., merchants, meat suppliers, miners) this can be inferred; for 1880, some individuals can be found in the census record. (The 1880 census takers did not record the value of personal property and real estate as did the 1870 census takers.) An example of the economic differentiation as reflected in the 1880 census schedules is shown in Table 9.

Merchants — The Euroamerican description of "merchant princes of the mountains" in Pierce (Goulder, 1875) suggests that Chinese merchants were clearly

Table 9. 1880 Assessment of Property Held by Chinese
in the Pierce Locality[a]

Name	Value	Items
Ah Gong	$3050	real estate ($275), merchandise ($1500), debts ($1200), 2 horses ($50), household ($25)
Quong Gee Long	$2840	2 houses & lot ($300), merchandise ($2000), solvent debts ($500), 2 horses ($40)
Hong Yune	$2700	real estate ($350), merchandise ($1500), debts ($800), 2 horses ($50)
Too Shong	$2490	house & lot ($250), merchandise ($1500), gold dust ($200), solvent debts ($500), 2 horses ($40)
Gin Fook	$3700	2 ditches ($3000), money ($700)
Ah Loy	$1000	2 ditches, water right ($1000)
Fook & Hong	$1000	1 ditch ($1000)
Ah Long	$500	2 ditches ($500)
Lune Fook Hong	$450	1 ditch water right ($450)
Ah Toy	$200	1 ditch ($200)
Lip Toy	$100	1 ditch ($100)
Ah Chom	$550	2 horses ($100), hogs ($450)
Jimmy Fee	$200	house & lot ($150), household ($50)
Tong Lee	$200	house & lot ($200)
Ah Sam	$120	house & lot ($100), horse ($20)
Sing Lee	$100	house & lot ($100)
Ah Sing	$150	garden & improvements ($150)
Ah Yen	$100	garden & house ($100)
Ah Yee	$50	1 garden ($50)
Ah Allen	$100	blacksmith shop ($100)
Ah Hang	$100	blacksmith shop ($100)

[a]Information from the Shoshone County Annual Assessment Records, 1880 (Shoshone County Records, 1861-1884).

distinct from Chinese miners. Further, assessment records indicate that there were two types of Chinese merchants in Pierce, ones with inventories that had a high assessed value, and ones with inventories that had a low assessed value. Whether this dichotomy was due to the nature of products sold, or simply the size of the retailing operation is not known. Trull (1946) suggested the latter, stating, "The stores varied from poor ones with only the very cheapest Chinese foods of tea, rice, cheap pottery and clothing, to the larger ones which were very exclusive" (Trull, 1946:43). We do not know whether the merchant actually owned the merchandise, or whether he was merely working for a larger company. Overseas Chinese literature in general states that the merchants were part of larger organizations; for Pierce there is little evidence suggesting that the Pierce Chinese stores were owned by people who lived elsewhere. Trull states that the stores were "company stores" (Trull, 1946:43), but then talks about the merchants growing wealthy (Trull, 1946:43-47); this suggests that there was a degree of entrepreneurship involved in being a merchant in an Idaho mining camp.

Miners — Social differentiation within the general overseas Chinese mining population is suggested by the existence of men who oversaw the mining operation (Barth, 1964:115). Individuals have also been described as miners of "the better class" (Borthwick, 1857:263). For Pierce, the 1870 census and the county assessment records provide evidence of the economic differentiation among the Chinese miners in that only a few had assessable property (Tables 8 and 9).

The Pierce Mining District records provide additional insight based upon the values of placer mine purchases (actually, they were paying for the mineral rights and usually miscellaneous things such as tools, cabins, sluice boxes, and ditches). The price of mining properties ranged from $10 to $9200; transactions over $1000 are shown in Table 10. All of the larger transactions involved major water ditches and many claims spread across several gulches. Although most of the larger purchases were made during the first years that the Chinese moved into Pierce, three of the four largest were made after 1878; these three sales represented the last major European holdings in the Pierce locality, though many Euroamericans continued to mine there throughout the 1880s.

Purchases over $1000 accounted for nearly 71 percent of the total mining purchases (in dollars) made by the Chinese; these accounted for less than 11 percent of the total number of mining claim purchases. As shown in Table 10, few individuals made more than one or two purchases above $1000 (although the problems associated with Chinese names discussed earlier may have skewed this analysis somewhat). When the number of purchases valued under $1000 made by the same individual are calculated, a similar pattern emerges. Nearly 60 percent of the individuals recorded as purchasing mining claims only made one purchase; only 22 percent made more than two purchases (Table 11). This pattern of many rather than a few individuals purchasing claims to mines may reflect a social

Table 10. Chinese Mining Purchases over $1000[a]

Price	Year	Name	Number Purchased Over $1000[b]
$9200	1867	Ah Quay	1 (unless same as Ah Qui)
$9000	1879	Lip Ky	1
$9000	1882	Ah Loy	1
$8000	1882	Ah Fong	1
$4800	1867	Ying Foo	1
$4500	1867	Ah Yee	2
$4400	1867	Lee Chee	2
$3600	1866	Cheung Tuk	1
$3500	1866	Mon Dock	2
$3000	1878	Ah Sam	1
$2960	1867	Ah Qui	1 (unless same as Ah Quay)
$2700	1869	Yim Hee	1
$2500	1867	Ah Yee	2
$2500	1874	Ah Wing	2
$2100	1870	Ah Toy	3
$2000	1871	Mee Cue	1
$1800	1866	Lem Long	2
$1600	1882	Fook Sing	1
$1500	1872	Ah Toy	3
$1500	1866	Tim Hoy	1
$1500	1871	Ah Hoy	1
$1500	1870	Ah Fook	3
$1500	1867	Lee You	1
$1500	1867	Lee Chee	2
$1400	1868	Ah John	1
$1400	1869	Ah Fook	3
$1400	1867	Ang Guwn	1
$1300	1868	Ah Wing	2
$1275	1869	Lem Long	2
$1250	1867	Mon Dock	2
$1250	1870	Hung Sin	1
$1200	1867	Ah Leon	1
$1200	1867	Ah Fook	3
$1200	1866	Ah Mong	2
$1200	1866	Ah Mong	2
$1200	1875	Ah Toy	3
$1200	1876	Ah Hung	1
$1200	1887	Ah You	1

[a]Based on bills of sale found in the Pierce Mining Records (1861-1890).
[b]Indicates the number of times each name was associated with a purchase over $1000 and hence, the number of times the name appears in this table.

Table 11. Numbers of Mining Purchases Under
$1000 Made by Individuals with the Same Name[a]

Number of Purchases	Occurrences	Percentage
1	98	59
2	31	19
3	12	7
4	6	4
5	8	5
6	6	4
9	1	<1
10	1	<1
12	1	<1
21	1	<1

[a]Based on bills of sale found in the Pierce Mining Records (1861-1890).

system far different from the centralized system often described by overseas Chinese researchers.

DISCUSSION

The purpose of this chapter was to produce a diachronic description of the Chinese in an Idaho mining camp. Such knowledge is important to overseas Chinese research because few in-depth descriptions of the Chinese in mining camps exist. Documentary data were used to describe patterns in population makeup, household composition, professions, the local economy, and in inter-ethnic relations. As research continues in Pierce and elsewhere, the significance of these patterns will become more clear.

The documentary data have been particularly valuable to the archaeological study of the Pierce locality in that we now have a greater appreciation for the complexity of the Chinese community. We now know, for example, that there were not just one or two types of Pierce Chinese mining households. The data indicate that there were households both large and small; households associated with rich mines, poor mines, large operations, and small operations; households of miners and non-miners; households with mine owners or overseers; and households with Chinese and Euroamericans. Thus, before making any definitive statements about Chinese miners in Pierce based upon the archaeological record, we must be certain that we understand the nature of the sites from which the data are recovered.

The documentary data have also stimulated the formulation of several questions which will guide future study, much of it archaeological, concerning the Pierce community. Among these are questions about the lifeways of the mine owners or overseers, the relationship of house size and number to household size, possible changes in mining technology, and possible changes in Chinese trade networks. As answers to these questions become clear, questions of greater anthropological significance can be pursued archaeologically.

Finally, the documentary study of Pierce also led to the development of several propositions concerning the Chinese, which will hopefully stimulate future research in Idaho and elsewhere. The first relates to ethnic relations within the community. Evidence from Pierce suggests that during the 1870s and early 1880s, membership in the community overshadowed ethnic categorization. This is suggested by the increase in Chinese/Euroamerican households during the 1870s and by documents which indicate that Shoshone County supported several indigent Chinese during this period (Shoshone County Records, 1861-1884). Moreover, when an Irish outsider murdered a local Indian supplier of fresh vegetables, the Euroamerican residents saw to it that the man was taken to trial and eventually sentenced to hang (Stapp and Spencer, in press). These apparent breakdowns in ethnic barriers stand in stark contrast to most descriptions of life in western mining camps. Perhaps the rural nature of the community or the general deterioration of economic conditions during this time prompted such behavior.

Second, patterns such as the increase in assessed Chinese merchandise, the increase in Chinese merchants and decrease in Chinese gamblers and prostitutes, the lag between the purchase of mining properties and town properties by Chinese, and the changes in household size suggest that a shift occurred in the economic organization within the Chinese community. It is proposed that this shift reflected a normal evolution of Chinese mining communities, whereas during the early boom period, "Situation A" existed, and as things calmed down, "Situation A" changed to "Situation B." The following scenario, based upon general knowledge of resource-oriented communities, is offered for consideration by overseas Chinese researchers:

1. When a mining district opened to the overseas Chinese, large tightly controlled Chinese mining companies purchased mines and dominated Chinese activities in the locality.
2. Once profitability fell below that which was acceptable to the large companies, both labor and equipment were moved to other mining districts.
3. Some Chinese stayed in Pierce out of choice or necessity, becoming entrepreneurs, forming partnerships, or finding employment with smaller mining companies or in the service sector.
4. Those remaining continued to work in the locality until economic conditions forced them to move on.

What is being proposed here is that following an initial economic boom, the Chinese economic system became less "corporate-like" and more "individual-like"; a process of entrepreneurialism set in.

Alternatively, the proposed change in economic structure may have been due to a change in the dominant Chinese group. Perhaps one dominant group, Group A, moved into Pierce at the outset of the Chinese occupation, and once the major deposits were extracted moved to another mining district that had greater promise, leaving Pierce to Group B, which previously had been in the minority. These hypothesized groups might have represented social groupings based upon language, regional roots, family associations, economic organizations, or political organizations.

Hopefully, this study will encourage researchers to examine other communities and compare them with Pierce. Studies are needed to determine whether the patterns observed at Pierce are anomalous or characteristic of other overseas Chinese resource-oriented communities. Data from other communities may hold the answers to explain the conditions under which changes such as the ones described herein took place. Were the changes simply due to decreases in population size? Were some changes related to the fact that the Chinese were a majority rather than a minority in Pierce? Were the relative numbers of gamblers and prostitutes a function of population size, or did they reflect certain community economic organizations such as secret societies or district associations? Did household size undergo similar shifts in other mining communities and non-mining communities? Does the ratio of assessed merchandise to population size reflect trade networks? Did all Chinese placer mining camps experience similar changes? As these and other questions are answered, progress will be made toward understanding the overseas Chinese experience in America and elsewhere.

REFERENCES CITED

BARTH, GUNTHER
 1964   *Bitter Strength: A History of the Chinese in the United States, 1850-1870,* Harvard University Press, Cambridge, Massachusetts.
BORTHWICK, J. D.
 1857   *The Gold Hunters: A First Hand Picture of Life in California Mining Camps in the Early Fifties,* MacMillan Co., New York.
BOYD, JOSEPH H.
 1924   Reminiscences of Joseph H. Boyd, *Washington Historical Quarterly, 15,* pp. 243-262.
DAILY OREGONIAN
 1866   Salmon River Mines, *Daily Oregonian,* Portland, p. 1, November 21.
FRENCH, ALLISON
 1891   Pierce City Mines, *Spokesman Review,* Spokane, p. 6, August 6.

GOULDER, W. A.
1875   North Idaho News, *Idaho Tri-Weekly Statesman*, Boise, p. 3, November 13.
1909   *Reminiscences: Incidents in the Life of a Pioneer in Oregon and Idaho*, Timothy Regan, Boise.
LOUIE, EMMA WOO
1985-   A New Perspective on Surnames among Chinese Americans, *Amerasia*, *12*:1,
1986   pp. 1-2.
PAUL, RODMAN WILSON
1974   *Mining Frontiers of the Far West 1848-1880*, University of New Mexico Press, Albuquerque.
PIERCE MINING RECORDS
1861-   Collection of primary documents relating to the Pierce Mining District,
1890   located at the Clearwater Historical Society, Orofino, Idaho.
SHOSHONE COUNTY RECORDS
1861-   Miscellaneous records relating to the operation of Shoshone County, located
1884   at the Clearwater Historical Society, Orofino, Idaho.
SPACE, RALPH
1957   How Louis Baker Fell in the Well; Yarns of Pierce in the '90s, *Idaho Yesterdays*, *1*:1, pp. 11-18.
STAPP, DARBY C.
1987   The Pierce Mining District Records, Alfred W. Bowers Laboratory of Anthropology, University of Idaho, *Letter Report*, No. 87-2, Moscow, Idaho.
1990   The Historic Ethnography of a Chinese Mining Community in Idaho, Ph.D. dissertation, University of Pennsylvania, Philadelphia.
STAPP, DARBY C. and JULIA G. LONGENECKER
1984   1983 Test Excavations at 10-CW-159, The Pierce Chinese Mining Site, *University of Idaho Anthropological Research Manuscript Series*, No. 80, Moscow, Idaho.
STAPP, DARBY C., and ROBERT W. SPENCER
In press   The First White Man in Idaho Convicted of Murdering an Indian, to appear in *Idaho Yesterdays*, 1992.
TRULL, FERN COBLE
1946   The History of the Chinese in Idaho from 1864 to 1910, Master's thesis, University of Oregon, Eugene.
U.S. BUREAU OF THE CENSUS
1870   *9th Census, 1870*. Idaho (Territory) Vol. 1. (Population schedules. Washington) Photographed in microfilm lab., Bureau of Census. (n.d.) National Archives. Microform publications.
1880   *10th Census, 1880*. Idaho (Territory) Vol. 1. (Population schedules. Washington) Photographed in microfilm lab., Bureau of Census. (n.d.) National Archives. Microform publications.
1897   *Report on the Population at the Eleventh Census: 1890*, Government Printing Office, Washington, D.C.
1900   *12th Census, 1900*. Idaho Vol. 1. (Population schedules. Washington) Photographed in microfilm lab., Bureau of Census. (n.d.) National Archives. Microform publications.

1910   *13th Census, 1910.* Idaho Vol. 1. (Population schedules. Washington) Photographed in microfilm lab., Bureau of Census. (n.d.) National Archives. Microform publications.

1922   *Fourteenth Census of the United States Taken in the Year 1920: Population,* Government Printing Office, Washington, D.C.

1931   *Fifteenth Census of the United States Taken in the Year 1930: Population,* Government Printing Office, Washington, D.C.

WELLS, MERLE

1963   Rush to Idaho, Idaho Bureau of Mines and Geology, *Bulletin* No. 19. Moscow, Idaho.

CHAPTER 2

Archaeological Evidence of Chinese Use along the Lower Salmon River, Idaho

David A. Sisson

BACKGROUND AND PURPOSE

This study of Chinese sites was initiated in response to the Bureau of Land Management's Lower Salmon River Cultural Resource Management Plan (the Plan) (Sisson, 1983). The Plan forms the framework for the management of over 200 cultural sites spanning 10,000 years of occupation.

The Lower Salmon River is located mid-way between Boise, Idaho and Spokane, Washington (Figure 4). The Bureau of Land Management (BLM) administers a half-mile-wide corridor along 205 miles of river from French Creek, twenty miles east of Riggins, Idaho, to the confluence of the Salmon and Snake Rivers. The BLM-administered land is intermingled with private lands in the corridor.

The majority of the canyon is grassland that has been modified from native species through heavy livestock use. Forested land is scarce throughout most of the canyon, although some pockets of trees can be found on north-facing slopes or sideslopes of the canyon. The area from Riggins to French Creek has greater amounts of forested land. Generally, hackberry (*Celtis douglasii*) trees are located on the terraces adjacent to the river.

Data on the Chinese sites have been gathered from cultural resource inventories conducted for the Plan, cultural resource site monitoring studies, and site-specific management actions including structural recording, mapping, and surface collections of artifacts exposed from natural erosion, recreation use, and livestock use. No excavations have been conducted on any of the Chinese sites. Therefore, all

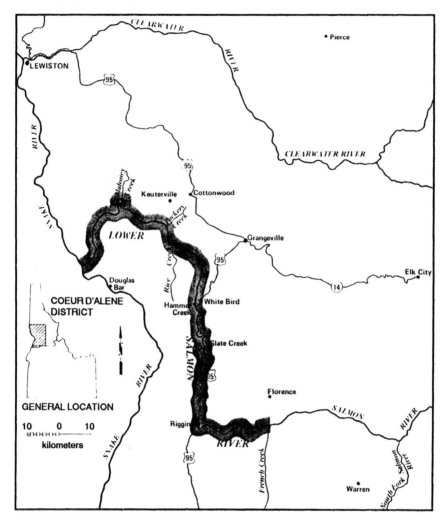

Figure 4. General location of the Lower Salmon River study area.

information and conclusions on Chinese sites along the Lower Salmon River are based solely upon surface features, exposed artifacts, and limited historical accounts.

GENERAL HISTORIC SETTING

Gold was first discovered in north Idaho at Pierce in 1860. The gold rush followed and other major deposits were soon found at Elk City in 1861, Florence in 1861, and Warren in 1862. The Slate Creek area was established in 1861 as a distribution point of supplies for the mines.

The bars along the Lower Salmon River were mined for gold in the early 1860s. Low bar placer deposits were worked with rockers or large hydraulic mining equipment when the Elk City and Florence mining districts were at their height (Lisle and Bradley, 1904:12). The production of the placers decreased in the mid-1860s but mining continued through 1900. There was another influx of mining in the 1930s during the Depression.

The first Chinese in the area reportedly arrived in Lewiston, Idaho, on steamboats in 1865 (Elsensohn, 1970:14). Some Chinese settled in Lewiston, north of the Salmon River, but many passed through that town on their way to the newly discovered gold fields.

Chinese were initially excluded from the Florence Mining District. In 1869 Chinese miners were allowed into the Florence district, and by 1880 the Chinese were said to virtually have complete control of the placer field (Elsensohn, 1970:43). There continued to be Chinese entries in the Florence mining records into the 1890s.

Elsensohn (1970:43) has reported that the mining districts along the Lower Salmon River had always permitted Chinese miners. The mineral values along the Lower Salmon River were never as high as those of the surrounding districts. Burnett (1978:17) reports that a group of Chinese were mining near Hammer Creek in 1893. Intensive Chinese use of the area between Rice Creek and Maloney Creek along the Lower Salmon River south of Keuterville was reported to have occurred in the 1880s through the 1890s.

Apparently, from the few historical accounts available, the Chinese population got along well with the local ranchers. In 1896 a local rancher helped Ah Can, a Chinese miner along the Lower Salmon River south of Keuterville, pack goods down to the river from the top of the canyon. Around 1900, Lee Tann was working for some of the local ranchers as well as mining along the river south of Keuterville; he died in 1918 in the Salmon River Canyon (Elsensohn, 1970:72). A popular route used by the packers taking goods to the Chinese was down Packers Creek, which was named for them. The Chinese miners also went up to the ranches to get goods. They bought hogs and drove them back down the canyon where they were slaughtered. Occasionally wheat or sacks of potatoes were purchased (Elsensohn, 1970:68).

Not all of the relations with the local people were so friendly. At Hammer Creek, near White Bird, the Chinese were reportedly kicked off their mining claim in 1893 by one of the local Euroamerican miners (Burnett, 1978:17). At Douglas Bar, on the Snake River south of the Salmon and Snake River confluence, thirty-two Chinese miners were massacred in 1885. Eight cowboys killed these men while stealing their gold (Elsensohn, 1970:74).

There is one account of a quarrel among the Chinese miners along the river south of Keuterville. Lee Tann could read and write, so he did much of the supply ordering for the local Chinese miners. On one occasion the other Chinese felt they were cheated and attacked Lee Tann. He sought refuge with a local rancher, who helped settle the dispute (Elsensohn, 1970:71).

In summary, based upon general historical accounts, the greatest concentration of Chinese use along the Lower Salmon River occurred south of Keuterville from the 1880s to the 1890s. Chinese use also occurred along other segments of the river. It is apparent that the Chinese obtained a variety of goods, including hogs, potatoes, and wheat from local ranchers. Elsensohn (1947:92) also reported that the Chinese, farther upriver from what is considered the Lower Salmon, had their own gardens along the South Fork of the Salmon River where they raised vegetables for the Warren Mining District. Salmon were also reportedly sold to the Chinese for ten cents a pound along the South Fork of the Salmon River (Elsensohn, 1947:92). Therefore, the Chinese used a variety of goods depending upon the local conditions supplementing others imported from China.

The Chinese in this area had many of the same experiences as other Chinese throughout the western United States. They were excluded from some of the major mining districts until the easily obtainable gold was exhausted, they were kicked off their mining claims, and they were sometimes even murdered. But they also often had good relationships with some of the local people, as well as with each other.

GENERAL BUILDING CHARACTERISTICS IN CHINA

A brief exploration of China's vernacular architecture was undertaken to aid in evaluation of historic sites along the Lower Salmon River. Generally most over-seas Chinese sites in a rural western United States setting have unique artifact assemblages that are typically easy to identify. Along the Lower Salmon River however, there are many sites with a paucity of artifacts. Also, if the Chinese immigrants adopted the use of many Euroamerican goods, or if Chinese goods were not available, it would then be difficult to identify ethnic Chinese sites based solely upon artifactual evidence. Therefore, if unique features of Chinese ver-nacular architecture could be identified, they would aid in future evaluations of other historic sites along the Lower Salmon River.

The following general Chinese building characteristics are summarized by Mirams (1940:10-11). The dwelling consisted of a wooden building with wooden support posts built upon a mud or stone platform. The walls could be made of stone, brick, or wood framing, but the wall usually did not provide any support. The plan was typically rectangular or square (Mirams, 1940:25). Knapp (1986:54) suggests that most rural buildings depended on load bearing walls. Most buildings faced south (Bushell, 1904:677, Mirams, 1940:25).

Rural dwellings in north China are traditionally one-story, single room, and rectangular. These would be extended into multi-bay dwellings (the most common had three bays) when possible. In most northern dwellings the ridgepole runs east-west, with the door and the windows facing south (Knapp, 1986:26). Chinese from the north brought the rectangular northern house layout when they migrated to southern China (Knapp, 1986:39). In southern China this pattern was adapted to the local site and conditions but did not necessarily face south (Knapp, 1986:51).

The foundation is tamped earth which is level or slightly elevated. Often a stone foundation is raised above the ground along the edge of the foundation to prevent water damage to the walls (Knapp, 1989:68).

Mirams (1940:27) mentions a peasant hut made of mud. Conwell (1871: 130-133) described a Chinese dwelling of around 1870 as a long hut with a hip style roof and with walls of beaten mortar attached to corner posts. The hut had four rooms, each reported to be eight feet square with beaten earth floors, and each occupied by one family of about eight people. The walls were seven feet high, the entrances two and one-half feet wide. There was only one small window that consisted of a hole cut in the wall for each room.

Mawson (1926:12), as reported in Ritchie (1986:47), describes Chinese structures around Canton as low, windowless, and constructed of sun dried and fired brick. Traditional houses in town were reported by Boyd (1962:76-77) as rectangular with courtyards. Entrances were located either in the middle or the corner of the south walls. The Chinese houses could be built without nails, hinges, clamps, or other iron artifacts (Hommel, 1937:283). Cave dwellings described by Boyd (1962:109), as well as dwellings consisting of a tent of straw matting about four feet high (Conwell, 1871:132), have also been reported.

Kitchens were generally located outside the structure. Conwell (1871:134-135) reported that all cooking took place at the back side of the house. Some kitchens were built on the veranda or, in some cases, in an outbuilding (Boyd, 1962:83). Hommel (1937:148) reports some kitchens with stoves built inside the houses.

Conwell (1871:135) has stated that there was never a fire inside a Chinese house. Hommel (1937:149) has observed that there was generally no provision for heating the houses in central and southern China since the winters were not severe, although some chimneys were seen. Hommel also remarks that the Chinese were familiar with chimneys 2000 years ago, but used them infrequently, possibly because of a fuel shortage. Boyd (1962:82) and Speiser (1965:390) report an absence of chimneys in Chinese houses.

The general method of heating appears to have been portable heating units described as charcoal braziers by Boyd (1962:82). Hommel (1937:309) described them as hand and foot warmers in the form of portable earthenware pots and portable stoves. The houses in northern China were reported to have a raised platform, heated from underneath, in a portion of the room (Boyd, 1962:82). The smoke from the portable heating units was allowed to rise to the roof rafters and through crevices in the roof's ridge or sides, or through a small, purposefully made opening (Hommel, 1937:136; Speiser, 1965:390). Both Hommel (1937:390) and Mirams (1940:31) report that warm clothing was worn by the inhabitants of the houses.

The typical north China dwelling of three bays had two bedrooms divided by a central room. In the central room there was often a low brick stove on each side of the entrance that provided heat in the dwelling and was used for cooking (Knapp, 1986:26).

Another feature in the Chinese house is described as follows (Hommel 1937:311):

> . . . there is usually a small stove to be found in the Chinese kitchen, built against the wall without any provision to carry off the smoke. A structure about 2-1/2 feet high is erected, consisting of three brick walls like a chimney but with the front open. The top opening is usually just large enough to hold the brass tea kettle. A little lower down protruding from the back wall is a brick ledge and at the same height in front, extending from one side wall to the other, an iron bar or sometimes a brick arch. Ledge and bar, or ledge and brick arch, as the case may be, form the support of the wrought iron grate. . . . A wood fire is made on this grate, off and on during the whole day with brush wood, as it is essential to the well-being of the Chinese to have hot tea all day long.

This feature was evidently not used to heat the house; instead, it was used to warm tea, although it undoubtedly provided some heat.

The privy was a separate structure placed over a rectangular hole about two feet deep. The sewage in towns was disposed of by transporting it to the nearby countryside as fertilizer (Boyd, 1962:83).

The technique of rammed earth construction is common throughout China. Hommel (1937:294-296) describes one method of construction and Knapp (1986:54-55; 1989:70) describes a slightly different method. Earth was dug and piled into V-shaped or H-shaped wall supports. It was then pounded with rammers until compacted. Additional earth was piled on top and the ramming process repeated. When completed the walled supports were removed, leaving a compacted earth wall.

Besides the structures themselves, another aspect of Chinese house construction has been considered. This is *feng shui,* a way of both perceiving and dealing with reality (Feuchtwang, 1974:14). It stands for the total, composite power of the natural environment. If one places oneself well within the environment, it will bring good fortune (Feuchtwang, 1974:2). Therefore, *feng shui* was a method of locating a house, village, or city in the environment.

The ideal *feng shui* site is protected on three sides; the side the structure faces should be open (Feuchtwang, 1974:60). The front of the structure should always face south. The front of the structure is symbolic of south, even if it is impractical to face south (Feuchtwang, 1974:2). It is considered good to have water in front, if it is calm and smooth (Feuchtwang, 1974:134). A point along the bank of a fast-running stream is generally undesirable (Feuchtwang, 1974:121). The confluence of streams is considered very desirable since it symbolizes a concentration of influence. A location at branching streams symbolizes dispersal of influence and is not desirable (Feuchtwang, 1974:130).

Towns are planned on a north-south axis whenever possible (Feuchtwang, 1974:3). The town plan, as well as the dwelling, is square (Feuchtwang, 1974:91). The resemblances of certain landscapes to forms in the Chinese culture, such as the White Tiger or the Green Dragon, is also an important part of *feng shui* (Feuchtwang, 1974:113).

Although the ideas set forth under *feng shui* were the ultimate goal, it was often not practical to follow them exactly. Divergence from the ideals was often unavoidable, but any potential catastrophe could be avoided by planting trees, building embankments, or placing a board with charms painted on it in the proper location (Feuchtwang, 1974:115).

It is evident that there was a variety of Chinese building characteristics, including mud structures, brick structures, one room structures, and multi-room structures sharing common walls. Some authors state that chimneys were never used, while others have noted they were used, albeit rarely. Some state that cooking was done entirely outside, while others document kitchens inside. Some have noted small windows in structures; others have described structures as windowless. A standard unit of measure does not seem to exist; the Chinese "foot" appears to be quite variable (Hommel, 1937:255). While the concepts of *feng shui* were probably carried with the immigrants to the United States, it is uncertain how discernible these ideals may be in the archaeological record, since undesirable influences could be compensated for when necessary. Boerschmann (1911:546) has noted that food and clothing, as well as styles of buildings, varied considerably throughout China. From a review of the literature, it would indeed appear that this variability does exist.

THE ARCHAEOLOGICAL EVIDENCE—HISTORICAL SITES

Although archaeological data have been generated by various reconnaissance surveys since 1958, historic sites were at first ignored. An archaeological survey completed for the Bureau of Land Management in 1980 along the Lower Salmon River recorded all sites encountered including historic sites. Survey results, Bureau of Land Management inventories, and site monitoring since 1983 have provided the information used in this study (see Table 12).

Site-specific management actions have provided more detailed information than the reconnaissance surveys. These actions have included detailed structural recording, limited archival research, feature and contour mapping, and surface collection of artifacts. Surface artifacts were collected because of damage created from livestock use, displacement or removal by recreationists, and damage created from above-average flows of the Salmon River. The collected artifacts provide temporal, functional, and ethnic information on specific sites. Both Chinese and

Table 12. Lower Salmon River Chinese Site Summary

Site Number	Structure	Other Features/Comments	Rescaled Exposure[a]
10-IH-60	—	Rock walls, hydraulic mine ditches, cutbanks, tailings piles, and pressure box. Chinese occupation 1890–1893.	90
10-IH-363	Three; one with a niche and a chimney adjacent to the entrance. All structures excavated into the ground.	Ditch, pond, rock-lined cistern, leveled area.	90
10-IH-724	—	Nine rock-walled terraces, 1-1.5 meter wide, apricot and plum trees on terraces. Hydraulic mine cutbanks. Common name is "China Gardens."	90
10-IH-750	Three; two with rock outcrops for back walls. All structures excavated into the ground.	Rock walls and terrace.	30
10-IH-779	Seven; two with chimneys in back wall opposite entrance. All structures excavated into ground.	Hydraulic mine cutbanks. Rock wall; standing circular rock feature (1.00 meter tall, 0.75 meter diameter).	90
10-IH-780	Three; all structures excavated into the ground.	Hydraulic mine ditch, reservoir, tailings piles. Chinese occupation—1890s.	93
10-IH-782	One; chimney adjacent to entrance.	Veranda and steps. Chinese occupation—1890s-1918?	147
10-IH-791	One; structure excavated into ground.	Rock walls and leveled areas. Chinese occupation—1890s	128

Table 12. (Cont'd.)

Site Number	Structure	Other Features/Comments	Rescaled Exposure[a]
10-IH-794	—	Hydraulic mine cutbanks.	144
10-IH-1161	One; structure excavated into ground.	—	150
10-IH-1162	One; rockshelter with rock wall. Chimney adjacent to entrance.	—	138
10-IH-1187	—	Rockshelter possibly associated with 10-IH-782. Complete mining rocker found in shelter.	137
10-IH-1199	—	Artifact scatter.	162
10-IH-1208	One; has two rooms and is excavated into ground.	Hydraulic mine ditch, cutbank, and tailings piles. Late 1880-1890 Chinese occupation.	91
10-IH-1222	One; used rock outcrop for back wall. Structure excavated into the ground.	—	132
10-IH-1225	One; excavated into ground with portion of roof remaining. Entrance and chimney in long side wall.	Hydraulic mine cutbank and tailings piles.	89
10-IH-1260	One; possibly with two rooms. Excavated into ground.	Hydraulic mine cutbanks, two ditches, reservoir, four terraces.	90
10-IH-1279	—	Rockshelter and rock wall.	96
10-IH-1328	Two; both excavated into ground.	One hearth, two mine shafts, hydraulic cutbanks.	146

[a]See Discussion, p. 47ff.

Euroamerican manufactured items are found on all the Chinese sites except 10-IH-1279 which only has opium cans.

Individual Chinese sites are briefly summarized in Table 12. A more detailed description of selected sites is provided in the following narrative. The Bureau of Land Management (1991) has a complete record of all Lower Salmon River sites referenced in this report.

10-IH-780

This site is located on a river terrace between Rice Creek and Maloney Creek. It consists of three rock structures and several other badly deteriorated features of unknown function. A mining reservoir, ditch, and hydraulic mine tailings are also associated with the site. The rock structures, all excavated into the ground, are built in a row along the edge of the terrace. All are oriented to the Salmon River, and the walls are aligned to the cardinal directions. The walls consist of rock with dirt piled against the outside of the wall for support. There are no chimneys in the structures. The plan view of structure 780/4 (Figure 5) is typical of most structures along the Lower Salmon River. Numerous artifacts, both Chinese and Euroamerican, have been collected from in front of the terrace because of the continuing erosion problem. The Bureau of Land Management completed a stabilization project in 1989 that has protected this site from further deterioration (Sisson, 1989). One bottle base has the embossing "M G W," which Toulouse (1971:362) suggests has an unconfirmed ca. 1889 manufacturing date.

10-IH-782

This site, located between Rice Creek and Maloney Creek, contains a rock structure, leveled area, and stone steps. The rock structure, 782/1, is unique in that it was excavated between two large boulders (Figure 6). These boulders form the east and west walls with cobbles piled on top. The north wall, made of rock, is excavated into the ground. A rock chimney is built inside, immediately to the right of the structure's entrance (Figure 7). The chimney feature is formed by a portion of the east wall, a portion of the south wall, and a small extension of rock perpendicular to the south wall that forms the west wall of the feature. The north side of the chimney opens into the structure, therefore giving the appearance of a three-sided feature. It is 0.51 meter wide at the base, narrows to 0.27 meter at the top, and is 2.03 meters high. Another larger three-sided feature is connected to the outside front of the structure. The outside feature faces southwest and is 1.27 meters wide. A leveled area, much like a veranda, extends from the front of the structure to the edge of a river terrace. A series of stone steps leads from the veranda down the terrace to a small permanent creek. Both Euroamerican and Chinese artifacts have been located. An embossed side panel of a "Hamlin's Wizard Oil" bottle was found on the site. This bottle type was first made in the early 1890s (Wilson and Wilson, 1971:41). Artifacts found in a nearby rockshelter

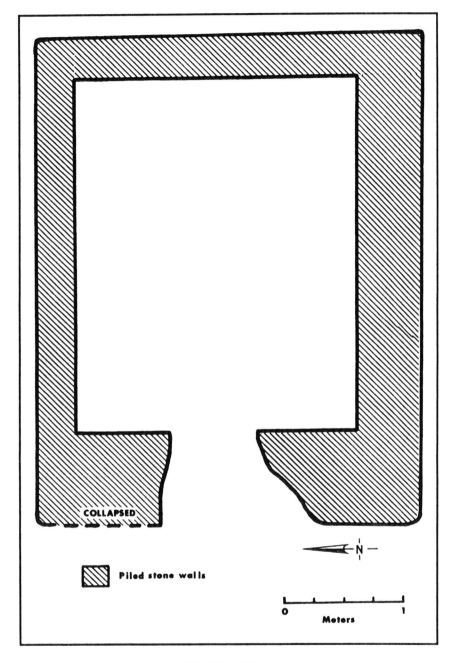

Figure 5. Plan of structure 10-IH-780/4. (This structure represents the typical form of the majority of Chinese habitations along the Lower Salmon River.) Drawn by Steve Wright.

Figure 6. Structure 10-IH-782/1 looking southwest.
(Note the chimney adjacent to the entrance.)

Figure 7. Chimney feature found on structure 10-IH-782/1. (The chimney is 0.51
meter at the base, narrows to 0.27 meter at the top, and is 2.03 meters tall.)

(10-IH-1187) may be associated with this site. They include a mining rocker and tobacco cans.

The General Land Office survey plats show the structure in 1909, and the survey notes indicate that the occupant was Lee Fenn (United States Department of the Interior 1909:Plat). This is also the general area where Lee Tann lived and worked during the same time. It is possible that the structure was his, but his name may not have been correctly recorded by the surveyor.

10-IH-1162

Located between Rice Creek and Maloney Creek, this is the only known Chinese habitation site that consists of a rockshelter with a rock wall enclosing an area around the shelter (Figure 8). The south and west walls are partially free-standing, while the wall opposite the entrance (east wall) is excavated into the ground. The rockshelter forms the north side of the habitation. The east wall continues up into the rockshelter. Mud mortar has been used in this wall. A chimney is located to the left of the structure entrance. The feature has a three-sided appearance with the open side facing into the structure. The chimney feature is about 0.53 meter wide. One small log that formed part of the roof still remains. It apparently rested on top of the west wall and was leaned against the overhang of the rockshelter. Both Euroamerican and Chinese artifacts have been located on the site.

10-IH-1225

This site is located between Rice Creek and Maloney Creek across the river from 10-IH-779. This single rock structure has been built in the middle of hydraulic mine tailings, at the edge of a high terrace that drops straight down to the Salmon River. Some Chinese artifacts have been found at the base of the terrace, but only Euroamerican artifacts have been found immediately around the struc-ture. This structure, which is excavated into the ground, is unique for several reasons. First, this is the only rock structure along the Lower Salmon River that still has the wooden framework of the roof. The framework is similar in style to the shed roof pattern (Wyatt, 1987:Fig. 6s), and is made of milled lumber. No roofing material was observed on the site. This site also has the entrance con-structed in the long side wall instead of the end wall. A chimney is located to the right of the entrance in the same long wall. This is not a three-sided opened chimney feature, but instead it is partially enclosed. A hole continues up through the wall that probably held a stove pipe. The bottom of the chimney feature is open, which probably allowed a stove to be placed in it; numerous stove parts remain in the structure. The Euroamerican artifacts located around the structure suggest that it was reoccupied in the early 1900s or 1930s.

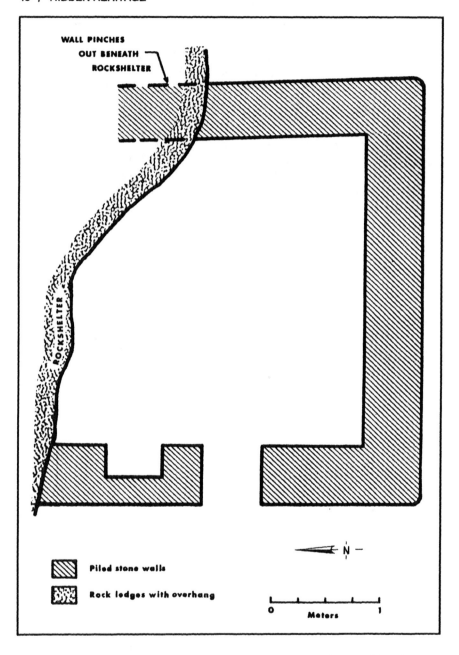

Figure 8. Rockshelter site (10-IH-1162) with rock wall built around it to form the habitation. (Note the chimney to the left of the entrance.)
Drawn by Steve Wright.

10-IH-1328

This site is located near the confluence of the Salmon and Snake Rivers. It consists of two rock structures, two mining shafts, hydraulic mine cutbanks, and one unidentified rock feature. The rock structures, which are excavated into the ground, have badly deteriorated rock walls. Both structures are open at the front; neither has a chimney. One structure is oriented almost due south and the other structure is oriented southeast. The rock feature has been referred to by some local people as the "Chinese Shrine" (Figure 9). It is 2.6 meters wide at the base, tapers to about 0.52 meter wide at the top; and is 1.6 meters high. A small rock and dirt ramp about 1.3 meters wide, 0.57 meter high at its junction with the main rock wall, and 1.63 meters long leads up to the south side of the feature. No oral or written documentation has been located to indicate the possible function of the feature; it may be a hearth. Both Euroamerican and Chinese artifacts have been found on the site.

DISCUSSION

The Chinese structures have a number of architectural characteristics in common. These will be summarized, and the following discussion will address exposure, pit and wall construction, area of the habitations, rockshelters, roof construction, chimney features, and miscellaneous features.

Exposure or orientation of the sites was measured to indicate possible tendencies to any of the cardinal directions (Table 12). Exposure is measured on United States Geological Survey (U.S.G.S.) 7.5 minute topographic maps using a protractor to calculate the angle of a line that is drawn perpendicular to the elevation contour lines through the center of the site. Site exposure was measured on a scale of 0-360 degrees. These data were later rescaled to range from 0-180 degrees with 0 degrees indicating north and 180 degrees indicating south; values near 90 degrees will indicate either east or west. Exposure of the site is used in the comparison rather than using that of the individual structures, since site exposure generally reflects the exposure of the structure. The only exception is feature 10-IH-1328/2 which is oriented 180 degrees, whereas the site is oriented 214 degrees.

The relationship of the total number of sites to exposure shows that only one site is oriented in a northerly direction (Figure 10). Nine are oriented either east or west with the remaining nine sites oriented southwest, southeast or south. Therefore, it would appear that there is a tendency to select sites with a south, east or west exposure.

The Salmon River can be seen from the entrance of any of the rock structures or rockshelters. Most entrances are directly facing the river although a few are placed at a slight angle to the river. Even in those circumstances where the structures could be oriented south they were not, instead they opened to the river. Excellent

Figure 9. Unidentified rock feature (possibly a hearth) located at 10-IH-1328. Drawn by Steve Wright.

examples are sites 10-IH-779 and 10-IH-780. In both circumstances the sites are situated on river terraces and are built along the terrace edge. All the structures are oriented west, towards the river. The river flows in a south to north direction so that structures could have easily had the entrances placed in the south wall. Since orientation to the south is one of the principles of *feng shui*, one might expect all the structures to be oriented to the south. But it must be remembered that other factors were part of *feng shui*, such as facing an open area, facing water, and being protected from behind. The front of the structure could symbolize all the good of the south even if it was not facing south. Since the primary purpose of the Chinese was to mine for gold, the critical factor for settlement would therefore have been the location of the mineral resource, not whether the area was exposed to any specific cardinal direction.

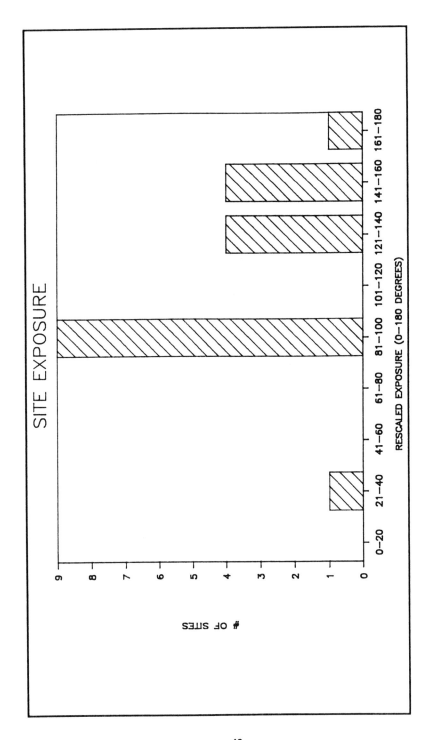

Figure 10. Site exposure showing the range of sites rescaled from 0-180 degrees.

49

The rock structures along the Lower Salmon River were each made by excavating a rectangular pit. The depths of the pits varied. Rock walls were constructed along the inside of the pit combining angular basalt and dirt. Rarely were river cobbles used. The angular basalt has flatter surfaces and was therefore easier to stack and more stable. The rock walls were often built above the pit, and the dirt piled against the outside of the rock wall for support. One rockshelter site (10-IH-1162) does have two partially free-standing walls. The east wall of this structure is excavated into the ground. A portion of the wall extends up on a ledge in the rockshelter and mud mortar has been used in the wall.

All habitation structures have been excavated into the ground. Only sites 10-IH-1187 and 10-IH-1279, both rockshelters, are not excavated into the ground. Rockshelters constitute a small percentage of the habitation sites. Of the three recorded rockshelters, one (10-IH-1187) was probably only used for storage and another (10-IH-1279) had only opium cans on the floor of the structure, suggesting its use was only for opium smoking.

The average area of the structures including the rockshelters has been computed (Table 13). All are internal measurements that should reflect the actual living space. Generally only one measurement each was taken for the width and the length. Occasionally two measurements were taken and averaged to arrive at a value. The insides of the rock walls of the structures are generally very irregular, which can create wide variability in measurements; therefore the calculated area cannot be considered an "absolute" value. Instead, it provides some comparative information. Excavations probably would provide more accurate information on the actual floor areas. The average internal area of the habitation sites is 9.52 square meters. Two structures (10-IH-1208 and 10-IH-1260) may have had two rooms. All of the other structures are single room dwellings. Site 10-IH-1260 is badly deteriorated, making it difficult to determine if the dwelling had two rooms or is composed of two habitations that share a common wall. None of the other rock structures share a common wall.

The area of rockshelter 10-IH-1279 has been included in the comparison of average area of the sites, as has that of rockshelter 10-IH-1162, a habitation site with a rock wall built on three sides forming the living area. The area of rockshelter 10-IH-1187 is the largest recorded for any of the Chinese sites but it was unsuitable for occupation because of the substantial amount of large rockfall; its area was not included in determining average habitation area. The areas of the other two rockshelters are each smaller than the average habitation site along the Lower Salmon River. In fact, 10-IH-1279 is the smallest of all. The smaller areas may be a result of the need to conform to the natural overhang and the rocky terrain.

There is little evidence of roof construction on any of the structures. The rockshelter site (10-IH-1162) has one pole that probably rested on top of the wall and was placed against the overhang of the rockshelter. There were probably other poles laid in a like fashion, forming a framework to which a roof covering was

Table 13. Lower Salmon River Chinese Structure Summary

Site Number	Feature Number	Area (Square Meters)	Entrance Location	Fireplace Location
10-IH-363	363/A	12.00	A	C
	363/C	9.00	A	N
	363/D	13.64	A	N
10-IH-750	750/1	11.51	A	N
	750/2	13.43	A	N
	750/3	5.85	A	N
10-IH-779	779/2	17.80	B	N
	779/3	6.82	A	N
	779/4	15.64	A	N
	779/5	6.50	A	N
	779/6	4.92	A	E
	779/7	11.61	A	N
	779/8	9.25	A	E
10-IH-780	780/1	6.27	B	N
	780/2	4.44	A	N
	780/4	7.25	A	N
10-IH-782	782/1	10.50	A	C
10-IH-791	791/1	5.25	A	N
10-IH-1161	1161/1	13.45	A	N
10-IH-1162	1162/1	8.26	A	D
10-IH-1187[a]	1187/1	39.00	—	N
10-IH-1208	1208/1	9.69	A	N
10-IH-1222	1222/1	12.41	A	N
10-IH-1225	1225/1	7.07	B	C
10-IH-1260	1260/1	20.72	A	N
10-IH-1279	1279/1	4.20	—	N
10-IH-1328	1328/1	4.21	A	N
	1328/2	5.33	A	N

[a]10-IH-1187 is a rockshelter that appears not to have been used as a habitation, therefore its area was not included in determining the average area of the Chinese habitations along the Lower Salmon River.
A = Entrance in end of structure.
B = Entrance in side of structure.
C = Chimney to right of entrance.
D = Chimney to left of entrance.
E = Chimney in wall opposite entrance.
N = No chimney present.

attached. There is no evidence of the type of roof covering used along the Lower Salmon River. A wooden framework still exists on one structure (10-IH-1225). The framework is milled lumber constructed in the shed-style roof design. It is uncertain whether this roof framework was left by the Chinese or by other miners, since this site was probably reoccupied later. The type of roof support used on the other structures is unknown.

Chimney features are not common on all the Chinese sites; the majority of habitations do not have chimneys (Table 13). There is also little surface evidence of chimneys or other cooking facilities separate from the structures. The one exception may be the possible hearth in Figure 9. There are occasionally unidentified features such as leveled areas or rock walls that could be related to cooking or any number of other functions.

A total of six structures have a chimney built into one wall. The location of these chimneys varies within the structures. Two chimneys are found in walls opposite the entrance; four are adjacent to the entrance (Table 13). Only Chinese structures are known to have the chimney feature located adjacent to the entrance. Two other structures (10-IH-1205 and 10-IH-1239) along the Lower Salmon River have similar chimney placement, but ethnic or temporal data have not been obtained on these sites.

Because of their appearance, these features are presumed to be fireplaces or chimneys. Fuel was either burned in the features or wood burning stoves could have been placed in some of them. The rocks that make up these features, at least those observable on the surface, do not show any evidence of discoloration from burning. Any evidence of burning or smoke staining may have weathered away, since these features have all been exposed for the last 100 years. Chimneys located in Euroamerican structures along the Lower Salmon River also do not show any evidence of burning.

The unique chimney features themselves are generally three-sided with the front open. They vary in width, and are as tall as the walls of the structure since the structure walls form their sides. These features would appear to be similar to the three-sided feature mentioned by Hommel (1937:311) and previously described.

The chimney adjacent to the entrance on site 10-IH-1225 does not have the three-sided appearance. Instead, the feature is partially open at the base, which would have permitted a fire or the back of a stove. A hole, about the size that would accommodate a stovepipe, then passes up through the rock wall. The fireplace in structure 10-IH-779/6 is built in the same fashion but is located in the wall opposite the entrance. Site 10-IH-1225 was probably reoccupied in the early 1900s, so it is not certain whether the feature has been modified. Stove parts were found in both structures.

As mentioned, two of the Chinese structures have a chimney in the wall opposite the entrance, a location more commonly associated with Euroamerican use along the Lower Salmon River. Both Chinese structures with this type of chimney are located at site 10-IH-779. All of the structures located at that site were built along the edge of the terrace except for structure 779/6 which was built near the back of the terrace. Its chimney was described in the previous paragraph. The chimney in structure 779/8 has the three-sided appearance with the front of the feature open, but is located in the back wall rather than adjacent to the entrance. Whether structure 779/6 is indeed a Chinese structure is actually somewhat questionable since it is set apart from the other structures and no Chinese artifacts were found in direct association with it.

Entrances to the structures are almost exclusively placed at their ends. Only three of the recorded structures have entrances located in the side, or long wall (Table 13). This preference for building the entrances in the ends of the structures may have allowed better utilization of the interior space.

No evidence of window construction is found on any of the rock structures, although some flat glass has been located at 10-IH-779. There is no information on whether floors were constructed since no excavations have been undertaken. The structure floors are now covered with vegetation and rubble from deteriorating rock walls. One site, 10-IH-782, does have evidence of an area leveled in front of the structure that could have been used like a veranda.

COMPARISON TO OTHER REPORTED CHINESE SITES

A comparison between the Lower Salmon River Chinese sites and other reported sites spread over a wide geographical area should further assist in identifying any unique overseas Chinese architectural patterns. This comparison should avoid the possible sampling problems which arise from using only Lower Salmon River data. If similar architectural characteristics are found over a widespread geographical area, it may indeed suggest that there is a unique vernacular overseas Chinese architectural pattern.

The Chinese habitations along the Lower Salmon River are all excavated into the ground and are generally rectangular. But this is also characteristic of Euroamerican rock structures along the Lower Salmon River. Ritchie (1986:147) found that 70 percent of the Chinese structures at Cromwell in New Zealand were excavated into the ground and were rectangular. At Arrowtown, however, only one Chinese hut was excavated into the ground (Ritchie, 1984:41). LaLande (1981:304) also reports Chinese habitations excavated into the ground in southwest Oregon. Rock outlined areas for tents, as well as excavated half dugouts which may have been used for habitations, were both described by Briggs (1974:47-122) in Val Verde County, Texas. Structure S-14 in the Cortez Mining District, Nevada, was described as excavated into the ground (Hardesty and Hattori, 1983:28). Therefore, Chinese sites are found to be excavated into the ground as well as built with little or no surface modification. Almost all of the habitations appear to be rectangular.

Sleeping platforms were not identified on any of the Lower Salmon River sites. Ritchie (1986:108) found that the back parts of structure floors were often 0.30

meter higher than the fronts, possibly indicative of sleeping platforms. Sleeping platforms were situated opposite the doorway in possible Italian habitations reported by Rossillon (1984:64). Further research is required to determine if sleeping platforms occur elsewhere, and if they are characteristic of only certain ethnic groups, or of particular locations.

The habitations along the Lower Salmon River consist of rock and earth walls upon which a wooden framework was probably built. Rock was probably used because it was abundant and usually easy to work with. Trees were difficult to obtain, making the use of logs generally unfeasible. Milled lumber also would have been difficult to obtain, but certainly not impossible. Driftwood would have been abundant. See Ritchie (Chapter 13 herein) for a discussion of building materials used in New Zealand.

Building materials used in the United States appear to be quite varied. Chinese structures in the nearby town of Lewiston, Idaho, were described as small mud houses or log cabins (Wynne, 1964:56). Elsensohn (1970:19) also described the structures in Lewiston as excavated into the ground, with soil then placed on the wooden roof.

Tents were made available to the Chinese on the railroad in Texas, but Briggs (1974:23) reported that many preferred to live in dugouts. Hardesty and Hattori (1983:24-26) describe the use of dugouts with reinforced side walls of dry-laid rock and brick in Shoshone Wells, Nevada. Leveled areas, possibly used as tent platforms, are also sometimes associated with Chinese sites. Probable tent pads in California are reported by Tordoff and Maniery (1986:1-5; 1989:5) and Tordoff and Seldner (1986:5-19). LaLande (1981:304) has found that some Oregon Chinese miners used rectangular platforms excavated into slopes usually with dry-stone reinforcing walls. In Texas, masonry structures, sometimes with their backs built against a natural rock outcrop, are reported by Briggs (1974:122-123). Adobe structures were also used (Greenwood, 1978:43; Hardesty and Hattori, 1983:26-28) in both urban and rural settings in California and Nevada, respectively.

Some structure walls along the Lower Salmon River may have been built using the rammed earth technique. Undoubtedly, the reservoirs found on several of the sites were built using this construction technique. Tordoff and Seldner (1986:5-50) report a rammed earth structure probably built by the Chinese. Costello (1988:29) describes a rammed earth Chinese store in California.

The Chinese use of log cabins in California is reported by Elston, Hardesty, and Clerico (1981:147-148). LaLande (1981:298) also describes the Chinese use of log cabins in southwest Oregon. Some of the log cabins were occupied by the Chinese after their original Euroamerican occupants moved. But the Chinese also built their own log cabins, using the techniques of the local Euroamericans. Excavations near Pierce, Idaho indicate that the Chinese habitation there was constructed of framed lumber (Stapp and Longenecker, 1984:93).

Jack, Holmes, and Kerr (1984:51) report that some of the Chinese structures in Australia were made of thatched grass or wood and bark. One habitation, a structure belonging to a man named Ah Toy, was constructed of corrugated iron. Jack (1986:2) also describes a Chinese habitation made from an iron water tank.

The previously described habitations are located in rural settings. The wide variety of construction materials reflects the adaptability of the Chinese and their ability to use whatever was available. Materials used in urban habitations probably varied depending upon how well-established the urban center was. Some of the early structures in Sacramento, California were made of wood and canvas; later, brick buildings became more prominent in the Chinese part of town (Praetzellis and Praetzellis, 1982:21). This change probably reflects a more permanent population.

Roofing materials were probably as variable as the structural materials used. Minimal evidence of roof construction materials or techniques remains on most structures. Because of a lack of trees around the site area, canvas roofs may have been used over the habitations in Val Verde County, Texas (Briggs, 1974:118). One Chinese structure in the United States Forest Service's Payette National Forest still has the roof remaining. The structure consists of rock walls about one meter high and was probably used for storage. The roof is made of logs laid horizontally across the walls, with soil placed over the top of the logs (Fee, 1982:Part C).

Most of the habitations appear to be single rooms. Two of the dwellings along the Lower Salmon River may have been two-room structures, but because of their deteriorated nature it is difficult to determine. Most of the reported Chinese structures are evidently single room residences and do not share a common wall with other structures. The one major exception appears to be in New Zealand. Some of the structures at Cromwell are built back-to-back, thus sharing a common stone wall. Most mud wall structures at Arrowtown did not share common walls (Ritchie, 1986:147).

The average area of Chinese habitations is variable. The average area of Chinese dwellings at Cromwell is 8.3 square meters, and at Arrowtown it is 7.3 square meters. Historic records indicate that between two and eight people shared a single hut (Ritchie, Chapter 13 herein). Three people was the most common number per hut (Ritchie, 1986:149). The average internal area of Chinese habitations along the Lower Salmon River is 9.52 square meters. Chinese sites reported by Briggs (1974:52, 118-133) and Hardesty and Hattori (1983: 24-29) are generally larger, with most structure areas ranging between 10 and 20 square meters. Chinese habitations south of the Lower Salmon River in the Payette National Forest average about 23 square meters. The structure excavated by Stapp and Longenecker (1984:93) near Pierce, Idaho was about 7.20 square meters. Jack, Holmes, and Kerr (1984:53) report a structure near Palmer, Australia of about 9.00 square meters. As one can see, the average internal area of Chinese structures is variable.

Windows do not appear to be a common feature. Ritchie (1986:149) describes vents or windows located above the entrances of structures which were observed in old photographs. Windowpane glass was located with the structure excavated at Pierce, Idaho by Stapp and Longenecker (1984:93), and flat glass was found on one site along the Lower Salmon River. Ritchie (1984:41) also reports window glass at most huts in Arrowtown and at two huts in Cromwell. Habitations in the Warren, Idaho area were described in the following manner: "Occasionally one finds windowless cabins, not much larger than dog houses, once the homes of Chinese miners" (Shenon and Reed, 1936:122). The evidence of windows is possibly not well represented in other samples of archaeological materials recovered, and is therefore not reported from other locations.

References to chimneys, fireplaces, or hearths have been made by several authors when describing Chinese habitations. Research conducted by Ritchie (1986:148 and Chapter 13 herein) has provided field observations and historic photographs of Chinese dwellings with chimneys in New Zealand. The Cromwell habitations had chimneys located immediately to the right of the entrance as one enters the structure, while those at Arrowtown had similar chimney features located either to the left or right of the entrance in about equal numbers. The chimney features described by Ritchie have the same three-sided appearance and are located in the same position as some of those previously described along the Lower Salmon River.

Work completed by Briggs (1974:122-124) in Val Verde County, Texas identified fireplaces or hearths in the northwest corners of some habitations adjacent to the entrances. Several of these were described as small fireplace alcoves with thermally fractured rock. This evidence was found in the corners adjacent to the entrances of a number of other structures, except there were no alcoves. One feature did not have any evidence of burning. Archaeological excavations of a structure at Shoshone Wells, Nevada revealed a fireplace or collapsed chimney in the southwest corner adjacent to the entrance. Other structures did not have the chimney feature (Hardesty and Hattori, 1983:25).

Anderson (1983:25) describes a variety of habitations at Promontory Point, Utah. Some of the habitations had chimneys built into the structure. These chimneys were located in the walls opposite the entrances. No definite Chinese use was attributed to the structures, but the Chinese did work in the area. Recorded Chinese habitations in the Payette National Forest also had chimneys located in the walls opposite the entrances. There were also habitations in both locations that did not have any chimneys.

Features referred to as hearths, ovens, or chimneys have been described by a variety of authors. Briggs (1974:132) describes a number of hearths located outside the structures. The hearths, some of which were roughly circular, were used for cooking. Briggs (1974:45) also describes double hearths that may be two hearths joined together and sharing a common wall. Outside ovens located in Australia had a variety of uses, including prayer burning, everyday cooking, and ore burning (Jack, 1986:2). Jack, Holmes, and Kerr (1984:53) state that there was probably no need for fireplaces in the structures located in warmer climates like the tropics. A stone-lined pit described by Hardesty and Hattori (1983:30) may have been used for an oven. Tordoff and Maniery (1986:1-1), as well as Tordoff and Seldner (1986:5-13), report hearths on several sites in California. Some of the hearths may have been constructed by Euroamericans and later used by the Chinese (Tordoff and Seldner, 1986:5-19). One hearth was excavated and the results described in Tordoff and Maniery (1989:6). Johnson and Theodoratus (1984:66) describe hearths which are frequently U-shaped and occasionally double hearths. Rock fireplace features near Sacramento, California are not in direct association with Chinese sites, although the Chinese were reportedly once in the area (Vaughan, 1986:71-74). One rock fireplace described by Vaughan (1986:21) is very similar to the rock feature from site 10-IH-1328 along the Lower Salmon River. The function of the Lower Salmon River feature, sometimes referred to as the "Chinese Shrine," is unknown. There is no direct evidence to suggest whether the feature is a "shrine" or a fireplace.

Wegars (1991) provides a thorough discussion of domed rock structures often referred to as "Chinese Ovens" and usually associated with railroad sites. No evidence was found to connect the Chinese with these features in the United States. There are no known domed rock ovens along the Lower Salmon River.

The chimney locations are as variable as the building materials. Some Chinese habitations have chimneys located adjacent to the entrance or in the wall opposite the entrance; some have no chimney at all. Many of the dwellings have outside features that were used for cooking. The chimney, or other evidence of burning adjacent to the entrance, appears to be widespread among habitations. To date, this feature only appears to be associated with Chinese residences. Although not all Chinese habitations have a chimney located adjacent to the entrance, the structures along the Lower Salmon River that do have this feature have all been Chinese.

Exposure also appears to be variable. Although tent outlines were oriented north, south, and northeast, the dugouts were all oriented west at Val Verde County, Texas (Briggs, 1974:46-52, 118-141). The dugouts at Shoshone Wells, Nevada were also oriented to the west (Hardesty and Hattori, 1983:24-30). A preference for a southern exposure was noted for sites in southwest Oregon (LaLande, 1981:305). Habitations at Cromwell and many other rural sites in New Zealand are oriented to the easterly quarter, whereas at Arrowtown most are oriented northwest (Ritchie, 1986:152). Exposure of the Lower Salmon River sites is predominantly east, west, and south. There generally is an avoidance of northerly exposure except for a few occasional exceptions.

Rock overhangs or rockshelters are another form of habitation and are only reported by Ritchie (1986:48-49) and along the Lower Salmon River. Rock walls were typically built up in front of the shelter, thus forming the habitation.

Anderson (1983:236) reports the use of caves with rock walls, but there is no direct association between the Chinese and these features.

Besides constructing their own dwellings, the Chinese often lived in structures they did not build. The mining records from Florence, Idaho show that the Chinese purchased mining claims including cabins from Euroamericans (Elsensohn, 1970:44). Wynne (1964:56) states that the Chinese also rented shacks. Adobes in California were sometimes reused by the Chinese (Greenwood, 1978:43). Housing was sometimes provided for the Chinese, especially those working on the railroad. Tents were provided while the Chinese were working for the Northern Pacific in north Idaho (Landreth, Boreson, and Condon, 1985:136). A translated 1862 circular described by Conwell (1871:154-155) encouraged the Chinese to work in Oregon, stating that good houses would be supplied. Prefabricated structures were also occasionally shipped to Chinese settlements (Ritchie, 1986:145; Spier, 1958:104).

Not only were the Chinese resourceful in building their own structures, they were also willing to obtain housing that was provided or already established. Such willingness to use what was available can lead to confusion when attempting to identify a characteristic building pattern among the Chinese.

As can be seen from this review of the literature, there is considerable variability in Chinese habitations. Such characteristics as the chimney adjacent to the entrance, the rockshelter with rock walls, or the various forms of outside fireplaces may reflect architectural features attributable only to the Chinese.

SUMMARY

The Chinese first entered the Lower Salmon River area in the late 1860s to mine gold in the placer deposits adjacent to the river. The peak of Chinese use occurred from the 1880s to the 1890s, but some individual Chinese remained in the area past 1900. This is supported by archaeological and historical data.

Chinese habitations along the Lower Salmon River are similar in that most are dry-laid rock walls in rectangular excavated pits. Some have chimneys located in the structures, and in several cases sites have features which may have been outside cooking facilities.

Building characteristics throughout China appear to have varied considerably. This variability is evident in the reported Chinese archaeological sites in the United States, New Zealand, and Australia. The variability ranges from the building materials to the internal area of the structures. But even with these variable characteristics, there appear to be some features unique to Chinese architecture. A vernacular overseas Chinese architectural pattern would provide important data that would assist in determining ethnic affiliations of sites along the Lower Salmon River and elsewhere.

A chimney adjacent to the entrance of the structure may be a feature unique to Chinese habitations. Not all structures have this feature; in fact, it is found in the minority of Chinese structures along the Lower Salmon River. The description of a three-sided chimney in some houses in China closely resembles the appearance of chimney features adjacent to the entrances of some overseas Chinese habitations. Evidence of these features has been found over a wide geographical area. It is uncertain why the chimney feature is located next to the entrance. It could reflect architectural practices in certain provinces or villages, or it could reveal certain beliefs related to *feng shui.*

Rockshelters with rock walls built around them to form the habitation may represent a unique Chinese building characteristic. This construction technique does not appear to be widespread, and has so far only been reported from New Zealand and the Lower Salmon River. Whether this building style is common in China is uncertain. Thus far this technique has only been associated with Chinese sites.

Fire hearths or ovens located outside the structures may potentially provide information on a unique architectural style common to the Chinese. Certain styles of hearths may be useful in identifying ethnic groups. The Chinese hearths thus far reported have a semi-circular appearance. More detailed descriptions and illustrations of these often ignored features are needed to make comparisons and conclusions.

Whether Chinese structures are always windowless is difficult to determine since most structures have deteriorated. The archaeological evidence should include window hardware or flat glass, assuming that a window was more than just a hole cut in a wall with only a paper or cloth covering. The Euroamerican structures along the Lower Salmon River do not appear to have had any windows.

Although a chimney adjacent to the entrance of a structure and the occasional use of rockshelters with rock walls may be characteristic of vernacular overseas Chinese architecture, these attributes are not found at every location. Even within the same locale, such as the Lower Salmon River, there are structures with chimneys located at various positions in the structure and structures with no chimneys at all. Even though these unique characteristics are not always present, it is important to note that they have been reported over a wide geographical area.

The Chinese were adaptable, used a wide variety of building materials, and adopted local building techniques. They also used existing structures or habitations supplied by the companies for which they worked. Many of the Chinese structures were reoccupied after the Chinese had left the area. The structures could have easily been modified to suit the needs of the new occupants. Chinese building techniques may have also been adopted by some Euroamerican individuals. All of these factors can make it difficult to identify Chinese sites solely upon architectural form. The information presented here should assist in identifying some Chinese sites based on their architectural characteristics.

Additional data from analysis of archaeological material together with historical research should be used to define the temporal, functional, and ethnic affiliation of similar archaeological sites.

The emerging pattern of vernacular overseas Chinese architecture will require further refining as other knowledge becomes available. More information on architectural styles and construction techniques in rural China could provide important data. There is a need to identify and describe Euroamerican structures from the same temporal period and functional setting (i.e., mining, charcoal-making, and so on). These facts would provide the information necessary for comparison purposes. More comprehensive studies using the "historic ethnography" approach suggested by Schuyler (1988), which can be seen in Stapp's (1990) excellent example of how such in-depth research can provide significant information, will greatly enhance our understanding of the overseas Chinese in the United States and abroad.

REFERENCES CITED

ANDERSON, ADRIENNE B.
  1983   Ancillary Construction on Promontory Summit, Utah: Those Domestic Structures Built By Railroad Workers, in *Forgotten Places and Things: Archaeological Perspectives on American History,* A. Ward (ed.), Center for Anthropological Studies, Albuquerque, pp. 225-237.
BOERSCHMANN, ERNEST
  1911   Chinese Architecture and Its Relation to Chinese Culture, *Smithsonian Institution Annual Report* 1911, Washington, D.C., pp. 539-567.
BOYD, ANDREW
  1962   *Chinese Architecture and Town Planning, 1500 B.C.-1911 A.D.,* University of Chicago Press, Chicago.
BRIGGS, ALTON K.
  1974   The Archeology of 1882 Labor Camps on the Southern Pacific Railroad, Val Verde County, Texas, Master's thesis, University of Texas, Austin.
BUREAU OF LAND MANAGEMENT
  1991   Bureau of Land Management Cultural Resource Site Records, on file at Cottonwood Resource Area Headquarters, Cottonwood, Idaho.
BURNETT, LARCIE
  1978   Cultural Resource Report for the Brust Recreation Site, ms. on file, Bureau of Land Management, Cottonwood, Idaho.
BUSHELL, STEPHEN W.
  1904   Chinese Architecture, *Smithsonian Institution Annual Report* 1904, Washington, D.C., pp. 677-697.
CONWELL, RUSSELL H.
  1871   *Why and How: Why the Chinese Emigrate and the Means They Adopt for the Purpose of Reaching America,* Lee and Shepard, Boston.

COSTELLO, JULIA G.
1988   *Archaeological and Historical Studies at the Chew Kee Store, Fiddletown,*
        Foothill Resource Associates, Mokelumne Hill, California.
ELSENSOHN, SISTER M. ALFREDA
1947   *Pioneer Days in Idaho County,* Vol. 1, Caxton Printers, Caldwell, Idaho.
1970   *Idaho Chinese Lore,* Caxton Printers, Caldwell, Idaho.
ELSTON, ROBERT G., DONALD HARDESTY, and SHERYL CLERICO
1981   *Archaeological Investigations on the Hopkins Land Exchange,* report sub-
        mitted to USDA Forest Service, Contract No. 53-91U9-0-80077, Tahoe
        National Forest, Nevada City, California.
FEE, JEFFREY M. (rec.)
1982   Intermountain Antiquities Computer System Site Form, Resource No.
        10VY512, on file with the Idaho State Historic Preservation Office, Boise.
FEUCHTWANG, STEPHAN
1974   *An Anthropological Analysis of Chinese Geomancy,* Vithagna.
GREENWOOD, ROBERTA S.
1978   The Overseas Chinese at Home, *Archaeology, 31*:4, pp. 42-49.
HARDESTY, DONALD L. and EUGENE M. HATTORI
1983   Archaeological Studies in the Cortez Mining District, 1982, *Contributions to
        the Study of Cultural Resources Technical Report,* No. 12, Bureau of Land
        Management, Reno.
HOMMEL, RUDOLF P.
1937   *China At Work,* M.I.T. Press, Cambridge, Massachusetts. (Reprinted 1969,
        John Day Co., New York.)
JACK, R. IAN
1986   The Overseas Chinese: Recent Work in Australia, paper presented at the
        Nineteenth Annual Meeting of the Society for Historical Archaeology Con-
        ference, Sacramento, California.
JACK, R. IAN, KATE HOLMES, and RUTH KERR
1984   Ah Toy's Garden: A Chinese Market Garden on the Palmer River Gold-
        field, North Queensland, *Australian Journal of Historical Archaeology, 2,*
        pp. 51-58.
JOHNSON, JERALD J. and DOROTHEA J. THEODORATUS
1984   Cottonwood Creek Project, Shasta and Tehama Counties, California: Dutch
        Gulch Lake Intensive Cultural Resource Survey, The Foundation of
        California State University, Sacramento and Theodoratus Cultural Research,
        Fair Oaks, California.
KNAPP, RONALD G.
1986   *China's Traditional Rural Architecture,* University of Hawaii Press,
        Honolulu.
1989   *China's Vernacular Architecture,* University of Hawaii Press, Honolulu.
LALANDE, JEFFREY M.
1981   Sojourners in the Oregon Siskiyous: Adaptation and Acculturation of the
        Chinese Miners in the Applegate Valley, ca. 1855-1900, Master's thesis,
        Oregon State University, Corvallis.

LANDRETH, KEITH, KEO BORESON, and MARY CONDON
1985   Archaeological Investigations at the Cabinet Landing Site (10-BR-413) Bonner County, Idaho, Archaeological and Historical Services Eastern Washington University, *Reports in Archaeology and History*, Cheney, No. 100-45.

LISLE, C. J. and L. G. BRADLEY
1904   Industrial Edition, *The Standard*, Grangeville, Idaho, pp. 1-73.

MAWSON, REV. WILLIAM and others
1926   *The Story of the Canton Village Mission of the Presbyterian Church of New Zealand*, Dunedin, New Zealand.

MIRAMS, D. G.
1940   *A Brief History of Chinese Architecture*, Kelly and Walsh Ltd., Shanghai.

PRAETZELLIS, MARY and ADRIAN PRAETZELLIS
1982   *Archaeological and Historical Studies of the IJ56 Block, Sacramento, California: An Early Chinese Community*, Anthropological Studies Center, Sonoma State University, Rohnert Park, California.

RITCHIE, NEVILLE A.
1984   *The Arrowtown Chinese Settlement: An Interim Report on the Excavation*, Lands and Survey Department, Dunedin, New Zealand.
1986   Archaeology and History of the Chinese in Southern New Zealand During the Nineteenth Century: A Study of Acculturation, Adaptation, and Change, Ph.D. dissertation, University of Otago, Dunedin, New Zealand.

ROSSILLON, MARY P.
1984   The Curecanti Archeological Project: The Archeology of Marion, An Historic Railroad Camp in Curecanti National Recreation Area, Colorado, *Midwest Archeological Center Occasional Studies in Anthropology* No. 9, National Park Service, Lincoln, Colorado.

SCHUYLER, ROBERT L.
1988   Archaeological Remains, Documents, and Anthropology: A Call for a New Culture History, *Historical Archaeology*, 22:1, pp. 36-42.

SHENON, PHILIP J. and JOHN C. REED
1936   Down Idaho's River of No Return, *The National Geographic Magazine*, 70:1, pp. 95-136.

SISSON, DAVID A.
1983   Lower Salmon River Cultural Resource Management Plan, report on file, Bureau of Land Management, Cottonwood Resource Area Headquarters, Cottonwood, Idaho.
1989   Packers Creek (10-IH-780) Project Plan, report on file, Bureau of Land Management, Cottonwood Resource Area Headquarters, Cottonwood, Idaho.

SPEISER, WERNER
1965   *Oriental Architecture in Color*, The Viking Press, New York.

SPIER, ROBERT
1958   Tool Acculturation Among 19th-Century California Chinese, *Ethnohistory*, 5:2, pp. 97-117.

STAPP, DARBY C.
1990   The Historic Ethnography of a Chinese Mining Community in Idaho, Ph.D. dissertation, University of Pennsylvania, Philadelphia.

STAPP, DARBY C. and JULIA G. LONGENECKER
1984   1983 Test Excavations at 10-CW-159, The Pierce Chinese Mining Site, *University of Idaho Anthropological Research Manuscript Series,* No. 80, Moscow, Idaho.

TORDOFF, JUDITH D. and MARY L. MANIERY
1986   *Analysis, Evaluation, Effect Determination and Mitigation Plan for Two Chinese Mining Sites in Butte County, California,* Public Anthropological Research, Sacramento, California.

1989   Data Recovery at Two Mining Sites in Butte County, California, *Public Anthropological Research,* Sacramento, California.

TORDOFF, JUDITH D. and DANA Mc GOWAN SELDNER
1986   Cottonwood Creek Project Shasta and Tehama Counties, California: Excavation at Thirteen Mining Sites in the Cottonwood Mining District, Vol. 1, The Foundation of California State University, Sacramento and Theodoratus Cultural Research, Fair Oaks, California.

TOULOUSE, JULIAN H.
1971   *Bottle Makers and Their Marks,* Thomas Nelson Inc., New York.

UNITED STATES DEPARTMENT OF THE INTERIOR
1909   General Land Office Plats and Notes, copy on file, Bureau of Land Management, Cottonwood, Idaho.

VAUGHAN, TRUDY
1986   Archaeological Investigations at a Sacramento River Mining Camp (CA-Sha-1450) Shasta County, California, ms. on file, Bureau of Land Management, Redding, California.

WEGARS, PRISCILLA
1991   "Who's Been Workin' on the Railroad?": An Examination of the Construction, Distribution, and Ethnic Origins of Domed Rock Ovens on Railroad-Related Sites, *Historical Archaeology, 25:*1, pp. 37-65.

WILSON, BILL and BETTY WILSON
1971   *19th Century Medicine in Glass,* 19th Century Hobby & Publishing Co., Amador City, California.

WYATT, BARBARA (ed.)
1987   Surveying and Evaluating Vernacular Architecture, Draft, *National Register Bulletin 31,* National Park Service, Washington, D.C.

WYNNE, ROBERT EDWARD
1964   Reaction to the Chinese in the Pacific Northwest and British Columbia 1850 to 1910, Ph.D. dissertation, University of Washington, Seattle.

CHAPTER 3

Idaho's Chinese Mountain Gardens

Jeffrey M. Fee

Chinese garden terraces of commercial capacity, developed by Chinese gold miners between 1869 and the 1920s, have been recorded in a remote area of the Payette National Forest in the Salmon River Mountains of Central Idaho (Figure 11). In addition, several small terraced garden plats cultivated for personal consumption are now a part of the official record. At present, research indicates that, collectively, these are perhaps the most extensive Chinese terraced garden developments recorded outside of Asia. Commercially, the Chinese cultivated approximately 250 terraces at five separate sites, totaling about 26 acres on the steep slopes of the South Fork of the Salmon River drainage. From these garden terraces the Chinese supplied the Warren Mining District with fresh vegetable and fruit produce.

During the early period of gold discoveries in Idaho, the Warren Mining District, a mountain wilderness laced in beauty at the end of the world, as some described it, was perhaps the most inaccessible, remote, and rugged of all the mining districts in the United States. From 1862 to 1946, population fluctuated with the price and quantity of gold recovered from the claims. During the first decade of mining activity, the Warren Mining District boasted a peak population of over 6000 miners. Soon after the initial gold rush population declined in the late 1860s, the Chinese became the majority from about 1870 until the turn of the century. During those three decades, the Warren Mining District was extensively influenced by Chinese culture and traditions. The significant Chinese presence in this mountain wilderness set the stage for some of the most interesting cultural contacts between Asian and American people ever recorded on the early western frontier.

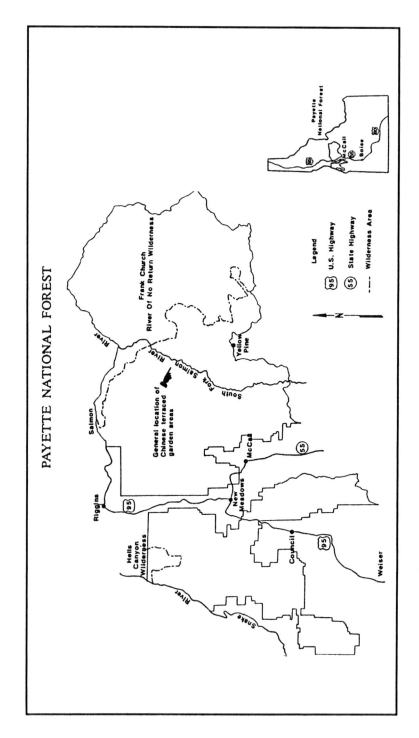

Figure 11. General location of the Chinese terraced gardens. (More detailed information may be requested through the Payette National Forest in McCall, Idaho.)

66

THE LEGENDARY AND "MYSTICAL" CHINESE
OF WARREN, IDAHO

By the late 1950s and early 1960s the mining town of Warren was a mere ghost, with the typical western fronts and boarded-up doors. Few people remained: only dedicated miners, old timers, summer residents, and on a seasonal basis, U.S. Forest Service personnel. My father Max Fee, a ranger, was among the latter group. At this point it must be understood that the term "mystical" Chinese, although in this case not negative, is an inaccurate stereotype of the Chinese people. However, the term is used by the author to reflect a perception passed on through folklore to an impressionable boy growing up during the 1950s in a ghost town such as Warren, Idaho.

It was during these summer months as a boy that I had heard fascinating tales of the Chinese from the old timers who actually knew those mysterious Asian people from a far-off land. Stories were told about the legendary heroine "China Polly" (Lalu Nathoy), who was purchased in a Chinese slave market and brought to Warren in 1872 to serve her Chinese master Hong King, a gambler and tavern owner. Ironically, Lalu arrived at a time when our country had just shed blood to abolish slavery. Years later, in another twist of irony, Lalu Nathoy's freedom was allegedly put up as high stakes in a poker game between Hong King and a rival gambler and tavern owner named Charley Bemis. Charley played for Lalu's freedom and won. Not long after, Lalu in turn saved Charley's life. In a shootout over a poker game, Charley received a lead ball which penetrated the cheek bone below the eyesocket and lodged near the lower back portion of his skull. Upon examination, Dr. Bibby, a Grangeville doctor summoned to Warren to treat the wound, diagnosed the injury to be fatal, and stated that he could do nothing for the dying Charley Bemis. With only a crochet hook, Lalu persevered, extracting bone fragments and lead. Using Chinese medical practices, Lalu nursed the ailing gambler back to health (McCunn, 1981:185-200; *Idaho County Free Press,* 1890:19 September). These events led to one of the most unusual marriages ever to take place on the early Idaho frontier, the union of an Asian woman (Figure 12), of whom there were very few, and a Euroamerican citizen.

Not all events concerning Chinese and U.S. citizen contacts were as dramatic and romantic as the relationship between Polly and Charley Bemis. A September, 1887 newspaper article stated (*Idaho County Free Press,* 1887:2 September):

> The Chinese in Warren camp had a grand festival last Sunday, the occasion being feeding of the dead. Several hogs and chickens were barbecued and taken to the burying ground and were then brought back and made a repast for the living.

Fred Sheifer, a long time Warren resident, remembered the Warren Chinese through the wide-open eyes of his boyhood in the early part of this century: the Chinese store; a tavern; opium dens; the hog slaughtering and butchering sheds;

Figure 12. A legend of the early West, Polly Bemis (Lalu Nathoy). She came into Warren in 1872, a Chinese slave girl in a "China pack train" on a mule called Polly after which she received her American name. Here she appears in her wedding dress in 1894, in her early forties. At that time she entered into holy matrimony with Charley Bemis, a gambler, saloon owner, and part-time sheriff. As legend has it, Bemis challenged Hong King (Polly's slave master) in a poker game for Polly's freedom and won. Later, after Charley was "given up for dead" by an American doctor, Polly saved his life by applying Chinese medical practices to the gambler, who had received a bullet wound to the head in a shooting over a poker game. Photograph courtesy Idaho State Historical Society, Boise.

burial grounds; the Chinese New Year celebrations; Fourth of July parades with traditional dress, dragons, and fireworks; and many other social events and feasts (Fred Sheifer, 1985:personal communication). In 1889 the *Free Press* reflected some of the activities Fred later witnessed in an article describing a Warren Fourth of July in which 200 Chinese participated, carrying gongs, playing stringed instruments, and floating dragon flags (*Idaho County Free Press,* 1889:12 July).

During the course of social conversation on the porch of a local Warren tavern in the summer of 1959, an early photograph was displayed of Sleepy Kan and one of several Chinese-owned pack trains. Sleepy Kan (Figure 13), Warren's legendary Chinese packer, made countless trips to and from other settlements, freighting thousands of tons of cargo on the backs of up to 150 pack mules, over hundreds of miles of treacherous trails winding through the Salmon River Mountains. Mention of those Chinese pack trains was made in an 1879 news article: (*Idaho Statesman,* 1878:2 October):

> In the Warren Mines ther[e] are at present about 800 Chinamen and some two or three hundred whitemen engaged in mining. The Chinese at Warrens are running several pack trains between that camp and the "Meadows" and the valleys of Weiser.

The late Otis Morris, who lived the majority of his eighty-plus years in Warren, told of the days when each spring the Chinese would make their annual hog drive, herding up to 200 hogs over the mountainous trails between Warren and Grangeville. The Chinese began the drive at dawn in order to herd the animals over the crusted snow in the high country before the afternoon sun would soften the crust, making it impossible to travel. Otis said that many of the Chinese were expert fishermen, often supplying Warren with fresh salmon, steelhead, and trout from the nearby Salmon and South Fork Rivers. I recall Otis's description of the Chinese as hard working good people with "strange and mystical ways," who worked long tedious hours on their claims and cultivated acres of gardens on the steep mountain slopes of the South Fork of the Salmon River (Otis Morris, 1959:personal communication).

During the 1950s, knowledge of Chinese gardening on the South Fork of the Salmon River during the early mining period was relatively common. However, only a few knew the exact location of just one of the five garden areas and even fewer people had any idea of the extent to which the Chinese developed agricultural land on the slopes above the river. Many people not familiar with cultivating areas of sloping land by means of terraces were skeptical. Comments were expressed, such as that the slopes in the South Fork Canyon were too steep for cultivation and the limited flat agricultural land along the river bottom was cultivated by U.S. citizens. Questions were raised; did Chinese gardens on the South Fork of the Salmon River really exist, and if so, where is the evidence?

Figure 13. Warren's Sleepy Kan, in a 1928 photo. Kan was one of a few
who could claim residency of the Mining District for sixty years.
A legendary packer of the early Warren mining period (1870-1900), Kan
packed incalculable tons of freight in and out of the District (as far as
170 miles one way) by means of pack trains (horses and mules) over the
hazardous trails of the Salmon River Mountains. During that period, such trails
were the only access that linked Warren with the civilized world. Photograph
donated by Herb McDowell to the Payette National Forest, McCall, Idaho.

In September of 1982, archaeologist Mark Arnold and I were doing a cultural resource inventory of a timber sale that included a portion of the area described by Otis Morris as the Chinese mountain gardens. We descended the steep slopes searching for evidence of cultivated soil. About midway down we stood in awe of the terraced agricultural lands of China, carved into the mountain slopes of the South Fork of Idaho's Salmon River (Figure 14).

HISTORICAL BACKGROUND

The end of the 1850s in the central mountains of Idaho marked the beginnings of the Salmon River gold rush. On July 22, 1862, a Florence gold miner by the name of James Warren was prospecting in the mountains south of the Florence Basin and across the Salmon River, when he discovered gold in a meadow that soon became the center of the Warren Mining District. Between 1862 and 1868, the population of the white miners in the Warren Mining District totaled approximately 1500. By 1869, with the rich pay dirt depleted, the population of the miners dwindled to a mere 400 (Elsensohn, 1965:100). One of the first clues to the arrival of Chinese in the Warren District appears in this 1869 newspaper article (*Idaho Statesman,* 1869:9 December):

> Our placer miners continue to yield fairly, the side claims paying well, the middle of the Creek having been worked out. The camp will be open for Chinamen next spring.

The Asian miners, most of whom were from China's Guangdong Province (U.S. Bureau of the Census 1870, 1880), were then allowed to lease and rework the abandoned Warren mining claims or pay a set price for whatever mineral content might remain on the claim. Incidentally, the 1870 census records for Idaho show a total of 14,999 residents. Of that number, 4,274 were Chinese, nearly one-third of the population (Elsensohn, 1970:15).

According to various and sometimes conflicting sources, the initial Chinese population in the Warren Mining District may have been between 800 and 1200. However, if the initial Chinese population estimates were anywhere near accurate, that figure remained short-lived. The census, taken in Idaho at the end of every decade, shows a population for the Warren Mining District in the summer of 1870 of 367 Chinese, 243 whites, three American Indians, and two African Americans (U.S. Bureau of the Census, 1870). An 1879 newspaper article claims Warren boasted about 800 Chinese and 200 to 300 white people (*Idaho Statesman,* 1879: 2 October). The 1880 census records for the area report 394 Chinese, eighty-three whites, one American Indian and three halfbreed American Indians (U.S. Bureau of the Census, 1880). In August, 1888 a *Free Press* article stated that there were about 100 white men and 300 Chinese living in Warren (*Idaho County Free Press,* 1888:23 August).

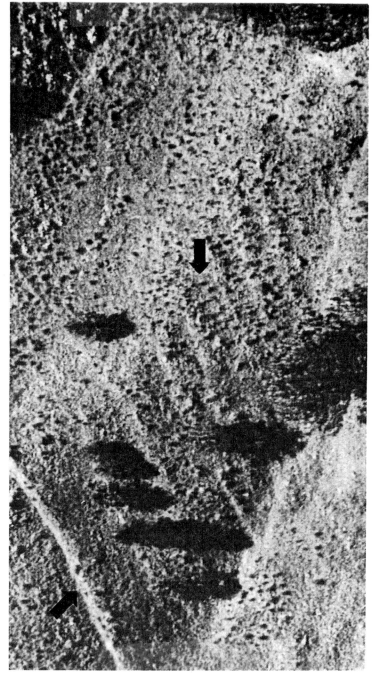

Figure 14. An overview of the China Bowl Gardens. Upper arrow points out a placer mining ditch which when tapped provided irrigation water to the terraces indicated by the lower arrow. This is the only terraced garden area known to be visible from the air; most of the terraced gardens are obscured by dense vegetation and the effects of erosion. Photograph courtesy *Idaho Statesman*, Boise.

Prejudice towards the Chinese in the Warren Mining District existed in various degrees. One Chinese man was hanged for stealing a pair of boots (Elsensohn, 1970:79) and two others were hanged in 1880 for unknown reasons (Idaho Genealogical Society, 1976:435).

Nearby, and from an unexpected source, a threat uncommon to most Asians on the early Idaho frontier made its presence felt. In the early spring of 1879, the Warren Chinese received the alarming news that five of their countrymen had been allegedly massacred by the Sheepeater Indians on Loon Creek, a tributary of the Middle Fork of the Salmon River nearly 55 air miles southeast. This event sparked the Sheepeater Indian Campaign in which five cavalry troops, totaling 180 men, pursued the Sheepeater Indians through an area noted as the most remote and rugged terrain in which to conduct a military campaign (Carrey, 1968:18-19). The area is now the Frank Church-River of No Return Wilderness.

In May, 1879, the entire Warren Mining District was put on alert when it was reported that the bodies of two white ranchers had been discovered at a ranch on the South Fork of the Salmon River, just a few miles from where the Chinese cultivated two of their terraced garden areas and worked their claims. The *Idaho Statesman* (1879:25 May) reported:

> Those who live on the South Fork in that vicinity have all moved into town, and night before last and yesterday morning signal fires and smokes were reported to have been seen on the mountain, showing that the Indians were returning probably in larger force.

In August of 1879 the South Fork residents again abandoned their claims, gardens, and ranches, and fled to Warren for military protection after the Indians attacked the James Rains Ranch on the lower South Fork of the Salmon River, killing Rains, wounding his brother-in-law, and setting fire to the ranch house (Yeckel, 1971:6). It was not until the first week of October, 1879, that sixty-five Sheepeater Indians surrendered to United States troops (Carrey, 1968:16). At the end of the Sheepeater War, the dead totaled ten whites and five Chinese. There were no recorded Sheepeater casualties.

The white and Chinese people of Warren, compared with those of some mining districts, lived in relatively peaceful co-existence, a co-existence which may be attributed to the fact that the Chinese were the overwhelming majority over a long period of time. By the turn of the century the Chinese majority had dwindled to a minority. Between 1910 and 1930 only ten to fifteen Chinese remained; most of them were old timers and veteran miners of the early Warren mining period. These longtime residents pursued their U.S. citizenships and persevered. As warm, friendly, and trusting relationships developed throughout the years, the Asian senior citizens were treated as local celebrities by the white citizens. A poem from local folklore reflects this atmosphere:

Figure 15. Ah Sam, honorary mayor of Warren, in 1931. Sam, standing near one of the local establishments, was greatly respected and loved by all Warren residents. Hours before dawn, on cold winter nights, Sam would go from one end of the sleepy Warren town to the other kindling dying embers in each stove so that the residents would have warm homes when they awakened. In return, the residents put out pastries, cold cuts, and other tasty foods. As the late Otis Morris described it, "Sam was just chuck full of breakfast by the time he opened the stove of that last house." Photograph donated by Herb McDowell to the Payette National Forest, McCall, Idaho.

In the wee hours of morning, over ice and snow
Comes Ah Sam from house to house
Blowing life back into dying coals.

The poem describes a daily ritual performed by Ah Sam (Figure 15), honorary mayor of Warren, in the winter months during the 1920s and 1930s for the sleeping residents of Warren who appreciated awakening to a warm fire. In the early morning hours Sam went to the home of each resident, building the fire back up in the stove. In return, the residents would leave out pastries, breads, cold cuts, and other treats the night before. Ah Sam, Warren's last Chinese resident, was laid to rest in American soil within the town's cemetery in 1938.

THE CHINESE CONTRIBUTION TO THE SETTLING OF THE WARREN MINING DISTRICT

Throughout the period from 1870 to 1900 the Chinese made major contributions not only in the gold production of the Warren Mining District, but also in the development of the settlement of Warren. An 1882 gold and silver production publication stated (Elsensohn, 1970:76-80):

> Placer mining in Warrens is mostly done by Chinese. Five companies in Warrens own over a mile of the creek bottom and employ about 200 men. They have reported the following production:
>
> | | |
> |---|---:|
> | Took Sing Company | $14,120 |
> | Lin Wo Company | 21,500 |
> | Hung Wo Company | 17,400 |
> | Wing Wo Company | 15,000 |
> | Shun Lee Company | 11,260 |
> | | 79,280 Total |
>
> In addition to this amount, other small companies produced $22,500, white men $12,500, and individual Chinese about $1,000, making the total productions of the district at $126,450.

Chinese business enterprises in Warren included a store, saloon, a laundry, supply pack trains, a doctor and pharmacy, mining companies, the nearby commercial terraced garden development, and the marketing of pork and fish. Occupations of the Chinese in the Warren Mining District are listed in the 1870 census records as 360 placer miners, two merchants, two cooks, one store clerk, one laundry washer, and one mule packer (U.S. Bureau of the Census, 1870). The 1880 census lists Warren Chinese occupations as 354 miners, five general merchants, five cooks, two general laborers, twelve gamblers, four farmers, three gardeners, two barbers, one housekeeper, one blacksmith, one mule packer, one laundryman, one prostitute, one woodchopper, one woodsawyer, one shoemaker, and one doctor (U.S. Bureau of the Census, 1880). Chinese work gangs were also responsible for many of the labor-intensive projects throughout the mining district, such as the construction and maintenance of much of the trail network connecting the settlement of Warren with the outside world.

Physical Setting

The South Fork of the Salmon River country, composed mostly of the Idaho batholith geological formation and relatively unstable granitic soils, is highly dissected by numerous creeks, streams, and ephemeral streams. Very little of the land is flat or even gently sloped; such lands are limited to either terraces created by former streams or alluvial fans occurring at the canyon bottom adjacent to the river.

The climate is characterized by hot dry summers, cold winters with twelve to twenty inches of snow, heavy rainfall in the spring with periods of rainfall throughout the summer, and moderate precipitation during the fall. Ponderosa pine and Douglas fir dominate the overstory, with vast grassy areas, bitter brush, and alder characterizing the understory. The Chinese garden areas are located along the west side of the South Fork on 12 to 45 percent slopes, at elevations between 3200 feet and 4700 feet. Most vegetables thrive in the South Fork River canyon, as do a variety of fruits including strawberries, blackberries, raspberries, grapes, peaches, cherries, plums, pears, apples, and walnuts.

Why a Terraced Garden Development?

In China's Guangdong Province, where most of the Warren Chinese originated, agricultural lands had to be extended onto the slopes of mountains and hillsides in order to produce enough food to feed a dense population. However, concentrations of people were obviously not a great problem on the early American frontier. So why would the Warren Chinese resort to terraced garden developments on the slopes of the South Fork when flat-land gardening might expend only half the amount of time and energy for perhaps the same yield? Preparing flat land for cultivation is relatively simple: clear the land and till. When preparing sloping land for cultivation, one must clear the land, excavate earth from the slope, then redistribute and level it, creating a terrace. Each terrace must then be tilled, planted, irrigated, hoed, and harvested by gardeners who must accomplish these tasks while constantly walking and working up and down hill.

The remote mining town of Warren was 150 tortuous mountain trail miles from the town of Grangeville, Idaho, the nearest, best-supplied trade center for the Warren and Florence mining districts. Transporting fresh produce, as well as any other cargo, on the backs of animals between Warren and Grangeville required a tremendous amount of time, energy, and cost, thus creating a need for a local supply of fresh produce.

The town of Warren, at 6000 feet, is located in a high valley of meadow lands surrounded by mountainous terrain. Throughout this district, land above 5000 feet becomes less productive for cultivation with increasing elevation. The South Fork of the Salmon River, the nearest river to Warren, has cut down through the earth to agriculturally-productive elevations. However, flat land within this elevation range is extremely limited and therefore very valuable. The flat productive land on the South Fork was either owned or occupied by U.S. citizens. A court decision concerning possession of land on American soil by a non-citizen was made clear in this 1890 news article (*Idaho County Free Press*, 1890:25 April):

> Ah Sing, et al, vs Flynn, et al. The Judge [Willis Sweet] delivered a lengthy opinion Monday morning in which he held that aliens had no right to occupy mining land of the United States. That the sale of mining claims to aliens of whatever nationality operated as an abandonment which subjected the claim to relocation by any citizen. The Judge further held, following the authority of the Supreme Court of Idaho, that to maintain a suit for possession of mining land, plaintiffs must allege citizenship or having declared intention to become such.

The case involved a mining claim located a few miles below the town of Warren. Although this particular case concerned mining lands, the law also applied to any land in Idaho. Therefore, the only option for the non-citizen Chinese was to apply the Asian horticultural method of terraced gardening to the sloped areas of the South Fork of the Salmon River.

Terraced garden developments, in steep and rugged terrain such as the South Fork River canyon, indicate the extent to which the Chinese were willing to expend time and energy to ensure an ample supply of vegetable and fruit produce. The high-in-fiber, rich-in-nutrient diet that vegetable and fruit produce provides is a traditional diet that many Chinese greatly valued, and may have required in order to maintain their health. An 1883 newspaper article implies the importance of vegetables in the diets of Chinese on the Canadian frontier (*Lewiston Teller*, 1883:29 March):

> A singular disease has made its appearance among the Chinese employed on the Canadian Pacific [Railroad], which terminates in death in the short space of a half an hour. The disease commences by swelling of the feet and legs and soon affects the whole body. The Celestials are scattering in terror from their camps. Want of vegetable food is supposed to have something to do with the disease. The telegraph announced this last Friday and the *Oregonian* received here on Monday confirms the announcement.

Chinese Occupancy on the South Fork of the Salmon River

Including the Chinese terraced garden sites, fourteen sites have been positively associated with Chinese occupancy along a 22 mile stretch of the South Fork of the Salmon River. Unlike the 1880 census, which did not record South Fork residents separate from the Warren residents, the 1870 census recorded a total of thirteen Chinese placer miners on the South Fork of the Salmon River (U.S. Bureau of the Census, 1870). The only other written information found to date regarding more than one or two Chinese on the South Fork was an August, 1879 news article quoting from the diary of an Army officer with a U.S. Cavalry detachment traveling down the river in pursuit of hostile Indians during the Sheepeater Indian War: "We then proceeded down the South Salmon about five miles, where we came upon eight Chinamen, and one white man engaged in mining" (*Idaho Statesman*, 1879:7 August).

Chinese Terraced Garden Sites

Five sites with Chinese terraced gardens, associated structures, and features have been recorded on the South Fork of the Salmon River. The terraces of the China Bowl Garden were cut into a bowl-like landform; the China Berry Garden, approximately 1 mile north, was named for the quantities of strawberries cultivated there. Fourteen miles down river and approximately .5 to 1 mile apart are the Celadon Slope Garden, named for the first ceramic sherd observed on the site; the Chi-Sandra Gardens, named after co-discoverer Sandra Hardin; and the Ah Toy site, named after the site's last occupant. These sites range in elevation from 3200 to 4700 feet, significantly lower than the town of Warren at 6000 feet. Selected features of the sites are compared in Table 14.

Evidence from three of the garden sites indicates that the Chinese irrigated the terraced gardens from the placer mining ditches routed to their early claims. It is most likely that each spring these miners and gardeners used the high water run-off simultaneously for both placer mining and irrigation.

China Bowl/China Berry Gardens — Although the upper China Bowl Gardens and lower China Berry Gardens differ by 800 feet in elevation and are one mile apart, both gardens were cultivated by China Bob and Ching Hai, who irrigated the gardens from the placer mining ditch routed to their nearby claim. Valuable insight into these two men was obtained through an interview with George Fritser, a long-time resident of the area. George was born on the Fritser Ranch on the South Fork of the Salmon River in 1902, at a period when the population of the Chinese placer miners on the South Fork had dwindled to about a half-dozen. By the time George was old enough to remember, China Bob and Ching Hai were the only remaining Chinese in that portion of the South Fork with which he was familiar.

The China Bowl Gardens (Figure 16) cover 2.5 acres, contain thirty-nine terraces, have a direct southern exposure, are located on slopes between twelve and 25 degrees, and are 3900 feet in elevation. Fritser speculated that only hardy vegetables were grown on these terraces. At 3100 feet in elevation, the lower China Berry Gardens are positioned on a more northerly slope averaging 18 degrees, and encompass 1.5 acres. Here eighteen terraces were cultivated for a strawberry crop. Fritser stated that as the vegetables matured and the berries ripened, the Chinese would transport the fresh produce on the backs of five to six

Table 14. Selected Characteristics of Five
Chinese Garden Sites

Characteristics	China Bowl Gardens	China Berry Gardens	Celadon Slope Gardens	Chi-Sandra Gardens	China Toy Gardens
Site acreage	2.5	1.5	12	3.5	3
Number of terraces	39	18	30	30-50	116
Average size (feet)	14 × 3.5	72 × 16.5	60 × 12	60 × 6	60 × 6.5
Average slope (deg.)	20	18	8	18	26
Aspect	Southern	Northern	SW	N & S	SE
Elevation (feet)	3900	3100	4700	4000	3400
Crops cultivated	hardy vegs.	straw-berries	unknown	unknown	apples grapes straw-berries rhubarb vege-tables
Miles to market	15	16	14	15	16
Transportation method	horses	horses	unknown	unknown	horses
Estimated period of occupation and/or cultivation	1880-1918	1880-1918	1870-1900	1880-1900	1890-1920
Dugout (feet)	none	4 × 6	12 × 24	none	12 × 18
Wood structure (feet)	none	cabin 12 × 27	probably unknown	none	none
Nails	none	cut/wire	cut	none	cut/wire
Irrigation/mining ditch	both	both	both	irrig.	both
mining evidence	none	tailings	placer	none	tailings
Other features	trail	trail	trail	trail	trail
Opium can fragments		1	2		
Opium pipe bowl sherds			3		13
Pig tusk			2		
Watering cans					12
Celadon glaze sherds			9		
Bamboo/Swatow sherds			9		1
Four Seasons sherds			2		
Brown glazed sherds	1	1	1	22	4

Figure 16. Closeup view of four terraces of the China Bowl Gardens. Note four young ponderosa pine trees growing on the first terrace and one young pine growing on the fourth terrace. Considering the trees are from fifteen to twenty years old and that the terraces were last cultivated in about 1918, it took approximately fifty years for conditions to be favorable for natural regeneration of these pines. Above these terraces, the water canal (trail-like feature) can be seen contouring around the slope. Miniature terrace-like patterns above the canal, to the right of the terraces, and just below the canal, are a network of winter range trails created by large herds of elk and deer. U.S. Forest Service photograph.

horses 16 miles into Warren where the produce was sold. When asked if he knew by what method Bob and Hai terraced the slopes, Fritser (1982) replied that he

> . . . was too young to know about those things, but I do remember the two Chinamen would every spring borrow Dad's plow to turn the soil in their gardens up there. By the time I was old enough to hike to the upper gardens nothing grew up there and I don't think that the lower gardens had any strawberries growing at that time.

Fritser described the two Chinese as having no queues and wearing American-style clothing; both spoke good English as well as Chinese. Ching Hai stood out at an unusual 6 feet 4 inches in height and had only one eye. According to Fritser, ". . . the two Chinese, in their late forties or early fifties, left the South Fork in 1918 and went home to China, where I think they had wives."

Although George would not speculate when the gardens were first terraced, architecture and datable artifacts associated with the nearby mining claim indicated a possible 1880s period. Other than a terraced garden spot and one brown glazed fragment of a Chinese liquor bottle, evidence of Chinese occupation of the China Bowl Gardens is minimal compared to that of the China Berry Gardens. The latter have definite Chinese architecture, but only one brown glazed fragment and one piece of a brass opium can. It is fairly certain that the gardeners had no residential structures at the China Bowl Gardens, choosing to live on their mining claim adjacent to their China Berry Gardens. It is likely that the China Bowl Gardens were irrigated and cultivated in conjunction with the constant maintenance of the two-mile-long placer ditch.

The architecture associated with the China Berry Gardens consists of a rock-walled dugout (Figure 17) and evidence of a decomposing cabin. For the purposes of defining Chinese architecture in the South Fork Canyon, a dugout in most cases is an excavation into a slope. The excavation is lined with rock walls and in many cases a rock fireplace has been constructed on the back wall. Most dugouts were constructed for occupancy; others appear to have been used for storage. The China Berry dugout is approximately 4 by 6 feet and kidney-shaped, with a double rock wall and no fireplace. Twenty feet east of the dugout are the almost totally decomposed logs of a 12 by 12 foot cabin. Adjacent to and south of the cabin are four small terraced areas where herbs and other medicinal plants may have been cultivated for personal use or for sale to Chinese doctors in Warren. Cultivating plants close to a living structure indicates that the plants may have required special care and perhaps protection against rodents and insects.

Although the dugout is definitely of Chinese origin, the cabin was probably constructed by the original Euroamerican claimant who later leased the claim and cabin to China Bob and Ching Hai. The cabin had a cobblestone fireplace constructed on the back wall. A log wall with a cut-out doorway divided the structure into two rooms; the front room contained a wood stove. During cold spells the

Figure 17. Astonishing preservation. Last utilized in about 1918 by China Bob and Ching Hai ("high pockets"), the sod roof of this stone and earthen structure near the China Berry terraces was almost completely intact in 1982. It apparently served as a cooler for produce and other food storage. The sod roof dissipated heat while porous double rock walls allowed for maximum ventilation. Note how the rock walls have been extended out on both sides of the entryway. Perhaps this was also designed to dissipate heat and/or to create an air flow through the structure similar to a draft in a fireplace.
Photograph courtesy Payette National Forest, McCall, Idaho.

back room, with a drafty, wood-depleting fireplace, may have been abandoned for the more efficiently heated front room.

Celadon Slope Garden Site — Approximately thirty large terraces are cut on a southwest 9 degree slope within an area of 8-10 acres. At 4700 feet in elevation this is the highest and largest terraced garden site recorded on the South Fork. The only visible Chinese-associated structure on this site is a 12 by 24 foot dugout overgrown with thick brush and dense grasses. Numerous cut nails of various sizes amidst several Chinese ceramic fragments observed ten meters downhill from the dugout suggest that the Chinese may also have had one or several wood structures.

During the 1930s, local informant Jim Bragg, a long-time South Fork cowboy, observed evidence of a decomposed woven willow and brush fence. He said the fence appeared to have enclosed the entire garden area (Jim Bragg, 1983:personal communication). Given the area's current growth of dense brush in nearby draws, it is possible that the Chinese may have used this abundant resource to fence their hogs and other domestic stock, and wild animals, out of the gardens.

The absence of wire nails and the presence of numerous cut nails found on the surface in association with the Chinese structures indicate that the Chinese may have cultivated the site as early as the 1870s and may have abandoned the gardens sometime prior to the time in the 1890s when the use of wire nails became dominant. Payette National Forest records indicate that the Chinese definitely had abandoned the Celadon Slope Gardens by 1903. In that year, a U.S. citizen decided that the Celadon Slope was a choice area to exercise his squatter's rights. The squatter ignored the terraces and planted seed which yielded 12 tons of hay for the winter feed of seventeen horses. On the more level areas he cultivated and harvested one ton of vegetables per year. In 1908 the squatter relinquished the Celadon Slope area to the U.S. Forest Service. Between 1908 and 1918 the Forest Service raised hay for government stock that wintered on the garden site. Stock raising and hay harvest by local ranchers continued on the slope until about 1940. These types of exploits have undoubtedly modified the terraces and may have totally obliterated others. Presently, the terraces can be observed beneath the dense, high grasses as vague to definite level areas cut into the slope. Many of the terraces now contain encroaching and relatively uniform rows of young ponderosa pine.

Chi-Sandra Gardens — Although the 3.5 acre Chi-Sandra Gardens are not associated with any known nearby structures, the gardens had been conveniently cultivated along the Old China Trail, about midway between the Celadon Slope and Ah Toy Gardens. The Old China Trail, named by the late John Lawrence, a local informant and longtime South Fork resident, was a trail approximately 1.5 miles long, constructed by the Chinese to reach the Celadon Slope and Ah Toy Gardens (Payette National Forest, 1985).

The Chi-Sandra terraced garden area is actually divided into two gardens, each with an opposite growing condition. The two gardens, located on the same level and approximately 150 feet apart, have been cultivated on the north and south slopes of a ridge running east and west. Eight to ten terraces, composed of a very rich organic, dark, and moist soil, covering about 1 acre, have been cut into a 14 degree slope on the more shady, cool, north side of the ridge. These terraces, compared to most others, must have been constructed with relative difficulty due to the very dense brush and other understory which develop thick networks of woven and matted root systems not easily extracted from the soil. The opposite conditions exist on approximately 2.5 acres of terraced land on the south slope. Here there is a sunny 25 degree slope, creating a soil condition which is more dry, sandy, and less stable. Extensive terrace erosion on this slope makes it difficult to estimate the number and size of the terraces. However, fifteen terraces are obvious, eight features may have been terraces, and a portion of the slope which appears to have been cleared for cultivation may have contained another thirty to fifty terraces.

Unlike the other South Fork Chinese terraced garden areas, the north and south slopes of the Chi-Sandra Gardens are not associated with mining activities and were irrigated from a ditch constructed solely for the purpose of garden irrigation. A reservoir of about 500 gallon capacity was constructed in an ephemeral gully approximately 200 feet west of the south slope terraces. Each spring the water from melted snow and heavy spring rains was retained in the reservoir which when tapped, flowed down a ditch with a 5 degree gradient to the top of the garden on the south slope and continued on around the ridge to the top of the north slope garden. The south slope garden probably required frequent irrigation; the soil on the north slope garden retained water for a much longer period of time. Perhaps, during most of the growing season, this garden survived on precipitation.

The Chi-Sandra terraces are located at an elevation of 4000 feet. The gardeners who exploited the opposite but versatile growing conditions probably cultivated the garden terraces for plants which adapted best to the conditions of that particular slope. It is possible that the plants on the sunny south slope were harvested early in the spring, giving the gardeners the advantage of capitalizing on the fresh produce market early in the year. Cooler conditions on the north slope gardens possibly allowed for an extended crop harvest. Garden plants on this slope may have begun to mature as garden production on the south slope declined due to the increasingly warmer temperatures of summer.

Ah Toy Gardens — One hundred sixteen terraces are presently visible within the three acre development of the Ah Toy Gardens. These gardens are located approximately one and one half miles down the Old China Trail from the Celadon Slope Gardens on a north-facing slope averaging 28 degrees at 3400 feet elevation. Some terraces on this site contain the only visible evidence that rock walls were used to retain the soil.

The 1910 memoirs of Walter Mann, an early forest ranger, reveal some rare and interesting glimpses of Toy, his gardens, and a horse Toy sold to Ranger Mann (Mann, 1969):

> I had bought this horse from Old Toy, a Chinaman. Toy had a garden spot on the slopes of the South Fork of the Salmon River where he raised vegetables and strawberries. Toy packed his vegetables on horseback out to the mines where he sold them at a good profit. However, this horse, he would not trust to carry his vegetables, so he used him as a saddle horse. The horse would buck and throw Toy off. Then Toy would tie the horse to a tree, get a club and beat him, yelling "Ki Ti, Ki Ti" at every whack. Toy could then ride the horse.

After Mann bought the horse, he appropriately named him Ki Ti. While at the forest headquarters in McCall, Idaho, Mann tried his hand at packing supplies on the untrustworthy animal (Mann, 1969):

> The pack was all on and I was starting to throw the diamond hitch, when away Ki Ti went—bucking, running, kicking, squalling. He bucked all over the little town of McCall, Idaho. He dumped the camp bed, scattered the sugar and flour, but for some reason the pack bags stuck to the saddle. Then the carton of matches caught fire and smoke came pouring out of the bags. I wondered if the horse would burn up. A crowd had gathered—everyone yelled—they gave me advice—it was fun for them. It was a great exhibition.

As it turned out, Ki Ti didn't burn and Ranger Mann had many eventful years with the horse that Ah Toy would not miss.

Lavel Thompson, an informant whose father had a ranch on the South Fork, stated "in the 1930s my brother and I dug clumps of rhubarb from Toy's lower terraces and transplanted them onto our father's ranch" (Lavel Thompson, 1982:personal communication).

Johnny Lawrence, referred to in the Chi-Sandra Garden discussion, had heard that a few fruit trees were also known to exist on Toy's garden area. During investigations of the site by the author in July, 1983, a small vineyard covering Toy's 12 foot by 18 foot rock-walled dugout bore several hundred grapes, dwarfed presumably from the lack of water. It is possible that the vineyards not only produced grapes but created a cooling effect on the dugout by shading the structure from the hot summer sun. Nearly forty yards down from the dugout is a rock-walled terrace 9 feet by 12 feet. The terrace was cut to the slope almost directly over a small artesian spring currently laden with a thick carpet of watercress. The water appears to have trickled at one time over the entire terrace, constantly saturating the contained soil.

Although it is likely that artifact collectors have visited the site, the collapsed dugout does not appear to have been tampered with, and broken glass and tin cans remain. The presence of a dozen or so five gallon kerosene cans perforated at the bottom (Figure 18), and with extra long bailing wire carrying straps attached at the top (Figure 19), suggests that two kerosene cans on a neck yoke (Figure 20) may have been an irrigation method. Ruthanne Lum McCunn, a Chinese American who wrote *Thousand Pieces of Gold,* informed this author that Chinese to this day still use kerosene cans and a yoke for irrigation (McCunn, 1986:personal communication). In addition, a flood irrigation method was used by tapping water from the nearby placer mining ditch routed nearly one-half mile to the nearest stream. Artifacts, such as cut and wire nails associated with the dugout, indicate a possible 1890-1915 occupation. It is not certain whether Ah Toy was the only one, or one of a group that originally cut and cultivated the terraces of the Ah Toy

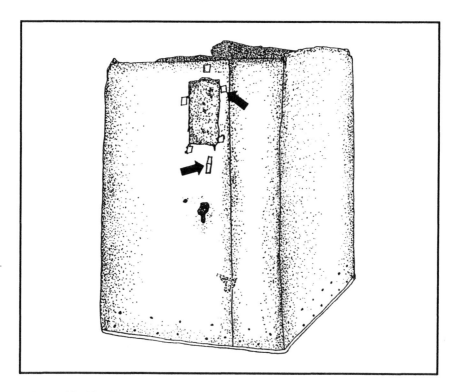

Figure 18. Modified kerosene can. A midden just meters in front of the Ah Toy earthen dwelling contained a dozen or so kerosene cans apparently modified to hold or dispense water. Holes in this can were punched with what appeared to be a cut nail. The pattern on the bottom sides, plus similar perforations totally covering the bottom of the can, are evidence that this container dispensed water or other liquids in sprinkling-like action. Brass brads (indicated by arrows) cut from an opium container were used to fasten a "tin" patch over a hole cut into the upper side of the can. Drawn by Colleen LeClair.

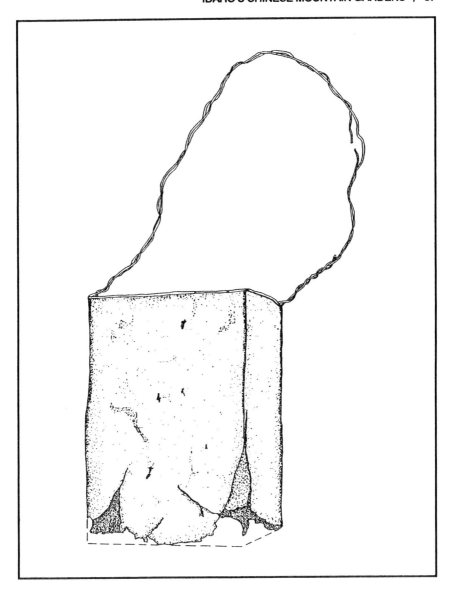

Figure 19. Kerosene can with wire handle. Cans modified in this way are too long for most humans to carry without dragging the can on the ground, so were most likely designed to hang from the ends of a neck yoke. Transporting water to each plant and irrigating it from the can (versus flood irrigation) was a method most likely preferred for the maximum conservation of water and, more importantly, the prevention of terrace erosion. Drawn by Colleen LeClair.

Figure 20. Ah Lee (Lee Dick), in Warren, Idaho, 1890, in front of what was then the Idaho County courthouse. Lee is seen going for water carrying a yoke with hanging kerosene cans. Archaeological evidence indicates that such a device was a method of irrigating terraced gardens in the nearby South Fork Canyon. As a medic in the Salmon River mountain areas, Lee Dick used Chinese medical practices which were preferred by many non-Chinese residents over conventional medical practices. He made countless "errands of mercy" into the remote areas of the Warren Mining District by foot, horseback, or snowshoe in emergency situations to administer treatment to victims near death.
Photograph donated by Herb McDowell to the Payette National Forest, McCall, Idaho.

Gardens. However, an early settlement document (Payette National Forest, n.d.) indicates that Ah Toy was settled at the Ah Toy Garden site by 1901.

Actual or Possible Small Terraced Gardens in the South Fork Drainage

The following describes a possible terraced garden plat associated with what is known as the Tong Yan Earthen Home (Fee, 1991:115-116):

> A small 1.2^2 m (4^2 ft.) by 1 m (3.3 ft.) high rock platform, perhaps part of a sluice operation, is located a few yards south of the earthen home. Several terraced features have been created adjacent to or near the earthen structure. Approximately 90 m (300 ft.) north along the high water level is a 3 m (10 ft.) by 4 m (13 ft.) rock terraced feature. Directly north of and adjacent to the earthen structure is a half acre consisting of a row of rocks along the north end and some very faint terrace-like formations indicating the rocks may have been cleared away for perhaps a small terrace garden development.

Located on the Krassel Ranger District, this earthen home, like the Ah Toy earthen dwelling, has been excavated and reconstructed, and is now a public interpretation site. Several miles from the Tong Yan site, although not found in direct association with Chinese evidence, is a likely Chinese terraced garden site (Dureka and Mesrobian, 1989):

> . . . 9 small flattened areas dug out of an approximately 35-degree slope, adjacent to a ferny, permanently-moist drainage. Several of the terraces were once joined but have been separated by a slope failure (landslide), now revegetated.

Definitely associated with Chinese occupation along the Pony Creek area is the following small terraced garden development (Fee, 1991:108):

> Directly in front of the cabin were observed numerous ceramic fragments including celadon, "[B]amboo" pattern, liquor bottle, other brown utilitarian ware, and the fragments of at least two opium pipe bowls. On a 20° slope, directly southeast of and approximately 30 m (100 ft.) from the cabin are approximately 12-15 garden terraces averaging 0.5 m (1.6 ft.) in width and 7 m (23 ft.) [long] within an 8^2 m (2.5^2 ft.) area.

Along Warren Creek are the charred remains of what was perhaps the "principal lodging and storehouse of the Fook Sing claims" (*Nez Perce News,* 1886:11 March). Recently the site of an annual University of Idaho archaeological field school, a terraced garden development was recorded in connection with the storehouse (Fee, 1991:82):

Four or five garden terraces cut to a 15% slope a few meters north of the structures measure approximately 10 m (33 ft.) in length and 1 m (3.3 ft.) in width. The terraces cover an area of approximately 10^2 m (33^2 ft.). Buckets, perhaps containers for night soil, have been inset into the ground at each end of the upper terrace.

Actual or Possible Recorded Chinese Terraced Gardens in Other Locations

Along the Lower Salmon River, Bureau of Land Management archaeologist David Sisson has recorded a terraced garden plat that very likely was developed by the Chinese. In 1979 he recorded "nine terraces averaging 1.5 feet wide, the longest 180 feet long, the shortest 40 to 50 feet, within a 100 by 180 foot area" (Sisson, 1991:personal communication). More recently, Chuck James, an archaeologist for the Plumas National Forest in north central California, located and recorded Chinese terraced gardens on that forest. He estimated the gardens to be (James, 1990:personal communication):

> . . . one tenth of an acre . . . on a very gentle slope. So far we've identified 11 terraces—dimensions in feet area; 13×20; 12×14; 8×16; 16×16; 13×27; 13×20; 9×20; 9×16; 13×20; 16×18; and 10×27 . . . Chinese habitation site near here is early, ca. late 1850s-1860s.

Other indications of possible Chinese terraced garden developments in northern California are referred to in certain archaeological site reports. A cultural resource inventory of the New Melones, California project area located "five terraces reinforced by stone walls" (Moratto and Greenwood, 1982:243) interpreted as a "Chinese truck garden(?)" (Greenwood and Shoup, 1983:372). In a survey of the Dutch Gulch Lake region survey, a combination of archaeological evidence and ethnohistory indicated a garden on a terrace (such as a river terrace) or terraced gardens (terraces cut into a slope specifically for cultivation) (Johnson and Theodoratus, 1984:70-71).

Chinese terraced gardens have also been recorded in other countries of overseas Chinese exploits, New Zealand and Canada. Located on New Zealand's South Island, in Central Otago province, is a plat described by archaeologist Neville Ritchie (1985:personal communication):

> We then moved on to a single terrace located halfway up the slope and about 100m downstream of the Chinatown residential area. This area is known to be an area where the Chinatown Chinese had apple and plum trees; there are still remnants. We also found no apparent soil modification. They just planted the trees in the sandy slope and I believe, largely used unmodified terracettes. They may have cut into the slope a bit to widen the terraces but I could not positively ascertain this.

In Barkerville, British Columbia, a guidebook describes the Barkerville Terrace Gardens (Wright, 1984:80):

> On the hillside above and behind the empty lots south of the Kwong Sang Wing Store is the rock work of Chinese Terrace Gardens. Though the growing season at this elevation of 4500 feet is short, the terraces served to trap warm air and delay frosts on chilly nights. There is no record and no sign of what was grown here, but the crops would probably have been mainly root vegetables. In the *Cariboo Sentinel* [a local newspaper] there is mention of the Chinese taking over the fresh vegetable market, so these gardens must have been successful.

Terrace Construction, Patterns, Dimensions, Shapes, and Condition

Currently, the research conducted on the Chinese terraced garden developments on the South Fork of the Salmon River has not revealed actual dates for when the terraced development began. Considering that the census records are one of the most reliable resources, approximate dates can be inferred. Both the 1870 and 1880 censuses taken in the Warren Mining District list the occupation of every Chinese who could be found within the District. That portion of the South Fork of the Salmon River where the terrace garden areas are located 14 to 16 miles from the town of Warren, is included within the Warren Mining District.

The list of Chinese occupations recorded in the 1870 census shows no agricultural employment, indicating that terraced gardens were not developed prior to 1870. The 1880 census list of Chinese occupations includes four farmers and three gardeners, indicating that the Chinese developed terraced gardening on the South Fork prior to 1880. Looking collectively at twenty-three datable surface artifacts from all four terraced garden sites, an 1875 to 1910 occupation period can be inferred.

Although there is presently no knowledge of the methods by which the Chinese developed the 26 acres of terraced gardens on the South Fork, a local informant remembers that on one of the terraced garden areas a horse and plow were used to till the soil each spring (George Fritser, 1982:personal communication). Chinese work gangs in the Warren Mining District were utilized in large-scale construction projects such as local roads, trails, ditches, and extensive mining projects (Elsensohn, 1970:76-80). Perhaps a large scale project such as terracing 26 acres of steep and rugged slopes required a highly organized work force.

In most cases, the terraces were cut almost horizontally along the slope with a slight gradient for more effective irrigation. Those terraced areas that can be seen from an aerial view appear as step-like patterns contouring to the landforms. Generally, but not in all cases, the narrower and more numerous terraces have been cut to the steeper slopes; wider terraces were spaced further apart and tailored to the more gentle slopes. This pattern may be due to the fact that construction of wide terraces on steep slopes requires that a larger volume of earth be excavated and leveled, with a greater risk of terrace soil erosion. At this point, it must be remembered that most of the Warren Chinese during the early Idaho mining period had intentions of returning to their homeland as soon as possible; although terrace erosion could have been almost totally prevented by the construction of rock retaining walls, it is conceivable that most of the gardeners had neither the time nor the extra energy to develop what would have amounted to permanent terraces on foreign soil.

Some garden areas have long, uniform rows of terraces ranging from 12 feet in width to 60 feet in length. Other terraces are no wider than the width of the hand and are 75 feet long. Most of the terraces are rectangular; others are tailored to a particular landform in square-like, half-moon, or kidney shapes. In all instances the terraces are constructed to make the most efficient use of agricultural space.

Natural plant succession is evident on all terraced areas. Many terraces are obvious while others, because of dense vegetation, can go unnoticed until they are observed from the proper angle, or have been exposed in the fall after the leaves have been shed from the brush. In other areas, winter reveals more definite shapes of the terraces as the snow flattens the thick, high grasses.

Over the decades since the Chinese abandoned their gardens, terrace erosion has occurred. Erosion is more extensive on steeper slopes with southern exposures where the soil is relatively dry, sandy, and unstable. On north-facing slopes, the rapid succession of natural vegetation has almost totally prevented erosion.

UNIVERSAL AND LOCAL COMPARISONS

Terracing slopes for agricultural purposes has been a method of horticulture throughout the world, particularly in highly populated areas such as Asia. After nearly 4000 years of developing agricultural lands in China, terraced gardening was common. In the Happy Valley of Hong Kong Island sometime before 1911, F. H. King recorded the art and perfection of Chinese gardening (1911:65, 67-68):

> . . . around Happy Valley on Sunday afternoon, looking down upon its terraced gardens and tiny fields, we saw men and women busy fitting the soil for new crops, gathering vegetables for market, feeding plants with liquid manure and even irrigating certain crops, not withstanding the damp, foggy, showery weather. . . . How thorough is the tillage, how efficient and painstaking the garden fitting, and how closely the ground is crowded to its upper limit of producing power [can be observed] . . .; and when one stops and studies the detail in such gardens he expects in its executor an orderly, careful, frugal and industrious man, getting not a little satisfaction out of his creations however arduous his task or prolonged his day. . . . Not only are these people extremely careful and painstaking in fitting their fields and gardens to receive the crop, but they are even more scrupulous in their care to make everything that can possibly serve as fertilizer for the soil, or food for the crop being grown, do so

unless there is some more remunerative service it may render. Expense is incurred to provide such receptacles . . . for receiving not only the night soil of the home [human manure and urine] and that which may be bought or otherwise procured, but in which may be stored any other fluid which can serve as plant food. . . . Generally the liquid manures must be diluted with water to a greater or less extent before they are "fed," as the Chinese say, to their plants, hence there is need of an abundant and convenient water supply. . . .

Ruthanne Lum McCunn described terraced gardening in a letter to the author (1986:personal communication):

> As a child growing up in Hong Kong, I saw Chinese carving out hillsides for roads and terrace gardens and housing projects, and no machinery was used at all—and no animals—just muscle, picks, shovels, and the yokes with baskets at either end. It was really awesome.

Extensive contributions to the development of flatland farming by the Chinese in Idaho and other western states was relatively common throughout the American frontier period (Lin, 1986:20):

> The agricultural skills of the Chinese in the area of vegetable gardening [are] clearly documented in the histories of Orange County. Henry Sienkiewicz, while in San Francisco, noted the awesome fruits and vegetables the Chinese had managed to coax out of the arid dunes and sandy hills of San Francisco. According to him, strawberries grown by the Chinese were the size of small pears, while cabbages assumed proportions four times the size of European cabbages. Likewise, Sienkiewicz describes pumpkins the size of wash tubs. . . . In San Francisco, as in Los Angeles, the Chinese dominated market gardening.

FUTURE RESEARCH

Although relatively few Chinese terraced garden developments have been located or recorded outside of Asia, it is likely many more exist, especially in remote areas with steep terrain and growing conditions similar to the Warren Mining District. Using the information gathered from the terrace garden sites on the South Fork of the Salmon River, a predictive model may be of use for any future studies conducted in similar climate and/or terrain in other locations of overseas Chinese exploits. Other than basic data recorded through the Intermountain Antiquities Computer System, archaeological information on each of the terraced garden areas is limited. Testing and/or excavation of terraces, including samples of pollen and macrofossils taken from terraces, may provide information concerning both the methods and materials used in terrace construction as well as the crops cultivated.

Excavation and/or testing of associated structures and features will, of course, reveal information on the gardeners themselves and the structures they built and occupied. More complete archaeological information would provide comparative data and show relationships between the five garden areas discussed herein. Further research conducted through literature searches and oral histories should reveal more precise dates on terrace garden development and abandonment, names of the developer or developers, names and numbers of gardeners, market competition, economics, and the major consumer groups.

In 1988 and 1989 the Payette National Forest developed a self-service interpretation center at Hays Ranger Station. Although the center interprets other past human events in the area, it focuses on the China Mountain terraced gardens. On a self-guided tour beginning at Hays Station (Celadon Slope), one can walk down through terraces, view a replica of a Chinese earth home, see an old restored ranger station, and travel the old "China trail" which winds its way down through several other terraced areas to the excavated and reconstructed Ah Toy earthen home. A report of the Ah Toy excavation results may be requested from the Forest Archaeologist, Payette National Forest, McCall, Idaho.

IN RETROSPECT

Much has been said about the Chinese being a resourceful and diligent people; the Chinese who worked and lived on the South Fork of the Salmon River are classic examples. Miners, gardeners, fishermen, and businessmen, these Asians made major contributions to Warren Mining District gold production and to the development of the mining district as a whole. They supplied the district with critical vegetables and fruit produce, pork, and fish. These resourceful people irrigated their terraced gardens from the same ditch they constructed for placer mining their nearby claims, and caught salmon, steelhead, trout, and whitefish for commercial and personal consumption in the adjacent river and its tributaries. The terrace gardens remain quiet and clothed in natural vegetation yet visibly carved into those Salmon River mountains. Here we have a glimpse of China in the backcountry of Idaho; a constant reminder of Asian contributions on American soil. Warren may prove to be a mining district in which the cultural contacts between Chinese and Americans lay etched in time; a unique human drama recorded in a mountainous land of gold, so far away from civilization, so rugged and remote, that some called it the end of the world.

REFERENCES CITED

CARREY, JOHN
    1968   *Sheepeater Indian Campaign,* Idaho County Free Press, Caldwell, Idaho.

DUREKA, JAMES THOMAS and ANN MESROBIAN
1989   IMACS Site Form, 10 VY 637, Hamilton Gardens, on file at Payette National Forest, McCall, Idaho.

ELSENSOHN, SISTER M. ALFREDA
1965   *Pioneer Days in Idaho County,* Vol. I, Caxton Printers, Caldwell, Idaho.
1970   *Idaho Chinese Lore,* Caxton Printers, Caldwell, Idaho.

FEE, JEFFREY M.
1991   A Dragon in the Eagle's Land: Chinese in an Idaho Wilderness, Warren Mining District, ca. 1870-1900, Master's thesis, University of Idaho, Moscow.

FRITSER, GEORGE
1982   Transcript of an interview conducted by Jeffrey M. Fee, ms. on file, Payette National Forest, McCall, Idaho.

GREENWOOD, ROBERTA S. and LAURENCE H. SHOUP, with contributions by others
1983   *New Melones Archeological Project, California: Review and Synthesis of Research at Historical Sites,* final report of the New Melones Archeological Project, Vol. VII, Infotec Development, Huntington Beach, California.

IDAHO COUNTY FREE PRESS
1887-   Various issues, "Warren News," Grangeville, Idaho.
1890

IDAHO GENEALOGICAL SOCIETY
1976   *Idaho Territory Federal Population Schedules and Mortality Schedules 1880,* Idaho Genealogical Society, Boise.

IDAHO STATESMAN
1869-   Various issues, "Warren News," Boise, Idaho.
1879

JOHNSON, JERALD J. and DOROTHEA J. THEODORATUS
1984   *Cottonwood Creek Project, Shasta and Tehama Counties California: Dutch Gulch Lake Intensive Cultural Resources Survey,* the Foundation of California State University, Sacramento, and Theodoratus Cultural Research, Fair Oaks, California.

KING, F. H.
1911   *Farmers of Forty Centuries or Permanent Agriculture in China, Korea and Japan.* Mrs. F. H. King, Madison, Wisconsin, reprinted 1927, Harcourt, Brace and Company, New York.

LEWISTON TELLER
1883   Untitled article about Chinese diet, March 29, Lewiston, Idaho.

LIN, PATRICIA
1986   The Chinese in Orange County: 1875-1910, ms. photocopy on file at the Asian American Comparative Collection, Laboratory of Anthropology, University of Idaho, Moscow.

MANN, WALTER
1969   Ki Ti the Bucking Horse, "Memoirs of an Early Forest Ranger," ms. on file, Payette National Forest, McCall, Idaho.

Mc CUNN, RUTHANNE LUM
1981   *Thousand Pieces of Gold,* Design Enterprises, San Francisco, reprinted 1983, Dell Publishing Co., New York.

MORATTO, MICHAEL J. and ROBERTA S. GREENWOOD,
with contributions by others
  1982   *New Melones Archeological Project, California: Research Background,* final
          report of the New Melones Archeological Project, Vol. III, Infotec Develop-
          ment, Huntington Beach, California.
NEZ PERCE NEWS
  1886   11 March, Lewiston, Idaho.
PAYETTE NATIONAL FOREST
  n.d.   History of the Idaho National Forest, ms., 1680 files, McCall, Idaho.
  1985   Intermountain Antiquities Computer Systems form for PY-794, ms., 2360
          files, McCall, Idaho.
U.S. BUREAU OF THE CENSUS
  1870   *Federal Population and Mortality Schedule, Idaho Territory,* Idaho State
          Library, Boise, Idaho.
  1880   *Federal Population and Mortality Schedule, Idaho Territory,* Idaho State
          Library, Boise, Idaho.
WRIGHT, RICHARD THOMAS
  1984   *Discover Barkerville, A Gold Rush Adventure: A Guide to the Town and its
          [Time],* Special Interest Publications, Vancouver, British Columbia.
YECKEL, CARL
  1971   The Sheepeater Campaign, *Idaho Yesterdays, 15*:2, pp. 2-9, Summer.

CHAPTER 4

The Study of Faunal Remains from an Overseas Chinese Mining Camp in Northern Idaho

Julia G. Longenecker and Darby C. Stapp

In 1983, the University of Idaho began a long-term anthropological study of Pierce, Idaho, an historic placer gold mining community (see Stapp, Chapter 1 herein, Figure 1). Research to date has concentrated on the Chinese who inhabited the locality between 1864 and 1932. This chapter focuses upon one aspect of the Pierce Chinese diet, meat consumption; documentary data are used to describe the manner in which the Pierce Chinese obtained, prepared, and consumed meat products. To identify the meat system, we have integrated the documentary and oral historical data from the Pierce locality with basic information about animal husbandry, meat, butchering, cooking, and Chinese foodways. We then move to the archaeological database and evaluate it within the context of the proposed meat system. A major concern here is to identify contributions that the archaeological record can make to the definition of the meat system. A second concern is the application that the faunal data may have for answering other questions regarding the Chinese experience in Pierce. We then conclude with a design for future faunal studies in Pierce, which may have application to research being conducted in other areas.

HISTORICAL OVERVIEW

The Euroamerican history of the Pierce locality began in 1860, when placer gold was discovered by Elias D. Pierce; within a few months, the area was filled with Euroamerican miners. New discoveries in the region fueled a migration to the

Clearwater and Salmon River mountains during the 1860s. The Chinese were at first excluded from the mines, but as the gold reserves were depleted, the Chinese were allowed to purchase mining properties and a new rush to the region began.

In contrast to their European counterparts, the Chinese maintained a distinct presence during their stay in America. The Chinese kept much of their traditional lifestyle by living together and importing some of their material culture from China. Elements of American culture were adopted, but the impact of these adaptations was apparently minimal. The diet was one area in which there were changes, although the significance of these changes is unclear.

Accompanying the Chinese miners to Pierce were Chinese merchants, gardeners, a doctor, gamblers, prostitutes, and others who supplied a variety of goods and services to the community. By the late 1860s, the Chinese in Pierce numbered over 500, accounting for approximately 80 percent of the Pierce population. As the gold was mined, population declined, and by 1900, only sixty-four Chinese remained in Pierce. A more complete description of the community and the changes that occurred over time is provided elsewhere (Stapp, Chapter 1 herein; Stapp, 1990).

HISTORIC MEAT SYSTEMS IN PIERCE

The first step in defining the Pierce meat system was to identify the various elements and arrange them in a logical order. The system began with the demand for the product, meat. Although there is presently no known record of the diet in 19th-century Kwangtung, Anderson and Anderson (1977:336) concluded that the meat consumed in the traditional Chinese diet was primarily fish, where locally available, and fresh pork, with chicken and beef accounting for minor percentages. Also important was a variety of specialty meats; although these were only a small part of the diet, they were important culturally and socially. Preserved meats used by the overseas Chinese included dried seafoods such as oysters, shrimp, and cuttlefish (Spier, 1958a:80); dried duck and giblets (Spier, 1958a:80); duck eggs (Anderson and Anderson, 1977:336); and Chinese bacon and sausage (Spier, 1958b:130). Whether demand existed for American preserved meats such as hams and bacons, canned fish items, and canned beef, is not known.

The Meat Supply Networks

A major component of a meat system is the meat supply network. For the Pierce system, the supply network was broken into two segments: one that supplied fresh meat and one that supplied preserved meat. As the Chinese moved into Pierce during the 1860s, they created a high demand for fresh pork. The local ranchers initially could not meet this demand because of low inventories (Table 15). To supply the Chinese miners with pork, the Euroamericans and Chinese probably brought hogs to Pierce from other areas during the late 1860s; this apparently

Table 15. Annual Totals of Livestock Assessed to Euroamericans and Chinese in the Pierce Locality between 1863 and 1882[a]

Year	Cows		Cattle		Hogs		Chickens	
	Euroamerican	Chinese	Euroamerican	Chinese	Euroamerican	Chinese	Euroamerican	Chinese
1863	7	—	9	—	2	—	—	—
1865	12	—	367	—	—	—	—	—
1867	6	—	41	—	60	—	—	—
1873[b]	100	—	59	—	134	23	—	—
1874	23	—	109	—	255	23	—	—
1875	26	—	113	—	88	102	—	—
1878	36	—	186	3	71	—	—	—
1880	24	—	303	—	20	150	61	—
1882	13	—	448	—	146	—	20	—

[a]Based on information extracted from the Shoshone County Annual Assessment Records (Shoshone County Records, 1861-1884).
[b]Four sheep were assessed to a Euroamerican this year.

99

became a common practice during the 1870s, as suggested by the following article (*Idaho Tri-Weekly Statesman,* 1875):

> The Chinese population is rather on the increase, they seem to have taken deep and permanent root in the soil. They are engaged in all the different occupations. There are two Chinese stores in Pierce City competing fiercely with the three "Melecan" stores. Some of the Celestials are engaged in butchering, driving hogs from the Walla Walla valley and selling meat to the rest.

Given the probable shortage of pork during the early years, the Chinese may have adapted by substituting other types of meat such as chicken and beef, or they may have purchased hams and bacon. Chicken, for example, was a traditional food for both Chinese and Euroamericans. An oral history source indicates that during the early 1900s, the Chinese in Pierce ate chicken regularly (Ralph Space, 1984:personal communication). Occasional references to various chicken "ranches" in the Pierce locality also are found, but the assessment records do not confirm large numbers of chickens (Table 15). Furthermore, many of the chickens raised were probably egg producers and not used for meat. Poultry was at least occasionally supplied by outside sources, as indicated in the following account (Goulder, 1875):

> Four prairie schooners . . . went into Pierce City the other day, through a fierce snow storm, loaded with poultry, eggs, butter, etc. They are all married men, far from their dear ones at home, and in a strange port. The Chinamen, touched with the liveliest sympathy for their distressed condition, went promptly forward and bought their cargoes, giving good prices.

We do not know how regular such trips were, or how dependent the Chinese were upon them.

Beef was available in good supply from the nearby ranches (Table 15). Most of the beef animals were probably targeted for the Pierce and adjacent localities during the early years. During the 1880s, demand for beef from outside the region increased, and the ranchers adjusted their operations accordingly.

Mutton consumption by the overseas Chinese has been documented archaeologically in New Zealand (Piper, 1984), but was not common in the nineteenth-century traditional diet. Apparently, mutton was generally not available in Pierce because in the fifteen years for which we have records; sheep are only documented during one year (Table 15). It is somewhat surprising that there was no Euroamerican demand for mutton by the Pierce residents, many of whom were Irish.

The networks through which the various meat products flowed are shown in Figure 21. Fresh meat was supplied through the local and regional networks, which consisted of the local and regional ranchers who transported their products

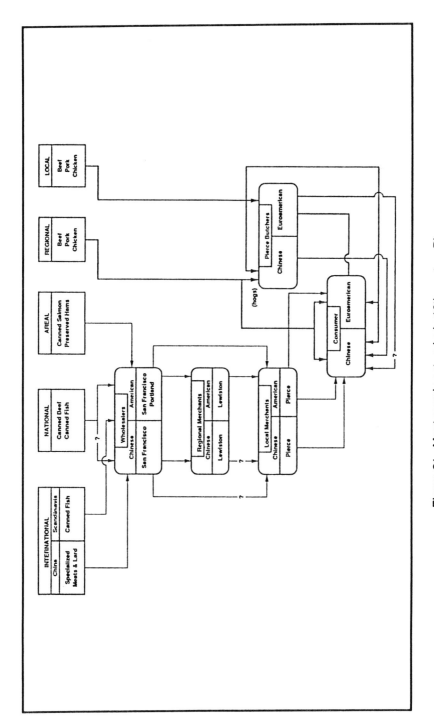

Figure 21. Meat supply networks in 19th century Pierce.

to Pierce and either sold their goods directly to the consumers or sold them to the local butchers. The butchers probably supplied most of the fresh meat to the consumers, though there are presently no data to determine the actual proportion. Presumably, the butcher offered for sale beef, pork, and game animals when available. Chinese merchants may have offered pork for sale.

The international, national, and areal networks were all associated with the preserved meat varieties. Most of the products from each source flowed through the major areal wholesalers, located in San Francisco and Portland. The Euroamerican wholesalers did not own the Pierce stores; whether the Chinese wholesalers had an interest in the Pierce stores is not known. Other unknowns relate to whether the Chinese wholesalers purchased Euroamerican goods, and whether the Euroamerican wholesalers purchased Chinese goods. We do have documentation that an American merchant in Pierce carried Chinese goods (Shoshone County Records, 1885), but we do not know the source of the goods.

The Consumer

Although Figure 21 identified only one type of Chinese and Euroamerican "consumer," in actuality there were many types. The range of consumer types is important to establish because it was the nature of the consumer that determined specific aspects of the meat system. The type of consumer was largely determined by the household in which he lived. Such factors as household location, household size, household wealth, and degree of household independence to a large extent determined the type of meat consumed and the manner in which it was obtained. These four factors are discussed below.

Household Location — The Chinese households can be divided into the following three groups based upon their location: 1) those in Pierce City, 2) those adjacent to Pierce City, and 3) those located away from Pierce City. Presently, no direct evidence exists to indicate that household location affected the foodways of household members; however, we believe that it quite likely did, based upon the preservation problems associated with fresh meat. Fresh meat spoils quickly if not kept at temperatures of 40 degrees or less. Hence, because fresh meat was readily available from butchers in town, individuals living in town (and probably those living within a short distance from town) would not have had the preservation problems of those who lived away from town, because they could purchase meat whenever needed. On the other hand, those at some distance from town would either have had to come to town regularly to obtain their meat supply, devise methods of preservation (e.g., cold storage, smoking, salting), or adjust their diets by eliminating meat at times or consuming preserved varieties.

Another characteristic of town life that would have affected the foodways of those with ready access to Pierce City was the existence of restaurants. Although there is no record of a Chinese restaurant in Pierce City, some of the local establishments such as the hotel, brothel, or gambling hall likely served meals to their clients. The clients, for the most part, were the Chinese miners who would come to town on their work breaks to stock up on supplies, repair equipment, and recreate. We do not know if the Chinese miners followed the Euroamerican pattern of heading to town every Sunday, nor do we know what percentage came to town regularly.

Household Size — The size of a household (i.e., the number of household members) will generally affect the purchasing pattern of the household members because purchasing patterns are often based upon economics and convenience. These two factors will often determine whether a household regularly purchases small or large quantities of meat.

Federal census records provide information about the number of occupants in each Pierce locality household. The number of individuals in a household ranged from one to fourteen, with an average of around four in 1870 and seven in 1880. To determine the quantity of meat consumed weekly by different size households it is necessary to know the amount of meat consumed daily by an individual. While Euroamericans during this time probably consumed between half a pound and one pound of meat per day, we do not know how much meat the Chinese ate. Anderson and Anderson state that in southern China today, only the wealthier households have meat regularly with their rice dishes (1977:319). Since most of the Pierce mining population was from the poorer class, meat may have been only a small part of the diet. However, the greater availability of meat in America combined with a steady income might have altered this traditional pattern.

If we assume that two ounces of meat was the daily average consumed by a Chinese individual in Pierce, the weekly needs ranged from nearly a pound for a household of one to nearly ten pounds for a household of twelve; the meat needed to supply these quantities would range from a few pork steaks to a few large pork roasts, respectively. Given the preservation problems associated with fresh meat, we would not expect that any Chinese households purchased meat in large units (i.e., quarters or halves) unless either larger numbers were being fed, or the individual meat consumption was greater than 4 ounces per day.

Degree of Household Independence — Another factor that would have affected meat purchasing patterns was the degree of household independence. Was each household independent in terms of food procurement, preparation, and consumption, or were some households linked to centralized distribution or eating locations? It has been suggested, for example, that overseas Chinese mining populations lived in clusters based upon some common link such as regional origin or dialect (Hardesty and Hattori, 1984). And in Pierce, records of mining purchases indicate that some sales included dozens of placer claims (Stapp, 1987), which must have involved many miners living in different households; it would not be surprising if these households were linked in some way to reduce food expenses.

Household Wealth — A final factor affecting meat consumption patterns was the degree of household wealth. Annual assessment records suggest that there were some Chinese individuals in Pierce who had greater disposable incomes than others (see Stapp, Chapter 1 herein). These included the merchants and other business people in Pierce, and the households of mine owners and foremen. There must also have been some households of miners with more income than others, either because they worked for themselves (rather than for a large company or vice versa), or because they worked in a successful mine. The amount of disposable income might have affected the foodways of the household members because more income would have made it possible to obtain preferred types of foods. For example, as mentioned earlier, there were many foods from China available to the overseas Chinese. At least in San Francisco, such foods as dried and salted meats, pumelos [sic], dried bean curd, bamboo shoots, narrow leaved greens, yams, ginger, sweetmeats, dried fruits, salt ginger, salt eggs, tea oil, dried turnips, bettlenut [sic], chestnut flour, birds' nests, fish fins, bean sauce, lily seed, Salisburia seed, and seaweed were available (Spier, 1958a:80). These items were undoubtedly relatively expensive and thus may only have been available to those with higher incomes.

Disposable income would also have allowed an individual to purchase the quantity and quality of meat desired. The quality of meat ranges considerably, as all meat-eaters know, and quality is nearly always reflected in price of various cuts. In beef records from Pierce for example, two prices were listed, one at 20 cents and one at 15 cents per pound. We interpret these prices as reflecting tender and less tender cuts, respectively, though this could also reflect bone-out and bone-in cuts. We do not have any figures for pork, but assume that because some cuts are more tender than others, that the tender cuts were more expensive and hence more readily obtainable for those with more disposable income.

Butchering Technology

At least some Chinese must have brought their traditional butchering technology with them from China. The best source we have found for any sort of detailed account of butchering methods is Levine (1921).[1] According to Levine, the butcher's tools used for slaughtering a pig were a "good sticking knife, a cleaver, a 14-inch steel on which to sharpen the knives, hog hooks, bell-shaped

---

[1] It must be noted that Levine was observing the methods of students and teachers at Canton Christian College while he was studying Chinese butchering and curing techniques in southern China. The practices he observed may not have been carried out by the common household members or butchers of Canton and southern China. However, in lieu of any evidence to the contrary, we assume in this study that most of the techniques varied little from traditional ways.

scrapers, meat saw, and gambrel" (1921:8). Saws were used for specific tasks during the slaughtering process and for cutting the carcass into primal units. After death the hog was scalded and scraped, hung and gutted. The head was removed by use of a knife. The pelvic bones were split either with a saw or cleaver (Levine, 1921:11) but the breast bone and back bone were usually split with a saw (Levine, 1921:12).

Cutting the pig into primal and smaller cuts required a different tool kit (Figure 22). Not shown in Figure 22 was the saw mentioned by Levine as part of the butcher's toolkit; perhaps the saw was only used for separating the large primal cuts. After the carcass was divided into halves and cooled, it was further cut with a knife and a saw into three parts: the shoulders, middle, and hams. Levine (1921:13) noted that "a heavy knife with a curved blade was best for cutting through the flesh," and that "a saw would be used in cutting through the bone." Cleavers and knives were used to complete the butchering process.

In comparing Levine's (1921) observations of Chinese butchering methods to a standard American text of the same time period (Helser, 1923), major differences in tool use were noted. The sticking knife, a tool used to bleed the animal, was considerably different in design (Figure 22m). In China, the knife blade was 8 to 9 inches long and tapered "from two inches wide at the handle to a long, narrow point . . ." (Levine, 1921:9). The Euroamerican sticking knife was approximately 8 to 9 inches long but had a straight blade with parallel sides and was tapered, just distally, more so at the bottom than at the top to form a point (Figure 23c).

Also, the Chinese cutting and scraping knives (Figure 22k and l) are quite different from the other Euroamerican knives (Figure 23a, b and d). Note the Chinese knife for cutting bone and the heavy knife for cutting meat (Figure 22i and j). Nowhere in the American documentary record have we found implements resembling the Chinese tools used for cutting bone and meat. To the Chinese, the cleaver was a most important tool for dressing and especially butchering hogs (Levine, 1921:8). The only identified Chinese cleaver illustrated by Levine (1921:Plate III) has a medium to narrow blade and a straight to slightly humped back (Figure 22h). The cleaver and knives were the implements used to cut the large primal sections into secondary cuts of meat and then into cooking-size portions. Cleavers were not the most common tool type used by Euroamericans; saws and knives were used more often.

Although the Chinese in China certainly had a standard way, or ways, of butchering an animal, it is not clear whether these techniques were commonly used by those overseas. Most of the overseas Chinese had probably never butchered an animal before, hence butchering may have been a trial and error process. One description of an overseas Chinese butchering practice in San Francisco gives a different picture from that left by Levine (Lloyd, 1876:251, as cited in LaLande, 1981:242):

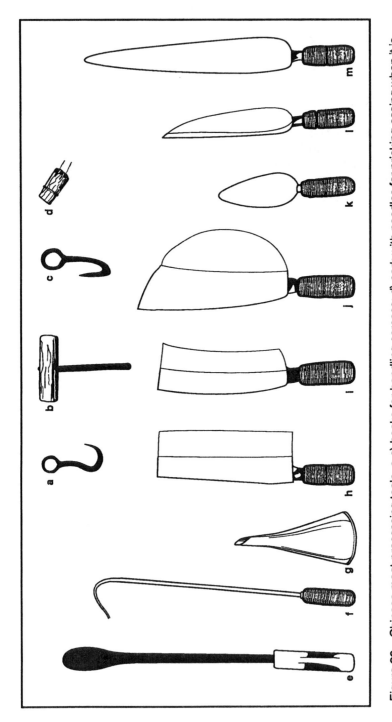

Figure 22. Chinese meat processing tools. a-c) hooks for handling carcass; d) cork with needles for pricking casing when it is being filled in order to let out the air; e) tool used for roasting meat; f) hook used for handling meat that is being roasted; g) funnel for stuffing sausage casing; h) cleaver; i) knife for cutting bone; j) heavy knife for cutting meat; k-l) cutting and scraping knives; m) sticking knife (drawn from Levine, 1921:Plate III).

106

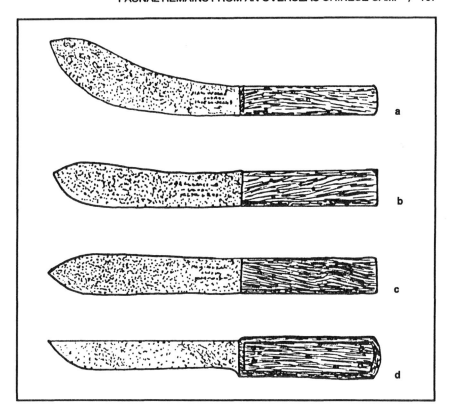

Figure 23. American meat processing knives: a) skinning knife;
b) butcher knife; c) sticking knife; d) boning knife (based on drawings
in Sears, Roebuck and Company catalog 1902:485; 1926:788).

A Chinese meat-market, although perhaps a legitimate exhibition in China-town, is a repulsive show. . . . Pork constitutes the greatest part of the stock, but it would be difficult to recognize one's pet pig after it had passed over the dissecting block of a Chinese butcher-shop. They seem to have no idea of the anatomy of the animal. With their heavy cleavers they cut and slash indiscriminately, apparently ignorant of the process of disjointing. The choicest morsels are so hacked and bruised that they are offensive to look upon. The walls and floors of the shop are besmeared with blood, grease and fragments of flesh, and everything about the premises looks jumbled and out of place.

The faunal remains from sites occupied by the overseas Chinese should reveal whether or not this account accurately represents the overseas Chinese "method" of butchering.

THE FAUNAL REMAINS FROM PIERCE
ARCHAEOLOGICAL SITES

Faunal remains from archaeological sites in the Pierce locality were studied to answer the following questions concerning the meat system:

1. What types of fresh meat were consumed by the Chinese in the Pierce locality, and in what proportions?
2. What types of preserved meats were consumed by the Chinese in the Pierce locality? Were these meats only from China, or were some American and European? If American and European meats were obtained, were these substitutes for Chinese varieties?
3. Were households independent in terms of meat procurement and consumption?
4. Is there any evidence to indicate how the meat was purchased; for example, did the Chinese purchase small retail cuts as needed, or large portions such as primal butchering units, quarters, or whole animals?
5. If meat was obtained in large quantities, how was it preserved?
6. Is there any evidence to suggest that certain cuts of meat were preferred over others?
7. Is there any correlation between the answers in 1 through 6 above and the following factors: distance of the household from town, size of the household, degree of household independence, or relative wealth of the household members?

The faunal remains discussed here are from two sites. The faunal remains recovered from 10-CW-159, an 1870s Chinese mining habitation and blacksmithing site, are more fully described elsewhere (Stapp and Longenecker, 1984). The second site, 10-CW-436, was a large late-1880s habitation site associated with Chinese miners (Stapp, 1988). Both habitations were located within one mile of Pierce City.

The primary research objectives that have guided the Pierce faunal research are common to most faunal analyses:

• The first objective was to determine the relative proportion of animal species consumed, as indicated by the faunal assemblage. This was accomplished by identifying the species of each bone, and then calculating different measures to document the relative proportion of each species.
• The second objective was to document the range of meat cuts that were consumed by identifying the skeletal elements represented in the faunal assemblage.
• The third objective involved examining the skeletal elements for insight into the manner of meat procurement; that is, to determine whether the site inhabitants were obtaining their meat supply by 1) purchasing live animals,

2) purchasing large sections of carcasses such as quarters, or 3) purchasing small retail cuts.

- The fourth objective was to determine the relative quality of the meat represented by the faunal remains as indicated by the presence of bones from "tender cuts" and the ages of the animals when slaughtered.
- The fifth objective was to identify cooking methods. This was attempted by recording evidence of cooking techniques and the size of the skeletal element. Methods which may have been used at Pierce include traditional techniques such as boiling, steaming, and stir frying (Anderson, 1988:152); roasting techniques may also have been used.
- The sixth objective was to determine if there is any variation in faunal assemblages from Pierce among sites from the same time period or among sites from different time periods. To meet this objective requires data from a variety of sites from each historic phase of settlement; thus this is a long-term objective and could only be addressed in a preliminary way with the data from 10-CW-159 and 10-CW-436.

Description and Analysis

The faunal remains from each site were recovered from two types of features. At 10-CW-159, virtually all of the bones were recovered from a habitation/industrial area refuse dump. At 10-CW-436, the majority of bones was recovered from three distinct areas of the site. The major portion of the collection came from Area F, where shallow pits filled almost entirely with bones were recovered adjacent to a building. Smaller collections were recovered in two refuse dumps located in Area G and Area M; these dumps were similar in character to the dump at 10-CW-159 (Table 16).

Table 16. Faunal Remains Recovered from Two Sites in the Pierce Locality

| | 10-CW-159 | | 10-CW-436 | |
	Feature 12	Area F	Area G	Area M
Number of bones recovered	192	475	246	131
Weight of bones recovered (grams)	4352	5075	1473	529
Bones (grams)/ All artifacts (grams)	.11	.80	.10	.15
Estimated bones in feature[a]	870	760	160	180

[a]Features were not completely excavated.

The proportion of species consumed at the two sites, as reflected by the faunal remains, is shown in Table 17. Several patterns deserve comment. One is the near absence of fowl in the faunal assemblages. The use of chicken and duck is well documented in the Chinese diet, but, as indicated by the documentary and archaeological data, fowl was not readily available in Pierce during the 1860s and 1870s (Tables 15 and 17). Fish was also not a large part of the diet, as only one fish bone and a few fish cans have been recovered at Pierce. The absence of sheep bones is consistent with the near-absence of sheep in the historical records.

The ratio of beef to pork bones at 10-CW-436 indicates a difference between Area F and Areas G and M in terms of the proportion of beef in the diet (Table 18). This difference is probably related to the fact that Area F was a different type of archaeological feature, and hence represents a different type of food-related behavior. This is explored in greater detail later in this chapter.

The use of beef by the overseas Chinese was due either to personal preference, availability, or economics. During the early period of settlement, the Chinese may not have had much choice, as pork was probably in short supply. By the time of the 10-CW-436 occupation (ca. 1880s), however, this was not a problem. Pork probably was more expensive than beef, but whether the price difference was enough to make a difference in purchasing patterns is not known. The most likely explanation for beef in the Chinese diet is simply that it was desired.

Both the presence and absence of skeletal elements were examined for insight into the manner of meat procurement. To determine whether animals were slaughtered at the site, the number of bones which are normally disposed of during the slaughtering and primary butchering process was counted; this only applies to beef as virtually the entire hog is edible, and primary hog butchering does not usually create skeletal waste. Not surprisingly, the near absence of bone from beef slaughtering indicated that live steers were not slaughtered at the site. While the presence of a few carpals could reflect slaughtering, in this case they are believed to have come from a shank cut because of the absence of other bones associated with slaughtering. Moreover, the small number of elements represented indicates that retail cuts were likely obtained by the inhabitants. The skeletal representation for beef is presented in Table 19. It is clear that at both sites only selected cuts of beef were obtained, indicating that beef was likely purchased from the local butcher.

The frequency of pork elements recovered from the two sites is shown in Table 20. To determine if whole hog carcasses were obtained by the inhabitants, the minimum number of animal butchering units from the secondary butchering process was calculated. If whole carcasses or halves were always purchased, we would expect there to be an equal proportion of butchering units represented. Some evidence, however, shows an imbalance of butchering units in all of the 10-CW-436 areas (Figure 24), with picnic shoulders, hams, and heads represented more often than the other meat units.

Table 17. Species Represented at Two Sites in
the Pierce Locality

| | 10-CW-159 | | 10-CW-436 | |
	Feature 12	Area F	Area G	Area M
Pork				
Number of bones	101	293	68	66
Weight of bones (grams)	1450	3954	558	476
Average bone weight (grams)	14	13	8	7
Min. number of individuals[a]	4	11	4	3
Min. number butchering units[b]	13	35	4	10
Medium Mammal				
Number of bones	111	150	121	29
Weight of bones (grams)	216	157	64	40
Average bone weight (grams)	2	1	1	1
Beef				
Number of bones	33	21	16	7
Weight of bones (grams)	2401	949	798	277
Average bone weight (grams)	72	45	50	40
Min. number of individuals[a]	2	1	1	1
Min. number butchering units[b]	12	8	8	6
Large Mammal				
Number of bones	23	2	1	7
Weight of bones (grams)	258	47	15	163
Average bone weight (grams)	11	24	15	23
Fowl				
Number of bones	12	—	—	—
Weight of bones (grams)	14	—	—	—
Average bone weight (grams)	1	—	—	—
Min. number of individuals[a]	1	—	—	—
Min. number butchering units[b]	3	—	—	—
Unidentified				
Number of bones	9	—	—	29
Weight of bones (grams)	13	—	—	6

[a]Minimum number of individuals based upon sizing and pairing sided bones.
[b]Minimum number of butchering units based upon Lyman (1979).

Table 18. Ratios of Pork to Beef Bones Recovered at 10-CW-159 and 10-CW-436

Ratio of Pork to Beef[a]	10-CW-159 Feature 12	Area F	10-CW-436 Area G	Area M
Bones	4	19	11	7
Weight (grams)	1	4	1	1

[a]For this analysis, medium mammal was grouped with pork and large mammal grouped with beef.

Table 19. Anatomical Distribution of Beef and Large-Sized Mammal from Pierce Sites

Element	Beef 10-CW-159 Feature 12	Beef 10-CW-436 F	Beef 10-CW-436 G	Beef 10-CW-436 M	Large-Sized Mammal 10-CW-159 Feature 12	Large-Sized Mammal 10-CW-436 F	Large-Sized Mammal 10-CW-436 G	Large-Sized Mammal 10-CW-436 M
Scapula	4	—	—	—	—	—	—	1
Humerus	—	2	—	—	—	—	—	2
Ulna	1	—	—	—	—	—	—	—
Radius	1	—	—	1	1	—	—	—
Carpal	6	—	—	2	1	—	—	—
2nd & 3rd	—	—	1	—	—	—	—	—
4th	—	1	—	—	—	—	—	—
Phalanx	—	—	—	—	—	—	—	—
1st	1	—	—	—	—	—	—	—
Pelvis	1	2	2	2	—	1	—	—
Femur	4	1	2	—	—	—	—	—
Tibia	7	—	—	1	—	—	—	—
Patella	—	1	1	—	—	—	—	—
Tarsal								
Astragalus	1	—	—	1	—	—	—	—
Calcaneum	1	—	—	—	—	—	—	—
Vertebra	1	1	—	—	2	—	—	—
Atlas	—	—	—	—	—	—	—	—
Thoracic	1	2	—	—	—	—	1	1
Lumbar	—	4	—	—	—	—	—	—
Rib	1	4	10	—	1	—	—	3
Long bone	2	—	—	—	13	—	—	—
Epiphysis	—	—	—	—	—	1	—	3
Metapodial	1	—	—	—	—	—	—	—
Nondiagnostic	—	3	—	—	5	—	—	4

Note: Numbers represent number of bones recovered.

Table 20. Anatomical Distribution of Pig and Medium-Sized Mammal from Pierce Sites

	Pig				Medium-Sized Mammal			
	10-CW-159	10-CW-436			10-CW-159	10-CW-436		
Element	Feature 12	F	G	M	Feature 12	F	G	M
Skull	15	32	4	14	10	—	17	6
Mandible	4	26	8	8	—	—	—	—
Maxilla	2	5	9	4	—	—	—	—
Teeth	25	38	21	20	1	—	2	2
Scapula	1	25	3	10	—	—	—	—
Humerus	9	31	—	—	—	—	—	—
Ulna	2	11	—	3	—	—	—	—
Radius	4	6	3	—	—	—	—	—
Ulna/Radius	—	—	—	—	1	—	—	—
Carpal	1	—	—	—	2	—	—	—
Radial	—	1	—	—	—	—	—	—
Metacarpal	—	4	—	—	—	—	—	—
4th	—	2	—	—	—	—	—	—
Phalanx	—	—	—	1	—	—	—	—
1st	1	—	—	—	—	—	—	—
2nd	1	—	—	—	—	—	—	—
Pelvis	7	35	4	1	2	—	—	1
Femur	12	18	2	2	1	—	—	—
Tibia	9	16	6	2	2	—	—	—
Patella	1	—	—	—	—	—	—	—
Fibula	1	—	—	—	1	—	—	—
Tarsal								
Astragalus	1	—	—	—	—	—	—	—
Calcaneum	1	—	—	—	—	—	—	—
4th	1	—	—	—	—	—	—	—
Metatarsal	—	3	—	—	—	—	—	—
Vertebra	—	3	—	—	5	2	—	1
Atlas	—	3	—	—	1	—	—	—
Axis	—	—	—	—	1	—	—	—
Cervical	—	4	—	—	—	—	—	—
Thoracic	—	5	—	—	—	—	—	—
Lumbar	—	23	3	1	—	—	—	—
Sacral	—	—	—	—	—	—	—	1
Rib	1	—	—	—	9	8	6	3
Sternum	—	2	—	—	—	—	—	—
Long bone	1	—	—	—	45	47	12	6
Epiphysis	—	—	—	—	2	—	—	—
Metapodial	1	—	—	—	—	—	—	—
Nondiagnostic	—	—	—	—	15	93	84	9
Unidentified	—	—	—	—	13	—	—	—

Note: Numbers represent number of bones recovered.

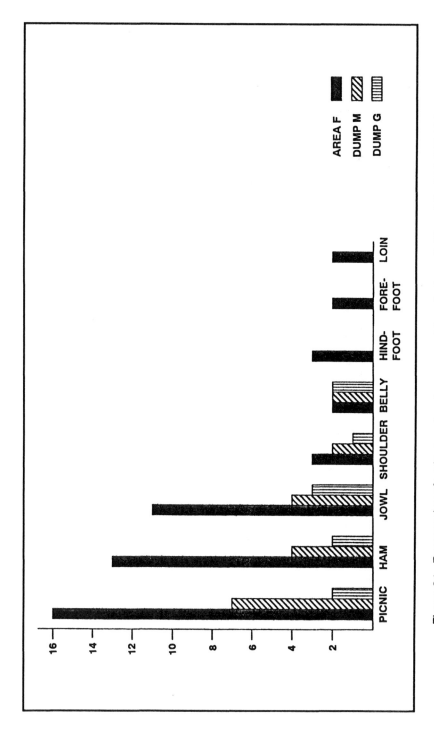

Figure 24. Frequencies of various pork units recovered from features F, M, and G at 10-CW-436.

The frequencies of bones within each butchering unit were then examined to determine if the entire unit or only retail portions from the butchering unit were being obtained; this was only done for Area F due to the small sample size of the other collections. The recovery of complete scapulas and cervical vertebrae, including atlases, suggests that pork shoulders were obtained in complete units. Picnic shoulders were also purchased in complete units, though the underrepresentation of proximal humeri indicates that smaller retail portions were also purchased. The loin was represented only by a few retail cuts, as no ilia were found and only one thoracic vertebra was recovered. Too few sparerib bones were recovered to indicate whether or not a complete slab of ribs was obtained by the site inhabitants. The hams were consistently purchased in complete units, as all of the bones were represented in equal frequency. Finally, hog heads were not always purchased as complete units; the mandibles, which include the pork jowl meat cut, were five times as common as the maxilla. The evidence indicates that those who produced the Area F deposits might have been purchasing some of their pork in large units, although it is clear that some retail portions were occasionally purchased.

Meat Quality

The two characteristics used to measure meat quality were the age of the animal when slaughtered and the tenderness of the meat cut. The few ageable beef bones recovered from both sides indicated that the animals were probably two to three years old when slaughtered (Silver, 1978), which is a good age for quality beef. The cuts from both sites were from the hindquarter and forequarter, and contained a mix of good quality and fair quality cuts.

Only two bones were recovered at 10-CW-159 that could be used to age the hogs at the time of death. One long bone indicated that one hog had been less than three years old; the other bone indicated an age of over three years old. The ages of the hogs whose bones were recovered at 10-CW-436 were based upon ageable mandibles (Table 21; Grant, 1982) and long-bone epiphyseal fusion (Silver, 1978). The tooth wear analysis of the mandibles showed that all but one of the hogs ranged in age from nearly two years to nearly three years old. The majority of long bones indicates that two-thirds of the animals were over three years in age, while the recovery of several unfused distal humeri suggested that approximately 20 percent of the animals were less than one year old. Also of interest is the fact that one-third of the animals were female (based upon the canine teeth that were recovered); these were probably the older hogs, as young female hogs were usually kept for breeding purposes by those who raised hogs.

Whatever the true proportion of young hogs to old hogs was, it is clear that much of the pork obtained by the Chinese at 10-CW-436 was from animals too old to produce top-quality pork. This could indicate that there was an oversupply of hogs in the locality at this time, as the most economic time for a rancher to sell his

Table 21. Ages of Hogs Based upon Mandibles Recovered from 10-CW-436[a]

				Number of Months Old								
<12	22	23	24	25	26	27	28	29	30	31	32	33
Mandibles 1	3	3	—	1	2	—	—	1	1	—	—	1

[a]Based upon methods described in Grant (1982).

hogs is between eight and twelve months, which is also the age when the meat is most palatable. The evidence suggests that the miners opted for price over quality when purchasing their pork, assuming that the meat from the older hogs actually sold for less.

Dividing the pig into high and low quality cuts is difficult, and we have no information regarding overseas Chinese preference. But if we were to select one butchering unit of the hog as having the highest quality meat, hence being the most expensive, it would be the loin. As previously shown, the loin was under-represented at both 10-CW-436 and 10-CW-159. This could be due to post-depositional factors, secondary butchering techniques, or simply because these cuts were not obtained. Piper (1984:22), for example, suggested that the Chinese did not desire the loin because it was too fatty. The loin aside, the evidence indicates that the inhabitants from 10-CW-159 and 10-CW-436 consumed good quality cuts of pork.

Relevant Non-Faunal Remains

Insight into the meat systems can also be gained from the non-faunal archaeo-logical record by looking at such things as dinnerware, eating utensils, food containers, butchering tools, and the general context in which the faunal remains were recovered.

The dinnerware assemblages from both sites were consistent in terms of form, with individual-sized rice bowls being the dominant vessel recovered. Large serving bowls were recovered along with a few dinner plates and an assortment of smaller saucers and dishes. For some reason, the dinner plates were Euroamerican in origin, there apparently not being a Chinese analogue. Whether or not this signifies a change in the traditional diet or serving methods is something that needs clarification. The major differences in the dinnerware from the two sites were that there was proportionately more Euroamerican whiteware recovered at 10-CW-436, and there was a total absence of "Bamboo"-patterned ware at 10-CW-436. While these differences probably do not have much to do with the meat systems, they could signify important differences between the occupants at the two sites.

Tableware and butchering tools were rare at both sites. At 10-CW-159, one Chinese cleaver and one Chinese knife were recovered (Figure 25); their occurrence appeared to be related to the blacksmith shop, as both were broken. The only eating utensil was a table knife recovered at 10-CW-436. Presumably, chopsticks were the common eating utensils of the Chinese miners and we would not expect to recover these perishable items archaeologically.

Food containers provide considerable information about the diet. The brown stoneware soy sauce and dried/pickled food storage vessels document the use of food products from China; the quantities of these items, however, do not appear to have been great. Even fewer green-glazed ginger jars were recovered. Whether such items were normally used sparingly, or cost restricted their use, needs to be determined. Several of the large rectangular cans probably contained cooking oil from China, presumably for use in the wok. A substantial amount of preserved food consumed at both sites was American or European in origin. The evidence indicates that a large quantity of canned vegetables and fruits was consumed; the bulk of these probably functioned as simple replacements for traditional foods. A few fish cans, some of which may actually be Chinese, were also recovered from 10-CW-436. No "exotic" type food containers were recognized. Glass food vessels were also found, but not in large numbers.

Figure 25. Chinese artifacts from 10-CW-159: (top-cleaver; bottom-knife).

Context

Finally, the contexts which produced the faunal remains indicate that there were at least two food behaviors in place among the Pierce Chinese. In three of the four contexts (10-CW-159; Areas M and G, 10-CW-436) the faunal remains were found amongst the regular household rubbish. This pattern suggests that food preparation and consumption occurred in the general vicinity of the living quarters. The faunal remains from Area F, however, were not associated with other household rubbish, but rather were recovered in bone pits with few non-faunal remains. Moreover, the pits were associated with a structure in which baking powder cans were recovered, leading credence to the suggestion that the structure was a cookhouse. The remains from Area F are the first evidence from Pierce that a Chinese habitation site had a specialized cooking location.

CONCLUSIONS

The paucity of archaeological data from Pierce requires us to be conservative in assessing the significance of any patterns observed to date. We have been particularly hesitant to bring data in from other localities, primarily because such data relate to systems which may or may not be analogous. With the exception of Gill (1985) and Piper (1984), there are no major faunal studies related to rural overseas Chinese sites. Studies involving faunal remains from urban Chinese sites are more plentiful (see Gust, Chapter 7 herein), but a greater understanding of rural and urban archaeological contexts will be required before any meaningful comparisons between the two can be made. Our strategy has been to move slowly in elucidating the meat system until the database is large enough for true patterns to be discerned.

The objectives outlined earlier in this chapter can now be reviewed within the context of the archaeological data presented above.

1. What was the proportion of animal species consumed? The faunal remains indicate that pork was the major meat consumed by the Chinese in Pierce. Beef may have accounted for as much as 20 percent of the meat consumed, although those who were served at the 10-CW-436 Area F cookhouse may have consumed more. The minor consumption of specialty fish products was documented at 10-CW-436. There is no archaeological evidence for the consumption of significant amounts of poultry. If major quantities of bone-less cuts of meat were purchased, if certain types of bones, such as poultry bones, were pulverized for some reason, or if certain types of bones disintegrated, the proportions of meat types would differ from those calculated.

2. What was the range of meat cuts consumed? The range of pork cuts was in general quite wide; hams and pork shoulders predominated, and the loin was underrepresented. Beef cuts were diverse with no one cut particularly common.

3. What strategy of meat procurement was used? No evidence was recovered which suggested that live animals were slaughtered at the sites. The nearly complete range of pork bones associated with edible quantities of meat could indicate that a whole carcass was purchased at 10-CW-436, but the imbalance of certain bone elements indicates that this was not the norm. The predominance of small sections of bones from three dumps (Areas G and M at 10-CW-436, and 10-CW-159) indicates that these bones were probably from smaller cuts purchased by the inhabitants. The predominance of whole bones from Area F at 10-CW-436 suggests that large units of pork, if not quarters or sides, were purchased. All of the beef cuts were retail steak, roast, and stew cuts.

4. What are the social and economic implications of the faunal remains? The evidence indicates that the occupants had adequate quality meat in their diet. Although we cannot suggest how much meat was eaten without knowing the number of occupants and the length of occupation, it certainly appears that meat supplies were plentiful.

5. What cooking methods were used? No clear evidence of cooking methods was recovered. Probable cans of cooking oil suggest stir frying. A small percentage of bone was burned, indicating that some roasting may have occurred.

6. Are there significant variations in the Pierce faunal assemblages? There were without question differences between the four faunal assemblages reviewed here. The greatest variation was between the assemblages from the three dumps and the assemblage from Area F. We have suggested that this correlates with functional, rather than temporal, differences between the features. Whether the minor differences between the three dumps are significant will become clearer as more assemblages are studied. We are convinced that in time there will be several archaeological faunal patterns documented within the Pierce locality that will have both temporal and social significance.

The intent of this chapter has been to put the archaeological food remains within the context of the overall meat system that existed in 19th-century Pierce. At this early stage of research, perhaps the contribution of this approach is not so much in the interpretation of the archaeological remains, but rather in the questions which have been raised. Some of the questions asked in the first part of this chapter have been tentatively answered. Those not answered deserve a final comment.

Were households independent in terms of meat procurement and consumption? The evidence from both sites indicates yes, although the discovery of a specialized eating and cooking location at 10-CW-436 suggests some inter-site centralization of this activity. We need to determine under what conditions centralized eating and cooking locations occurred.

How was meat preserved? We have found no evidence for meat preservation methods; however, since both of the sites were located within a mile of town, we should not have expected any. If we are to answer this question, we will have to investigate a site in one of the areas located away from town.

Does distance from town, size of household, degree of household independence, or relative wealth of household members affect the purchasing patterns of the site occupants? The faunal assemblage associated with the cookhouse at 10-CW-436 had faunal remains that differed from those in the three household dumps. If we assume that the need for the cookhouse was due to the large size of the household, then household size did affect purchasing patterns. But there could be other reasons for the cookhouse pattern, and this question really should be examined further. The only other comment we have regarding this complex question regards household wealth. Although neither site produced evidence of obvious wealth, the quantities and diversity of refuse indicate that the inhabitants were not destitute. Since both sites were located in one of the richest parts of the mining district, we can suggest that these sites are on the upper side of the wealth scale; perhaps wealthy people did not live there, but the occupants were at least comfortable. It will be useful to compare the archaeological remains from these sites with the remains from sites in mining areas that were less productive to test the proposition that wealth affected purchasing patterns.

In closing, we have found that it is advantageous to study faunal assemblages within the context of the local meat system. This approach allows for substantive interpretations of the faunal remains and contributes ideas regarding the relationship of particular sites to the locality. The approach has stimulated the formulation of numerous questions about the archaeological patterning of overseas Chinese sites which we, and hopefully other archaeologists and faunal analysts, will strive to answer in the future.

REFERENCES CITED

ANDERSON, E. N.
   1988   *The Food of China,* Yale University Press, New Haven.
ANDERSON, E. N., JR. and MARJA L. ANDERSON
   1977   Modern China: South, in *Food in Chinese Culture,* K. C. Chang (ed.), Yale University Press, New Haven, pp. 317-382.
GILL, ANNE L.
   1985   A Pound of Pork and a Pinch of Puffer: Subsistence Strategies in a Chinese Work Camp, Master's thesis, California State University, Hayward.
GOULDER, WILLIAM A.
   1875   The Pierce Mines, *Idaho Tri-Weekly Statesman,* Boise, p. 3, December 16.
GRANT, ANNIE
   1982   The Use of Tooth Wear as a Guide to the Age of Domestic Ungulates, in Ageing and Sexing Animal Bones from Archaeological Sites, B. Wilson, C. Grigson, and S. Payne (eds.), *BAR British Series, 109*:91-108.

HARDESTY, DONALD L. and EUGENE M. HATTORI
1984   Rural Chinese on the Nevada Mining Frontier: Archaeological and Historical Perspectives, paper presented at the 17th Annual Meeting of the Society for Historical Archaeology, Williamsburg, Virginia.
HELSER, MAURICE D.
1923   *Farm Meats,* Macmillan, New York.
IDAHO TRI-WEEKLY STATESMAN
1875   Notes from Pierce, *Idaho Tri-Weekly Statesman,* Boise, p. 3, October 12.
LALANDE, JEFFREY M.
1981   Sojourners in the Oregon Siskiyous: Adaptation and Acculturation of the Chinese Miners in the Applegate Valley, ca. 1855-1900, Master's thesis, Oregon State University, Corvallis.
LEVINE, CARL OSCAR
1921   Butchering and Curing Meats in China, *Canton Christian College Bulletin,* No. 27, Canton.
LLOYD, B. E.
1876   *Lights and Shades in San Francisco,* A. L. Bancroft and Company, San Francisco.
LYMAN, R. LEE
1979   Available Meat From Faunal Remains: A Consideration of Techniques, *American Antiquity, 44*:3, pp. 536-546.
PIPER, ANDREW K. D.
1984   Nineteenth Century Chinese Goldminers of Central Otago: A Study of the Interplay between Cultural Conservatism and Acculturation through an Analysis of Changing Diet, B.A. (Hons.) dissertation, University of Otago, Dunedin, New Zealand.
SEARS, ROEBUCK AND COMPANY
1902   *The 1902 Edition of the Sears Roebuck Catalogue,* No. 111, 1969 reprint, Bounty Books, New York.
1926   *Sears, Roebuck Catalogue,* Spring and Summer.
SHOSHONE COUNTY RECORDS
1861-   Miscellaneous records relating to the operation of Shoshone County. Located
1884   at the Clearwater Historical Society, Orofino, Idaho.
1885   Probate file of David M. Fraser. Located at the Shoshone County Courthouse, Wallace, Idaho.
SILVER, I. A.
1978   The Ageing of Domestic Animals, Approaches to Faunal Analyses in the Middle East, R. H. Meadow and M. A. Zeder (eds.), *Peabody Museum Bulletins, 2,* Harvard University Press, Cambridge, Massachusetts, pp. 283-302. Also exists in earlier publication, 1969, *Science in Archaeology* (D. Brothwell and E. S. Higgs, eds.), pp. 283-302 [cited by Gust, this volume.]
SPIER, ROBERT F. G.
1958a   Food Habits of 19th Century California Chinese, *California Historical Society Quarterly, 37*:1, pp. 79-84.
1958b   Food Habits of 19th Century California Chinese, *California Historical Society Quarterly, 37*:2, pp. 129-136.

STAPP, DARBY C.
  1987   The Pierce Mining District Records, Alfred W. Bowers Laboratory of
           Anthropology, University of Idaho, *Letter Report*, No. 87-2, Moscow, Idaho.
  1988   An Overseas Chinese Mining Camp: Excavations at 10-CW-436, Alfred W.
           Bowers Laboratory of Anthropology, University of Idaho, *Letter Report*,
           No. 88-20, Moscow, Idaho.
  1990   The Historic Ethnography of a Chinese Mining Community in Idaho. Ph.D.
           dissertation, University of Pennsylvania, Philadelphia.
STAPP, DARBY and JULIA G. LONGENECKER
  1984   1983 Test Excavations at 10-CW-159, The Pierce Chinese Mining Site,
           University of Idaho Anthropological Research Manuscript Series, No. 80,
           Moscow, Idaho.

PART TWO
Urban Contexts

Many of the Chinese who settled in the United States and Canada gravitated to urban areas. There they usually became part of a larger Chinese community, and also functioned in relationship to non-Chinese society. In both cases, they made significance contributions to community formation and development, clearly indicated in numerous reports that combine historical research with archaeological excavation from a variety of urban sites.

One large urban project was the excavation of a Chinese site in El Paso, Texas, intriguing in part because of the possibility of Chinese immigration over the border from Mexico. Edward Staski explores the concepts and processes of ethnicity and assimilation by integrating information from both the documentary and archaeological records to reach conclusions regarding the El Paso Chinese maintenance of ethnic separation from the dominant society.

Some significant work in northern California has focused on translating Chinese-language inventories of goods, particularly ceramics and opium, stocked by the Kwong Tai Wo general store between 1871 and 1883. For ceramics, Chinese names for some of the patterns sold were identified, and their relative worth was established. This chapter is particularly important because of its potential effect upon terminology; authors Ruth Ann Sando and David L. Felton have found, for example, that the pattern which archaeologists first termed "Three Circles and Dragonfly," then "Three Circles and Longevity," was actually called "Bamboo" in the store inventories. The inventories also indicate that opium was the most expensive item stocked, and that there was a great variation in its quality and price. Because opium cans were often stamped with "brand names" or manufacturers' marks, other researchers will be able to compare the opium inventory records with archaeologically-recovered cans to see which brands were most popular on particular sites.

In contrast with the earlier chapter on faunal materials from rural Chinese sites, Sherri M. Gust presents a comparative assessment of the faunal remains from five urban locations in California, Nevada, and Arizona. Chinese food preferences are shown to have differed at the various sites, a phenomenon based more upon economic considerations than ethnic ones. An examination of cleaver and saw marks showed that butchering patterns varied both over time and with the type of meat represented.

CHAPTER 5

The Overseas Chinese in El Paso: Changing Goals, Changing Realities

Edward Staski

In 1983, New Mexico State University conducted archaeological investigations at locations in El Paso, Texas about to be impacted by downtown redevelopment. A research plan was developed and preliminary archival research for three site locations was conducted (Sick et al., 1983). Subsequently, archaeological testing was carried out at all three sites (Figure 26), and the results led to the recommendation for mitigation, again at all three sites. Detailed reports and two lengthy monographs contain the descriptive results of these investigations (Sick, Staski, and Batcho, 1983; Staski, 1984a; 1984b; 1984c; 1985; Staski and Batcho, 1983).

The sites in downtown El Paso contained a wealth of cultural material, and it has been possible to address such research issues as the ecological history of the area, changing patterns of refuse disposal in the growing city, and developing trade and economic conditions. Yet, the most exciting and fruitful research undertaking has been the attempt to study changing ethnic relations in this multi-cultural west Texas city, primarily because the recovered materials represent activities once carried out by the three largest ethnic groups ever to inhabit the area. These groups were Euroamericans, Mexicans, and overseas Chinese. It is this last group of immigrants which is the focus of the present chapter.

The distinctive Chinese artifacts were recovered from the Cortez Parking Lot site, named after the adjacent and historically significant Cortez Hotel. Fieldwork resulted in the recovery of a large and diverse collection of overseas Chinese material.

This chapter begins with a consideration of certain basic concepts. Next, a brief history of the Chinese in El Paso is presented. Following is a discussion of the nature of the material recovered from the Cortez Parking Lot. Finally, these

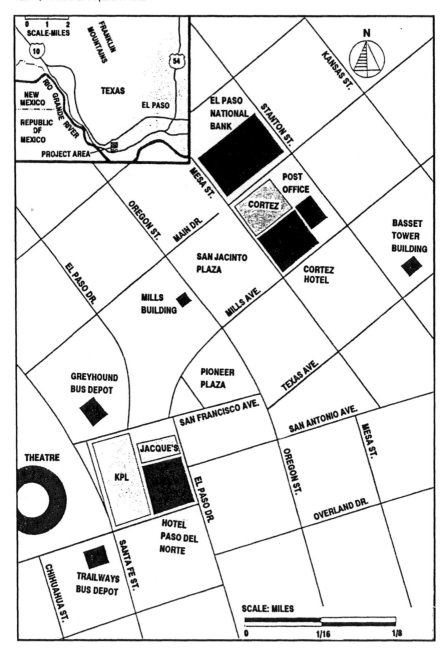

Figure 26. Downtown El Paso archaeological sites. Stippled areas indicate
locations of excavations. "Cortez" is the Cortez Parking Lot site,
from which all the Chinese material was recovered.

artifacts and observed artifact patterns are interpreted with reference to current research emphases among those who have studied the overseas Chinese archaeologically, focusing on questions regarding the nature and extent of assimilation that this population might have undergone. In particular, it will be shown that El Paso's Chinese community exhibited behavioral patterns that were in many ways similar to those of other Chinese groups, though in certain important ways they might have responded distinctively to unique circumstances. It is thought that the results of work in El Paso will contribute to a broader, more accurate image of the overall Chinese role in America.

CONCEPTS AND DEFINITIONS

The study of culture change by assimilation has a long history in anthropology and the other social sciences (e.g., Park and Burgess, 1921; Mead, 1932; SSRC Seminar, 1954). Yet, substantive study of contact and assimilation is a fairly new endeavor for archaeologists, primarily because of the difficulty of recognizing ethnic or cultural groups in many prehistoric contexts. The recent and rapid growth of historical archaeology, with its ability to identify ethnic and cultural variations by reference to documentary materials, has altered this situation in dramatic fashion (Staski, 1990).

A number of relevant organizational principles and general concepts have appeared in the historical archaeological literature (e.g., McGuire, 1979, 1982; Schuyler, 1980). For example, it is generally accepted that cultural materials can be sensitive indicators of whether ethnic groups maintained separation, or significantly assimilated with each other or into the host society. Furthermore, the most valuable archaeological measure of these processes appears to be reached by analyzing patterns of material which best correlate with ethnically distinct patterns of behavior (e.g., faunal remains indicative of diet, architectural reflections of the use of domestic space). Such an approach has proven more useful than the simple search for specific objects of obvious ethnic affiliation, which often have limited distributions in the archaeological record (Wobst, 1977).

Assimilation studies in historical archaeology have developed, in fact, to a point where general theoretical models of assimilatory processes have been advanced (McGuire, 1982). Nevertheless, a systematic archaeological approach to issues of ethnicity and assimilation has yet to be developed. The lack of rigor in our methods, and the absence of substance in our theories, is most obviously reflected by the inability of archaeologists to reach a consensus, or even an awareness, of just what such concepts as ethnicity and assimilation mean. The following brief discussion is meant to help correct this state of affairs.

As a first step, it seems appropriate to propose an explicit definition of *ethnic group,* and by extension, *ethnicity.* Foremost, this definition must be consistent with historical and sociological facts as presently understood. Only secondary consideration can be given to the inherent strengths and weaknesses of archaeology, and to our variable ability to observe and measure a limited number of sociocultural phenomena. We cannot allow the limitations of our discipline, whatever they are perceived to be, to play a greater role in determining our concepts than does sociocultural reality.

Such a task is not as straightforward as many might believe, including numerous historical archaeologists who have uncritically used the concept of the ethnic group, along with other related concepts. Throughout the past several decades, a good number of definitions for ethnic group and ethnicity have been offered, however, stressing such diverse factors as the patterns of ecological-economic interdependencies (Barth, 1969:7-38); the persistence of psychological identification and a shared sense of "peoplehood" (Gordon, 1964:24-29); the quest for political and social power through exploitation of ethnic identity (McGuire, 1982); and the structural composition of and interaction between various social groupings (Gordon, 1964:30-53). Deciding what should be emphasized, when considering ethnic experiences in the United States specifically, is not accomplished without effort.

Following Gordon (1964), and to some extent Barth (1969), it is argued here that the most sound sociological definition of the ethnic group is one that recognizes two related functions: 1) providing individuals with an ascriptive and exclusive group with which to identify, and 2) allowing individuals to confine primary relationships to others within that group. Primary relationships are those which are personal, intimate, often informal, and face-to-face, and require the involvement of the entire personality (Gordon, 1964:32). The recognition of the ethnic group thus serves to channel these relationships towards those who claim the same identification, that is, ethnicity.

These two functions appear to be the most significant contributions of ethnic groups, particularly in the modern world where economic and political systems are quite impersonal and assume global proportions. The fact that these functions might not always be directly or easily translatable into archaeological measures presents a methodological challenge to archaeologists, not a requirement for them to distort sociocultural reality.

Having thus defined ethnic group and ethnicity, it is now appropriate to consider the precise meanings of *assimilation* and *acculturation*. These meanings must logically follow from the previous discussion. Thus, assimilation is defined here as a series of processes which, if completed, totally eliminate the need for and operation of the two most significant ethnic group functions, described above. Acculturation, in contrast, is considered merely one of these processes: the one which eliminates particular behavioral patterns which serve to identify those who are within or without the ethnic population. The balance of assimilatory processes—structural assimilation, marital assimilation, and others—involve structural changes necessary to alter patterns of primary social relations, as discussed in detail by Gordon (1964:61-81). Changes in both identifying behaviors (acculturation) and structural relations (the other types of assimilation) seem to be appropriate and manageable subjects for archaeological study.

While many archaeologists have used the term acculturation consistently in their writings, it should now be clear why reference is made to assimilation throughout this chapter. Assimilation is, after all, the more inclusive term. Nevertheless, it is recognized that those archaeologists studying the overseas Chinese should not be unfairly criticized for focusing on acculturation. It is well established that the Chinese assimilated relatively little during their first eighty years in the United States, and changes in behavioral identifiers usually are the first steps towards further assimilation. Proper research questions regarding the overseas Chinese, then, might appropriately focus on degrees of acculturation. Still, other groups, particularly those who originated from European countries, appear to have assimilated significantly in both behavioral and structural ways. The attempt to reach a unified archaeological approach to ethnic issues requires that the more inclusive term be used.

The preceding discussion makes it necessary to now briefly consider whether 19th-century Chinese immigrants to the United States did indeed represent a legitimate ethnic group. This question might at first glance seem trivial, and the answer obvious. Indeed, historical archaeologists have generally assumed the answer to be yes. Yet, other social scientists have recently raised important questions regarding two critical issues: 1) the relevance or impact of ethnicity in general, relative to other social categories such as class and status (Wilson, 1980), and 2) the significance of ethnic identification for particular groups of people, given the colonial nature of their transfer to and experiences in North America (Blauner, 1972). While the first issue has been raised for all observable groups, the second has focused on those with distinctive physical characteristics, including the Chinese. It is thus appropriate to ask whether these Chinese were indeed an ethnic group as defined above, before considering the degrees or types of assimilation they experienced.

The answer seems to be that the overseas Chinese were a legitimate ethnic group in all important respects. Being recognized as Chinese, or more precisely South Chinese, was to all people an ascriptive and exclusive categorization. Furthermore, the vast majority of these Chinese immigrants found it both adaptive and necessary to restrict primary relationships to others of Chinese origin: adaptive because such interactions aided in economic and social survival, and necessary because these relationships could not be shared with the non-Chinese. The limitations on primary group membership can be seen in various social practices, ranging from the economic and social separation of Chinese from non-Chinese railroad labor gangs (Mark and Chih, 1982:8-11) to the widespread occurrence of segregated urban "Chinatowns" (e.g., Great Basin Foundation, 1987; Lister and Lister, 1989). Such limitations seem to have been in operation in the El Paso case as well, at least until the early 20th century.

Finally, the conclusion that the Chinese were a true ethnic group, as defined above, is supported by the fact that these people strongly identified with ascriptive and exclusive categories of kin while still in South China, that is, before emigration to the United States. In contrast to the Japanese, the most powerful identification for a person near Canton was with the local village, and not the nation (Lyman, 1968; cf. Daniels, 1988). As a result, the Chinese emphasized ethnicity long before they arrived in the New World, and most effectively transferred this primary identification when they moved.

The notion that the overseas Chinese were forced to participate in the internal colonial system of the United States, thus having experiences more similar to those of African Americans than to those of European people, is a possibility raised by several students of contemporary race relations (e.g., Blauner, 1972). As a result, it has been questioned whether the concepts of ethnicity and assimilation, originally intended to apply to European immigrant history, are valid given that the dynamics of colonialism and free immigration are not the same. This important issue is the focus of much current debate among sociologists, and cannot be addressed adequately in this chapter. It can be pointed out, nevertheless, that the Chinese appear to have come to North America by choice, if only to stay temporarily. Although many became economically dependent on other people to complete the trip, and started out unaware of the poor treatment to come, few were forced to take the journey. In all of these respects the overseas Chinese experience mirrors that of the vast majority of European immigrants.

THE CHINESE IN EL PASO

No aspect of El Paso's history can be understood without a clear appreciation of the remarkable impact of the railroad. That is certainly true for the history of the Chinese in the city, who might very well never have settled there if the railroad did not arrive. As with many other areas of the American West, the Chinese moved into west Texas initially as laborers along the railroad line (in this case, the Southern Pacific). Others followed via the railroad after the community was established.

The Southern Pacific, arriving from the west on or around May 19, 1880 (Leach, 1965, Sonnichsen, 1982), was only the first of five approaching rail lines to arrive. Within three years the city was connected to major trade centers to the east, north, west, and south. The impact this transportation revolution had on El Paso's demographic, economic, and social growth cannot be overstated. What in 1880 was still an insignificant point along trade routes became an "Instant City" (Barth, 1975; Staski, 1984c) of regional importance. Population climbed from 736 in 1880 to over 11,000 in 1888. The cattle, mining, and manufacturing industries became significant sources of national economic growth nearly overnight. Finally, the diversity of cultural and economic groups within the city expanded dramatically.

Yet it was not within El Paso, but rather some 400 miles to the east, that circumstances led to the establishment of a Chinese community there. The Southern Pacific finally met the west-moving Galveston, Harrisburg, and San Antonio near Pecos, Texas, to complete the second transcontinental railroad. As they had done numerous times before, railroad officials then summarily dismissed many of the Chinese laborers, as their efforts were no longer needed. These Chinese were left poor, without work, and without any means of returning to California, from where they originated. They settled in the nearest community of any size, El Paso, in the hope of finding any kind of employment.

Documentary evidence suggests that life was quite foreign and difficult for the Chinese in El Paso, at least at first. Dwellings were crowded, and sanitary conditions were terrible. Few Chinese women were ever present. The non-Chinese community was hostile and resisted giving the immigrants either social or economic support (Farrar, 1972; Rhoads, 1977). Yet, perhaps most disturbing to the residents of this small Chinatown, was the initial inability to acquire Chinese goods and live in a traditional Chinese manner.

This initial isolation of the community is foremost evidenced in various city directories and business listings. Chinese merchandise stores, carrying goods from China which were not available in other establishments, were apparently not in operation until several years after initial settlement in the city. Only three such stores are reported in 1886 (Farrar, 1972:7). The number of such establishments grew to seven by 1892, however, and then to eight by 1907 (Rhoads, 1977:13). Obviously, the inability to create exchange networks with China, and acquire desired Chinese goods, was only a temporary situation.

Indeed, these records are evidence for a gradual though steady increase in the degree of self-sufficiency experienced by the Chinese, brought about by the growing capability to create ties to the West Coast and the Old World. Such trends clearly occurred when it came to the availability of goods, an important point to be brought out later in this chapter by the results of the El Paso archaeological investigations. Other documents, regarding other community developments, also support these apparent trends.

As with all Chinese in the United States and elsewhere, El Paso's Chinese community found it necessary to form social alliances among its members which reflected or at least substituted for those left behind. The rigors of emigration, and particularly the absence of many women and other kin, made it impossible to maintain previous social relations. In their place, the overseas branch of the revolutionary Triad Society (the Chee Kung Tong) gradually became a central institution for the El Paso community. The importance of this ritual brotherhood cannot be overemphasized. Being one of the most influential secret societies in South China, and having had many members who fought in the Taiping Rebellion and the Red Turban Uprisings in Guangdong, the Triad Society was the first to be formed by immigrants in the United States (Mark and Chih, 1982:56). Nevertheless, it took nearly a decade for a significant portion of the Chinese population in

El Paso to join (Rhoads, 1977). Its influence, particularly its role in giving economic support to members, continued growing throughout the remainder of the 19th and early 20th centuries.

In yet another enterprise, the smuggling of Chinese into the United States, it is obvious that El Paso's Chinese community only gradually became more independent of the balance of the city. Illegal entry, of course, became a regular endeavor after the passage of the Exclusion Act of 1882, at nearly the same time that El Paso's Chinatown came into existence. Yet, smuggling operations in the city did not reach their well-known enormous proportions until the early 20th century (Rhoads, 1977:16). From 1905 until about 1915 El Paso's Chinese ran the largest port of entry for illegal Chinese immigrants arriving via Mexico, supporting the notion that the community had developed an effective, integrated system by that time.

Finally, growing hostile attitudes within the non-Chinese community of El Paso further encouraged isolation and self-sufficiency. By the turn of the century the general perception of Chinatown was that it was a place of moral degradation, filth, and crime (Farrar, 1972:12). The "opium problem," for instance, was perceived as growing increasingly worse through the late 19th century and into the 20th century, and legal penalties for selling, receiving, or smoking the drug became more severe through time. Violence and danger were, in addition, viewed as becoming more common in the streets of Chinatown, and efforts to further restrict the geographical extent of the Chinese community became more frequent. In the face of these official and unofficial anti-Chinese attitudes, the Chinese found it necessary to become increasingly independent.

This growing independence did not result in the establishment of a permanent Chinese community in El Paso. For various reasons, including a possible increase in the degree of assimilation, discussed below, this west Texas Chinatown vanished during the first half of the 20th century. The precise time of the demise of El Paso's Chinatown is a matter of debate, with dates given as early as 1917 (Farrar, 1972:33) and as late as 1938 (Rhoads, 1977:18). Certainly, however, a number of specific events can be held partly responsible for the decline and disappearance of the community. Included is the Mexican Revolution, which made life intolerable for Chinese immigrants in northern Mexico and thus curtailed the flow of illegal Chinese aliens through Juarez and El Paso. Also playing a significant role was the continuing enforcement of the various federal exclusion laws, which disallowed the legal arrival of additional Chinese people, particularly women. With both illegal and legal entry brought almost to a standstill, El Paso's Chinese population became static and eventually declined.

THE ARCHAEOLOGICAL RECORD

A total of fifty-seven feature designations were assigned during the combined efforts of archaeological testing and mitigation at the Cortez Parking Lot site, "feature" being defined broadly to denote any separate and identifiable archaeological formation that is useful in site interpretation. Twelve features contained direct material evidence of the presence of the Chinese community, including five refuse pits (purposefully dug pits most likely designed for refuse deposition), six trash concentrations (naturally or accidentally occurring concentrations of refuse), and one privy filled with Chinese material culture. Complete descriptions of all recorded features are presented elsewhere (Staski, 1985:131-227).

Five of these Chinese features were relatively small, highly disturbed, or otherwise determined insignificant, and little or no additional work was conducted on them after initial testing. The remaining seven, however, were remarkable for their large size, the amount and density of material culture within them, the uniform nature of their functional associations, and the wide range of depositional dates they represented. Several hundred kilograms of material were recovered from these seven features alone. All except one (number 38) appeared to have been sealed deposits in clear association with a number of Chinese laundries and residences known to have once stood on the block. Dates of deposition can be confidently placed between ca. 1890 and ca. 1915, with intermediate dates occurring within this twenty-five-year period. Basic data concerning this small though highly useful sample of deposits are summarized in Table 22.

There is one temporal pattern in these basic data requiring explicit consideration. When the estimated dates of deposition are compared with the mean bottle manufacture dates, the former are all significantly more recent than the latter, with estimated lag times ranging from ten and one half to sixteen years. "Estimated Date of Deposition" is, in all seven cases, a strong inference based on several sources of information, including documented dates of associated structures and activities, stratigraphic relationships, and several artifact attribute relative frequencies. It is thought to be the most reliable temporal indicator of deposition. "Mean Bottle (Ceramic) Dates" are, in contrast, merely mean manufacture dates determined by following the methods of Henry and Garrow (1982:269-292), previously derived from South's mean ceramic dating formula (South, 1977). Bottles were relied on more frequently than ceramics for this analysis because only two deposits (numbers 18 and 38) contained enough tightly datable ceramic material to make the technique useful.

These apparent dating discrepancies suggest that the mean dating formula might not be an accurate or sensitive indicator of actual feature formation date, especially when applied to later 19th and early 20th century bottles. Similar results have been obtained when applying South's original method to later 19th century ceramics (Henry and Garrow, 1982). Indeed, a systematic investigation of glass container manufacture-deposition lag time shows that numerous social and economic factors might play a role in postponing deposition by a similar number of years as observed in El Paso (Hill, 1982, especially Table 12.26). Clearly, such lag time needs to be considered in all such analyses.

Table 22. Descriptive Data for Significant Chinese Features

Estimated Date of Deposition	Feature Number	Feature Type	Functional Association	Mean Bottle (Ceramic) Dates
1890-1895	17	Trash pit	Laundry/ residence	1884.5
1895-1900	16	Trash pit	Laundry/ residence	(insufficient data)
1900	3-3/ 14-14[a]	Trash pit	Laundry/ residence	1887.4
1900	15a	Trash concentration	Laundry/ residence	1887.0
1900	18	Trash pit	Laundry/ residence	1887.1 (1883.5)
1910-1915	26	Trash concentration	Laundry/ residence	(insufficient data)
1910-1915	38	Trash concentration	(unclear)	1899.0 (1895.4)

[a]This single feature has three numerical designations due to the fact that it was perceived as potentially being three separate features during archaeological testing.

In the case of the Chinese deposits, it appears that reuse and recycling of bottles by Chinese residents might have played an important role in the postponement of deposition. As discussed in detail elsewhere (Staski, 1985:127-128, 229-235), the vast majority of glass containers used by the overseas Chinese was of American manufacture, primarily because the glass industry in late 19th century China was nearly nonexistent. In addition, there is convincing evidence that the Chinese were using a number of these bottles for purposes other than those for which they were originally intended.

A number of remarkable artifacts give direct and incontrovertible evidence of reuse. One is a patent-extract bottle which contains traces of bluing, a preparation of blue dyes commonly used in laundries to counteract yellowing of white fabrics. Others include two American-made bottles upon which Chinese labels are adhered. These artifacts not only indicate reuse, but also suggest that reuse and recycling were occurring among the overseas Chinese in both a widespread and organized fashion.

The label on one American-made beer bottle advertised a "wine" considered by the Chinese to be useful in promoting male virility (Figure 27). The brand name, type of alcohol, and supposed effects of its consumption are all described. A

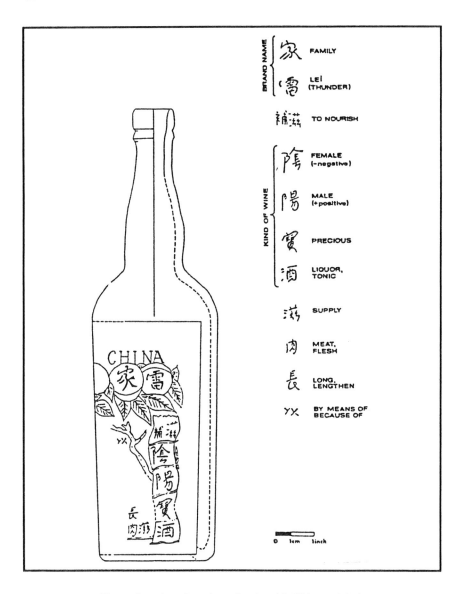

Figure 27. American beer bottle with Chinese label.

similar artifact consists of a familiar Dr. J. Hostetter's Stomach Bitters bottle, with a Chinese label advertising some sort of liquid useful for the cleaning of clothing (Figure 28).

These artifacts make it seem likely that Chinese entrepreneurs had to buy empty bottles wholesale, or at least collect them rather systematically once emptied of

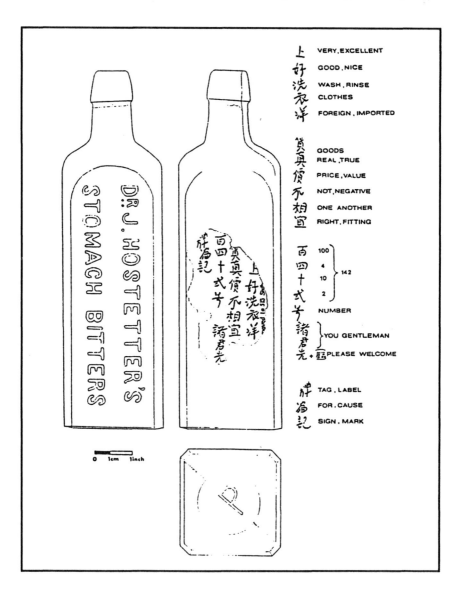

Figure 28. Dr. J. Hostetter's Stomach Bitters bottle with Chinese label.

original contents. It was, in addition, necessary for these same or other Chinese businessmen to have access to the resources required for label production. The bottles had to be filled with a product known to be in demand among the overseas Chinese. Finally, the bottles most likely had to be shipped to various Chinese settlements across the United States. The economic capabilities of small Chinatowns like El Paso's, although quite developed by the turn of the century, were probably never adequate for a market venture of this kind. Rather, the products probably were prepared and bottled in one of the larger and more established Chinatowns (such as San Francisco), and distributed from there.

Because the Chinese use of American-made bottles was widespread and intensive, and because the systematic, organized reuse of these bottles required economic efficiency, it is likely that many bottles were used for such purposes. Although there is presently no way of determining what percent of all bottles recovered from the Cortez Parking Lot were reused, it can nevertheless be argued that a significant number of them were. Such a conclusion calls into question any interpretation of product preference and use among the overseas Chinese which has exclusive dependence on the analysis of bottle types. All such analyses were done with caution. Whenever possible, analyses were conducted with reference to artifact classes other than glass.

The two labeled bottles are also highly significant because they are part of a body of evidence suggesting that a certain amount of assimilation—more specifically, acculturation—might have been occurring among El Paso's Chinese residents.

ASSIMILATION AMONG THE OVERSEAS CHINESE

At the present time it appears difficult, if not impossible, to measure archaeologically the precise degrees and types of assimilation experienced by any minority group. Yet, it is possible to recognize in patterns of material culture whether assimilation into a dominant society was a major or insignificant factor in the lives of a group of people. Such an analysis of the El Paso material begins with consideration of the two labelled bottles described previously.

Careful observation reveals that the Chinese labels not only have Chinese characters on them, but English words as well. The beer bottle has the word "CHINA" clearly written along the top (Figure 27), and the Hostetter's bottle has a portion of an English statement ". . . moved to 513 Sixth . . ." written along one side (Figure 28). It is intriguing to ask for whom those statements were intended. Obviously, the bottles, and the contents within them, were intended for the overseas Chinese. There is thus the possibility that the English messages were intended for these Chinese as well, suggesting some degree of literate bilingualism and thus some degree of assimilation. This suggestion, recognized as initially based on little evidence and weak inference, can nevertheless be explored in a more systematic and reliable fashion by reference to other material evidence recovered from the Cortez Parking Lot.

Artifact Relative Frequencies

Archaeological data suggesting that the Chinese experienced little assimilation include the relatively large amounts of Chinese ceramic material always recovered from overseas Chinese sites. The El Paso collection is no exception, with the majority of ceramics (measured by weight for this analysis) from most Chinese deposits being of Chinese manufacture (Table 23). Yet, it appears that the degree of dependence placed on either Chinese or non-Chinese ceramic items changed through time, in a way which complements the documentary history of the city's Chinese community.

As discussed earlier in this chapter, a major theme emerging from the documentary record is that it took a number of years, up to two decades, for El Paso's Chinese to gain employment and some economic stability, create internal social institutions thought necessary, effectively aid other Chinese who wanted to enter the country, and establish a reliable economic network to the West Coast so that desired Chinese merchandise could arrive in adequate quantities. The delay in this community's establishment, caused by poor economic conditions, small population size, and the great distance between El Paso and the West Coast, is suggested somewhat in the archaeological record.

The data (Table 23), restricted here to ceramics because of the complexities of American bottle reuse, suggest that just over half of all ceramic material available to the Chinese laundry workers was coming from China during the early 1890s (Feature 17). By the late 1890s, this figure appears to have climbed to over 60 percent (Feature 16). Then, by the turn of the century, over 85 percent of the ceramics available to, and used by, some of these same workers were manufactured in China (Features 3-3/14-14 and 15a). It seems that the gradual growth of self-sufficiency in El Paso's Chinese community, most obviously the improving economic ties to the West coast and the increasing number and efficiency of Chinese merchandise stores, is indeed archaeologically observable.

It can be further concluded from both the documentary and archaeological records that El Paso's Chinese were going to great lengths to maintain ethnic separation from the dominant society, and becoming more successful at this endeavor as the 19th century was coming to a close. Yet, it is possible to suggest that other forces were at work as well, and observe that only some members of the community were depending on Chinese ceramics to a greater and greater extent as availability improved. Others, apparently, began depending on these Chinese goods less and less.

Fewer than 50 percent of the ceramics from one deposit are Chinese, and this trash pit (Feature 18) is thought contemporary with Features 3-3/14-14 and 15a. In contrast, a deposit dating to the second decade of the 20th century contained

Table 23. Artifactual Data from Significant Chinese Features

Estimated Date of Deposition	Feature Number	Chinese Ceramic within Total (percent)	Porcelain within Chinese (percent)	Rice Bowls within Porcelain (percent)	Serving Bowls within Porcelain (percent)	Liquor Containers within Stonewares (percent)	Food Storage Jars within Stonewares (percent)	Soya Sauce Containers within Stonewares (percent)
1890-1895	17	54.6	47.2	40.4	32.5	18.3	16.6	29.5
1895-1900	16	62.1	3.3	0.0	37.1	0.0	63.2	2.0
1900	3-3/ 14-14[a]	86.1	18.5	31.6	43.9	58.9	19.5	10.7
1900	15a	85.4	19.9	41.6	34.5	47.7	15.4	5.9
1900	18	47.4	23.0	17.3	21.5	9.6	50.0	15.4
1910-1915	26	100.0	48.9	38.5	38.0	0.0	11.9	49.0
1910-1915	38	10.4	67.1	75.4	0.0	16.5	4.5	5.4

[a]This single feature has three numerical desginations due to the fact that it was perceived as potentially being three separate features during archaeological testing.

139

nothing but ceramics of Chinese manufacture (100 percent; Feature 26). Finally, just over ten percent of the ceramics from Feature 38, contemporary with number 26, were manufactured in China. Thus, the apparent pattern is one of a growing diversity or range of dependence on Chinese goods, after an initial overall increase in such dependence. Percent of total ceramics that are Chinese is the only measure exhibiting any apparent chronological trend (Table 23).

Clearly, sample size might be responsible for the pattern that has been observed. It is also possible that an additional though as yet unrecognized variable led to the apparent distributions. Additionally, it must be mentioned that the inference being made concerning assimilation is fairly weak, and requires further confirmation before being accepted without question. Nevertheless, the possibility exists that a portion of El Paso's Chinese community had increasing access to Chinese ceramics (and their contents) but chose not to depend on them to as great an extent as would otherwise be expected. The factor of choice suggests that assimilation within this portion of the community was occurring, and is being observed archaeologically.

Diet

Other data sources support the notion that some assimilation, in the form of acculturation, might have been occurring. One of these is the large quantity of faunal material recovered. It is well known that dietary patterns are some of the most enduring aspects of an ethnic group's behavioral separation from the host society (Baer, 1981, 1991). If important dietary changes can be observed archaeologically for any ethnic minority, it is reasonable to conclude that a high degree of acculturation was taking place. For this reason, along with the fact that traditional South Chinese dietary patterns are well documented (Anderson, 1988; Chang, 1977) and known to have been highly distinctive from common American foodways, archaeologists have devoted considerable time to the study of Chinese diet in America (Evans, 1980; LaLande, 1982; Langenwalter, 1977, 1978, 1980; McEwan, 1984, 1985).

The material recovered from the Cortez Parking Lot is similar to that from other overseas Chinese sites, in that the faunal assemblage can be easily distinguished from non-Chinese faunal collections. Emphasis on sea fauna, fowl, and pork stands in striking contrast to the typical non-Chinese diet of turn-of-the-century El Paso, with its almost exclusive reliance on beef. Yet, there are some intriguing differences between the data from El Paso and other overseas Chinese sites, and it does seem as if the dominant dietary regime was influencing Chinese patterns (LaLande, 1982; McEwan, 1984, 1985).

From the material examined—to date restricted to that recovered from Feature 3-3/14-14, one of the deposits thought to have dated to ca. 1900—the following observations can be made. Pig (*Sus scrofa*) was the predominant species recovered. Pig remains comprise nearly 20 percent of the individuals and 25 percent of the estimated biomass. Yet, fully 57 percent of the pig bone with evidence of butchering was cut with a non-Chinese saw, and not in a traditional Chinese manner. The remaining 43 percent was cut with the use of a cleaver. Thus, although pork was common in the El Paso Chinese diet, preparation techques and cuts might often have been quite different than those of South China.

Supporting the notion that some change in dietary patterns was occurring is the fact that cow (*Bos taurus*) was the second most important contributor to the diet, based on biomass estimates. In addition, over 80 percent of the recognizably butchered beef elements (only 3% of the total, it should be noted) were prepared with non-Chinese implements. All recognizable cuts were identified as typically Euroamerican, and it appears that the Chinese in west Texas were eating different quantities of food types, possibly in what was to them a foreign manner.

The analysis of the faunal material from the Cortez Parking Lot will remain incomplete until assemblages from additional features are taken into account. Further evidence that some diet-related behavioral changes might have taken place is available now, however, and can be gleaned by considering patterns of alcohol consumption among the overseas Chinese. The evidence from El Paso is neither incontrovertible nor clear in many respects, given the fact that the extent of bottle reuse remains unknown. Still, if the assumption is made that even a minority of bottles did contain originally intended contents, then it can be argued that non-Chinese alcohol was an important element in the Chinese diet. This argument is reasonable, because so many alcohol bottles were recovered.

The rate and quantity of alcohol consumption among the overseas Chinese have received some attention in the archaeological literature. Alcohol has been ". . . an integral part of Chinese culture for several thousand years" (LaLande, 1982:44), and archaeological evidence indicates that the immigrants consumed both Chinese and American alcoholic beverages. What is most fascinating is that the rate and quantity consumed, as suggested by archaeologists, appear much greater than that described in written records and reflected in popular perceptions. Much of the documentary evidence depicts the Chinese as relatively light or moderate drinkers, with a low incidence of pathological drinking behaviors. Archaeological data from El Paso, in contrast, suggest that relatively heavy drinking might have been the norm.

An explanation for this discrepancy between the documentary and archaeological records is found when the nature of both drinking behavior patterns and drunken comportment are considered (MacAndrew and Edgerton, 1969). Non-Chinese culture of the western frontier prescribed drinking in public groups, and the public display of drunkenness was not considered horrible or highly immoral. In contrast, the overseas Chinese generally drank in private, hidden from the non-Chinese population. They seldom displayed the effects of consumption publicly. The apparent "sobriety" of the Chinese in the non-Chinese mind was thus the result of an effort by the immigrants to keep their drinking practices secret (LaLande, 1982:44-46).

Similar contrasts between public and private drinking behaviors have been discussed for the Navajo and Hopi (Levy and Kunitz, 1974), and 19th century Irish and Jewish immigrants to the United States (Staski, 1983). It has been concluded that most available measures of alcohol consumption rates are reactive to the public, social environment. Archaeological investigations, of course, are non-reactive and thus more accurate when it comes to the study of actual drinking behavior (Staski, 1983).

When considering drinking in relation to assimilation, both the actual patterns of consumption and the publicly displayed patterns of use must be taken into account. The first is a measure of behavior while the second is a measure of perceptions and attitudes. Clearly, assimilation involves changes in both behaviors (acculturation) and attitudinal repertoires (primarily what Gordon (1964:71)) calls "Identificational Assimilation," though behavioral changes are involved as well). Alcohol consumption appears to be a most appropriate subject of inquiry for assimilation studies, precisely because the related actions and attitudes are quite distinctive.

Nevertheless, a number of caveats in this analysis must be pointed out immediately. First, it is at this time impossible to estimate changing rates of alcohol consumption among individuals, or even groups, since no accurate correlations between number of responsible people, actual duration of deposition, and particular trash deposit can be made. Second, it should be pointed out that no measure of ethanol consumption was attempted. Since different alcoholic beverages contain different amounts of the drug (i.e., have different "proofs"), it follows that any measure of alcohol consumption requires knowledge of these percents. It was decided that any estimation of Chinese alcohol proofs would be difficult to confirm. Third, as already mentioned, the presence of American bottle reuse among the Chinese clearly presents a problem since glass alcohol containers comprise a large portion of the data under analysis. Finally, accurately estimating numbers of functional bottle and ceramic types from an urban setting, necessary for the analysis to be complete, is highly problematic given the complex nature of urban depositional histories.

Despite these problems, and the recognized substantial limits imposed on the analysis, it is still intriguing to note that chronological relative frequencies of estimated total alcohol containers from China and the United States exhibit a remarkably similar pattern to that displayed when the weights of all ceramics are considered (compare Tables 23 and 24). During the 1890s, it appears that a relatively large amount of the alcohol consumed by El Paso's Chinese was American-made (Features 17 and 16; see Table 24). This dependence on American beverages most probably resulted because few Chinese goods, including liquor, were available in El Paso at the time. By the turn of the century, however, there seems to have been relatively greater use of Chinese spirits, reflecting the growing self-sufficiency of the community (Features 3-3/14-14 and 15a). Finally, beginning with and continuing into the early 20th century (Features

Table 24. Absolute Numbers and Percents of Chinese and
American Alcohol Bottles

Feature Number	Number Chinese Liquor Containers	Number American Alcohol Bottles	Total	Percent Chinese of Total		Percent American of Total
17	13	27	40	32		68
16	0	4	4	0	1	100
3-3/ 14-14[a]	117	57	174	67		33
15a	56	18	74	75	2	25
18	20	87	107	19		81
26	0	2	2	0	3	100
38	1	9	10	10		90

1 = Evidence of nonavailability of Chinese goods
2 = Growing availability, little or no assimilation
3 = Growing availability, greater assimilation
[a]This single feature has three numerical designations due to the fact that it was perceived as potentially being three separate features during archaeological testing.

18, 26, and 38), use of American liquor predominated once again. This time, however, the apparent overwhelming use of non-Chinese beverages was most probably the result of choice, not merely availability. Assimilation is suggested once again.

It must be noted that the general pattern is similar when total ceramic weight artifact frequencies and estimated number of alcohol bottles are compared, though the particular patterns exhibited by individual features are not. For example, Feature 26 contained Chinese ceramics exclusively, yet all recovered alcohol-containing vessels are American made. The former measure indicates little or no assimilation among those responsible for feature formations, while the latter measure suggests significant behavioral changes. Clearly, the processes of culture change and assimilation are mosaic in nature, with different behaviors changing at different times and rates. Nor are they easy to reconstruct on any but a very general level of abstraction. Nevertheless, the fact that both total artifact weights and estimated numbers of alcohol bottles reveal similar general patterns lends strength to the suggestion that some significant changes were occurring among portions of the Chinese community. The observation that these patterns are similar also suggests that the distorting influences of the caveats mentioned previously might not be as significant as thought.

The other aspect of alcohol consumption needing consideration is that involved with attitudes regarding public displays and comportment. As stated earlier, the Chinese had an image of being light to moderate drinkers because they kept their drinking hidden most of the time. Yet, this proclivity to hide activities is also an ethnic or cultural marker, and changes in attitudes are as indicative of changes in ethnic identification (i.e., assimilation) as are changes in actual behavior. Unfortunately, the documentary record concerning the public display of Chinese behaviors is so distorted and incomplete that not even general conclusions can be reached at this time. Perhaps further research will suggest methods to retrieve more information from the few available documents.

CONCLUDING DISCUSSION

To this point, this chapter has been concerned with 1) defining such concepts as ethnicity and assimilation, and determining that the Chinese in late 19th century America were indeed an ethnic group, 2) tracing the general history of the overseas Chinese experience in El Paso, and 3) examining the archaeological record and the patterns of behavioral changes it possibly reflects. It is now necessary to consider how these behavioral changes might have related to the processes of assimilation, and what these relations can tell us about the dynamics of both assimilation and ethnic boundary maintenance.

First, it is clearly the case that the inferred changes experienced by at least a portion of El Paso's Chinese community could not possibly have been any type of assimilation other than acculturation. No significant alterations in social structure are apparent in either the archaeological or documentary data, and the vast majority of Chinese seem to have restricted primary relationships to within their community. They did so, furthermore, during the entire time they lived in the city, even when they might have found it difficult. For example, only one marriage of a Chinese man to a non-Chinese woman (apparently legal in El Paso) is recorded over a period of approximately thirty-five years, despite the fact that only four Chinese women were ever reported to be present. Needless to say, and for numerous reasons, these records might be inaccurate, but certainly not to the extent necessary to distort the general pattern.

A situation of "acculturation only" (Gordon, 1964:77) is not uncommon, and does not contradict the general definitions presented previously. In addition, some reflection on the dynamics leading to this situation naturally leads to a consideration of theories regarding the underlying causes of ethnic boundary maintenance. Three influential theories are discussed here.

Barth (1969), with his ecological orientation, claims that the degree of boundary maintenance is determined by the extent of overlap between each group's economic activities. The greater the overlap, he argues, the weaker the boundary. In contrast, Spicer (1971, 1972) sees boundaries strengthening among minorities as a powerful group increases its attempts to absorb the smaller groups. Opposition to such attempts is, for Spicer, the proximate cause of the persistence of ethnic diversity. Finally, McGuire (1982), one of the few archaeologists to consider the theory of ethnic group dynamics, regards degrees of disparity in the distribution of power as the critical factor determining the strength of ethnic boundaries. It is intriguing to consider the El Paso situation with each of these three theoretical views in mind.

The archaeological and documentary records regarding the Chinese in El Paso do not support the argument put forth by Barth. Ethnic boundaries between these people and others remained high, as suggested by the fact that only a certain amount of acculturation is indicated. Yet, there was a significant amount of overlap in the economic activities of the Chinese and other groups, particularly Mexicans. Records indicate that there were numerous instances of resentment, and even violence, resulting from competition for jobs in such areas as laundry service, restaurant operation, and truck farming. Only gradually did the Chinese establish monopolies within these occupations, and for most of their stay they had to struggle with others doing the same sort of work (Rhoads, 1977).

Nor does the evidence support the model developed by Spicer. There is absolutely no indication that the non-Chinese population had any interest in absorbing, or assimilating, the overseas Chinese. Rather, all efforts were directed at keeping these people separated from the balance of the community. Clearly, the lack of assimilation other than some acculturation was not the result of Chinese opposition, as defined by Spicer.

McGuire's model cannot be rejected so completely. There is no question that the distribution of power was unequal in turn-of-the-century El Paso, and the Chinese had very little, if any, influence on general metropolitan policies or directions. They were always relatively few in number, never elected one of their own to political office, appear not to have contributed any leaders to the outside community, and had no means of curtailing the various discriminatory actions taken against them. Certainly, this unfair situation might have encouraged the Chinese to maintain strong ethnic boundaries.

What McGuire fails to mention, and what the El Paso material seems to suggest, is that certain amounts of acculturation can occur even when the disparity of power is great and not decreasing. Put another way, it appears as if behavioral and cultural patterns might not be very important in maintaining strong ethnic boundaries. Rather, these boundaries are maintained most effectively by avoiding structural assimilation, that is, by limiting primary social relationships to those within the group. This interpretation does not contradict the view that a disparity of power creates the need to maintain or strengthen the boundaries. Neither does it weaken the general opinion that structural assimilation is the "keystone" of all assimilation (Gordon, 1964:81). Indeed, it lends support to this observation.

If this conclusion is correct, then archaeologists wishing to study ethnic group dynamics will have to look more often for patterns of social structure, rather than limiting themselves to the investigation of changing behavioral repertoires. Such an approach might help us better understand both the distribution of power and the composition of primary groups, as reflected in a number of both historical and prehistoric archaeological settings.

SOURCES CITED

ANDERSON, E. N.
1988   *The Food of China,* Yale University Press, New Haven.
BAER, ROBERTA D.
1981   The Effects of Social and Cultural Variables on Food Consumption Patterns and Dietary Adequacy, ms. on file, Arizona State Museum, Tucson.
1991   Cultural Factors Affecting Relationships between Household Refuse and Household Food Consumption, in "The Ethnoarachaeology of Refuse Disposal," E. Staski and L. D. Sutro (eds.), *Anthropological Research Papers,* No. 42, Arizona State University, Tempe, pp. 5-12.
BARTH, FREDRIK
1969   Introduction, in *Ethnic Groups and Boundaries,* F. Barth (ed.), Little, Brown, Boston, pp. 7-38.
BARTH, GUNTHER
1975   *Instant Cities: Urbanization and the Rise of San Francisco and Denver,* Oxford University Press, New York.
BLAUNER, ROBERT
1972   *Racial Oppression in America,* Harper and Row, New York.
CHANG, K. C. (ed.)
1977   *Food in Chinese Culture: Anthropological and Historical Perspectives,* Yale University Press, New Haven.
DANIELS, ROGER
1988   *Asian America: Chinese and Japanese in the United States since 1850,* University of Washington Press, Seattle.
EVANS, WILLIAM S.
1980   Food and Fantasy: Material Culture of the Chinese in California and the West, circa 1850-1900, in *Archaeological Perspectives on Ethnicity in America: Afro-American and Asian American Culture History,* R. L. Schuyler (ed.), Baywood Publishing Co., Amityville, New York, pp. 89-96.
FARRAR, NANCY
1972   The Chinese in El Paso, *Southwestern Studies Monograph,* No. 33, Texas Western Press, The University of Texas at El Paso.
GORDON, MILTON M.
1964   *Assimilation in American Life: The Role of Race, Religion, and National Origins,* Oxford University Press, New York.

GREAT BASIN FOUNDATION
1987   *Wong Ho Leun: An American Chinatown,* 2 vols., Great Basin Foundation, San Diego.
HENRY, SUSAN L. and PATRICK H. GARROW
1982   The Historic Component, in "City of Phoenix Archaeology of the Original Townsite, Blocks 1 and 2," J. S. Cable, S. L. Henry, and D. E. Doyel (eds.), *Soil Systems Publications in Archaeology,* No. 1, Phoenix, pp. 183-382.
HILL, SARAH H.
1982   An Examination of Manufacture-Deposition Lag for Glass Bottles from Late Historic Sites, in *Archaeology of Urban America: The Search for Pattern and Process,* R. S. Dickens, Jr. (ed.), Academic Press, New York, pp. 291-327.
LaLANDE, JEFFREY M.
1982   "Celestials" in the Oregon Siskiyous: Diet, Dress, and Drug Use of the Chinese Miners in Jackson County, ca. 1860-1900, *Northwest Anthropological Research Notes, 16*:1, pp. 1-61.
LANGENWALTER, PAUL E. III
1977   The Archaeology of 19th Century Chinese Subsistence at Lower China Crossing, Madera County, California, Unpublished manuscript, National Park Service, Interagency Archaeological Division, San Francisco.
1978   A Late 19th Century Chinese Store in the Sierran Foothills, paper presented at the 1978 Annual Meeting of the Society for California Archaeology, Yosemite National Park, California.
1980   The Archaeology of 19th Century Chinese Subsistence at the Lower China Store, Madera County, California, in *Archaeological Perspectives on Ethnicity in America: Afro-American and Asian American Culture History,* R. L. Schuyler (ed.), Baywood Publishing Company, Amityville, New York, pp. 102-112.
LEACH, JOSEPH
1965   Farewell to Horseback, Muleback, Footback, and Prairie Schooner: The Railroad Comes to Town, *Password,* El Paso Historical Society Publication.
LEVY, JERROLD E. and STEPHEN J. KUNITZ
1974   *Indian Drinking: Navajo Practices and Anglo-American Theories,* John Wiley and Sons, New York.
LISTER, FLORENCE C. and ROBERT H. LISTER
1989   The Chinese of Early Tucson: Historic Archaeology from the Tucson Urban Renewal Project, *Anthropological Papers of the University of Arizona,* No. 52, University of Arizona Press, Tucson.
LYMAN, STANFORD M.
1968   Contrasts in the Community Organization of Chinese and Japanese in North America, *The Canadian Review of Sociology and Anthropology, 5.*
MacANDREW, C. and R. B. EDGERTON
1969   *Drunken Comportment: A Social Explanation,* Aldine, Chicago.
MARK, DIANE MEI LIN and GINGER CHIH
1982   *A Place Called Chinese America,* Kendall/Hunt Publishing Co., Dubuque, Iowa.

McEWAN, BONNIE G.
1984   Appendix C: Faunal Analysis, in "Beneath the Border City, Volume One: Urban Archaeology in Downtown El Paso," by Edward Staski, *University Museum Occasional Papers*, No. 12, Las Cruces, New Mexico State University, pp. 271-301.
1985   Appendix B: Faunal Analysis, in "Beneath the Border City, Volume Two: The Overseas Chinese in El Paso," by Edward Staski, *University Museum Occasional Papers*, No. 13, Las Cruces, New Mexico State University, pp. 262-283.

McGUIRE, RANDALL H.
1979   Rancho Punta de Agua, Arizona State Museum, *Contribution to Highway Salvage Archaeology in Arizona*, No. 57, Tucson.
1982   The Study of Ethnicity in Historical Archaeology, *The Journal of Anthropological Archaeology, 1*, pp. 159-178.

MEAD, MARGARET
1932   *The Changing Culture of an Indian Tribe*, Columbia University Press, New York.

PARK, ROBERT E. and ERNEST W. BURGESS
1921   *Introduction to the Science of Sociology*, University of Chicago Press, Chicago.

RHOADS, EDWARD J. M.
1977   The Chinese in Texas, *Southwestern Historical Quarterly, LXXI*:1, pp. 1-36.

SCHUYLER, ROBERT L. (ed.)
1980   *Archaeological Perspectives on Ethnicity in America: Afro-American and Asian American Culture History*, Baywood Publishing Company, Amityville, New York.

SICK, DEBORAH, MICHAEL ROBERTS, DAVID BATCHO, and WILLIAM A. TIMMONS
1983   *Documentary Research, Photo Documentation, the Research Design and Plan for Public Programs for the City of El Paso Downtown Revitalization Project*, report prepared for the City of El Paso by the Cultural Resources Management Division of New Mexico State University, Las Cruces.

SICK, DEBORAH, EDWARD STASKI, and DAVID BATCHO
1983   *Archaeological Testing of 41EP2370, the Kohlberg Parking Lot Site, El Paso, Texas*, report prepared for the City of El Paso by the Cultural Resources Management Division of New Mexico State University, Las Cruces.

SONNICHSEN, C. L.
1982   *Tucson: The Life and Times of an American City*, University of Oklahoma Press, Norman.

SOUTH, STANLEY
1977   *Method and Theory in Historical Archaeology*, Academic Press, New York.

SPICER, EDWARD H.
1971   Persistent Cultural Systems, *Science, 174*, pp. 795-800.
1972   Plural Society in the Southwest, in *Plural Society in the Southwest*, E. H. Spicer and R. H. Thompson (eds.), Interbook, Inc., New York, pp. 21-64.

SSRC SUMMER SEMINAR ON ACCULTURATION
1954   Acculturation: An Exploratory Formulation, *American Anthropologist, 56*, pp. 973-1002.

STASKI, EDWARD
 1983　　Patterns of Alcohol Consumption Among Irish-Americans and Jewish-Americans: Contributions from Archaeology, Ph.D. dissertation, Department of Anthropology, University of Arizona, Tucson.
 1984a　*Archaeological Testing of the Jacque's Bar Site, El Paso, Texas,* report prepared for the City of El Paso by the Cultural Resources Management Division of New Mexico State University, Las Cruces.
 1984b　*Archaeological Testing of the Cortez Parking Lot Site, El Paso, Texas,* report prepared for the City of El Paso by the Cultural Resources Management Division of New Mexico State University, Las Cruces.
 1984c　Beneath the Border City, Volume One: Urban Archaeology in Downtown El Paso, *University Museum Occasional Papers,* No. 12, New Mexico State University, Las Cruces.
 1985　　Beneath the Border City, Volume Two: The Overseas Chinese in El Paso, *University Museum Occasional Papers,* No. 13, New Mexico State University, Las Cruces.
 1990　　Studies of Ethnicity in North American Historical Archaeology, *North American Archaeologist, 11*:2, pp. 121-145.
STASKI, EDWARD and DAVID BATCHO
 1983　　*A Preliminary Report on Archaeological Testing of the Cortez Parking Lot Site, Mills Block 3, West Half,* report prepared for the City of El Paso by the Cultural Resources Management Division, New Mexico State University, Las Cruces.
WILSON, J. W.
 1980　　*The Declining Significance of Race,* University of Chicago Press, Chicago.
WOBST, H. M.
 1977　　Stylistic Behavior and Information Exchange, in "For the Director: Research Essays in Honor of James B. Griffin," *Anthropological Papers,* No. 61, C. E. Cleland (ed.), University of Michigan, Ann Arbor, pp. 317-342.

CHAPTER 6

Inventory Records of Ceramics and Opium from a Nineteenth Century Chinese Store in California

Ruth Ann Sando and David L. Felton

The past twenty years have witnessed increasing interest in the history and archaeology of the overseas Chinese communities that were common throughout much of the western United States during the late 19th century (cf. Praetzellis and Praetzellis, 1990:9-12). Most of the resulting studies concentrate on analysis of English-language documents that reflect the Chinese presence, or on description of the physical remains of these neighborhoods and settlements. The studies provide important insights into the demographics and material culture of the Chinese in America. Nevertheless, these avenues of inquiry by themselves often provide only limited information about Chinese individuals or their establishments, daily life in an overseas Chinese community, or Chinese perceptions of life and identity in America (cf. Praetzellis, Praetzellis and Brown, 1987:38-40). Our understanding of these aspects of overseas Chinese life should be enhanced through analysis of Chinese-language records, but this approach has been limited both by the scarcity of historic Chinese document collections in the United States, and by the fact that many of the researchers active in this field are not fluent in Chinese. The senior author's translation of sections of a collection of 19th century California Chinese business records of the Kwong Tai Wo Company, and our analysis of the data provided, are efforts to broaden our research base. These documents have yielded a considerable amount of information about both the economic development of an overseas Chinese mercantile venture and the range of goods commonly made available by Chinese merchants to their countrymen.

The Kwong Tai Wo Company (Kuang T'ai Ho) operated a general store in northern California during the last half of the 19th century. The store sold a wide range of goods, probably both wholesale and retail, to the Chinese residents of the area. The records of the company have outlasted both the owners and the store itself, and are now preserved in the manuscript collections of the Bancroft Library at the University of California in Berkeley (Kwong Tai Wo Company, 1871-1883). These business records constitute a rare and valuable resource; relatively few such collections are available outside Asia (Gardella, 1982:63).

The location of the Kwong Tai Wo store is uncertain; the manuscripts are simply labeled "Grass Valley?" Although historical research to confirm the location of the business was not successful, it is most likely that the store was situated in Marysville rather than Grass Valley. Wells, Fargo & Company directories of Chinese businesses for the years 1878 and 1882 list no firms by the name "Kwong Tai Wo" in Grass Valley, Nevada City, or Marysville (Wells, Fargo & Company Express, 1878, 1882). The 1878 directory, however, lists a "Quong Ty & Co." in Marysville (Wells, Fargo & Co., 1878). The store's business records include, among the Chinese documents, several loose shipping bills and orders in English, which refer variously to "Mr. Quong Ty," "Quong Ti," "Q. T." and "Quong Hi." Two of the bills, dated December 6 and 20, 1880, are for shipment of goods by steamer from San Francisco to Marysville.

Although we know little of the company or the manner in which these documents came to the attention of manuscript collectors, the records tell a great deal about the range of goods made available by overseas Chinese merchants, and about the evolution of this particular commercial venture. The Kwong Tai Wo documents consist of twenty-two volumes dated from 1871 to 1896. The majority of the volumes are daily sales records, but also included are records of purchases from other merchants, pawn records, payroll, and inventories (two volumes). The books are of standard size and appearance; their bindings are sewn by hand. All are written in Chinese.

The range of goods sold by the Company is comprehensive, and includes food, tools and hardware, household goods, clothing, personal accessories, books, drugs, and ceremonial items. Food items include such staples as rice, oil, tea, vegetables, pork, fish, sauces and spices, fruit, wine, sugar, salt, and flour. Hoes, axes, shovels and other tools, rope, and nails are listed. Household items include ceramic tableware, soap, lanterns, wicks, brooms, comforters, kerosene, mahjong sets, scissors, door locks, mirrors, iron woks, tin teapots, scrub boards, dusters, measuring weights, dresser sets, and chopsticks. Among the clothing carried were trousers, shirts, shawls, slippers, boots, silk ribbons, belts, padded jackets, vests, underclothes, shoes, and Shanghai-style hats. Personal accessories ranged from fans and earrings to tobacco, guns, and a few opium pipes.

THE INVENTORIES

The Kwong Tai Wo inventories (Volumes 6 and 7) hold the greatest immediate value for historical archaeologists and historians. They provide vernacular names for artifacts recovered on overseas Chinese archaeological sites, objects that until now have been referred to in the archaeological literature simply by descriptive terms. A potentially more significant contribution of the inventories lies in the quantitative data given on the values of different classes of artifacts. While all of the goods in stock are listed in the inventories, complete translation was limited to ceramic objects and opium.

The two volumes of the Kwong Tai Wo inventories which cover the years from 1871-1883 are each approximately eighty pages long, with thirty entries per page. The format of the entries is standardized, with the page arranged in vertical columns divided across the middle into two sets (Figure 29). At the top of each entry is written the unit price, usually as cost per item or set. Below is the name of the item with a short description ("four-flower rice bowl"). In some cases this includes a measurement ("7-inch plate"), or even place of origin ("Japanese blue-flower teacups"). The description is followed by the quantity in stock. Ceramics are listed either as individual vessels or sets of ten items each, while opium is listed by weight. Finally, the total value of the goods in stock is given in American dollars.

Comparison of these inventories with the records of daily sales indicates that the inventory prices are wholesale. Unfortunately, the surviving Kwong Tai Wo store records are incomplete. Most of the daily sales records represent the period following 1880, thus providing little potential for direct comparison of daily retail sales and wholesale inventory records.

The inventories appear to have been prepared annually, for the most part by one person. The handwriting changes rarely, a consistency which aided in translation. Most of the problems in translation developed from the style of handwriting. Characters in handwritten Chinese are often simplified and abbreviated. For example, the five stroke character for "four" becomes a spiraling line written in a single stroke. Such simplification presented some difficulties, but translation was greatly helped by the consistency in use and the uniformity of handwriting.

CERAMIC TABLEWARE

Translations were made of all ceramic tableware inventory entries, which represent a total of 5253 vessels (Table 25). A variety of ceramic vessels is listed: tea and liquor cups; tea and liquor pots; bowls (large, medium, rice); plates (2-, 3-, 5-, and 7-inch sizes); and spoons. The largest category of ceramics in stock was bowls, with tea and liquor cups following in importance. There were relatively few spoons, teapots or liquor servers. The styles of decoration on these vessels are described with at least seventeen different terms (Table 26), although some may be variant descriptions of the same style. Many styles are clearly identifiable with

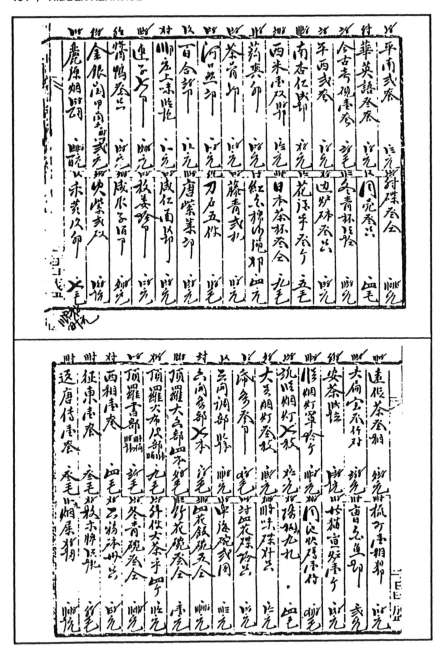

Figure 29. Kwong Tai Wo inventory, Vol. 6, pages 30-31, 1881.
The two rows of entries per page read from top to bottom, right to left.
(Courtesy Bancroft Library.)

Table 25. Ceramic Tablewares, Kwong Tai Wo Inventories, 1871-1883

Vessel Forms:

	Bowls					Cups		Plates				Pots		Spoons	Totals
	Bowl	Large	Medium	Rice	Cup[a]	Tea	Liquor	2-inch	3-inch	5-inch	7-inch	Tea-pots	Liquor Servers		
Winter Green	603				130	445	10								1188
Green	268														268
Bamboo	1061														1061
Double Happiness	15														15
Happiness	245														245
Prosperity (3)	10														10
Prosperity (2)	107														107
Prosperity (large)	15														15
Four Flower design	140		20	222							16				398
Flowers of Four Seasons	70														70
With Design	10	10	70	125		40	450	10	10	86	80		4	150	1045
Simple Flower design													6		6
Gold & Color Rim design					60										60
Gold Rim design						12									12
Japanese						120									120
Japanese Blue Flower design						17									17
Blue Flower design						45									45
(no style listed)		51	52			100	15	30	210	30		2	1	80	571
Totals	2544	61	142	347	190	779	475	40	220	116	96	2	11	230	5253

[a]Style not stated.

155

Table 26. Chinese Characters Used to Describe Ceramic Tablewares Listed in the Kwong Tai Wo Inventories

English Translation	Transliteration Pinyin [Wade-Giles]	Characters
Winter Green	dōng qīng [tung ch'ing]	冬青
Green	qīng [ch'ing]	青
Bamboo Design	zhú huā [chu hua]	竹花
Double Happiness	shuāng xǐ [shuang hsi]	双喜
Happiness	xǐ [hsi]	喜
Four Flower design	sì huā [szu hua]	四花
Flowers of the Four Seasons	sì jì huā [szu shi hua]	四季花
With design	huā [hua]	花
Simple Flower design	tán huā [tan hua]	簡花
Prosperity (2)	fú [fu]	福
Prosperity (3)	fú [fu]	
Prosperity (large)	dà fú [ta fu]	大福
Gold and Color Rim design	cǎi jīn kǒu fāng [tsai chin k'ou fa]	彩金口方
Gold Rim design	jīn kǒu [chin k'ou]	金口
Japanese	rì běn [jih pen]	日本
Japanese Blue Flower design	rì běn lán huā [jih pen lan hua]	日本竹花
Blue Flower design	lán huā [lan hua]	竹花
Barbarian Plates	fān dié [fan tieh]	番石碟

Table 26. (Cont'd.)

English Translation	Transliteration Pinyin [Wade-Giles]	Characters
Bowl (crude, no base)	bō [po]	砵
Bowl	wǎn [wan]	石宛
Bowl, large	dà wǎn [ta wan]	大石宛
Bowl, medium	zhōng wǎn [chung wan]	中石宛
Bowl, rice	fàn wǎn [fan wan]	飯 碗
Cup	bēi [pei]	杯
Cup, tea	chá bēi [ch'a pei]	茶杯
Cup, liquor	jǐu bēi [chiu pei]	酒杯
Plate, 2-inch	èr cùn dié [liang ts'un tieh]	川寸 石某
Plate, 3-inch	sān cùn dié [san ts'un tieh]	川寸 石某
Plate, 5-inch	wǔ cùn dié [wu ts'un tieh]	夕寸 石碟
Plate, 7-inch	qī cùn dié (ch'i ts'un tieh]	二寸 石碟
Pot, tea	chá hú [ch'a hu]	茶壺
Pot, liquor	jǐu hú [chiu hu]	酒壺
Spoon	chí [ch'ih]	是匕

the ceramics found on archaeological sites in the western United States (Figure 30), increasing both our interest in these records and their value to archaeologists.

Winter Green — The greatest number of ceramic inventory entries is for the "Winter Green" (*dōng qīng) [tung ch'ing]* style; 1188 vessels are represented. This category includes bowls, tea cups, and liquor cups. Winter Green is among the most costly groups of tableware listed; the wholesale values of the bowls range from 6.6 to 8.7 cents apiece. In common with other items in the inventories, these

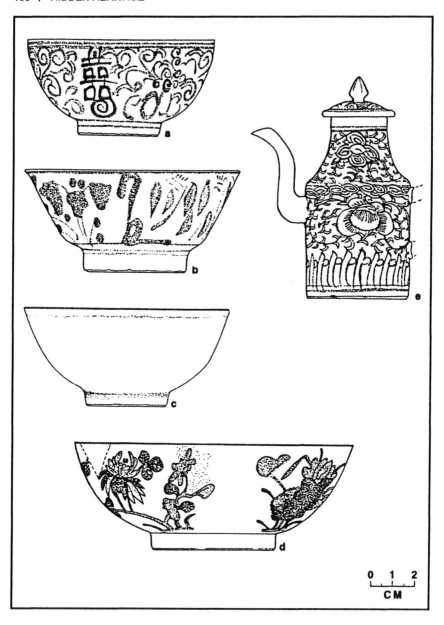

Figure 30. Archaeological ceramic tablewares represented in the
Kwong Tai Wo Company inventories. a) Double Happiness Bowl;
b) Bamboo bowl; c) Winter Green bowl; d) Four Flower design medium bowl;
e) Simple Flower design liquor server (reproduced from Felton,
Lortie and Schulz, 1984:37).

ceramics show a general decline in price beginning in the mid-1870s, dropping further in the first two years of the 1880s. It seems apparent that the Winter Green style vessels are those commonly referred to in the archaeological literature as "Celadon." The exteriors of these wares are covered with a light bluish-green glaze, but bear no additional decoration (Figure 30c). The correlation of the Winter Green inventory group with the archaeological specimens is based on both the color of the glaze and the range of vessel forms present. This style makes up a high percentage of the bowls and cups in both the inventories and overseas Chinese archaeological assemblages.

While most archaeologists have assumed that "Celadon" vessels recovered from overseas Chinese sites are of Chinese origin, one study of stylistic attributes and elemental analysis suggests that most if not all of this material is, in fact, of Japanese origin (Stenger, 1986 and Chapter 12 herein). Other Japanese tablewares are specifically identified in the Kwong Tai Wo inventories, although the Winter Green vessels are not described as such. Further evaluation of this hypothesis requires more complete presentation of Stenger's data, including explicit information on the sources of presumably non-archaeological control specimens used to establish the elemental ratios that purportedly distinguish Japanese and Chinese green glazed wares.

Green — A group of 268 bowls referred to simply as "Green" ($q\bar{\imath}ng$) [*ch'ing*] in the Kwong Tai Wo documents may also be present but as yet unidentified among the archaeological Celadon ceramics. Each bowl is valued at only about half as much as a Winter Green bowl. We can only speculate on the difference between Winter Green and Green ceramics, as an archaeological correlate of the latter has not yet been identified. It seems clear that they are distinct groups, however, rather than variant names for the same style.

The Kwong Tai Wo bookkeeper consistently used distinct characters to differentiate the more highly priced (and more numerous) Winter Green vessels from the Green bowls. Although both listings can be translated simply as "green," the characters for Winter Green are those used in China to describe a tree with bluish-green foliage. While the inventory descriptions only suggest a difference in color, the consistent difference in the values and differences in the variety of vessel forms represented also indicate that the Winter Green and Green inventory categories are distinct. The relative prices indicate that Winter Green represents a higher quality product.

Our inability to distinguish archaeological specimens of the Green and Winter Green styles is perplexing. Frierman (1983:198) has hypothesized that the green wares may include both true Celadon glazes and other similarly colored but technically distinct glazed wares. Perhaps stylistic and elemental analyses begun by Stenger (1986 and Chapter 12 herein) and others suggesting a Japanese origin for green glazed tablewares on overseas Chinese archaeological sites will eventually help identify the distinct varieties included among this group of ceramics.

Bamboo — About 20 percent of the ceramic entries (1061 vessels) are of the "Bamboo" design (*zhú huā*) [*chu hua*]. We believe this is the pattern variously referred to in the archaeological literature by the names "Three Circles and Dragonfly," "Three Circles and Longevity," and "Swatow," among others (e.g., Chace, 1976:523; Olsen, 1978:15). The hand-painted patterns include what appear to be bamboo leaves, as well as other design elements (Figure 30). The Bamboo design is listed only for bowls in the inventories. This is also true of most archaeological assemblages, although a few plates with a related pattern have been reported from San Francisco and Southeast Asia (Pastron, Gross, and Garaventa, 1981:428; Willetts and Poh, 1981:10, 62). These bowls, while not the cheapest in the inventories, were not far from it; they are valued at about half that of the costly Winter Green bowls.

Double Happiness, Happiness — A stylistic group of considerable archaeological interest is "Double Happiness" (*shuāng xī*) [*shuang hsi*]; archaeological specimens are clearly marked with the same character (Figure 30a). Only one entry for this style, dated 1873 and listing fifteen bowls, is found in the inventories. These vessels make up less than one-third of one percent of the Kwong Tai Wo ceramic inventory. The value of the Double Happiness bowls is even less than that of the cheap Bamboo pattern.

Works by Chace (1979), Praetzellis and Praetzellis (1982) and Felton, Lortie, and Schulz (1984:94) indicate that Double Happiness is one of the few overseas Chinese ceramic styles for which a restricted temporal distribution can be demonstrated. It occurs in high frequencies on sites occupied prior to about 1870, but is scarce in later assemblages; Double Happiness appears to have been superseded by Bamboo style bowls after about 1870 (see discussion of ceramic values below).

Two hundred and forty-five bowls with the "Happiness" character are itemized in the inventories. At present, we cannot positively identify an archaeological correlate for these vessels. The characters used to describe this group are the same as those translated as Double Happiness bowls, although the initial character indicating "double" is not included. We can only suggest that the "Happiness" and "Double Happiness" inventory entries might be slightly different terms referring to vessels of a single style (i.e., Double Happiness). Both "Double Happiness" and "Happiness" bowls are in the same low price range, and occur in listings for different years (Double Happiness—1873 only; Happiness—1872, 1876, 1878, 1880). This interpretation would, however, suggest a longer survival of this style after 1870 than is indicated by archaeological evidence.

Four Flower Design and Related Styles — Another major class of ceramics present in both the Kwong Tai Wo documents and overseas Chinese archaeological assemblages is identified variously in the inventories as "Four Flowers Design" (*sì huā*) [*szu hua*]; 398 vessels) and simply "With Design" (*huā*; 1045 vessels). In all likelihood, these groups are the ceramics referred to in the archaeological literature as "Four Seasons" (Figure 30d). This assertion is based on the range of vessel forms of these styles present in both the inventories and the archaeological assemblages. Most of the large and medium size bowls, and especially the plates recovered from overseas Chinese archaeological sites, are of the "Four Seasons" pattern; these vessel forms are also prominently represented in the Four Flower Design and With Design inventory groups (Table 25).

We suspect that at least some of the inventory listings for which no pattern names are given also refer to ceramics identified in the archaeological literature as "Four Seasons." This inference is again based on the vessel forms identified in the inventories: this is the only style group, besides the two mentioned above, which includes the plates and large and medium bowls commonly associated with the archaeological "Four Seasons" pattern.

One additional inventory designation, "Flowers of the Four Seasons" (sì jì huā) [szu chi hua], may also include archaeological "Four Seasons" ceramics. This group includes only seventy bowls and is mentioned only during the years 1872 through 1874. These bowls were valued the same as the Four Flower Design bowls listed separately for 1872. The distinction in this case may be attributable to bookkeeping inconsistencies in the terms used to describe the same style.

Simple Flower Design — Another inventory pattern that can be identified archaeologically is translated as "Simple Flower Design" (tán huā) [tan hua]. The only vessels of this style included in the inventories are liquor servers, archaeological examples of which are most commonly decorated with a hand-painted blue floral pattern (Figure 30e). A variety of vessel forms with the same and similar motifs are sometimes referred as "Shanghai Ware" by collectors (Willetts and Poh, 1981:13-14, 69-81).

Prosperity (fú) Character Bowls — One hundred and thirty-two bowls decorated with the character fú (prosperity) are listed in the Kwong Tai Wo inventories. Three different variants, based on the number and size of fú characters, are listed (Table 25). Most of these (107) apparently were decorated with two fú characters. Ten are listed as having three fú characters; fifteen are described simply as large fú character bowls. The fú character bowls make up about 2.5 percent of the total number of vessels listed in the Kwong Tai Wo inventories.

The character used for "bowl" (bō) [po] in most of the fú vessel listings differs from that used for bowls (wǎn) [wan] of most other stylistic groups. The more common of the two, wǎn, indicates a bowl with a base. The other character, bō, is apparently a Cantonese slang term referring to very cheap, poor quality bowls with smooth bottoms (no base?) and rims which curve slightly inward.

While there is no clear reference to fú bowls in the published archaeological literature consulted for this study, a number of 19th century stoneware pieces bearing fú characters have recently been reported from Southeast Asia: "Fu plates with biscuited bands," "block-printed wares" (Willetts and Poh, 1981:14, 15, 82, 89, 90, 92). All of these have unglazed (i.e., biscuit) bands on the bottom of the vessels' interiors. It seems likely that the "crude, cheap, no base" description in the Kwong Twi Wo inventories is in reference to this attribute.

Although not yet widely recognized, it appears that *fú* vessels may occur in small frequencies on archaeological sites in the western United States. Pastron, Gross, and Garaventa (1981:428-430) refer to five "bat or knot pattern" plates or shallow dishes with unglazed rings from a dump in San Francisco. Fragments of block printed bowls with biscuit rings and what may be a *fú* character on the interior were recovered in small quantities from excavations on the site of a late 19th century fishing village at China Camp State Park in California (Peter D. Schulz, 1986:personal communication). Pieces of stoneware vessels with unglazed interior rings have been observed at a number of pre-Gold rush sites in California (e.g., La Purisima Mission, Lompoc; Cooper-Molera Adobe, Monterey). These are fragmentary and have not been studied systematically; it is not clear whether these early pieces also include the *fú* character. While it seems likely that the *fú* bowls listed in the Kwong Tai Wo inventories are represented by some of the archaeological specimens with unglazed rings discussed above, further identification and analysis of pertinent artifact assemblages is called for before the inventory listings can be identified with confidence.

Gold (and Color) Rim Design — Seventy-two cups with "gold rim" (*jīn kŏu*) [*chin k'ou*] and "gold and color rim" (*căi jīn kŏu fāng*) [*tsai chin k'ou fang*] designs are listed in the Kwong Tai Wo inventories. Only twelve tea cups are listed for 1876 simply as "gold rim design;" the majority are described as "gold and color rim cups," and are listed in 1875, 1877, 1878 and 1880. As is the case with several other classes of ceramics in the inventories, the similarity of the descriptive terms employed, the price ranges indicated, and the fact that both terms are not used in entries for the same year all suggest that both are alternate terms for vessels of the same style. We are not yet able to hypothesize an archaeological equivalent of these inventory styles.

Japanese Ceramics — The Kwong Tai Wo Company also stocked a few Japanese and European or American products. The only Japanese ceramic imports identified as such in the inventories are teacups, listed simply as "Japanese" (*rì bĕn*) [*jih pen*]; 1878-1880, 1882) or "Japanese blue flower design" (*rì bĕn lán hūa*) [*jih pen lan hua*]; 1877).

We suspect that one other group of teacups listed only as "Blue Flower Design" (*lán hūa*) may also be of Japanese origin. In addition to the common use of the "blue flower" description, they are also similar in value to the verifiably Japanese cups, and are included only for two years (1875-1876) during which no other Japanese cups are listed. Other considerations (e.g., Stenger's hypothesis regarding Japanese origin of Celadons, 1986 and Chapter 12 herein) also suggest that the Japanese origin of other ceramics may not always have been explicitly identified in the inventories.

We have not identified the archaeological correlates of the Japanese cups listed in the Kwong Tai Wo inventories. Relatively little has been published on Japanese ceramics from archaeological contexts in North America. One notable exception is a monograph on Japanese ceramic assemblages from Walnut Grove, California (Costello and Maniery, 1988), although most of the deposits reported post-date the period represented by the inventories. Costello and Maniery (1988:24) describe rapid expansion of the Japanese ceramic industry beginning about 1870, a factor that may account for the appearance of Japanese ceramics only after 1875 in the Kwong Tai Wo inventories. They also illustrate a number of vessels that might be described as having a "blue flower design" (1988:74-77), although before hypothesizing that any of these represent the cups listed in the Kwong Tai Wo inventories, we must await their discovery with overseas Chinese assemblages securely dated to the 1870-1880 period.

Euroamerican Ceramics — No European or American-made ceramics were identified in the inventories, although the daily sales records for 1881 include a group of five non-Chinese (probably British) plates selling for 75 cents. The description reads "barbarian plate" (*fān dié*) [*fan tieh*], which reflects the perspective of the overseas Chinese of the time.

Ceramic Values

Analysis of the values of the ceramics in the Kwong Tai Wo inventories illustrates meaningful trends both for the study of this particular company and for the interpretation of archaeological assemblages from overseas Chinese sites. Our initial quantitative analyses have focused on bowls, which make up over half of the total number of vessels listed in the inventories. Large and medium bowls have been excluded from the following discussion, as the values listed are considerably higher than those for vessels listed simply as "bowl" or "rice bowl." Comparisons of the values of different styles of bowls are based on mean annual value per vessel, as calculated from the inventory data.

Most of the bowls listed in the inventories fall into two distinct price categories (Figure 31). The most expensive styles (Winter Green, Four Flower, Large Prosperity Character, Flowers of the Four Seasons, and With Design) range in value from 6.5 to 8.7 cents per bowl. Vessels in the cheaper category (Bamboo, Green, Double Happiness, Happiness, Two Prosperity Characters, and Three Prosperity Characters) have average values ranging from 2 to 5 cents each. In both groups, there is a general downward trend in the mean values during the mid-1870s and into the early 1880s. While we are not prepared to explain this decline, we have noted that it parallels the general downswing in wholesale prices in the United States during the period 1865-1896 (cf. Robertson, 1964:414).

Almost 59 percent of the total number of bowls and rice bowls fall into the cheaper category; about 41 percent are of the more costly varieties. Apparently the

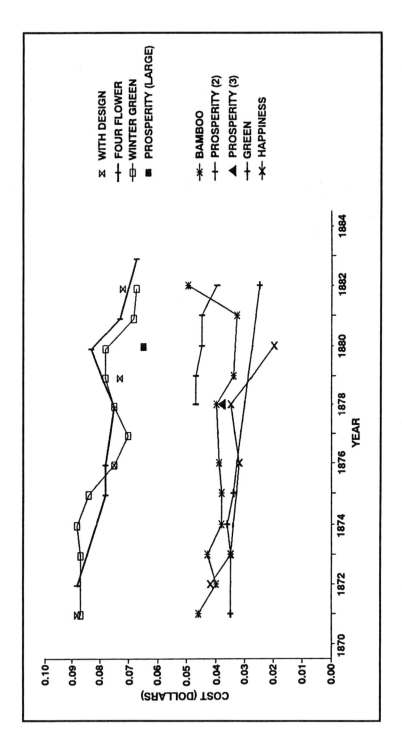

Figure 31. Average values of bowls listed in the Kwong Tai Wo Company inventories, 1871-1883. Includes vessels listed as "bowls" and "rice bowls;" "large bowls" and "medium bowls" are excluded. The "Four Flower" group includes "Flowers of the Four Seasons" patterns.

store owners perceived a part of the community as sufficiently well-off to be interested in buying relatively expensive dishes. While costly wares are well represented, the fact that the majority are of the less costly varieties indicates that most of the store's clients could purchase only the cheapest of supplies.

A closer study of the relative numbers of cheap and costly bowls across time suggests that the market being served by the Kwong Tai Wo store was not only varied but changing. While many more cheap than costly bowls were listed in the inventories for the years 1871-1875, costly bowls were stocked in comparable or greater numbers from 1876 to 1882 (Figure 32). There are several possible explanations for this trend. The simplest is that the market during the earlier period was made up primarily of a large number of relatively poor consumers, while during the late 1870s the size of the market decreased as the relative well-being of the consumers improved. Another possibility is that the Kwong Tai Wo Company itself, and not just the population it served, was changing. Perhaps limited capital initially forced the merchant to stock low-priced goods, which were later replaced by more costly commodities aimed at more affluent markets as the company grew. Similar patterns are apparent in the quality of the opium listed in the inventories. There is a dramatic and as yet unexplained decrease in the number of both cheap and costly bowls for 1877, compared to preceding and subsequent years (Figure 32). We do not know if the number of vessels stocked declined, or if data for that year are simply missing.

Archaeological studies have shown that various kinds of Chinese ceramic tableware are distributed differently on different kinds of sites (cf. Felton, Lortie, and Schulz, 1984:88-98). It is probable that these distributions are related to the cost of the ceramics and the wealth and occupations of the inhabitants. The value distinction between the cheap Bamboo and expensive Winter Green bowls provided by the Kwong Tai Wo inventories fits nicely with archaeological distributions of these artifacts. These patterns are far more common than the other styles of bowls in both the inventories and overseas Chinese archaeological sites. The cheaper Bamboo bowls constitute up to 80 percent of the Chinese tableware on an 1880s railroad camp and other post-1870 rural construction and mining sites (e.g., Briggs, 1974), while the Winter Green (Celadon) vessels are more common on many post-1870 village and urban sites. It is probable that occupants of rural work camps were chiefly low-paid workers, which could explain the predominance of cheap bowls in the resultant archaeological sites.

At earlier railroad camps of the 1860s in California, cheap Double Happiness bowls, rather than Bamboo bowls, make up the bulk of the Chinese ceramic assemblages (Chace and Evans, 1969; Evans, 1980). Considering the comparably low monetary values and similar archaeological contexts in which Double Happiness and Bamboo bowls are recovered, it seems likely that the Double Happiness style was largely replaced by Bamboo as the most common tableware among low-paid Chinese workers after about 1870 for as yet undetermined reasons. The

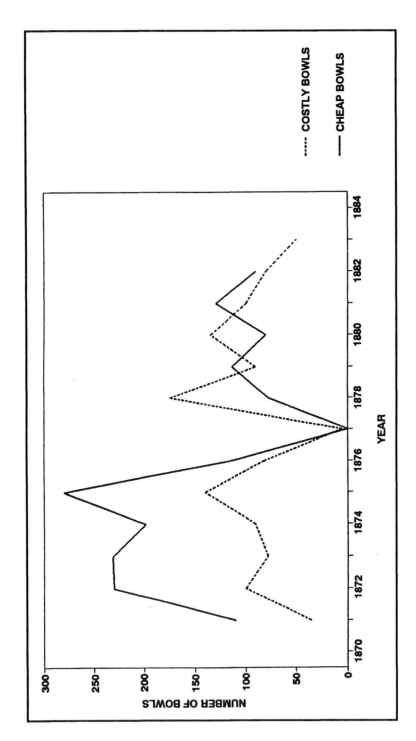

Figure 32. Total numbers of cheap and expensive bowls listed in the Kwong Tai Wo Company inventories; "large bowls" and "medium bowls" are excluded. Note large numbers of cheap bowls in stock before 1876.

limited occurrence of Double Happiness and the large number of Bamboo bowls in the post-1870 Kwong Tai Wo inventories seem compatible with this temporal interpretation of the archaeological evidence. Evaluation of this interpretation will require further studies of the inventories and archaeological specimens to determine whether inventory entries for Happiness and Double Happiness represent the same pattern.

With the information on the relative values of these and other artifacts provided by the Kwong Tai Wo inventories, it should be possible to begin to quantify and compare the values of different archaeological assemblages, and perhaps to gain some insight into ways that social stratification is reflected in the archaeological record of this group of immigrants. This "economic scaling" strategy has been used very successfully on British ceramics by George L. Miller (1980, 1991) and others.

Use of the Kwong Tai Wo ceramic data for economic scaling analysis will require further archaeological and technical studies to help correlate ceramic styles and technologies represented in the inventories with specimens from archaeological sites. Key areas of concern are the differentiation of the cheap Green bowls and the more costly Winter Green vessels, as discussed above, and archaeological identification of the vessels described simply as Happiness in the inventories.

PREPARED OPIUM

In spite of the thousands of ceramic items carried by the Kwong Tai Wo store from 1871 to 1883, the total value represented by their ceramic stock during this period amounted to only $266.80. An examination of the records revealed that not all categories of stock were of such small value. In fact, by far the most expensive item carried was opium, worth over ten times as much as the ceramics. From 1873 to 1883, the total value of the opium inventoried exceeded $2850.00.

Opium prepared for smoking is listed in the Kwong Tai Wo inventories by brand and weight. It usually appears in the daily sales records by the can, presumably corresponding to the small brass containers described in historical literature (e.g., Culin, 1891:498), artifacts which are frequently recovered from overseas Chinese archaeological sites (Figure 33). Each can contained 5 liǎng, or Chinese ounces. One liǎng (also referred to as tael) was the equivalent of approximately 1.333 ounces avoirdupois. The total amount of opium listed in the inventories in 2337.1 liǎng, or about 194.7 pounds.

Anti-Chinese Opium Legislation

Widespread use of opium was a prominent feature of life in America throughout the late 19th century, among both Chinese and non-Chinese alike. Opium was primarily ingested as a medicine by most white Americans, although smoking the

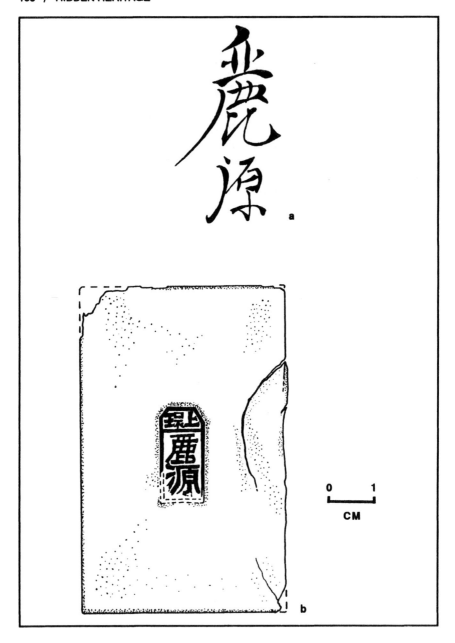

Figure 33. "Source of Beauty" (*lì yuán*) brand opium. a) as listed in the
Kwong Tai Wo Company inventories; b) stamped opium can lid
bearing the "Source of Beauty" brand name (Opera House site,
Woodland, California; P327-24-7).

drug in a social context was a common method of consumption among the Chinese throughout the period, and had become popular among some non-Chinese groups as well by the end of the century. The procedures and reasons for smoking, and the evolution and eventual replacement of this habit by even more dangerous forms of opiate use, is well beyond the scope of this chapter (cf. Brecher, 1972; Courtwright, 1982; Felton, Lortie, and Schulz, 1984:98-106; Wylie and Fike, Chapter 10 herein). Nevertheless, some knowledge of the changing commercial and legal status of the drug is needed as a background against which to view its place in the Kwong Tai Wo Company inventory.

The possession and use of smoking opium was legal during the period represented by the Kwong Tai Wo inventories. Although the smoking of opium was documented among the Chinese in California during the 1850s, it did not become an object of major moral or legal concern in the United States until the 1870s. Various scholars have attributed this increased visibility to a number of factors, including increased anti-Chinese sentiment among Americans during this period, Chinese merchants' response to the depression of the 1870s, increased use of this form of the drug by whites, and increases in the supply by the British opium growers in India, among others. Whatever the case, this concern was quickly translated into legislation. In 1875, the city of San Francisco adopted an ordinance prohibiting the use of opium in smoking houses or dens (Brecher, 1972:42). Other cities and states followed suit, and in 1881 the State of California passed a law making it a misdemeanor to operate or frequent ". . . any place where opium, or any of its preparations, is sold or given away to be smoked at such place . . ." (Kane, 1882:4).

In spite of these laws, the possession and sale of opium prepared for smoking was still legal. Further attempts to control opium during the next thirty years seem to have been aimed as much at harassing the Chinese as inhibiting opium consumption by the population at large. In 1883, Congress raised the tariff on smoking opium precipitously, and raised it even higher in 1890. The primary result of this effort was to make smuggling more profitable, and to cut drastically the amount of legal smoking opium reported to U.S. Customs. No similar increase in tariff was instituted for non-smokable forms of the drug. In 1887 Chinese were restricted from importing smoking opium into the United States; thereafter, legal opium was channeled through non-Chinese merchants. By 1897, the ineffectiveness of these measures had been demonstrated, and tariffs were reduced to pre-1883 levels. In 1909, however, a federal law prohibiting all importation of smoking opium was passed, although domestic production by non-Chinese was still legal. The Harrison Narcotic Act of 1914 finally made simple possession of opiates illegal, creating a ready market for the cheaper, stronger, and more easily smuggled injectable variants, such as the newly-perfected heroin (Brecher, 1972:44-45).

Opium Brands and Grades

The most valuable data about opium provided by the Kwong Tai Wo inventories are the names of specific brands being sold, and information regarding variations in quality and price (Table 27). Opium ranged from expensive, high-quality grades to what were literally the dregs. Much as the tobacco user today asks for a pack of "Winston" or "Camel" cigarettes, the opium smoker or merchant at the counter of the Kwong Tai Wo store requested a can of "Source of Beauty" (*lì yuán*) or "Abundant Luck" (*fú lóng*) [*fuk lung*].

Table 27. Chinese Characters Used to Describe Opium Brands Listed in the Kwong Tai Wo Inventories.

English Translation	Transliteration Pinyin [Wade-Giles]	Characters
Abundant Luck (Listed Kane 1882; Anonymous 1874:a9. Less than 2% of total in inventories.)	fú lóng [fu (fuk) lung]	福 隆
Abundant Memory (Less than 2% of total listed in inventories.)	lóng jì [lung chi]	隆 記
Source of Beauty (Listed Kane 1882:31: Anonymous 1874:a9. Most common brand in inventories.)	lì yuán [li yuan, lai yun]	麗 源
Big Bamboo	dà zhú [ta chu]	大 竹
Combined Abundance	hé lóng [he lung]	合 隆
Everlasting Peace (Second most common brand in inventories.)	wàn hé [wan ho]	萬 和
"House Brand" (Less than 2% of total in inventories.)	zuò zì hào [tso tzu hao]	作 字 号
Opium Waste	yān shǐ [yen niao]	烟 屎
Second Quaility	èr gōng [erh kung]	二 公
. . . Origin (First element not yet translated.)	? yuán [. . . yuan]	𥹆 源

Note: Information on marked specimens recovered from archaeological contexts is available from the Asian American Comparative Collection, Laboratory of Anthropology, University of Idaho, Moscow.

The greatest amount of smoking opium stocked during the period covered by the inventories was 1185 *liǎng* (97.7 pounds) of the Source of Beauty brand. Source of Beauty was widely distributed in the last century, as witnessed by the frequent recovery of the stamped tops of these cans from archaeological sites (Figure 33b); Abundant Luck marks have also been identified archaeologically. Both Source of Beauty and Abundant Luck opium were prepared in Hong Kong, as indicated by the presence of both companies in business directories dating from 1867 through 1884 (Anonymous, 1867, 1872, 1873, 1874, 1877, 1884).

The Kwong Tai Wo store carried at least four other name brands of relatively costly opium in addition to Source of Beauty and Abundant Luck (Table 27). We are not aware of the occurrence of these marks in archaeological deposits, nor have we found reference to these brands in the Hong Kong directories. Good quality opium was also sold as what we might today call a "house blend" (*zuò zì hào*) [*tso tzu hao*], with no brand given. Similarly, an inferior product referred to simply as "Second Quality" opium (*èr gōng*) [*erh kung*] was also carried at about two-thirds the cost of the top quality brands. Finally, the poorest quality was represented by what the English language literature politely refers to as "opium refuse mass." This was made by scraping residue from used opium pipe bowls and recycling it, at less than one-third the price of the brand-name opiums. Obviously, it was weaker, and was reportedly more injurious to the health of the smoker than the more costly products (Kane, 1882:20).

Opium Merchandising

The opium stocked over the twelve-year period clearly indicates that the Kwong Tai Wo store moved into the selling of opium gradually (Figure 34). None is listed in 1871 or 1872. In the first year it appears, 1873, the inventory lists only twenty-eight *liǎng* of opium refuse mass. In 1874, the store continued to carry the low-grade product but added thirty-three *liǎng* of the more valuable Second Quality opium to their stock. By 1875, the owners had apparently decided that there was a market for more expensive types of opium—or had acquired the capital to enter that market—and added sixty *liǎng* of the more costly brands. Relatively large quantities of opium, mostly of the top grade, were stocked during the period between 1876 and 1883, although the amount on hand fluctuated from year to year. As an indication of the overall quality of the opium carried, less than one-fifth (17.1%) of the total listed belonged to the two cheapest categories (Second Quality and opium refuse mass).

The growth of the Kwong Tai Wo opium trade closely mirrors the rise in importation of this commodity into the United States. The greatest increases were between 1870 and 1883, at which time a drastic rise in the tariff decreased the amount of legally imported smoking opium being reported (cf. Courtwright, 1982:24; Wright, 1910:81-83). It appears that the gradual movement of the Kwong Tai Wo Company into the opium market may have been typical of other

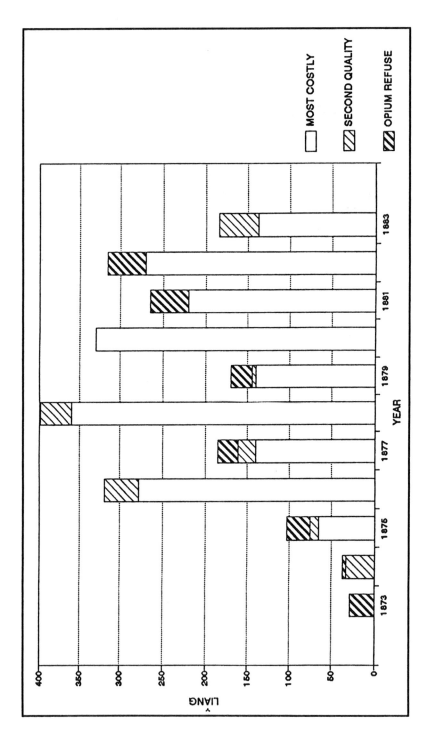

Figure 34. Quantities of opium of various grades stocked by Kwong Tai Wo Company, 1873-1883.

MOST COSTLY

SECOND QUALITY

OPIUM REFUSE

late 19th century Chinese commercial ventures in the United States (Culin, 1887:10-11; emphasis added):

> The store is the centre around which life in a Chinese colony revolves. As soon as several men have collected in a town or city, one of them will send to the nearest place of supply and purchase such Chinese groceries and other wares as may be needed. . . . Other opportunities for making money will not be lost sight of. The cellar will be fitted up with bunks for opium smoking and tables covered with matting for the convenience of those desiring to play dominoes; and *the profit on the opium consumed and the portion of the winnings set aside for the use of the tables soon constitute a more important source of revenue than the store itself.* . . .

Although comparisons of daily sales and inventories are tenuous because the records are incomplete, it appears that the markup on opium was considerably less than that on ceramics. While the historical literature frequently refers to the retail sales of opium in 25-cent increments, it appears that most of the Kwong Tai Wo opium was sold by the can. Perhaps the clients were distributors who broke it down into smaller units for sale in shops or opium houses. It may also be that the apparently modest markup is attributable to the large volume being sold, or to a rapid turnover in this commodity and subsequent decrease in overhead costs.

The Kwong Tai Wo records end at precisely the period that anti-smoking opium, anti-Chinese legislation, and tariffs began to seriously affect what had previously been a legal, above-board business venture. It is not clear from the available evidence what, if any, role the changing legal and economic status of opium played in the eventual demise of this company. Considering the high value of this commodity and the volume carried by the store relative to other less valuable goods (e.g., ceramics), it seems probably that the Kwong Tai Wo Company had to make fundamental adjustments in their operation to survive. These are no clear indications in the remaining records that the owner(s) were successful in this attempt.

CONCLUDING COMMENTS

The work reported here has only begun to realize the potential applications of the Kwong Tai Wo Company data to archaeological and historical studies of 19th century overseas Chinese communities. A number of problems remain, the foremost of which is the complete translation of the rest of the Kwong Tai Wo Company documents. Further study will be needed to identify the archaeological correlates of as yet unidentified ceramic styles. Understanding the distinction between Green and Winter Green tableware styles will be a key step toward application of relative cost data to quantitative comparison of different ceramic assemblages.

Many questions remain to be addressed regarding the economics and sociology of opium. These have to do with both the commercial networks by which it was delivered, and the socioeconomic factors that resulted in its heavy use by workers in the most arduous jobs, who could least afford the costly habit (cf. International Labour Office, 1935; Felton, Lortie, and Schulz, 1984:98-106). We hope that other Chinese business records representing different stores and time periods will be located and translated, providing a means of corroborating or refuting the trends and tentative conclusions drawn from this initial study of the Kwong Tai Wo documents.

REFERENCES CITED

ANONYMOUS
1867   *The China Directory for 1867*, A. Shortrese & Co., Hong Kong.
1872   *The Chronicle and Directory for China, Japan and the Philippines for the Year 1872*, 'Daily Press' Office, Hong Kong.
1873   *The China Directory for 1873*, 'China Mail' Office, Hong Kong.
1874   *The China Directory for 1874*, 'China Mail' Office, Hong Kong.
1877   *The Chronicle and Directory for China, Japan and the Philippines for the Year 1877*, 'Daily Press' Office, Hong Kong.
1984   *The Chronicle and Directory for China, Corea, Japan, the Philippines, Borneo, Annam, Cochin China, Siam, Straits Settlements, Malay States, &c . . . for the Year 1884*, 'Daily Press' Office, Hong Kong.
BRECHER, EDWARD M. and the Editors of Consumer Reports
1972   *Licit and Illicit Drugs*, Little, Brown and Company, Boston.
BRIGGS, ALTON KING
1974   The Archeology of 1882 Labor Camps on the Southern Pacific Railroad, Val Verde County, Texas, Master's thesis, University of Texas, Austin.
CHACE, PAUL G.
1976   Overseas Chinese Ceramics, in *The Changing Faces of Main Street*, R. S. Greenwood (ed.), Redevelopment Agency, City of San Buenaventura, Ventura, California, pp. 509-530.
1979   Note on "Double Happiness" porcelain, appended to Chace, 1976, copy from the author.
CHACE, PAUL G. and WILLIAM S. EVANS
1969   Celestial Sojourners in the High Sierras: The Ethnoarchaeology of Chinese Railroad Workers (1865-1868), paper presented at the 2nd annual meeting of the Society for California Archaeology, Tucson.
COSTELLO, JULIA G. and MARY L. MANIERY
1988   *Rice Bowls in the Delta: Artifacts Recovered from the 1915 Asian Community of Walnut Grove, California*, Occasional Paper 16, Institute of Archaeology, University of California, Los Angeles.
COURTWRIGHT, DAVID T.
1982   *Dark Paradise: Opiate Addiction in America before 1940*, Harvard University Press, Cambridge.

CULIN, STEWART
  1887   *China in America: A Study in the Social Life of the Chinese in the Eastern
          Cities of the United States,* paper read before the American Association for the
          Advancement of Science (Section of Anthropology), at the Thirty-Sixth
          Meeting, New York.
  1891   Opium Smoking by the Chinese in Philadelphia, *American Journal of Phar-
          macy, 63*:10, pp. 497-502.
EVANS, WILLIAM S.
  1980   Food and Fantasy: Material Culture of the Chinese in California and the
          West, Circa 1850-1900, in *"Archaeological Perspectives on Ethnicity in
          America,* R. L. Schuyler (ed.), Baywood Publishing Company, Amityville,
          New York, pp. 89-96.
FELTON, DAVID L, FRANK LORTIE, and PETER D. SCHULZ
  1984   The Chinese Laundry on Second Street: Archeological Investigations at
          the Woodland Opera House Site, *California Archeological Reports, 24,*
          pp. 1-120.
FRIERMAN, JAY D.
  1983   Chinese Ceramics in the New Melones Project Area, *New Melones Archeo-
          logical Project, California: Review and Synthesis of Research at Historical
          Sites* by R. S. Greenwood and L. H. Shoup, final report of the New Melones
          Archeological Project, Vol. VII, National Park Service.
GARDELLA, ROBERT P.
  1982   Commercial Bookkeeping in Ch'ing China and the West: A Preliminary
          Assessment, *Ch'ing-Shih Wen-ti, IV:*7, pp. 56-72.
INTERNATIONAL LABOUR OFFICE, LEAGUE OF NATIONS
  1935   Opium and Labour, "International Labour Office Studies and Reports,"
          Series B Social and Economic Conditions, No. 22, P. S. King & Son, Ltd.,
          London.
KANE, HARRY HUBBELL
  1882   *Opium-Smoking in America and China,* Arno Press Inc., New York. [Reprint
          edition.] (Reprinted by Arno Press, New York, 1976.)
KWONG TAI WO COMPANY
  1871-   Inventories (C-G 50, Volumes 6 and 7), ms. on file, Bancroft Library, Univer-
  1883   sity of California, Berkeley.
MILLER, GEORGE L.
  1980   Classification and Economic Scaling of 19th Century Ceramics, *Historical
          Archaeology, 14,* pp. 1-40.
  1991   A Revised Set of CC Index Values for Classification and Economic Scal-
          ing of English Ceramics from 1787 to 1880, *Historical Archaeology, 25,*
          pp. 1-25.
OLSEN, JOHN W.
  1978   A Study of Chinese Ceramics Excavated in Tucson, *The Kiva, 44:*1, pp. 1-50.
PASTRON, ALLEN, ROBERT GROSS, and DONNA GARAVENTA
  1981   Ceramics from Chinatown's Tables: A Historical Archaeological Approach
          to Ethnicity, in *Behind the Seawall: Historical Archaeology along the San
          Francisco Waterfront,* Vol. 2, A. G. Pastron (ed.), San Francisco Clean Water
          Program, San Francisco, pp. 365-469.

PRAETZELLIS, MARY and ADRIAN PRAETZELLIS

1982   *Archaeological and Historical Studies of the IJ56 Block, Sacramento, California: An Early Chinese Community,* Anthropological Studies Center, Sonoma State University, Rohnert Park, California.

1990   *Archaeological and Historical Studies at the San Fong Chong Laundry, 814 I Street, Sacramento, California,* Anthropological Studies Center, Sonoma State University, Rohnert Park, California.

PRAETZELLIS, ADRIAN, MARY PRAETZELLIS, AND MARLEY BROWN III

1987   Artifacts as Symbols of Identity: An Example from Sacramento's Gold Rush Era Chinese Community, "Living in Cities: Current Research in Urban Archaeology," E. Staski (ed.), Society for Historical Archaeology *Special Publication Series,* Number 5, pp. 38-47.

ROBERTSON, ROSS M.

1964   *History of the American Economy,* Harcourt, Brace, & World, New York.

STENGER, ALISON

1986   Japanese Ceramics from Chinese "Sojourner" Sites, paper presented at the 19th Annual Meeting of the Society for Historical Archaeology, Sacramento.

WELLS, FARGO & COMPANY EXPRESS

1878   *Directory of Chinese Business Houses,* Britton & Rey, San Francisco.

1882   *Directory of Chinese Business Houses,* Britton & Rey, San Francisco.

WILLETTS, WILLIAM and LIM SUAN POH

1981   *Nonya Ware and Kitchen Ch'ing,* The Southeast Asian Ceramic Society, West Malaysia Chapter, Selangor, Malaysia.

WRIGHT, HAMILTON

1910   Report on the International Opium Commission and on the Opium Problem as Seen Within the United States and its Possessions, *Senate Documents, Vol. 58,* pp. 1-83, Washington D.C.

CHAPTER 7

Animal Bones from Historic Urban Chinese Sites: A Comparison of Sacramento, Woodland, Tucson, Ventura, and Lovelock

Sherri M. Gust

Defining the characteristics of historic urban Chinese animal bone assemblages, particularly shared and distinctive features, is a primary purpose of this chapter. It has often been assumed that the Chinese in 19th century America continued their traditional food habits. This has been inferred from their conservatism in material remains, such as dishes, games, drugs, and clothing. In addition, documentary records such as ships' manifests and travelers' accounts, mostly from San Francisco, make it clear that traditional foodstuffs were imported and utilized. The evidence offered by the actual boney remains of meals has been neglected until relatively recently.

The bones analyzed herein all come from known Chinese sites and are associated with distinctly-Chinese artifact assemblages and site histories. I chose to include only domestic refuse from distinct Chinatowns to make the comparisons as viable as possible. Throughout this chapter, the sites being compared are referred to in chronological order, that is, Sacramento, 1850-1860; Woodland, 1870-1880; Tucson, 1880-1910; Ventura, 1890-1910; and Lovelock, 1920-1930. Three of the sites are located in California: Sacramento, Woodland, and Ventura. Lovelock is in northwestern Nevada and Tucson is in southern Arizona.

THE SITES

Sacramento

The bones from two trash pits, Features 5 and 11 from the excavations of the IJ56 Block, are the sample considered here. Feature 5 is superimposed upon Feature 11, but they are separated in time by only a few years. Feature 5 was deposited circa 1855, Feature 11 slightly earlier. Both were domestic trash deposits associated with Chinese merchants living, and doing business, on the site. Maps and more information are available elsewhere (Praetzellis and Praetzellis, 1982).

The site is located in the midst of Sacramento's original Chinatown. The Chinatown was established within a year of Sacramento's origin in 1848. The city was located on the confluence of two rivers amidst a rich agricultural valley, and was both a major supplier of miners heading to the gold fields and an important distributor of farm products (Praetzellis and Praetzellis, 1982:16).

By the middle of the 19th century, the Chinese called the city Yee Fow, or Second City (San Francisco being first). The population of Chinese in Sacramento was close to 1000 in 1860, and continued to grow thereafter. Chinese merchants, doctors, butchers, musicians, cooks, and teamsters all lived on the site's block during the 1850-1860 period, and many also worked there (Praetzellis and Praetzellis, 1982:22-29). Sacramento, including Chinatown, burned twice during the early 1850s. The high cost of rebuilding with brick and the replacement of housing by businesses gradually changed the makeup of the block. By 1857 Chinatown had moved elsewhere, although some Chinese continued to reside on the block (Praetzellis and Praetzellis, 1982:16-18).

Woodland

Only Feature 8/9 from the excavations of the Woodland Opera House site is considered here. This deposit was a filled cesspool or cellar associated with a Chinese laundry/residence. The washhouse was present on the site by 1870, but was moved to the Chinese quarter (northwest of the site) in 1880 (Felton, Lortie, and Schulz, 1984:28-32). These structural events, as well as artifact dates, define the time span of the deposit.

Woodland was established in 1855, became the county seat in 1862, and in 1869 was linked by rail to the transcontinental line between Sacramento and San Francisco. The area was primarily agricultural. The Chinese population of Woodland varied from sixty to 100 over the ten years between 1870 and 1880. According to the 1870 census, most Chinese occupants of the town were cooks or laundry workers (Felton, Lortie, and Schulz, 1984:11).

Tucson

Four Chinatown faunal samples excavated as part of the Tucson Urban Renewal (TUR) project were analyzed. All were located on Tucson Urban Renewal block 3, parcel (lot) 4, within about 150 feet of one another. Their official designations are TUR 3:4-2a, TUR 3:4-3a, TUR 3:4-5b, and TUR Trench 69-2. Site 2a was a filled privy and 3a was a filled well, while both 5b and 69-2 were trenches into trash deposits. All the sites, except TR 69-2, were dug in two foot levels.

The sites were located on a map of late 1960s Tucson and then relocated on a series of Sanborn fire insurance maps dating 1883, 1886, 1901, 1909, and 1919. They document the Chinese presence on block 3 from the 1883 map up to the 1901 map. By 1909, the Chinese were no longer present on this block.

Tucson's Chinatown began in the late 1870s as the southern transcontinental railway neared Tucson, and blossomed when the railroad arrived in 1880 (Fong, 1980:8). Some Chinese working for the Southern Pacific Railroad may have used Tucson as their home base, but others quit to settle in the city and pursue other occupations. Ethnographic data indicate that a few Chinese were present in Tucson even earlier (Tom, 1938:8). However, their number was very small as indicated by U.S. Bureau of the Census figures for all of Arizona: 1860—three persons; 1870—twenty persons; and 1880—1630 persons (Tom, 1938:8). The Chinese population of Tucson in 1880 was 159 (Fong, 1980:8) and had increased to 215 by 1890 (Fong, 1973:5). These Chinatown parcels were not owned by Chinese, but were held by members of the Stevens and Corbett families throughout Chinatown's existence (Wolf, n.d.). This Chinatown was demolished in 1909/1910 for construction of civic buildings. Most Tucson Chinese moved several blocks south along Main Street to new quarters (*Daily Star,* 1937:1).

The Sanborn maps demonstrate that buildings were constructed over the locations of sites 2a and 5b sometime between 1886 and 1901. The deposits must therefore predate 1901. The locations of sites 3a and 69-2 were cleared for future building between 1904 (correction of the 1901 map) and 1909, and therefore date before 1909.

Ventura

Two Chinese deposits, Features 24 and 25, were excavated as part of Ventura's redevelopment project. Feature 24 was a filled well behind a Chinese laundry in Ventura's second Chinatown, dating between 1905, when Chinese moved onto the property, and 1910, when the buildings were demolished. For the faunal analysis, the external fill around the well was excluded. Feature 25 was a small trash pit located behind an earlier Chinese laundry in the original Chinatown, and dates to the 1890s-1900s. A detailed report on the Features appears elsewhere (Benté, 1976). Chinatown maps showing the Features are also available (Greenwood, 1984:7).

The city of Ventura sprang up around Mission San Buenaventura in the late 1700s. Chinese settled in Ventura sometime after the Gold Rush and a Chinatown of some 200 men was well established by the 1870s (Wlodarski, 1976:445). This Chinatown was razed in 1905-1906, and a new, smaller one built several blocks away. The Chinese population had dropped to around 100 by this time (Greenwood, 1984:7).

Lovelock

Only the faunal materials from Well One and Well Two were used. The upper levels of each well were not considered due to mixture and contamination. The remaining levels, 10-12 in Well One and 5-12 in Well Two, were deposited into the well structures in the 1920s and 1930s. Well One was probably filled a few years earlier than Well Two. The deposits in both wells are primarily domestic, but Well Two also has refuse associated with a Chinese laundry. More detailed information and maps are available elsewhere (Jensen and Rusco, 1979:131).

Lovelock was settled in 1861, but the town grew up only after the Central Pacific railroad agreed to a passenger station there in the late 1860s. The town's major business was catering to travelers (Rusco, 1979a:2). By the 1870 census, Chinese residents numbered nineteen. Their population increased to a peak of about sixty during the period between 1910-1920. In the early years the Chinese were mostly general laborers, but by 1900 their occupations had diversified, with about 50 percent employed as cooks and over 10 percent as independent owners of stores, restaurants, or other businesses. In addition, by 1920 over 30 percent of the Chinese were women or children. The community declined during the 1930s and by 1940 few people remained (Rusco, 1979b:50).

ANIMALS REPRESENTED AND MEAT UTILIZED

The total faunal sample for each site by number of identified specimens (NISP) follows: Sacramento 631, Woodland 717, Tucson 2090, Ventura 919, and Lovelock 1096. At all five sites, cattle, pigs, and sheep dominate the faunas (over 50% of NISP). Sheep are the least significant of these, being present at all sites, but in very small quantities (Table 28). For all sites except Tucson, the number of pig bones is larger than that of cattle (Table 28A and C). The percent of total large mammal specimens for pigs varies from 97 percent for Sacramento to 31 percent for Tucson (Table 28C). Because the quantity of sheep bones is so small, the percentages change by only 2 percent if sheep are excluded (Table 28E).

A more accurate assessment of the relative importance of meat from large animals is obtained by calculating the meat weight (MTWT) in pounds (Lyman, 1979). I have slightly modified the calculation process by including weight of steaks. For instance, if there were five minimum butchering units (MBUs) and 119 steaks (of one bone, say scapula blade) for beef chuck, I calculated MTWT for the

Table 28. Large Mammals Represented at Urban Chinese Sites

Animal Type or Meat Type	Sacramento	Woodland	Tucson	Ventura	Lovelock
A. Number of Identified Specimens					
Cattle	7	45	1179	237	156
Pigs	547	301	573	362	430
Sheep	8	8	107	25	41
Unidentified	42	3	18	16	112
B. Meat Weight in Pounds					
Beef	20	432	1590	690	196
Pork	523	301	548	523	230
Mutton	10	13	78	17	31
C. Percent Number of Identified Specimens					
Cattle	1.5	13	63	38	25
Pigs	97	85	31	58	69
Sheep	1.5	2	6	4	6
D. Percent Meat Weight					
Beef	4	58	72	56	43
Pork	95	40	25	43	51
Mutton	1	2	3	1	6
E. Percent Number of Identified Specimens (Percent Meat Weight)					
Beef	1 (4)	13 (59)	67 (74)	40 (57)	27 (46)
Pork	99 (96)	87 (41)	33[a] (26)	60 (43)	73 (54)

[a]The percent number of identified specimens for Tucson given in Gust 1984, Table 4, was based on preliminary data and differ from these final results.

MBUs plus 2 pounds for each steak. I used very conservative values of 2 pounds for beef steaks, 0.5 pound for pork steaks, and 0.25 pound for mutton steaks. I think this provides a better estimate in many cases, especially those with very few or very many steak bones. For example, if the only beef bone from a site is from a sirloin steak, two pounds is a more realistic estimate of the amount of beef than the 32 pounds Lyman's calculation procedure would yield.

Since beef cuts weigh more than pork cuts, representation by meat weight justifiably increases the importance of beef relative to pork, as compared to NISP.

Using percent meat weight, only Sacramento and Lovelock have more than 50 percent pork. Woodland, Tucson, and Ventura have more beef than pork. However, the percent meat weight of beef and pork differ by less than 20 percent for Woodland, Ventura, and Lovelock (Table 28D) Sacramento has much more pork than beef, while Tucson has the opposite. Mutton is present in small meat weight quantities at all sites.

The smaller animals were quantified by NISP and minimum number of individuals (MNI) for all sites. Since small mammals, birds, and fishes were only available as whole carcasses, whether hunted or bought during the time represented by the sites, MNI is considered a good estimate of relative quantity (meat weight calculations would consist of the MNI multiplied by an edible meat weight for each animal (see White, 1953).

There is no uniformity in the types of small mammals and reptiles present in the various site faunas. The sample sizes are small, none totaling more than 4 percent of the NISP. Cut marks were present on ground squirrel bones from Woodland; cat bones from Woodland, Tucson, and Ventura; bobcat bones from Lovelock; dog bones from Sacramento; rabbit bones from Tucson and Lovelock; and pond turtle bones from Woodland and Lovelock. Due to the presence of butchering marks, all these animals are considered to have been food items. The paucity of remains indicates that they were merely occasional additions to the diet.

Other small animals present in one or more site faunas are dog, snake, and cuttlefish (Table 29). While it is possible that any or all of these animals were used as food, there is no direct evidence. Dog bones, snake bones, and cuttlebones were present at Tucson and Lovelock.

Many domestic and game birds are represented in the assemblages (Table 30). Birds were more frequent dietary additions than small mammals, as evidenced by MNIs as high as twenty-nine. Woodland, Tucson, and Ventura all possess bird MNIs over twenty, with many species present. Ducks and geese are not well represented in the dry-climate sites, namely Tucson and Lovelock. Chicken was the single bird with the highest MNI at Woodland, Ventura, and Lovelock. For Tucson, dove remains outnumbered those of chicken. Sacramento is the only site with few bird bones. This is probably due to its early time frame, before either poultry production or market hunting had become important commercial enterprises (see Simons, 1984:169).

Fish bones are present in all the faunas (Table 31), but those from Lovelock have never been identified. Sample size and MNI are small, reflecting occasional dietary use or, more probably, bias from lack of fine-screening during excavation. Fish apparently ranked between birds and small mammals in dietary importance. Both Tucson and Ventura have totally marine fish faunas. In contrast, Sacramento has 100 percent freshwater fishes and Woodland has 88 percent freshwater species.

A number of factors contribute to these results. All the sites are located with access to freshwater rivers or streams. However, freshwater fish faunas rich

Table 29. Small Mammals and Miscellaneous Animals Represented at Urban Chinese Sites Quantified by Number of Identified Specimens (NISP)/Minimum Number of Individuals

Taxon	Name	Sacramento	Woodland	Tucson	Ventura	Lovelock	Totals
Small Food Animals							
Spermophilus beechyii	ground squirrel		3/2				3/2
Felis catus	cat		3/1	24/4	1/1		28/6
Canis familaris	dog	2/1					
Lepus spp.	jackrabbit			14/2			14/2
Lepus/Sylvilagus	rabbit					33/?	33/?
Clemmys marmorata	pond turtle		14/?			6/?	20/?
Other Small Animals							
Canis familaris	dog			2/1		1/1	3/2
Lynx rufus	bobcat					2/1	2/1
Sepia spp.	cuttlefish			8/?		2/?	10/?
Serpentes	snake			3/?		2/?	5/?
Totals		2	20	51	1	46	116
Percent Total Faunal NISP		.3	3	2	0.1	4	

Table 30. Birds Represented at Urban Chinese Sites Quantified by Number of Identified Specimens (NISP)/ Minimum Number of Individuals

Taxon	Name	Sacramento	Woodland	Tucson	Ventura	Lovelock	Totals
Anseriformes	ducks and geese	4/2	36/4	1/1	99/8	12/2	152/17
Asio otus	long-eared owl			4/1			4/1
Branta canadensis	Canada goose		1/1				1/1
Columba livia	pigeon			11/2			11/2
Corvas brachyrhynchos	crow		1/1				1/1
Fulica americana	coot	1/1		14/1	1/1		16/3
Gallus gallus	chicken	2/1	176/11	17/7	144/12	257/10	596/41
Geococcyx californianus	roadrunner			7/1			7/1
Lophortyx californica	California quail		3/1				3/1
Meleagris gallopavo	turkey	1/1		12/3	1/1	7/2	21/7
Zenaidura macroura	dove		1/1	24/11			25/12
miscellaneous	other birds		3/2	3/2			6/4
Totals		8/5	221/21	93/29	245/22	276/14	843
Percent Chicken		25	80	18	59	93	
Percent Total Faunal NISP		1	31	5	27	25	

Note: Sacramento data from Simons 1982; Woodland data from Simons 1984; Tucson data from Alan Ferg 1980:personal communication; Ventura data and Lovelock data from Dwight Simons 1981:personal communication.

enough to support commercial fisheries were limited to Sacramento (Peter Schulz, 1989:personal communication). Of the sites studied, only Ventura is located on the coast with direct access to marine fish.

These locational and faunal richness factors are mitigated in the later sites by rail connections. The Sacramento deposit predates the railroad, probably limiting the populace to local fish. Woodland was connected to Sacramento by rail in 1869, and via Sacramento to San Francisco. Both local and intercontinental rail connections were also present in Tucson and Lovelock before the time of the deposits studied. The prevalence of freshwater fish at Woodland and marine fish at Tucson probably resulted from these being the kinds of fish available at the nearest commercial fishery, and therefore freshest upon delivery. The lack of fish species (such as cod) used for salt fish or canned fish is notable in all these sites.

Meat Cuts Utilized

Selection of various meat cuts was assessed by calculating percent meat weight for each cut (Table 32). Economic rankings for each type of meat from most expensive to least follow: beef—loin, rib, round, chuck, brisket, hindshank, and foreshank (Schulz and Gust, 1983a, 1983b); pork—loin, ham, shoulder, picnic ham, belly, and jowl (United States Department of Agriculture, 1957); mutton—loin, rib, leg, shoulder, breast, and foreshank (Oehl, 1936).

Relatively inexpensive cuts like chuck and round made up 50-60 percent of the beef at all sites except Sacramento. The percentage of expensive beef cuts (loin and rib) at Lovelock was double that of any other site. A different pattern was present for pork. The expensive cuts of pork (loin and ham) dominate at all sites except Ventura. Both Ventura and Lovelock have substantial percentages of picnic ham in addition. For mutton, no patterns are evident among sites. Overall, status as indicated by percentage of expensive meat cuts (beef, pork, and mutton) resulted in this order: Sacramento (80%), Lovelock (48%), Woodland (39%), Tucson (26%), and Ventura (23%).

The relative contribution of various cuts to the overall meat diet was computed as percent meat weight of all three types of meat (Table 32). Only percentages over 15 percent are considered for the "meat most often utilized" (MMOU) ratings which follow. Pork cuts, specifically loin and ham, were the meats most often utilized in both Sacramento and Lovelock. For Woodland the meat most often utilized was beef chuck, trailed by pork loin. Beef round and chuck were the meats most often utilized for Tucson. In Ventura, the meats most often utilized were beef round and chuck, with a lesser percentage of pork picnic ham.

Documentary Information on Meat

There is an overwhelming amount of evidence that pork was the preferred meat in China (Ball, 1906:287; Tingle, 1907:157; Wang, 1920:289; Buck, 1937:411; Koo, 1973:122). Indeed, even the word for meat (*rou,* or the Cantonese *yuhk*) is

Table 31. Fishes Represented at Urban Chinese Sites Quantified by Number of Identified Specimens (NISP)/ Minimum Number of Individuals

Taxon	Name	Sacramento	Woodland	Tucson	Ventura	Lovelock
Marine Species						
Amphistichus argenteus	barred surfperch				20/2	
Caulolatilus sp.	whitefish			7/1		
Centropomus sp.	snook			18/1		
Cynoscion nobilis	white seabass				3/1	
Cynoscion sp.	corvina			5/1		
Damalichthyes vacca	pile surfperch				1/1	
Eopsetta jordani	petrale sole				2/1	
Hexagrammos decagrammus	kelp greenling		3/1			
Leptocottus armatus	staghorn sculpin				1/1	
Lutjanus sp.	snapper			2/1		
Paralabrax sp.	seabass			1/1		
Paralichthys californicus	halibut			6/2	3/1	
Pimelometopon pulchrus	sheephead				1/1	
Scorpaenichthyes marmoratus	cabezon		2/1			
Sebastes spp.	rockfish		8/2		2/1	
Seriola sp.	yellowtail			4/1		
Serranidae	grouper			3/1		
Sphyraena argentea	barracuda			21/1		
Stereolepis gigas	giant seabass			1/1		
Tetradontidae	puffer			1/1	1/1	
Total Marine Fishes		0	14/5	69/12	33/9	0

186

Freshwater Species

		Sacramento	Woodland	Tucson	Ventura	Lovelock
Acipenser sp.	sturgeon	1/1				
Archoplites interruptus	Sacramento perch	14/3	18/4			
Catostomus occidentalis	Sacramento sucker		10/2			
Cyprinodea	minnows and suckers	3/?	48/?			
Gila crassicauda	thicktail chub		5/1			
Lavinia exilicauda	hitch		4/1			
Orthodon microlepidotus	blackfish		7/2			
Pogonichthys macrolepidotus	splittail	1/1	1/1			
Ptychocheilus grandis	squawfish		12/4			
Total Freshwater Fishes		19/5	105/15	0	0	0
Grand Totals		19/5	119/20	69/12	33/9	35 [not identified]
Percent Marine Fishes		0	12	100	100	?
Percent Freshwater Fishes		100	88	0	0	?
Percent Total Faunal NISP		3	17	3	4	0.3

Note: Sacramento data from Schulz, 1982; Woodland data from Schulz, 1984; Tucson and Ventura data from Kenneth Gobalet, 1980:personal communication; Lovelock data from Amy Dansie, 1979:personal communication.

Table 32. Meat Cuts for Urban Chinese Sites Quantified by
Percent Meat Weight

Meat Cut	Sacramento %MT	(%T)	Woodland %MT	(%T)	Tucson %MT	(%T)	Ventura %MT	(%T)	Lovelock %MT	(%T)
Beef										
loin			7	(4)	14	(9)	16	(9)	18	(7)
rib			5	(3)	1	(1)	3	(2)	20	(9)
round	10	(0.5)	14	(8)	31	(22)	27	(15)	16	(7)
chuck			60	(35)	31	(22)	29	(16)	27	(11)
brisket	10	(0.5)	5	(3)	1	(1)	3	(2)	12	(5)
hindshank			6	(3)	13	(9)	9	(5)	4	(2)
foreshank	80	(3)	3	(2)	9	(7)	13	(7)	3	(2)
Pork										
loin	18	(17)	47	(19)	35	(8)	14	(6)	30	(16)
ham	65	(61)	27	(11)	33	(8)	15	(6)	33	(16)
shoulder	3	(3)	6	(2)	11	(3)	15	(6)	8	(4)
picnic ham	12	(11)	12	(5)	14	(4)	49	(21)	26	(13)
belly			7	(3)	4	(1)	4	(2)		
jowl	2	(2)	1	(0.5)	4	(1)	3	(1)	3	(1)
Mutton										
loin	60	(1)			4	(0.2)	18	(0.2)		
rib			20	(0.5)	4	(0.2)	18	(0.2)		
leg			80	(1)	51	(2)	58	(1)	48	(3)
shoulder	40	(1)			32	(1)	1	(0.04)	46	(3)
breast					3	(0.2)				
foreshank					6	(0.3)	5	(0.06)	6	(1)

Note: Column labelled %MT contains the percent meat weight for each type of meat separately. For example, the percentages under pork for Sacramento total to 100%. Column labelled %T contains the percent of the total meat weight for each site. For example, the percentages under Sacramento have to be added across beef, pork, and mutton to total 100%. Within each type of meat, the cuts are ordered by expense.

taken to indicate pork unless modifiers are added (Croll, 1983:166). However, other meats like beef, mutton, fowl, and fish have always been eaten also (*Chinese Repository,* 1835:462-464; Buck, 1937:411; Huc and Gabet, 1987:72-73, 114-116, 272, 376; Koo, 1973:121-124).

A list of Canton prices for 1835 (*Chinese Repository,* 1835:471) from most expensive to least consisted of mutton, hams (cured pork), goat, pork, pigeon, sole fish, beef, pig's feet (pickled), geese, chickens, ducks, white rice fish, oysters, and eggs. In modern China, prices over the last thirty years show pork to be the most expensive meat, followed by beef, chicken, eggs, and fish, with mutton by far the least expensive (Croll, 1983:227).

Wild game including deer, hares, rabbits, wild cats, squirrels, ducks, quail, pheasant, and many types of fresh and marine fishes were taken (*Chinese Repository*, 1835:462-463). Dogs and cats were reportedly common food animals; these are available for purchase in the markets of Canton today (Peter Schulz, 1989:personal communication). Rats, mice, lizards, and such were eaten by the poor (*Chinese Repository*, 1835:463; Ball, 1906:287-288; Koo, 1973:123-124).

Accounts of Chinese foodstuffs in 19th-century America can be divided into those about San Francisco's Chinatown, an enclave of 22,000 Chinese in 1880 (Bee, 1971:8), and those about other places, where the Chinese community often consisted of 100 or fewer people. The general view that Chinese in the West ate only traditional foods, bought only from other Chinese, and did not use American goods (Spier, 1958a, 1958b) appears to be based on the highly atypical situation of San Francisco. The following quotes are indicative of this.

In describing a Chinese settlement of 1850, Goris noted that, "in the Chinese section, one sees only shops where all the products of China are sold. . . . Their principal meat was pork. As for fish, they are good fishermen and the bay is there in which to catch them. They grew their own Chinese vegetables . . ." (1958:338). Peabody, in speaking of Chinatown, found that "their provision-shops contain little except pork, and that, seldom in a form in which it would be recognized by an unpractised eye" (1871:661).

The testimony of a police officer given during an investigation of Chinese immigration is also informative: (Joint Special Committee to Investigate Chinese Immigration, 1877:219-229, Bainbridge testimony):

> A great quantity [of pork is used by the Chinese]. The better part of the pork is sent to white butchers in the market and cured by them. . . . They [wagons filled with hog carcasses in Chinatown] are intended for the pork-shops there, and if you stay until 3 or 4 o'clock in the morning you will see the hams and sides taken down to our curers here for sale. . . . I do not know that they furnished enough to supply all [the white butchers with pork exclusively], but I know that they supply the best part of the animal to our butchers. They buy from the killer and they sell to the curer.

Brooks (1882:14) adds the following:

> From the number of butcher and provision shops in Chinatown, it is quite evident that, in his way, John Chinaman lives well. They appear at almost every step, and all seem to be doing a good business. In the mornings, every spot of vantage is taken by fish dealers, who spread a by no means uninviting display of salt-water game. . . . Later in the day the butchers come in for their share of the public patronage. Butcher meat apparently means pork; they may stretch it to include beef and mutton sometimes, but there is nothing hereabouts which is not plainly pork, except one piece presided over by a

chap who doesn't seem to have anything else in that line; perhaps he is a specialist, and deals in beef.

Chinese living in small communities, whether in large cities or mining camps, generally bought from Euroamerican merchants. They used American goods, clothes, foods, and tools, and became increasingly American in their use of material goods. Speer illustrates this by recounting several communications of the time (1856:22-25):

> I have often enquired of merchants as to their business with the Chinese, and almost always been answered that their trade was very extensive and important; that while they consume large quantities of imported provisions from China, yet they purchase much that is American, often even that which is most expensive, even luxuries such as chickens, eggs, fresh meats in cans, pork, even when it might be twice as dear as beef, melons, fruits, &c.; that the Chinese would purchase when the expense was such as to deter Americans, for the Chinese would have what they wanted, cost what it may (traveler's letter).

> I have conversed with several of the mountain merchants, and they give it as their opinion that more than three-fourths of their sales to Chinamen are for American products. Almost every merchant in the mines has more or less Chinese trade, and a good many of them are dependent almost entirely on them for their business. The following are the kind of goods, provisions, &c., they consume the most of: potatoes, cabbage, pork, chickens, flour, and almost every article of vegetables raised in this State—they buy clothing, shoes, boots, blankets, American brandy, whiskey, gin, hams, beans, lard, codfish, lobsters, and almost every article of American production to some extent. As they become Americanized, the demand for American products increases with them. . . . The Chinamen say that the estimate is made that they spend in the country seven-tenths on an average of all the money they make. Dealers with them in the mines are of the opinion their estimate is nearly correct . . . (merchant's letter).

> I often sell as much as four hundred weight of beef a day to the Chinamen, and charge them sixteen to twenty cents a pound. They hardly ever ask for it less if they are treated fairly and get good weight. . . . They preferred pork, even at twenty-five cents a pound. I have sold in one day as high as fourteen hogs, averaging seventy-five pounds each. They will pay as high as a dollar a pound for nice dried sausage. They are very fond of fowls, and buy a great many. . . . They like fish too, whenever they can be got, and use dried or salt fish daily (butcher's account).

> The principal articles purchased by the Chinese population, in my line of business, take a very wide range, embracing nearly all those in use amongst our general population. . . . I find, on reference to my book, that the articles most permanent in my sales are, salt fish, pork, lard, salt, liquors, flour, tea, sardines, preserved meats, raisins, olive oil, maccaroni [sic], and vermicelli,

paper and matches, together with a great variety of other articles that are either the product of American industry, or pay a large profit in the way of trade (businessman's account).

An early butcher shop ledger (Mariposa County, 1867-1871) reveals that A. Chung bought only beef on 11 dates in one month. A California farmer testified to the committee investigating Chinese immigration as follows (Joint Special Committee to Investigate Chinese Immigration, 1877:793-795):

> I have known a Chinaman to pay $2.50 for a chicken. . . . I think they will have just what they want, cost what it will. . . . [Discussing Chinese who live at the farms they work] I feed my wife and the Chinaman alike. They do not sit at the same table, but they have the same food, prepared by the same hands. . . . [also] I have a table for my white laborers, and a table for my Chinamen, but they have the same kind of food, prepareed by the same hands. [Discussing Chinese who board themselves] . . . I sell them vegetables and meats when they board themselves in about the same way and proportion as those articles go on my table.

In addition to these accounts, a study of the diet of three groups of California Chinese in 1899 clearly shows inclusion of non-traditional food items such as butter and milk (Table 33) along with bread and cake (Jaffa, 1901:30, 33, 36). This study indicates variance in the relative amounts of beef and pork eaten (pork varies from 85% to 48%), as well as the dietary importance of fish (Table 33).

A more recent study compares the food practices of Chinese Americans with those of overseas (China-born) Chinese living in the United States (Howard, 1974:59-66). The results for meat indicated that pork and beef were used often by both groups, but that "variety meats" (e.g., tongue and tripe) were used much more frequently by overseas Chinese. For fish, the results indicate that all types were used less often by Chinese Americans, and that shrimp was the type used most often by both groups. Chicken was the preferred fowl, followed by duck, for both groups. The overseas Chinese used other varieties of poultry often.

Cooking practices were also surveyed in the study. Stir-frying was used most often by both groups. The only distinct difference between the two groups with respect to other cooking methods was that roasting was the second choice of Chinese Americans, but the last choice of the overseas Chinese.

Butchering of Major Meat Animals

Age at slaughter — Samples sufficient for calculation of slaughter curves from epiphyseal union times (Silver, 1969) at all sites exist only for pig bones. The cumulative slaughter curves show no uniform pattern. For Sacramento and Lovelock, less than 15 percent of pigs were slaughtered under the age of twelve months. Woodland, Tucson, and Ventura slaughtered over 45 percent of pigs during the first year. Over 95 percent of pigs were slaughtered before the second

Table 33. Dietary Studies of Chinese in 1899[a]

Animal Food	Dentist Grams	%	Laundry Grams	%	Farmers Grams	%
Meat	(21242)	35	(41087)	68	(44628)	67
beef	4045		21338		6583	
pork, fresh	14264		19749		38045	
sausage	454					
pig's feet	2479					
Poultry	(6681)	11	(3632)	6	(3632)	5
chicken	6681		3632		3632	
Fish	(11674)	19	(10102)	16	(18428)	28
smelt	6363					
perch			6810			
carp					2724	
shad					8172	
salt fish	1589		1135		4086	
dried squid	681		908		1362	
abalone			454		1362	
crab	2043					
shrimp	499		114			
dried shrimp	499		681		722	
Dairy	(20748)	34	(5902)	10	(0)	
eggs	2361		454			
butter	681		454			
milk	17706		4994			
Total	(60345)		(60723)		(66688)	
Beef[b]		19		52		15
Pork[b]		81		48		85

[a]Data from Jaffa 1901. Dentist's household in Chinatown, San Francisco, consisted of dentist, wife, cook, and seven male boarders ranging in age from fifteen to thirty. The San Francisco laundry group was ten male employees, living on the premises. The farmers were twelve men employed as laborers on a Berkeley truck (vegetable) farm. These men paid the owner (also Chinese) one day's pay per week to board them.

[b]These percentages are a subset of the Meat category at the top of the table and were calculated by taking the grams of the three types of pork versus the grams of beef. They contrast the amount of pork eaten with the amount of beef eaten.

year at Woodland, Ventura, and Lovelock. Sacramento and Tucson differed with only 75 percent slaughtered by twenty-four months. Virtually all pigs were slaughtered before reaching three years of age.

In addition to Chinese site curves, I plotted the curve for Euroamerican sites from Sacramento dating between 1870-1880s (author's unpublished data). The curve for Chinese Sacramento was identical to that for Euroamerican Sacramento. I believe this indicates that slaughterhouses in Sacramento had a uniform selection procedure, and slaughterhouses in other cities probably did too. The major pork slaughterhouses in Sacramento were operated by Chinese, who then supplied most of the butchers and curers in town (*Sacramento Union,* 1873:11 January). Similar data were not available for the other sites.

Butchering tools — Marks from handsaws, knives, and cleaver/ax-type tools were all represented in these collections. For the most part, the handsawn cuts were those of standard meat cuts. The cleaver and knife marks were more varied. The number of kinds of marks used to cut meat differed among sites. Percentages of cleaver and handsaw marks on beef, pork, and mutton bones (excluding ribs, vertebrae, foot, and miscellaneous bones for reasons of between-site consistency, and to remove splitting and skinning marks from the totals) show clear trends. There were slightly fewer cleaver marks than handsaw marks for Sacramento and Woodland. In contrast, for Tucson, Ventura, and Lovelock, there were mostly handsaw marks. Both types of marks show rough chronological trends—cleaver marks decreasing through time and handsaw marks increasing.

The frequency of tool marks varies according to meat type. On pig and sheep bones, cleaver marks account for roughly 20-40 percent of the cut marks, but on cow bone fewer than 10 percent of the marks were from cleavers (Figure 35). Approximately 90 percent of the cut marks on cattle bone were handsaw marks. The exception is the tiny butchered beef bone sample from Sacramento (NISP=7).

In addition, the pattern of the overall sample most closely reflects that of the pork bones (Figure 35). Both show Sacramento and Woodland as one cluster with nearly equal percentages of cleaver and handsaw marks, while Tucson, Ventura, and Lovelock form another cluster dominated by handsaw marks.

Cleaver and handsaw marks generally divide bone-meat portions. Scores (nicks from cleavers or knives), however, are evidence of carving meat away from the bone (on foot or skull bones, excluded here, these can be skinning marks). The inclusion of scores along with cleaver and handsaw marks changes the percentages of pork and beef marks very little. The percentage of scores on pork bone is greatest for Sacramento, about equal for Woodland, Tucson, and Ventura, and least for Lovelock, approximating a rough chronological trend. Beef bone scores are analogous to the percentages for cleaver marks; very few are present at any site.

Pork butchering — Pork is consistently present in large quantity at all five sites, so the emphasis of the butchering analysis is on this meat source. Comparison of butchering on bone fragments (Figure 36) gives detailed information on

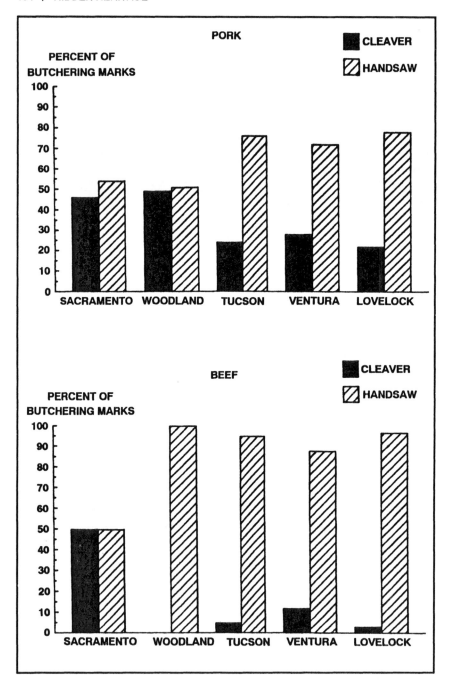

Figure 35. Comparison of beef and pork butchering marks.

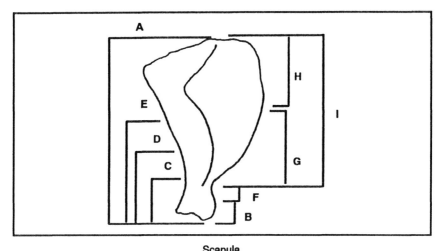

Scapula

Code	Bone Fragment	Sacramento b/unb	s	Woodland b/unb	s	Tucson b/unb	s	Ventura b/unb	s	Lovelock b/unb	s
A	whole					0/3					
B	glenoid	1/2				3/0		3/2		5/0	
C	ventral 1/4	2/1		1/0		4/0		6/0		1/0	
D	ventral 1/3					6/0		2/1		2/0	
E	ventral 1/2	0/2		0/1		3/1		1/0			
F	neck	0/1		2/0		1/0		9/0			
G	ventral blade	0/1		1/0		4/1					
H	dorsal blade			1/0		5/1		9/0		2/0	
I	blade	0/4		1/0	1	6/0	17	7/0	3	2/0	
Totals		3/11		7/1		49/6		40/3		12/0	
Percent Butchered		21		88		89		93		100	

Figure 36. Representation of butchered (cross cut by saw or cleaver) and unbutchered portions of major pig bones from five urban Chinese sites. (b = butchered, s = steak, unb = unbutchered; totals combine steaks into butchered category.)

cut marks present on specific bone portions and their quantity, as well as the degree of butchering. Generally, the degree of butchering increases through time, with the forelimb more intensely butchered than the hindlimb (see Figure 36, Percent Butchered rows, especially Forelimb Totals, Hindlimb Totals, and Grand Totals). The intensity of butchering, as expressed by the total percentages for each bone, is similar and low for Sacramento, Woodland, and Lovelock. Tucson and Ventura both have much more intense butchering. Sacramento is notable for the lack of retail butchering marks. Whole bones are present for all elements except the pelvis. Only the latter sites, Tucson, Ventura, and Lovelock, have steak bones.

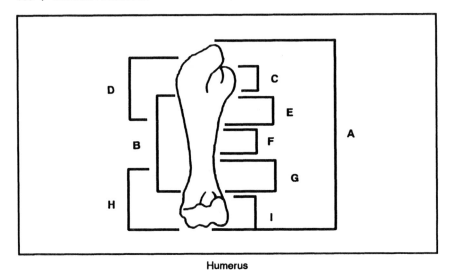

Humerus

Code	Bone Fragment	Sacramento b/unb	s	Woodland b/unb	s	Tucson b/unb	s	Ventura b/unb	s	Lovelock b/unb	s
A	whole	1/0				0/2		0/1			
B	complete shaft			1/0		2/0		2/0			
C	proximal end	1/3		0/1		1/2		1/3			
D	proximal end			2/0							
	and shaft					4/1		7/3		5/1	
E	proximal shaft	1/1				1/0		8/0		1/1	
F	midshaft	1/1		2/0		4/0		7/1		4/0	
G	distal shaft					4/0		14/5		3/0	
H	distal end										
	and shaft	5/5		2/1		6/1		13/3			
I	distal end	1/0		0/1		0/1		0/3		3/0	
Totals		10/10		7/3		22/7		52/19		16/2	
Percent Butchered		50		70		76		73		89	

Figure 36. (Cont'd.)

The butchering data were reanalyzed by placement of cut mark alone, without reference to the bone portion. The resulting pattern is an amazingly regular series of cuts down the length of each limb (Figure 37). In several cases, cuts that appear to cross more than one bone are seen. These illustrations reflect the actual cut marks observed on bones of these samples. However, note that many cuts on actual bones are obliquely placed, rather than strictly transverse. For example, I ended up with two summary diagrams of cut marks for the scapula, one showing cuts at about 45 degrees and another showing cuts at about 135 degrees from the transverse lines in Figure 37. The number of cuts for each position on the scapula

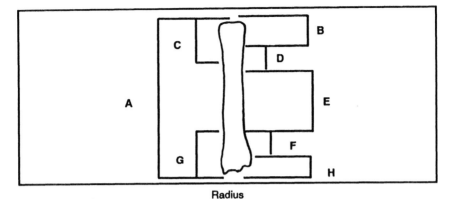

Radius

Code	Bone Fragment	Sacramento b/unb	s	Woodland b/unb	s	Tucson b/unb	s	Ventura b/unb	s	Lovelock b/unb	s
A	whole	1/1		1/0		3/0					
B	proximal end	1/1				1/0				1/0	
C	proximal end and shaft	1/1		2/0		1/2		4/2		4/2	
D	proximal shaft					1/0					
E	midshaft					1/0		1/0		3/0	
F	distal shaft					1/0				2/0	
G	distal end and shaft			1/0		1/1				5/0	
H	distal end	0/3				2/1		0/2			
Totals		3/6		4/0		11/4		5/4		15/2	
Percent Butchered		33		100		73		56		88	

Figure 36. (Cont'd.)

was nearly equal, indicating to me that the butcher's choice was very patterned as regards cut location, but that choice between the two types of obliqueness was random. It is important to remember that when butchers cut a chunk of meat, most of the bones are not directly visible. Perhaps the choice of which oblique angle cut to make was dependent on whether the butcher cut with the shank side toward him or away from him, or on the butcher's being right- or left-handed. However, the data show that the mental templates (see Deetz, 1967) of where to make the cuts were very similar for all the butchers who cut bone that ended up in these sites. I chose to represent the cuts as transverse lines, rather than one set for 45 degree obliques and another set for 135 degree obliques, to emphasize the patterning.

Each cut is identified by a letter, representing the element, and a number, sequenced from distal to proximal. The quantity of each coded cut mark was tabulated and compared between sites.

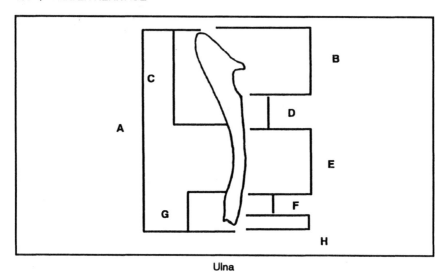

Ulna

Code	Bone Fragment	Sacramento b/unb	s	Woodland b/unb	s	Tucson b/unb	s	Ventura b/unb	s	Lovelock b/unb	s
A	whole			0/1		0/1					
B	proximal end	0/1				1/0		0/1			
C	proximal end and shaft	1/1		3/0		4/6		2/7		1/0	
D	proximal shaft	1/3		2/0		1/1		3/1		8/1	
E	midshaft	1/0		1/0		4/0		0/1		3/0	
F	distal shaft					0/1				1/0	
G	distal end and shaft			1/1		2/0		1/0		1/0	
H	distal end	0/1		2/0		0/2					
Totals		3/6		9/2		12/11		6/10		14/1	
Percent Butchered		33		82		52		38		93	
Forelimb Totals		19/33		27/6		94/28		103/36		57/5	
Percent Butchered		37		82		77		74		92	

Figure 36. (Cont'd.)

Cut S4 is the most frequent on the scapula and divides the bone in half. The "field" of cuts, S2-S4, make up 58 percent of the cuts on the scapula. On the humerus, the most frequent cut is H2. Cuts H1-H3 comprise 82 percent of the cuts and sever the foreshank from the arm. For the radius and ulna, cut RU6 is the most frequent, with RU4 and RU5 also common. I think these serve the same purpose as cuts H1-H3.

An analysis of the overall pattern for the pelvis shows that cuts P8 and P9 are the most frequent, followed by P6 and P7. These all appear to be variants

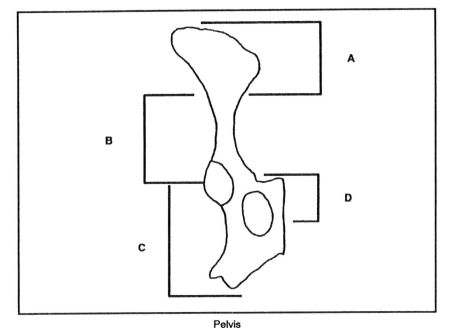

Pelvis

	Bone	Sacramento		Woodland		Tucson		Ventura		Lovelock	
Code	Fragment	b/unb	s	b/unb	s	b/unb	s	b/unb	s	b/unb	s
A	ilial blade	0/3		4/0		5/0	4	2/1	2	2/0	3
B	ilial shaft	9/5		1/0		2/0	1	2/0		7/0	2
C	ischium	11/22		2/2		8/2	1	3/0		2/1	
D	pubis	8/1		0/2						1/1	
Totals		28/31		7/4		21/2		9/1		17/2	
Percent Butchered		47		64		91		90		89	

Figure 36. (Cont'd.)

corresponding to the top cut for short cut ham. Femur cuts F2 and F3 are the most common. These correspond to removing the shank. Cuts F7 and F8 are also frequent and correspond to cuts removing the butt portion of the ham. Two-thirds of the cuts on the tibia serve to remove the lower shank and foot. These are coded T1-T4.

The only other limb bones with substantial numbers of butchering marks are the calcaneus and talus (Gust, 1982:5, Figure 5). All of these appear to be in the same class of cuts as T1-T4, severing the foot. About twenty axial bones also have butchering marks. Of particular interest are the marks on the skull and mandible showing splitting on the midline of both (illustrations available from author). Virtually all of the vertebrae were also split on the midline. Data on the ribs and

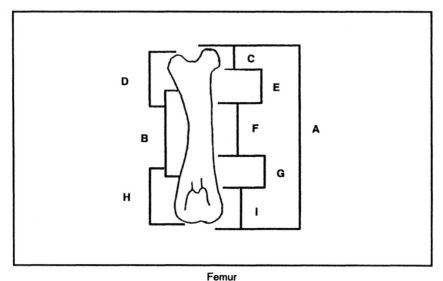

Femur

Code	Bone Fragment	Sacramento b/unb	Sacramento s	Woodland b/unb	Woodland s	Tucson b/unb	Tucson s	Ventura b/unb	Ventura s	Lovelock b/unb	Lovelock s
A	whole	0/1		0/1		0/4					
B	complete shaft	0/14				1/0					
C	proximal end	0/23		3/5		2/5		0/2		1/0	1
D	proximal end and shaft	1/2		1/0		4/0	1	3/0		0/4	
E	proximal shaft			1/1		3/0	1	1/0		1/0	
F	midshaft			1/0		2/0	1			3/0	2
G	distal shaft	1/0		1/1		3/0		2/0		1/0	1
H	distal end and shaft	2/3		1/1		4/0	2	2/0		1/3	
I	distal end	0/21		1/1		2/4		7/1		1/0	
Totals		4/64		9/10		26/13		15/3		12/7	
Percent Butchered		6		47		67		83		63	

Figure 36. (Cont'd.)

other elements are not presented because they were either incomplete, or recording varied from site to site.

Beef and mutton butchering — These two meat sources were represented less frequently than pork at all sites except Tucson. The butchering marks on both are mostly from Tucson and Ventura, with sparse additions from other sites (illustrations similar to Figure 36 are available from author). The beef and mutton butchering is standard 19th-century retail butchering.

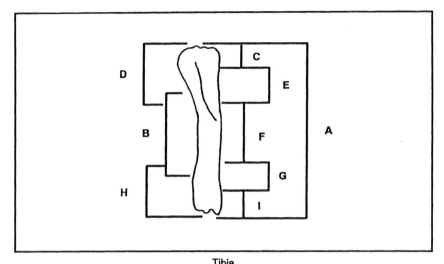

Tibia

Code	Bone Fragment	Sacramento b/unb	s	Woodland b/unb	s	Tucson b/unb	s	Ventura b/unb	s	Lovelock b/unb	s
A	whole	2/2		0/1		0/2				0/6	
B	complete shaft	1/0		2/0		1/0		1/0		1/0	
C	proximal end	0/26		0/5		0/2					
D	proximal end and shaft	3/5		2/0		3/1		1/2			
E	proximal shaft	1/2				1/0		1/2		1/0	
F	midshaft	1/5								0/1	
G	distal shaft					1/0					
H	distal end and shaft	4/3		1/1		4/1		4/3		6/0	
I	distal end	0/8		1/1		0/2		1/3			
Totals		12/51		6/8		10/8		8/10		8/7	
Percent Butchered		19		43		56		44		53	
Hindlimb Totals		44/146		22/22		57/23		32/14		37/16	
Percent Butchered		23		50		71		44		70	
Grand Totals		63/179		49/28		151/51		135/50		94/21	
Percent Butchered		26		64		75		73		82	

Figure 36. (Cont'd.)

Butchering of Minor Meat Animals

Butchering tools — The cleaver and the knife were the tools used to butcher small animals. None of the small animal bones show any evidence of saws. In a few instances, it could not be determined from the physical evidence which tool, knife or cleaver made a mark, and these were listed simply as cut.

Scapula

Number	Sacramento s	c	t	Woodland s	c	t	Tucson s	c	t	Ventura s	c	t	Lovelock s	c	t	Totals
1		1	(1)				4	1	(5)	5		(5)				11
2				2		(2)	3	1	(4)	16		(16)				22
3				1		(1)	3	1	(4)	12	2	(14)	4		(4)	23
4		1	(1)	5		(5)	22	1	(23)	19		(19)	3		(3)	51
5							5	2	(7)	3	2	(5)	1		(1)	13
6				3	1	(4)	18	1	(19)	4		(4)	2		(2)	29
7				1		(1)	5	1	(6)	6	2	(8)	1		(1)	16

Note: Some steaks were present at Woodland, Tucson, and Ventura (Figure 36 for counts); Tucson had one scapula with multiple knife scores.

Humerus

Number	Sacramento s	c	t	Woodland s	c	t	Tucson s	c	t	Ventura s	c	t	Lovelock s	c	t	Totals
1	4		(4)				2		(2)		3	(3)	3		(3)	12
2				1	3	(4)	5	3	(8)	38	4	(42)	8		(8)	62
3	1		(1)	2		(2)	3	2	(5)	6		(6)	1		(1)	15
4	1		(1)				3	2	(5)	20		(20)	2		(2)	28
5	1		(1)	1		(1)	5	3	(8)	17		(17)	5		(5)	32
6					1	(1)				9		(9)	3		(3)	13
7										4		(4)	1		(1)	5
8		2	(2)				3		(3)	2		(2)				7

Note: Sacramento had two humeri split vertically by cleaver.

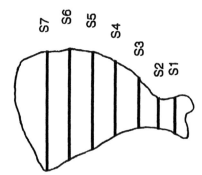

S7 S6 S5 S4 S3 S2 S1

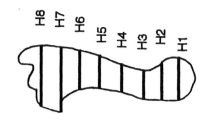

H8 H7 H6 H5 H4 H3 H2 H1

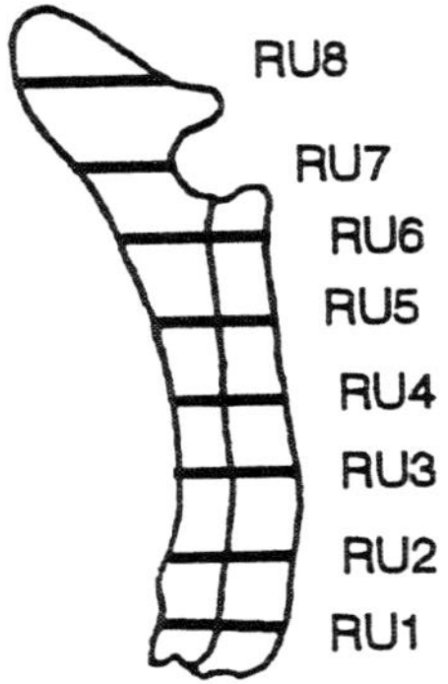

Radius and Ulna

Number	Sacramento s	c	t	Woodland s	c	t	Tucson s	c	t	Ventura s	c	t	Lovelock s	c	t	Totals
1				1	2	(3)		1	(1)				1		(1)	5
2					1	(1)		3	(3)		1	(1)	4	3	(7)	12
3					1	(1)	3	2	(5)				8	1	(9)	15
4	1	2	(3)	1	1	(2)		1	(1)		4	(4)	4	3	(7)	17
5							2	3	(5)	3	1	(4)	7	3	(10)	19
6		1	(1)	2	1	(3)	4	9	(13)		5	(5)	5	7	(12)	34
7			(1)		1	(1)		5	(5)		1	(1)				8
8								1	(1)							1

Note: Woodland had five radii/ulnae with cleaver/knife scores or scrapes; Tucson had two whole radii which were cleaver split vertically through the entire bone, two distal ends of radii which were cleaver split vertically, and eight bones with cleaver/knife scores or scrapes (these were concentrated near cut #8); Ventura had one bone with a cleaver/knife score.

Figure 37. Detailed butchering information on major pig bones from five urban chinese sites (s = sawn, c = cleaved, t = total butchered).

RU8
RU7
RU6
RU5
RU4
RU3
RU2
RU1

203

Pelvis

Number	Sacramento s	c	t	Woodland s	c	t	Tucson s	c	t	Ventura s	c	t	Lovelock s	c	t	Totals
1	3	5	(8)					1	(1)							9
2		1	(1)	1		(1)										2
3	1	1	(2)				1	1	(2)	1		(1)				5
4				1		(1)	4		(4)	2		(2)	2		(2)	9
5				1		(1)	2		(2)	2		(2)	4		(4)	9
6		7	(7)	2		(2)							3		(3)	12
7		2	(2)				4	1	(5)	5		(5)	6	1	(7)	19
8		1	(1)	2		(2)	2	1	(3)	1		(1)	1		(1)	8
9							3		(3)				1	1	(2)	5

Note: Steaks were present at Tucson, Ventura, and Lovelock (see Figure 36 for counts).

Femur

Number	Sacramento s	c	t	Woodland s	c	t	Tucson s	c	t	Ventura s	c	t	Lovelock s	c	t	Totals
1							1		(1)	4		(4)				5
2							8	1	(9)	4		(4)	1		(1)	14
3	1	1	(2)				7	1	(8)	1		(1)	1		(1)	12
4				2		(2)	1		(1)				1		(1)	4
5				1		(1)	4	1	(5)	1		(1)	2		(2)	9
6							2		(2)	1		(1)	1		(1)	4
7				2		(2)	6		(6)							8
8				2		(2)	6		(6)	1		(1)	2		(2)	11

Note: Steaks were present at Tucson and Lovelock (see Figure 36 for counts); Tucson had four femora with cleaver/knife scores or scrapes.

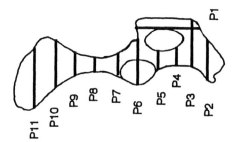

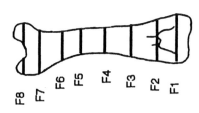

204

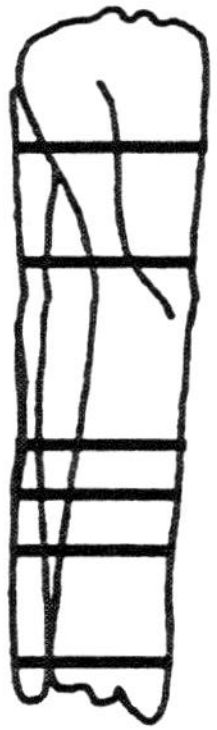

Tibia

Number	Sacramento			Woodland			Tucson			Ventura			Lovelock			Totals
	s	c	t	s	c	t	s	c	t	s	c	t	s	c	t	
1		2	(2)		1	(1)	3		(3)		1	(1)		1	(1)	8
2		2	(2)		2	(2)	2		(2)					4	(4)	10
3					1	(1)	3		(3)	1						5
4		1	(1)					3	(3)	3		(4)				8
5		1	(1)				2	1	(3)	1	1	(1)		1	(1)	6
6				2		(2)	3	1	(4)	1		(1)	2	1	(3)	10

Note: Sacramento had six tibiae with cleaver/knife scores or scrapes.

Figure 37. (Cont'd.)

T6
T5
T4
T3
T2
T1

205

Butchering marks — Seven bones of the jackrabbit from Tucson showed evidence of butchering. The marks on the scapula, humerus, and femur were concentrated near the ends of the bones, while the marks on the pelvis were in the middle region. All the marks were knife scores clearly intended to separate the meat from the bones; none of the rabbit bones was cross-cut. A Euroamerican sample from Old Sacramento (Gust, unpublished data in possession of author) exhibited a very different pattern, with many cross-cuts and few knife scores.

Both the Woodland and Tucson faunas contained butchered bones of the domestic cat. The Woodland bones were a pelvis with a cleaver cut through the iliac shaft, and a scapula that was cleaver cut through the ventral blade. The Tucson bones were a radius with knife scores on the distal shaft, an ulna with knife scores on the anterior and posterior of the olecranon process, and a vertebra that had been cut horizontally. Dansie (1979:377) reported two butchered bones of the bobcat, a distal humerus and an ulna, from Lovelock. Both had cleaver scores.

Two butchered bones of the domestic dog were present at Sacramento. An atlas was cleaver-split vertically on the midline and a pelvis was cleaver-cut through the acetabulum.

Two ground squirrel skulls from Woodland were cut in half (sagittally). One skull was also quartered (cut sagittally and coronally).

Documentary Information on Butchering

Very little information is available on the process of butchering as it was practiced in China or the United States during the middle to late 19th century. The following is the only actual 19th-century description I have seen (Huc and Gabet, 1987:278 [writing in 1844-46]):

> Every Mongol knows the number, the name, and the position of the bones which compose the frame of animals; and thus they never break the bone when they are cutting up an ox or sheep. With the point of their large knife they go straight and at once to the juncture of the bones and separate them with astonishing skill and clarity.

In those parts of early 20th-century China unaffected by Europeans and Americans there are some indications that the practice of cutting the meat away from the bone, rather than cross-cutting both bone and meat, was maintained. In a 1920s study of Chinese tools (Hommel, 1937), many kinds of saws are discussed under woodworking, but none are mentioned as food preparation tools. Consider the following (Hommel, 1937:134):

> In Canton and in Chekiang Province the straight-edged cleaver, Fig. 196, can be found in every kitchen and the peculiar thing about it is that this is the only cutting instrument used in the house except the fire-wood cutter. In Shanghai a cleaver with a curved edge is used. . . .

In discussing pork, Levine (1921:12-13)[1] noted:

> As a rule, the butchers in Canton cut up the carcass immediately after gutting. . . . It is the custom for butchers in Canton to remove all the meat from the ribs and backbone. The sides are then cut into strips about one inch wide, cutting from the top to the bottom, and used fresh or cured. The ribs and backbone are then cut into small parts and prepared in a very tasty way with a sweet dressing.

Some Chinese apparently did practice European butchering styles in catering to the local Europeans. Hong Kong, Macao, and Canton are very close to one another and had sizable English, Dutch, and Portuguese populations. The following price list was doubtless directed at these customers (*China Mail,* 1850:1; "c/catty" is cash per 1.12 pounds):

1850 PARTIAL MEAT PRICE LIST FROM HONG KONG

BEEF, loin	10 c/catty
steak	10 c/catty
shin	6 c/catty
soup	8 c/catty
HAMS, Nankin	25 c/catty
Kwang-se	22 c/catty
PORK, chop	10 c/catty
lean	11 c/catty
leg (fresh ham)	10 c/catty
pig's feet	8 c/catty
MUTTON, chop	24 c/catty
leg	24 c/catty
shoulder	20 c/catty

Even less direct information is available on Chinese butchering in the United States. Those few sources that can be found indicate that in butchering of fresh meats, the Chinese in the United States adopted American methods and tools.

The author interviewed Howard and Arthur Jan (father and son) of Wing Lee Meats, Sacramento, California in 1979. Wing Lee is a fictitious name for the family business, established in 1913 by Howard's father.

Howard Jan said that his father learned the business in San Francisco's Chinatown in the late 19th century. He learned using American tools and American butchering styles, specifically the San Francisco style. Arthur Jan said

---

[1] Levine has been cited as a source on Chinese butchering methods, however the information specifically cited as Chinese in the butchering section is limited to the one item quoted here. His preface makes clear that his intention was to provide a training manual for his Chinese students, not to document Chinese butchering. He states that he includes material from United States Department of Agriculture publications in his pamphlet.

that his father and grandfather had bought beef quarters and shipper-style pigs from local butchers and had cut American-style since the business was established in 1913.

CONCLUSIONS

The characteristics of the urban Chinese faunas from Sacramento, Woodland, Tucson, Ventura, and Lovelock have been well defined here. There appear to be few valid indicators of Chinese ethnicity for bone deposits, excepting butchering marks on cat and dog bones. Contributions of many other factors besides ethnicity confuse the picture.

The results often indicate two subgroupings of the urban Chinese sites used for this chapter. Subgroup one consists of Sacramento, Woodland, and Lovelock. Subgroup two contains Tucson and Ventura. Subgroup one has large amounts of pork, a large percentage of chicken, higher status meat cuts, and less intense butchering of pork. Subgroup two is opposite in all these features. I think that these features are interrelated in an economic fashion. Pork and chicken were more expensive than beef, high status cuts are more expensive than low status cuts, and large pieces of meat are more expensive than small ones. Relative to Sacramento, Woodland, and Lovelock, the Chinese who contributed to the Tucson and Ventura deposits seem to have been less well-to-do.

The only clear chronological trend is in the relative abundance of butchering mark types. High percentages of cleaver marks set the earlier sites apart from the later sites with their high percentages of handsaw marks.

The actual butchering marks themselves are, for the most part, standard Euroamerican butchering style. The only distinctive marks are cleaver scrapes and scores which seem to have resulted from removing meat from bones. However, these marks were neither found at all sites, nor in very great number.

Material acculturation is indicated by the bones and by the documentary information showing that towns with small Chinese populations, even though they were called Chinatowns, were vastly different from San Francisco's Chinatown.

REFERENCES CITED

BALL, J. DYER
1906   *Things Chinese,* Charles Scribner's Sons, New York.
BEE, FRED
1971   *The Other Side of the Chinese Question,* 1886. (Reprinted by R and E Research Associates, San Francisco.)
BENTÉ, VANCE G.
1976   Good Luck, Long Life, *The Changing Faces of Main Street,* R. S. Greenwood, (ed.), San Buenaventura Redevelopment Agency, Ventura, California, pp. 457-495.

BROOKS, WILLIAM
  1882   A Fragment of China, *The Californian,* 6:31, pp. 13-15.

BUCK, JOHN L.
  1937   *Land Utilization in China,* University of Chicago Press, Chicago.

CHINA MAIL
  1850   June 13, Hong Kong.

CHINESE REPOSITORY
  1835   Diet of the Chinese, *3*:10, pp. 59-471.

CROLL, ELIZABETH
  1983   *The Family Rice Bowl,* United Nations Research Institute for Social Development and Zed Press, Geneva and London.

DAILY STAR
  1937   February 20, Tucson, Arizona.

DANSIE, AMY
  1979   Beef, Bobcat and Other Beast Bones: Faunal Remains from Lovelock's Chinatown, "Archaeological and Historical Studies at Ninth and Amherst, Lovelock, Nevada," E. M. Hattori, M. K. Rusco, and D. R. Touhy (eds.), 2, *Archaeological Services Reports,* Nevada State Museum, Carson City, pp. 347-410.

DEETZ, JAMES
  1967   *Invitation to Archaeology,* Natural History Press, Garden City, New York.

FELTON, DAVID L., FRANK LORTIE, and PETER D. SCHULZ
  1984   "The Chinese Laundry on Second Street: Archeological Investigations at the Woodland Opera House Site," D. L. Felton, F. Lortie, and P. D. Schulz (eds.), in *California Archeological Reports, 24,* pp. 1-120.

FONG, LAWRENCE M.
  1973   Historical Explanatory Report (accompanying Chinese Manuscript Collection from the Tucson, Arizona, Urban Renewal Project) on file with Special Collections, University of Arizona Library, pp. 1-6.
  1980   Sojourners and Settlers: The Chinese Experience in Arizona, *The Chinese Experience in Arizona and Northern Mexico,* Arizona Historical Society, Tucson, pp. 1-30. (Reprinted from *The Journal of Arizona History.*)

GORIS, JAN A. (trans.)
  1958   A Belgian in the Gold Rush: A Memoir by Dr. J. J. F. Haine, *California Historical Society Quarterly, 37*:4, pp. 311-346.

GREENWOOD, ROBERTA S.
  1984   Chinatown in Ventura, *Gum Saan Journal, 7*:1, pp. 1-11.

GUST, SHERRI M.
  1982   Mammalian Remains, *Archaeological and Historical Studies of the IJ56 Block, Sacramento, California: An Early Chinese Community,* M. Praetzellis and A. Praetzellis (eds.), Anthropological Studies Center, Sonoma State University, Rohnert Park, California, pp. 87-112.
  1984   "Mammalian Faunal Remains at the Woodland Opera House Site," D. L. Felton, F. Lortie, and P. D. Schulz (eds.), in *California Archaeological Reports, 24,* pp. 181-192.

HOMMEL, RUDOLPH
1937   Handling of Meat, in *China at Work*, John Day Co., New York, pp. 134-137.
HOWARD, CONSTANCE
1974   Comparison of Food Practices and Customs of American-born and Overseas
           Chinese in Tucson, Master's thesis, University of Arizona, Tucson.
HUC, EVARISTE-REGIS and JOSEPH GABET
1987   *Travels in Tartary, Thibet and China, 1844-1846*, Dover Publications, Inc.,
           New York.
JAFFA, M. E.
1901   Nutrition Investigations among Fruitarians and Chinese, *U.S. Department of
           Agriculture, Office of Experiment Stations, Bulletin*, 107.
JENSEN, ANDREW and MARY K. RUSCO
1979   Archaeological Studies at Ninth and Amherst, "Archaeological and Historical
           Studies at Ninth and Amherst, Lovelock, Nevada," E. M. Hattori, M. K.
           Rusco, and D. T. Touhy (eds.), 1, *Archaeological Services Reports, Nevada
           State Museum*, Carson City, pp. 57-136.
JOINT SPECIAL COMMITTEE TO INVESTIGATE CHINESE IMMIGRATION
1877   44th Congress, session 2, report No. 689.
KOO, LINDA C.
1973   Traditional Chinese Diet and Its Relationship to Health, *Kroeber Anthropo-
           logical Society Papers*, No. 47-48, pp. 116-147.
LEVINE, CARL OSCAR
1921   Butchering and Curing Meats in China, *Canton Christian College Bulletin*
           No. 27, Canton.
LYMAN, R. LEE
1979   Available Meat from Faunal Remains: A Consideration of Techniques,
           American Antiquity, 44:3, pp. 536-546.
MARIPOSA COUNTY BUTCHER SHOP LEDGER
1867-   Call number cHD 9419 R421 #11, California Room, California State Library,
1871   Sacramento.
OEHL, E. J.
1936   Oehl's Meat Market, San Bernardino, California: Cards Showing Meat
           Prices, 1910-1912, ms. on file, Bancroft Library, University of California,
           Berkeley.
PEABODY, A. P.
1871   The Chinese in San Francisco, *American Naturalist, 4*:11, pp. 660-664.
PRAETZELLIS, MARY and ADRIAN PRAETZELLIS
1982   The Chinese on I Street, *Archaeological and Historical Studies of the IJ56
           Block, Sacramento, California: An Early Chinese Community*, M. Praetzellis
           and A. Praetzellis (eds.), Anthropological Studies Center, Sonoma State
           University, Rohnert Park, California.
RUSCO, MARY K.
1979a   Introduction, "Archaeological and Historical Studies at Ninth and Amherst,
           Lovelock, Nevada," E. M. Hattori, M. K. Rusco, and D. R. Touhy (eds.), 1,
           Archaeological Services Reports, Nevada State Museum, Carson City,
           pp. 1-4.

1979b   Counting the Lovelock Chinese, "Archaeological and Historical Studies at Ninth and Amherst, Lovelock, Nevada," E. M. Hattori, M. K. Rusco and D. R. Touhy (eds.), 1, *Archaeological Services Reports,* Nevada State Museum, Carson City, pp. 44-56.

SACRAMENTO UNION
1873   January 11, Sacramento, California.

SCHULZ, PETER D.
1982   Fish, Reptile, and Cephalopod Remains, *Archaeological and Historical Studies of the IJ56 Block, Sacramento, California: An Early Chinese Community,* M. Praetzellis and A. Praetzellis (eds.), Anthropological Studies Center, Sonoma State University, Rohnert Park, California, pp. 74-86.

1984   "Nineteenth-Century Fish Remains from Woodland, California," D. L. Felton, F. Lortie, and P. D. Schulz (eds.), in *California Archeological Reports, 24,* pp. 158-166.

SCHULZ, PETER D. and SHERRI M. GUST
1983a   Faunal Remains and Social Status in 19th Century Sacramento, *Historical Archaeology, 17*:1, pp. 44-53.

1983b   Relative Beef Prices in the Late 19th Century, *Pacific Coast Archaeological Review, 19*:1, pp. 12-18.

SILVER, I. A.
1969   The Aging of Domestic Animals, in *Science in Archaeology,* (2nd Edition), D. Brothwell and E. S. Higgs (eds.), Thames and Hudson, London, pp. 283-302.

SIMONS, DWIGHT D.
1982   Bird Remains, *Archaeological and Historical Studies of the IJ56 Block, Sacramento, California: An Early Chinese Community,* M. Praetzellis and A. Praetzellis (eds.), Anthropological Studies Center, Sonoma State University, Rohnert Park, California, pp. 71-73.

1984   "Avifaunal Remains at the Woodland Opera House Site," D. L. Felton, F. Lortie, and P. D. Schulz (eds.), in *California Archeological Reports, 24,* pp. 167-180.

SPEER, WILLIAM
1856   *A Humble Plea addressed to the Legislature of California in Behalf of the Immigrants from the Empire of China to this State,* The Oriental, San Francisco, copy in the Huntington Library, San Marino, California.

SPIER, ROBERT F. G.
1958a   Food Habits of Nineteenth-Century California Chinese (Part One), *California Historical Society Quarterly, 37*:1, pp. 79-83.

1958b   Food Habits of Nineteenth-Century California Chinese (Part Two), *California Historical Society Quarterly, 37*:2, pp. 129-136.

TINGLE, LILLIAN E.
1907   Food Notes in Shantung, North China, *The Boston Cooking-School Magazine, 12*:4, p. 157.

TOM, MAY Y.
1938   The Chinese in Tucson, Arizona, *Chinese Digest,* pp. 8-9, March.

UNITED STATES DEPARTMENT OF AGRICULTURE
1957   Prices of Hogs and Hog Products, 1905-56, *Agricultural Marketing Division, Livestock Division, Statistical Bulletin 205.*

WANG, CHI C.
1920   Is the Chinese Diet Adequate?, *Journal of Home Economics, 12*:7.

WHITE, THEODORE E.
1953   A Method of Calculating the Dietary Percentage of Various Food Animals Utilized by Aboriginal Peoples, *American Antiquity, 18*:4, pp. 396-399.

WLODARSKI, ROBERT J.
1976   A Brief History of Chinatown in Ventura, *The Changing Faces of Main Street,* R. S. Greenwood (ed.), San Buenaventura Redevelopment Agency, Ventura, California, pp. 440-456.

WOLF, ARTHUR
n.d.   Tucson Urban Renewal Project Title Search, ms. in anthropology class files, Arizona State Museum, Tucson.

PART THREE
Work and Leisure

The Chinese were widely known for their ability to work diligently under often adverse conditions. They were also believed to be heavily involved in the encouragement of opium smoking, gambling, and prostitution. While one description expresses virtues and the other, vices, both statements perpetuate stereotypes about the Chinese. Just as not all Chinese were diligent workers, not all participated in illegal activities. Opium smoking by the Chinese, for example, has long been both misunderstood and oversensationalized by the dominant white culture. Although some communities wrote ordinances prohibiting opium smoking within their boundaries, until mid-1909 the drug, prepared for smoking, could be legally imported into the United States.

As mention in the Introduction, the Chinese were employed in a wide variety of occupations. The best known, mining and railroad work, have been studied in some detail. Others are less well documented. Salmon canning, for example, was an industry that flourished in the Pacific Northwest, particularly on the Columbia River, but until the excavation of the Warrendale Cannery site very little was known about the Chinese laborers who performed most of the work. Using documentary research and interviews with informants, John Fagan describes what life must have been like for the cannery's Chinese work force; evidence from the archaeological excavations there adds an additional dimension to the historical accounts.

In contrast to the life of this exclusively male group, Priscilla Wegars presents an occupational profile of Chinese women in the West. Although most of the earliest arrivals were prostitutes, this was generally not by choice; Chinese women as a group entered other occupations as opportunities widened. Where there is little information about Chinese women in the documentary records, archaeological and other artifactual evidence may still attest to their presence on certain sites and in various localities.

Leisure activities are well-represented in the archaeological assemblages from Chinese sites. Opium paraphernalia is commonly recovered; such objects include opium cans, ceramic opium pipe bowls, metal fittings from opium pipes and opium lamps, and glass opium lamp components. Jerry Wylie and Richard E. Fike have examined numerous opium pipe bowls, from both archaeological and private collections, and have prepared a typology of forms and styles against which other archaeologists can compare their own finds. Documentary sources provide additional information on opium-smoking techniques and accoutrements.

CHAPTER 8

The Chinese Cannery Workers of Warrendale, Oregon, 1876-1930

John L. Fagan

The salmon canning industry on the Columbia River began in 1866 when Andrew S. Hapgood, accompanied by George, William, and Robert Hume of Hapgood, Hume, and Company, established the first cannery at Eagle Cliff (Smith, 1979:15-17). Within ten years, seventeen canneries were in operation, and by 1883 there was a record high of thirty-nine canneries on the Columbia River (*The Daily Astorian*, August 9, 1887; Smith, 1979: Appendix B).

Frank Manley Warren was one of the early cannery magnates who built his first cannery at Cathlamet, Washington, in 1871. In 1876 he established another cannery (35-MU-53) on the Columbia River at Warrendale, Oregon (Figures 38 and 39). Later still he developed another cannery in Alaska. Warren, an entrepreneur, capitalist, successful businessman, and inventor of a widely used retort for canning salmon, met an untimely end when the *Titanic* sank in 1912 (*The Oregonian*, April 21, 1912).

Upon the death of their father, Warren's sons took over the operation of the fish packing company (Donaldson and Cramer, 1971:17). After a few more blows, including increased competition for an ever decreasing number of salmon, more stringent regulation of commercial fishing on the Columbia River, and the outlawing of fishwheels (a water-powered device resembling a ferris wheel which scooped fish from the river as they swam upstream), business declined, and the Warrendale Cannery ceased operation about 1930.

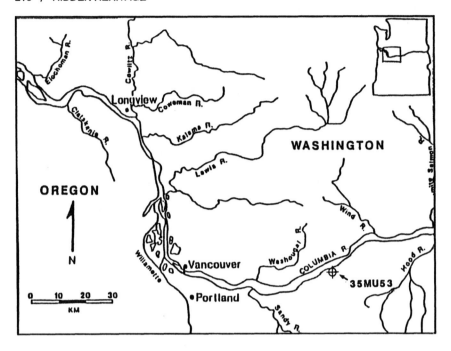

Figure 38. Map of the Lower Columbia showing the location of the
Warrendale Cannery (35-MU-53).

USE OF CHINESE LABOR ON THE COLUMBIA RIVER

Throughout the history of the salmon canning industry on the Columbia River, Chinese laborers provided the work force and performed all of the operations necessary for the processing of the salmon once they were caught and delivered to the canneries by the Scandinavian fishermen. At Warrendale, Chinese laborers were employed for about six months a year. The canning season began in early spring and continued into winter. Prior to the first spring fish runs, the Chinese laborers were kept busy making cans. Early accounts of the salmon canning process and the role played by the Chinese laborers are available for the 1873 (Nordhoff, 1874:340-341), 1888 (Jones, 1888:40), and 1897 (Jordan, 1897:8) canning seasons. The account of the 1873 season by Charles Nordhoff, as it appeared in *Harper's New Monthly* in 1874, vividly depicts the entire process and the predominant role played by the Chinese workers (Nordhoff, 1874:341) (Figure 40):

> The fishermen carry the salmon in boats to the factory—usually a large frame building erected on piles over the water—and there they fall into the hands of the Chinese, who get for their labor a dollar a day and their food.

Figure 39. Photograph of the Warrendale Cannery showing steamboats
at the dock. Photograph was taken in the early 1900s.
Courtesy of Ivan J. Donaldson.

The salmon are flung up on a stage, where they lie in heaps of a thousand
at a time . . . in such a pile you may see fish weighing from thirty to sixty
pounds. The work of preparing them for the cans is conducted with
exact method and great cleanliness. . . . One Chinaman seizes a fish and
cuts off his head; the next slashes off the fins and disembowels the fish; it
then falls into a large vat, where the blood soaks out . . . and after soaking
and repeated washing in different vats, it falls at last into the hands of one
of a gang of Chinese whose business it is, with heavy knives, to chop the
fish into chunks of suitable size for the tins. These pieces are placed
into brine, and presently stuffed into cans, . . . the top, which has a small
hole pierced in it, is then soldered on, and five hundred tins set on a form
are lowered into a huge kettle of boiling water, where they remain
until the heat has expelled all the air. Then a Chinaman neatly drops a
little solder over each pin-hole, and after another boiling . . . the process is
complete. . . .

Census records and government documents detailing the economic condition of
the Columbia River salmon industry attest to the large number of Chinese
employed in these establishments, which were so colorfully described by Charles
Nordhoff. Census records for the years 1870, 1880, and 1900 reflect the fluctua-
tions in the industry in ten-year increments as illustrated by the numbers of

Figure 40. Photograph of Chinese men working in a salmon cannery
ca. 1900. Oregon Historical Society photograph taken by
Wesley Andrews (OHS 238-A).

Chinese employed in the salmon canneries. The 1870 census lists fifteen out of
thirty-three Chinese involved in the cannery business in the four counties of
Oregon and Washington situated on the Lower Columbia River, while the 1880
census lists 2388 Chinese working in canneries in this region (Friday, 1982:39).
Referring to the salmon canning industry for the entire Columbia River below the
Cascades, Major W. A. Jones of the Corps of Engineers listed 3396 Chinese
employed in thirty-nine canneries in 1886 (Jones, 1888:62). The 1880 census
lists eighty Chinese laborers at the Warrendale Cannery, and the 1900 census
includes sixty Chinese—fifty-nine laborers and one foreman (U.S. Bureau of
the Census, 1880, 1900). Business records provide additional information.
For example, business records for 1908 and 1910 indicate that forty-four
Chinese worked at the Warrendale Cannery (Oregon Historical Society, n.d.:
Vol. 11; 1906-1910:Vol. 11). Thus, Chinese labor, important to the salmon canning industry before the enactment of the Chinese Exclusion Act of 1882, continued in importance into the 1900s. This, at least, was the case at the Warrendale
Cannery.

Few written records remain that shed light on the experiences and lives of these
Chinese laborers. In fact, these experiences were probably not even recorded by
the Chinese themselves. Documentary evidence for the most part is confined to

government and business records which provide, at best, some basic statistics. All of this information is useful, as are informant interviews in the interpretation of the archaeological data, but all of it suffers from a lack of emphasis on the Chinese worker's point of view.

Contract Labor

The most common system used to obtain Chinese workers for the canneries was through a labor contractor. Potential workers obtained passage money for the journey across the Pacific most frequently by borrowing the funds from an employer in the United States, or from agents of Chinese merchants or brokers in the United States working in Hong Kong. In either case, the borrowed funds were paid back within a set period of time, and were usually deducted directly from the employees' wages.

The average fare for passage from China to America in the mid-nineteenth century was about forty dollars, while the average yearly earnings in China amounted to twenty or thirty dollars (Perrin, 1980:11-12). Chinese laborers during this same period earned approximately one dollar per day (Corbett and Corbett, 1977:79). Wages for a single month during the canning season, thus equalled, or in some cases exceeded, yearly earnings back home. Reports of such high wages, good food, and available housing were spread by labor recruiters and returning laborers. These reports encouraged others to try their luck in America, which was referred to as the "Golden Mountain."

Business records for the Warrendale Cannery indicate that laborers were obtained through two labor contractors in Portland: Wang On Company and Wing Sing Long Kee Company (Oregon Historical Society, n.d.: Vol. 11). Workers were provided transportation to and from Portland at the beginning and end of each season. Accommodations at Warrendale for the Chinese crew consisted of the "China house" or bunkhouse for the Chinese workers (Figure 41), a garden patch, and a pig pen. In early spring the Chinese planted a garden. They also raised pigs for food, and butchered them as needed.

A cook was included in the Chinese crew. He tended the garden and pigs, and did the cooking with occasional help from some of the other Chinese cannery workers. Traditional Chinese food items were brought in bulk from Portland in baskets, large pottery jars, and sacks. These supplies generally were provided by the contractor, with the cost deducted from the salaries of all of the men at the end of the canning season. Thus, the cannery operator placed an order for the workers, and provided living quarters, a garden patch, a pig pen, and in some cases even pigs for the Chinese workers. A crew usually included a cook and a bookkeeper, as well as a foreman and laborers. At Warrendale in the early 1900s, the Chinese foreman was also a doctor.

Figure 41. Photograph of Warrendale Cannery taken in the early 1900s.
The bunkhouse for Chinese workers is the long white building
at the lower center. The Chinese gardens and pig pen
are to the right of the bunkhouse.
Photograph courtesy of Ivan J. Donaldson.

The Chinese were hired for the entire season at an agreed-upon price. The crew worked ten to eleven hours a day, six days a week. Payment for work was made at the end of the season to the contractor, who then paid the workers after making appropriate deductions for each person's share of the food expenses and cook's wages.

Interviews have supplemented historical documentation. Euroamericans who worked and lived in the area and at the cannery itself have identified all of the associated structures appearing in historic photographs, as well as some of the problematical artifacts. Their recollections and accounts have aided in the interpretation of the archaeological remains. Informants have included several non-Chinese Americans who either lived at Warrendale or visited the cannery as children. One Chinese American informant, Charles Koe, the son of a labor contractor, followed his father's profession and worked in canneries up and down the Columbia River. He lived in "China houses" at several canneries and has provided much information about the life of the Chinese laborer.

THE ARCHAEOLOGICAL SAMPLING OF THE
RIVERBANK TRASH DUMP

Examination of the riverbank revealed an area of dense historic remains consisting of broken bits of Chinese pottery, bottle glass, bricks, and rusty metal. The
area to the east of the pilings on which the main cannery buildings sat (Figure 42)
contained extensive scatters of Chinese ceramic fragments. The area around the
pilings and to the west side of the cannery contained bricks, American and English
pottery fragments, large quantities of tin can scraps, rusted metal fittings, bolts
and nails, and a few Chinese ceramic fragments. The distribution of the historic
trash reflected the segregation of the various ethnic groups represented at the
Warrendale Cannery.

By sampling and analyzing these trash deposits, more information has been
obtained about the Chinese cannery workers, the Scandinavian fishermen, and the
American owners and overseers. The sampling strategy included collecting a one
percent stratified random sample of cultural materials from the surface of five
trash clusters lying to the east of the former location of the main cannery buildings
(Figure 42). Collection units consisted of one-meter squares. All artifacts from the
surface and extending down into the beach gravels within each unit were collected. The stratified random sample was augmented by purposeful placement of

Figure 42. Photograph of the Chinese workers' dump area east of the
remaining pilings for the main cannery building along the riverbank.

sample units in high density areas not represented in the random sample. This included units situated on the beach, as well as submerged units below the low water line. Diagnostic artifacts falling outside of the sample units were collected and piece-plotted on the site map, and labeled according to their location from the datum and baseline.

Results of the Archaeological Investigations

This project was conducted to learn more about the Chinese cannery workers, how they lived, and how they adapted to the dominant American culture. The variety and types of artifacts of non-Chinese origin associated with artifacts of Chinese origin were expected to provide information about Chinese self-sufficiency and degree of acculturation. Based on the archaeological field investigation and laboratory analysis, it is possible to identify a specific range of artifacts attributable to the Chinese occupants of the cannery. We can also address some of the original study questions and hypotheses regarding ethnic identity and acculturation which were developed as part of the research design. In addition, information now available from the archaeological deposits gives us an idea about the day-to-day lives of the Chinese, who left no other record of their stay at the Warrendale Cannery.

Informants suggested that opium was occasionally used by the Chinese, however no written documentation has been found to support such claims. The artifact sample, on the other hand, suggests that opium was used extensively, as were traditional Chinese foods, tablewares, utensils, liquors, and medicines. Opium use is suggested by artifacts including pieces of brass opium cans, a metal fitting from an opium pipe stem, a piece of a glass opium lamp (Figure 43), and numerous fragments of a wide variety of opium pipe bowls (Figure 44).

Brown stoneware shipping and storage jars of several shapes and sizes (Figure 45) are well represented in the artifact sample, as are traditional Chinese cups, bowls, sauce dishes, and teapots. Numerous fragments of ceramic rice bowls of the "Bamboo" pattern; small "Celadon" ("Winter Green") cups (Figure 46) of at least two different sizes; "Four Seasons" ("Four Flower") pattern serving bowls, cups, and sauce dishes (Figure 47); and teapots and cups of other patterns, some of Japanese manufacture (Figure 48), are all present in the artifact sample. Fragments of ceramic liquor containers (Figure 45, top row far right) were especially abundant along the riverbank and in surface dumps around the "China house" (Reese, 1986, 1989; Sullivan, 1983). Other Chinese artifacts represented within the riverbank trash deposit include a coin, a medicine bottle, a Chinese padlock and brass key, a fragment of a ceramic ink box stained with red ink, a fragment of a ceramic spoon, and several glass gaming pieces resembling items from the game *wei-ch'i* (Japanese, *go*) (Aero, 1980:123-124) (Figure 43). Other artifacts of Chinese origin found around the Chinese laborers' bunkhouse and

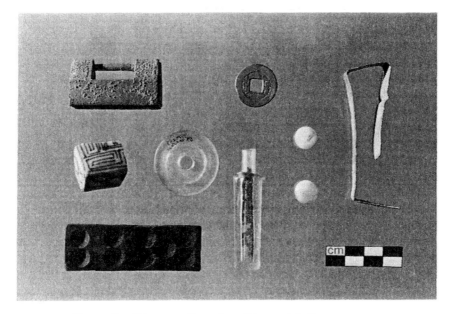

Figure 43. Chinese artifacts from Warrendale Cannery
(padlock, coin, opium can fragment, portion of a ceramic ink box, part of
a glass opium lamp, a medicine bottle, two gaming pieces, and a domino.)

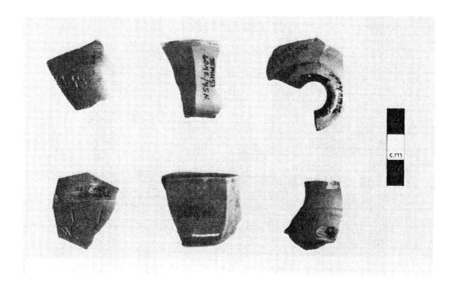

Figure 44. Opium pipe bowl fragments from the riverbank dump area.

Figure 45. Fragments of brown stoneware vessels from the
riverbank dump area.

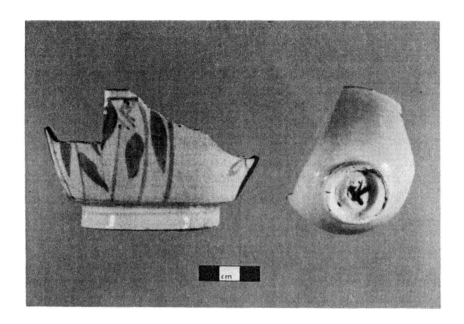

Figure 46. "Bamboo" pattern bowl and small "Winter Green" cup
fragments from the riverbank dump area.

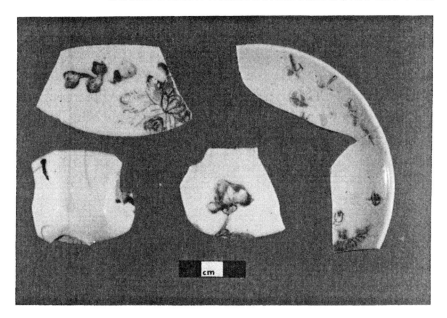

Figure 47. Fragments of "Four Seasons" pattern cup, bowls, and sauce dish from the riverbank dump area.

Figure 48. Fragments of teapots and cups from the riverbank dump area.

gardens include metal wok fragments (Sullivan, 1983) and a wooden domino (Figure 43).

Items of American manufacture associated with the Chinese ceramics and assumed to have been used by the Chinese include glass and rubber buttons; rubber and leather boot soles; glass beer, wine, and ale bottles; and a few fragments of white ironstone china and window glass.

In addition to the Chinese artifacts, there are a few fragments of Japanese rice bowls and cups (Figure 48, the two items at lower left). Business records for the cannery attest to the multi-ethnic mix of the workers which included Japanese, Korean, and Mexican laborers for the period after 1900. The ethnic groups present at the cannery between 1900 and the 1930s suggest that the Chinese were gradually being replaced by other ethnic groups. Perhaps, in part, this was a delayed reaction to the Chinese Exclusion Act of 1882. On the other hand, it may reflect the gradual change that occurred during the early to mid-1900s with the replacement of Chinese cannery workers by other nationalities and by American women and children.

CONCLUSIONS

The following conclusions regarding the Chinese laborers at the Warrendale Cannery can be offered. For the most part, the Chinese workers were "sojourners" who came to America to earn their fortunes before returning to China. While in America, and while working at the Warrendale Cannery, they comprised a male-dominated group devoid of Chinese women and children. They planned to stay only as long as it took to acquire adequate funds to assure a successful and well-respected life back home in China. Although this is probably true for the late 1800s by the early 1900s the Chinese were staying in America, and their children would become Americans.

Based on census records and informant interviews, the Chinese workers at Warrendale maintained their traditional Chinese culture and language. Few learned to speak English, and fewer still were able to read or write this foreign language. The Chinese maintained their traditional belief systems and, based on the archaeological record, continued to enjoy their own ethnic food prepared in traditional ways, using traditional utensils and cooking techniques, and served in familiar dishes.

Although work at the cannery required six ten- to eleven-hour days per week, the Chinese found time for gambling, drinking, and opium smoking. Although they consumed large quantities of both Chinese and American alcoholic beverages and frequently partook in opium smoking, their work was never reported to suffer from the effects.

According to informants, and as documented in historical photographs, the Chinese laborers wore American clothes (including shirts, pants, and leather and rubber boots) during working hours. During off-duty hours the Chinese workers changed into more comfortable traditional clothing, according to Eldon Sams, who recalled the period between 1918 and 1926. Sams also reported that several of the older men wore their hair in the traditional pigtail.

Acculturation was superficial. The Chinese workers only selected those few items of American culture which were indispensable for adapting to the particular job at hand: American work clothes, overalls, and rubber boots. They also consumed American alcoholic beverages as well as Chinese ones. Those who eventually left the United States endured their passage in the "land of the barbarians" until they were able to accumulate enough money to assure them of acquiring a wife and/or a secure retirement in China; they left America as soon as they could. Both those Chinese who left and those who stayed lived and worked within a traditional Chinese cultural system that operated within the dominant American culture but helped to isolate them from it. Chinatowns provided familiar places of refuge during the off-season, while alcohol, both American and Chinese, and opium might have eased the drudgery and tedium of cannery work.

REFERENCES CITED

AERO, RITA
    1980   *Things Chinese,* Dolphin Books, Doubleday & Company, Inc., Garden City, New York.

CORBETT, P. SCOTT and NANCY PARKER CORBETT
    1977   The Chinese in Oregon, c. 1870-1880, *Oregon Historical Quarterly, 78*:1, pp. 73-85.

THE DAILY ASTORIAN
    1887   Some Salmon Statistics Aggregate Pack for the Present Season Figures from Former Years of Business, manuscript in Oregon Historical Society vertical file: Salmon Fishing Industry, Astoria, August 9.

DONALDSON, I. J. and F. K. CRAMER
    1971   *Fishwheels of the Columbia,* Binfords and Mort, Portland, Oregon.

FRIDAY, CHRIS C.
    1982   Silent Sojourn: The Chinese along the Lower Columbia River, 1870-1900, unpublished Honors thesis, History Department, Lewis and Clark College, Portland.

JONES, W. A.
    1888   *The Salmon Fisheries of the Columbia River,* report of Major W. A. Jones, Corps of Engineers, 50th Congress, 1st Session, Senate Executive Document No. 123, Washington, D.C.

JORDAN, DAVID S.
    1897   The Columbia's Fish, *The Morning Oregonian,* Portland, Monday, May 31.

NORDHOFF, CHARLES
    1874   The Columbia River and Puget Sound, *Harper's New Monthly Magazine, 48*:285, pp. 338-348.

OREGON HISTORICAL SOCIETY
    n.d.   Frank M. Warren Packing Company Papers, MSS 1144, Portland, Oregon.

1906-   Warrendale Cannery Record Book, 1906-1910, MSS 1141, Portland, Oregon.
1910

THE OREGONIAN
1912   News item regarding the *Titanic* disaster and memorial services for the victims, April 21, Portland, Oregon.

PERRIN, LINDA
1980   *Coming to America: Immigrants from the Far East,* Delacorte Press, New York.

REESE, JO
1986   Microarchaeological Identification of Activity Areas in the Chinese Workers' Area at the Warrendale Cannery Site, Oregon, unpublished Master's thesis, Department of Anthropology, Washington State University, Pullman.
1989   Microarchaeological Analysis of the Chinese Workers' Area at the Warrendale Cannery Site, Oregon, *Contributions to the Archaeology of Oregon, 1987-1988,* R. Minor, (ed.), Association of Oregon Archaeologists, Occasional Papers No. 4, pp. 197-221.

SMITH, COURTLAND L.
1979   *Salmon Fishers of the Columbia,* Oregon State University Press, Corvallis.

SULLIVAN, DANIEL D.
1983   Archaeological Investigation of the China House at the Warrendale Cannery, 1876-1930, paper presented at the 16th Annual Meeting of the Society for Historical Archaeology, Denver.

U.S. BUREAU OF THE CENSUS
1880   Tenth Census of the United States, Population Schedules, Multnomah County, Oregon.
1900   Twelfth Census of the United States, Population Schedules, Multnomah County, Oregon.

CHAPTER 9

Besides Polly Bemis: Historical and Artifactual Evidence for Chinese Women in the West, 1848-1930

Priscilla Wegars

Although Chinese women have resided in the West for over 140 years, very little is known of them in general, and even less is known of particular individuals, especially those who were here before the turn of the century. If asked, some people could probably name Polly Bemis of Warrens, now Warren, Idaho, the subject of a non-fiction book (Elsensohn, 1979), a faithfully researched biographical novel (McCunn, 1981), and a recently released film based on the latter book. Besides Polly Bemis, however, few if any other names would come to mind. Most 19th century Chinese women were uneducated, and therefore would have been unable to keep journals or diaries of their experiences here; at least, none have yet been mentioned in the literature. No letters home are so far known to exist in China (Luchetti and Olwell, 1982:50), although a few have been located in the Federal Archives in Philadelphia (Judy Yung, 1987:personal communication) and elsewhere (Fisk University, 1946:34-35). Even where such documents do exist, however, they are likely to be written in Chinese.

The best hope for unearthing and deciphering such primary source materials is probably San Francisco's Chinese Women of America project (Novak, 1982:377). Some material from it has been effectively utilized in a pictorial history of Chinese women in the United States (Yung, 1986). Other relevant works are a collected biography of Chinese in the United States, including many women (McCunn, 1988); social histories of Chinese American women in Los Angeles (Cheng et al., 1984) and San Francisco (Yung, 1990); and a recent book on Chinese exclusion containing a lengthy chapter on this topic's effect upon Chinese women (Chan, 1991:94-146).

Previously, researchers had to rely on those books about the general Chinese experience in America with either a short chapter on Chinese women or occasional paragraphs about them in various places throughout the text (e.g., Daniels, 1988; Takaki, 1989). Some sources that discuss Chinese women unfortunately focus on them only as slave girls or prostitutes (e.g., Dillon, 1962:221-239). Works about women in the West, where one might expect to find information on Chinese women, often, disappointingly, have little (e.g., Jameson, 1988) or nothing (e.g., Blair, 1988).

This chapter will bring together some widely scattered information in both primary and secondary source materials in order to better document the presence of Chinese women in the West, and to chronicle their occupational transition away from enforced prostitution. A second aim is to examine the archaeological evidence for Chinese women in this country. Although Chinese women are often absent from the historical record, archaeological excavations on overseas Chinese sites have sometimes recovered artifacts indicative of their presence. These will be discussed in detail, as will relevant objects from museums and private collections.

IMMIGRATION—19th CENTURY

The first Chinese woman believed to have come to the United States, other than temporary entertainers (La Fargue, 1940:138; Lyman, 1970:23; Yung, 1986:14), landed in San Francisco in February, 1848. She arrived on the brig *Eagle* from Hong Kong, and had been brought over as a domestic servant by Charles Gillespie, an American missionary who was returning home (Chen, 1981:5). Other sources, while giving the same year, note that the woman's name was Maria or Marie Seise, and that Gillespie was an American lawyer and businessman, or trader (Char, 1975:42-43; Yung, 1986:14). Between 1848 and 1854 a total of only sixteen Chinese women immigrated to the United States, while during that same period 45,000 men arrived (McLeod, 1948:175; Dicker, 1979:7).

The reason for this large discrepancy in immigration figures lies in traditional Chinese customs and attitudes. In the first place, most of the Chinese men did not consider themselves immigrants; the vast majority of them originally came with the hope that they could earn more money here than in China, and then could return there with their savings. Not only did many of them have wives and families at home, it was also customary for the wife to reside with the husband's parents, serve her mother-in-law, have children (preferably boys), and venerate her husband's ancestors. At that time, custom required that Chinese women be subservient to men; a woman was expected to "serve her father when young, . . . her husband when married, and . . . her son when widowed" (Mark and Chih, 1982:61). So, while it was uncommon for a Chinese man to bring his wife with him to America, it would have been "unthinkable that any proper girl would go off on her own as an immigrant" (Chen, 1981:29).

Prostitution

A very few Chinese women did, however, come to the West on their own in the early years, mostly as prostitutes (Figure 49). Ah Toy or Ah-Choi (Hirata, 1979a:225) was one such woman. This legendary beauty was so famous in the early 1850s that block-long lines of men formed for the privilege of paying an ounce of gold worth $16, just to look at her (Yung, 1986:14). Ah Toy soon became the madam of her own brothel in San Francisco's Chinatown (McLeod, 1948:176-177; Chen, 1981:63). She represents one of "two distinct periods of prostitution in California" (Hirata, 1979b:7). The first was more of a free enterprise system, where the prostitute herself controlled her own services as well as the money she earned. This period was brief, lasting only until about 1854 (Hirata, 1979b:8). From then on, the prostitute became a commodity, owned and exploited by others, with no control over her own work or earnings. In Helena, Montana, for example, men controlled prostitution in Chinatown by 1880 (Petrik 1987:32).

By the mid-1850s young Chinese women began to arrive in the West in increasing numbers, often brought here by some of the tongs. Separate and distinct from the family-name and district-association groups to which most Chinese men belonged, the tongs were fraternal organizations or secret societies; most did not engage in illegal endeavors. (The word "tong" simply means "hall" or "parlor" (Tsai, 1986:51).) A few criminal tongs, however, controlled most of the under-world activities, particularly those related to gambling, opium smoking, and prostitution. This second, exploitative, period was much more the norm as far as Chinese prostitution was concerned. While prostitutes of other nationalities continued to be independent or were wage-earners, Chinese prostitutes during this era had virtually no control over their own destinies (Yung, 1986:18-20).

Imported by the tongs, supposedly to work as indentured servants, these women had been sold by poor parents in China, kidnapped, or lured with promises of lucrative employment (Yung, 1986:18) or marriage. Those servant girls (*mui jai*) (*mooi-tzai*), who were too young to become prostitutes upon arrival were virtual domestic slaves in their earlier years; later they might be resold into prostitution, often when they were still as young as twelve (Hirata, 1979a:229).

Some were luckier. Goon Gum-ying, or Martha Goon, who was born in China in 1884, was somehow in the Pacific Northwest in the 1890s when she was obtained by the entrepreneur Goon Dip as a servant girl for his wife. She was later adopted by the Goon family and married to Jue Wong-yuen, a protege of her adopted father (Lee, 1984:3-4).

For women sold into prostitution, an average sale figure was several hundred dollars; however, an exceptionally beautiful potential prostitute could be worth as much as $3000 (Mark and Chih, 1982:62). These transactions were extremely

Figure 49. Photograph of three Chinese prostitutes, "Marie," "Susie," and "Nellie," taken in 1866. Courtesy of Special Collections, University of Nevada-Reno Library, No. 1355.

profitable for the tongs. It was estimated, for example, that some 6000 women were imported by the Hip Yee Tong alone between 1852 and 1873, netting them $200,000 (Dillon, 1962:230-231); the name Hip Yee Tong translates, ironically, as "Temple of United Justice" (Dicker, 1979:8). The figure quoted seems rather low; however, it probably only reflects the profit after sale, once fares and bribes were paid. Other estimates suggest that even a lower-grade brothel with nine prostitutes, in 1870, would have netted the owner about $5000 per year (Hirata, 1979a:234).

Because this trade was so lucrative, inter-tong warfare over its control flared in San Francisco during the 1870s and 1880s (Yung, 1986:18). Lurid accounts in the popular press, together with anti-Chinese feelings, contributed to the then-prevalent notion that Chinese prostitution was somehow worse than any other kind (Yung, 1986:20). Laws were passed against Chinese prostitution, and, as Judy Yung points out (1986:20), ironically this "made immigration difficult for all Chinese women, thereby increasing the demand and raising the value of prostitutes." A need to control the "evils of Chinese prostitution" was one reason for passage of the 1875 immigration act that, in part, prohibited ". . . importation . . . of women for the purposes of prostitution . . ." (United States Code, 1875:477-478).

In terms of numbers, in 1860 there were over eighteen Chinese males for every Chinese female (Lyman, 1974:88); only 1784 Chinese women were registered in the United States (Luchetti and Olwell, 1982:50). By 1870, San Francisco's Chinatown had an estimated 159 brothels (Mark and Chih, 1982:62), and of 1769 Chinese females in that city who were over the age of fifteen, 1452 were prostitutes.

The Chinese generally recognized two types of prostitutes: higher-class ones, who had relations with Chinese men only, and lower-class ones, whose clientele included anyone who could pay their lower fees (Hirata, 1979b:13). The lower-class prostitutes were poorly-housed and badly treated. The upper-class ones, in contrast, generally lived in attractive surroundings and had fine clothes and jewelry; if they entertained at parties they were allowed to keep any gifts given to them (Hirata, 1979b:14). In general, however, these latter women were the exception. As prostitutes, Chinese women were usually condemned to suffer lives of unrelieved degradation (Yung, 1986:18-19).

During the years of various city "Expositions," Chinese women were brought to this country ostensibly to work as dancers in Chinese pavilions. However, they were often sold into prostitution even before reaching the event, or shortly afterwards. This trick was worked in the 1880s for at least one of several Atlanta fairs (Dillon, 1962:226), and surfaced again for later Expositions. For example, in 1894 a number of Chinese, most of whom were women, arrived in San Francisco for the Midwinter Fair. Suspecting deception, a special agent for the Treasury Department investigated the Chinese village and found only thirty-seven of the 257 Chinese who were supposed to be there (Dillon, 1962:319-320). Most of the women had been sold into slavery. In 1898, seventy "Oriental maidens" were admitted by a special Act of Congress for the Omaha Exposition; some thirty of them actually ended up in San Francisco (Martin, 1977:55-57).

Several factors aside from the substantial financial rewards contributed to this widespread immoral traffic in Chinese women. First, female children in China were usually considered more of a liability than male children, since "they were basically raised for the benefit of another family: once a woman married, she was considered a member of her husband's clan" (Dicker, 1979:7). In times of poverty, female children were sometimes sold into wealthier families, either as servants or as potential daughters-in-law; female infanticide was also practiced, at least among the poorest classes. Protestant missionaries estimated that the percentage of female infants killed was "as high as 70 percent" around 1836, and "up to 40 percent" in 1848 (Miller, 1969:67). Female children could also be sold to dealers who raised them as prostitutes, or to "prostitutes who adopted daughters to raise in their profession as support for their own old age" (Wolf, 1968:100). This "economic manipulation" of girls and women "could . . . yield resources convertible into property belonging to men" (Gates, 1989:814).

The life of an Idaho Chinese woman typifies the experiences of many. Polly Bemis, whose Chinese name was Lalu Nathoy, was born in China in 1853. Traded by her father for two bags of seed grain during a famine year, Polly was resold as a slave girl and later auctioned in San Francisco for $2500. She arrived at the mining camp of Warrens, now Warren, in 1872, the property of one Hong King, who had bought her as a hostess for his gambling hall and saloon. There is no evidence to suggest that she was ever a prostitute in the commonly-accepted sense; although she was Hong King's concubine, he seems to have kept her for his exclusive use. Her story has been much romanticized (Elsensohn, 1979) because she was reportedly won by Charlie Bemis in a poker game. In 1890, Bemis was shot over a gambling debt and Polly nursed him back to health; they were married in 1894. She obtained a certificate of residence in 1896, listing her occupation as "laborer" (Elsensohn, 1979:26). In her later years Polly Bemis was a beloved local celebrity; she died in 1933. Her life has since been portrayed in a well-researched fictionalized biography (McCunn, 1981), which was released as a movie, "1000 Pieces of Gold," in 1991.

The Presbyterian Mission Home — Concerned citizens of San Francisco, including many Chinese, were outraged at the continuing traffic in women, and in 1873 the Presbyterian Woman's Occidental Board of Foreign Missions founded a group that began to combat the evil practices they deplored (Martin, 1977:51). Beginning in 1874, these people established the Presbyterian Mission Home to care for the first slaves who were persuaded to run away from their masters. By the 1890s prostitutes and slaves were being actively rescued by this organization. In 1895, Donaldina Cameron came to help as an assistant to Margaret Culbertson, the Home's first Superintendent. Following Culbertson's death in 1897, Cameron succeeded her (Martin, 1977:21-22). Over the years, Cameron became an expert in leading daring night raids, accompanied by the police. She is credited, some say, with the rescue of nearly 3000 girls and women between 1895 and the late 1930s (Martin, 1977:23), not only in San Francisco, but in the East Bay, Fresno, Sacramento, Los Angeles, Red Bluff, Santa Barbara, and elsewhere (Martin, 1977:154, 166).

The rescued girls and women could choose whether they wished to remain in the United States or return to China. About half chose to return and, of the remainder, many were legally adopted by Miss Cameron. At the Home they learned English and were taught various skills, including sewing, cooking, and homemaking. Some married and raised families, while others went on to careers, becoming, in the 20th century, teachers, nurses, secretaries, seamstresses, and clerks. One, Tye Leung, who had run away to the Mission to escape an arranged marriage, was the Chinese interpreter and assistant to the matrons on Angel Island when it opened in 1910 (Lai, Lim, and Yung, 1980:16; Yung, 1986:54), while another earned her M.D. in the early 1930s (Martin, 1977:247).

It should be noted, however, that not all of the women welcomed rescue, and a few even refused it or ran away; the austerity of life in the Home may have compared unfavorably with the opulence that some of them had previously enjoyed. Among the working classes, the practice of prostitution in China did not carry the same stigma as it did, and does, in this country. For example, a study of a more recent Chinese farm family points out that, in China, a prostitute's "morality" and "respectability" are not based upon her profession (Wolf, 1968:103):

> Too many village girls have had to 'go out to work' to support aging parents or young siblings; . . . women become prostitutes . . . because their family is desperately in need of the income.

Because "Chinese children are expected to make great sacrifices for their parents," such women are not considered martyrs, and neither are they likely to be criticized, for they have, according to Wolf (1968:103), repaid the debt owed the parents

> . . . more fully than the daughter who remains at home can ever hope to do. By giving up her youth, the young prostitute has gained a certain amount of control over her future. In the village her respectability depends upon how careful she is to walk within the paths of traditional morality when she is home for a few days each month, how compliant she is in turning over the majority of her earnings to her parents, and how cautious she is with village males.

Traffic in women continued into the early 20th century and was greatly aided by the connivance and complicity of non-Chinese immigration, customs, steamship, and police officials, who regularly accepted bribes for their cooperation. In San

Francisco, for example, "a quarter of the profits made in the importation of prostitutes was earned by non-Chinese" (Mark and Chih, 1982:62).

Marriages — Prostitutes could later make respectable marriages, provided they had not "compromised their future by a series of abortions, illegitimate children, or the adoption of young girls for the support of their old age;" it was thought that such young women might be "less likely to succumb to temptation after marriage" (Wolf, 1968:107). In spite of their backgrounds, then, the women rescued by Donaldina Cameron were in demand as wives. For Chinese laborers, who were often forbidden by law from marrying white women, marriage to ex-prostitutes was far cheaper than bringing brides over from China (Judy Yung, 1986:personal communication).

Lucie Cheng Hirata's research (1979a:236-237) found that the number of Chinese housewives in California increased dramatically between 1870 (753, or 21%) and 1880 (1445, or 46%). She noted that the census enumerators assigned the designation "keeping house" only "to women who were not performing household functions for pay, and who reported no other occupations;" she speculated that a proportion of the married women were former prostitutes (Hirata, 1979a:237). Some of the Chinese women reported as "keeping house" might have been involved in polyandrous relationships such as those reportedly "encountered" by Henryk Sienkiwicz in 1880 (Lyman, 1970:50). The 1882 Chinese Exclusion Act, which barred entry into the United States for Chinese laborers, was also extended to their wives through a court interpretation that wives had the legal status of their husbands and could therefore be excluded as well (Lyman, 1970:50). Thus, Chinese men may have turned to ex-prostitutes for marriage partners more frequently due to the difficulty of entry for women from China, particularly during the exclusion period.

Not all brides, of course, were former prostitutes; some were from respectable Chinese families and came to this country for arranged marriages (Far, 1897: 60-62), or following such marriages. The "first Chinese wedding in California" and, therefore, probably in the United States, took place in Mokelumne Hill in August 1853, when "Keong Asking of Hong Kong and Tiss Ahew of Titsing, China were married by Judge Henry Enos" (Cunningham, 1986:1). From 1858 to 1886, eighteen Chinese marriages were recorded in Shasta County, California (Hoffpauir, 1986); from 1860 to 1882 an additional sixteen Chinese marriages were performed in California's Calaveras County (Cunningham, 1987).

Chinese women not only got married in this country, they also got divorced. When one did in California, it was news even in Moscow, Idaho (*Moscow Mirror*, 8(33):4, February 7, 1890):

> Fook Toy, a Chinese woman, has been granted a divorce from Fook Kan, at San Jose, Cal., on the ground of extreme cruelty. The parties were married by a justice of the peace about a year ago. This is said to be the first Chinese divorce in the state. The defend[a]nt did not appear.

Another divorce reported twenty years later, in 1910, was said to be "probably the first" Chinese divorce in the United States. Mrs. Josie Hung divorced W. Q. Hung, "the once wealthy resident of Denver's Chinatown," but would pay a high price in "social ostracism" for her decree. Her marriage to him, some eighteen years previously, was arranged by her parents, who "sold her to Hung for $750," when she was fourteen years old and he was thirty-four. She claimed that "all he wanted her to do was to work," and that he also had "a wife in China, to whom he sends money annually" (*Bonners Ferry Herald*, *20*(19):8, November 5, 1910).

Other Occupations

Chinese women turned away from prostitution in increasing numbers as other avenues beside marriage gradually became open to them. While California census records for 1860 and 1870 show that the majority of Chinese women were prostitutes, by 1880 prostitution took second place (24%) to "keeping house" (46%) (Hirata, 179a:228, 236). The California census lists additional occupations for Chinese women during 1860, 1870, and 1880 (Table 34). Only the top ten wage-earning categories are included. "Keeping house" was not considered a wage-earning occupation even though many of those women also took in sewing or did other work that was not counted; some had several boarders or lodgers in their own households (Hirata, 1979a:238-239). One woman, who came over to join her miner husband, made cigarettes and did sewing (Loomis, 1869:350), but she probably would have been listed as a housewife rather than as a wage-earner, if indeed the census taker even learned of her other activities (Cheng et al., 1984:7). Wives of small businessmen who helped their husbands were probably not paid; although they were certainly part of the work force, they would not have been so listed (Cheng et al. 1984:7).

As far back as 1860, twenty-eight women in San Francisco had occupations of laundress or washerwoman, gardener, fisherwoman, laborer, storekeeper, clerk, and tailoress (Hirata, 1979b:23). In 1880, census records there showed 250 United States-born Chinese women who were not prostitutes. Of these, "227 were housewives, while the rest were students, apprentices, housekeepers, and seamstresses" (Hirata, 1979b:21, 23). In comparison, the top occupational categories for white women for the years 1860-1880 included teaching and nursing (Hirata, 1979a:236), opportunities that were still not available to Chinese women.

The few women who were wives of Chinese merchants generally led more leisured, secluded lives revolving around their husbands and children. The home was most often a family quarters located upstairs from the husband's business. Those who had household servants "usually filled their leisure time with needlework" (Cheng et al., 1984:7). Until the birth of their first child, they were not often seen in public, and then only at Chinese New Year, weddings, and funerals, and sometimes at the (Chinese) theater (Cheng et al., 1984:7). It was said of Chinese wives living in America that, on the whole, they were pleased, mainly because

Table 34. Hierarchical Primary Occupations of Chinese Women in California
(Adapted from Hirata, 1979a:236)

1860	1870	1880
Prostitute[a]	Prostitute, 61%[b]	Keeping house, 46%[f]
Wife/possible wife	Keeping house, 21%[b]	Prostitute, 24%[g]
Laundress	Servant	Seamstress, $n = 192$[e]
Miner, $n = 63$[b]	Laundress	Servant
Servant	Seamstress, $n = 36$[e]	Laundress
Laborer	Miner, $n = 29$[b]	Cook
Seamstress	Housekeeper	Needlework
Housekeeper	Fisherman [sic]	Actress
Cook	Shoe binder	Laborer[h]
Gardener	Cook	Miner, $n = 11$[b]
Lodging house operator	Laborer	Lodging house operator
Total: 1784[c] or 2006[d]	3536 adults[d]	3171 adults; 3686 total[i]

[a]Inferred; not an occupational category in 1860. Probably close to the 85 percent postulated for San Francisco alone, since the figures for 1870 and 1880 for San Francisco's Chinese prostitutes are 71 percent and 21 percent of the Chinese female adult population (Hirata, 1979b:23-24).
[b]Hirata, 1979a:235.
[c]Luchetti and Olwell, 1982:50.
[d]Hirata, 1979a:227.
[e]Hirata, 1979a:239.
[f]Of 3171 adults (Hirata, 1979a:236).
[g]Of 3171 adults (Hirata, 1979a:228).
[h]Most were railroad workers (Hirata, 1979a:236).
[i]Hirata, 1979a:227-228.

they did not become subject to the husbands' mothers, as they would have had they remained in China (Far, 1897:60).

In 1882, the Chinese Exclusion Act was passed in response to the rising resentment felt by most white Americans against Chinese laborers. While it did not specifically prohibit the entry of women into the United States, decisions in subsequent court cases ruled that the Act also applied to wives of Chinese laborers, even if their husbands already resided there. Certain classes of people, particularly students, teachers, tourists, diplomats, and merchants, were still able to enter (Chen, 1981:148), as could their wives. Although passage of the 1875 immigration law made it harder for women to be brought in for "lewd and immoral purposes," the various exclusion laws did not halt the traffic in women, but made it more difficult, resulting in higher prices. For example, "slave girls, who brought $1000 before the exclusion law of 1882, ranged in price from $2000 to $3000 thereafter" (Palmer, 1934:25).

Increasingly, throughout the 19th century, Chinese women could be found in occupations besides prostitution. In addition, foreign-born Chinese women were beginning to take advantage of previously unavailable educational opportunities in the United States, perhaps paving the way for a more ready acceptance of American-born Chinese women into non-traditional fields during the 20th century. In 1885 Dr. King Ya-Mei, a Chinese woman adopted by Americans as a small child, was awarded a medical degree from Cornell, and in 1894 Dr. Hu King Eng obtained her degree from the same institution (Abbott, 1976:243). Both, however, returned to China once they had completed their education (Judy Yung, 1986:personal communication).

Judy Yung has commented that another stimulus to increasing numbers of Chinese women being educated both in China and abroad was China's Reform Movement (1898-1908), which advocated women's equality. She noted that missions in Chinatown encouraged women's education, and parents began to see the importance of a public school education for their daughters. By 1900, American-born Chinese females in the United States outnumbered those born in China (Judy Yung, 1987:personal communication).

IMMIGRATION—20th CENTURY

A 1910 survey of the marital status of Chinese laborers in five industries across several states showed that 67 percent (163 men) were married at the time; of these, only nine had wives in the United States (Lyman, 1974:90). In the early years of the 20th century, Chinese men in increasing numbers began sending to China for their wives and families. Because of the 1882 Exclusion Act, however, only United States citizens or merchants could bring in female family members, and from then until 1943 an average of only 215 Chinese women per year immigrated to the United States (Yung, 1986:42).

In the early years of the 20th century, those few women who were allowed to immigrate first had to endure the rigors of entry at Angel Island (Lai, Lim, and Yung, 1980). Once admitted, the women often joined their husbands at work, becoming waitresses, cooks, or store clerks, or washing and ironing in the laundries (Mark and Chih, 1982:66). Those whose husbands were not businessmen looked elsewhere for employment, working in the canneries, sewing, peeling shrimp, gathering watercress, or opening clams (Mark and Chih, 1982:67, 72); some also found jobs as fruit pickers (Martin, 1977:177). Contemporary photographs show Chinese women working in a variety of occupations; one of unknown date depicts "Chinese Mary," described as a laundress in Virginia City, Montana (Randall, 1961:24). Bilingual telephone operators (Dicker, 1979:109) and store clerks were hired in San Francisco's Chinatown, but these opportunities generally went to American-born Chinese women (Judy Yung, 1986, 1987: personal communications). Because immigrant Chinese women usually could not speak English when they arrived, were generally uneducated, and lacked skills marketable in the United States, domestic work jobs were most often the only ones open to them (Judy Yung, 1987:personal communication).

The "first modern-trained Chinese woman dentist in the world," (Chen, 1981:220), Faith So Leung, graduated from dental school in San Francisco in 1905 (Yung, 1986:50, 55). On May 14, 1912 Tye Leung Schulze of San Francisco was the first Chinese American woman to vote in a primary election (Yung, 1986:54; Soo, 1986:2), although another source says that 1920 was the first year that a Chinese American woman cast a ballot (Chen, 1981:220). This discrepancy can be explained by the fact that California gave women the vote in 1911, before the nation did in 1920. One source reported that the "first Chinese woman registered to vote" was Clara Lee of Oakland, California, who was born in Portland in 1886 (Gan, 1986:16).

Margaret Chung, the first Chinese American woman to become a physician, did so in 1916 (Yung, 1986:50). Her accomplishment went unrecognized by another source, who gives the honor to Dr. Rose Goong Wong in 1925 (Abbott, 1976:246). Although Chinese American women were finding educational opportunities beginning to open for them, employment was not yet keeping pace. Dr. Chung, who graduated from the University of Southern California's medical school, could not find work in Los Angeles and had to go instead to San Francisco (Cheng et al., 1984:23). Carolyn Chan, a 1920s graduate of the University of Southern California, had secondary school teaching credentials but could not find a secondary teaching job in either the Los Angeles or San Francisco area; the best she could hope for was teaching English to immigrant Chinese women (Cheng et al., 1984:24). Effie Chew was more fortunate. She was able to begin her teaching career at Oakland, California's Lincoln School in 1918 (Soo, 1976:255).

In the mid-1920s actress Anna May Wong began to win national recognition for her work (Chen, 1981:221), appearing in some 100 films between 1919 and 1942 (McCunn, 1979:125). Louise Leung Larson became a Los Angeles journalist, Katherine Cheung was a daring aviatrix, and Soong Yee was a successful flower farmer (Cheng et al., 1984:24, 72-74). The fullest account of the pre-war accomplishments of these and other Chinese-American women can be found in Yung (1986:48-66).

Pioneering Chinese-American women had begun to participate in many facets of American life during the pre-war years; for most others, the coming of World War II was the turning point. Primarily due to China's wartime alliance with the United States, American attitudes toward China and Chinese Americans improved significantly (Judy Yung, 1986, 1987:personal communications).

The 1882 Exclusion Act was extended in 1888, renewed in 1892 and in 1902, and was extended indefinitely in 1904 (Wegars, 1991:566-587). Anti-Chinese hysteria reached a new peak in 1924 when the Immigration Act of that year was passed. This "Second Exclusion Act," as it was sometimes called (Chen, 1981:176), meant that even Chinese who had been born in America could not bring over wives or children who had been born in China (Chen, 1981:176). From

1924 to 1930, no Chinese wives legally entered the United States (Mark and Chih, 1982:61). This was a devastating blow to the Chinese community, since by then many men were working and saving for the day when they could afford to send for their families, rather than just visiting them every few years as had been customary. Judy Yung notes, however, that except for brief periods during exclusion when their admittance was being contested, merchants' wives (Figure 50) were always allowed entry (Judy Yung, 1987: personal communication). These injustices lasted until 1943 (Yung, 1986:42).

Lucie Cheng et al. describe an even more discriminatory result of the exclusion laws. Under the provisions of the Cable Act of 1922, enforced until 1930 (Judy Yung, 1987:personal communication), a woman of Chinese ancestry born in the United States could be stripped of her citizenship if she married a person who was not eligible for citizenship. Prior to her marriage, Alice Mar Wong, born in Weaverville, California, was an American citizen with the right to vote and the right to purchase property. In 1924, she lost her citizenship because of her marriage to a non-citizen, and only was able to regain it through naturalization following the repeal of the Chinese Exclusion Act in 1943 (Cheng et al., 1984:9-10).

With the repeal of the Exclusion Act, the Chinese could apply for admission to the United States under the quota laws, but these allowed the admittance of only 105 Chinese persons per year. Chinese women benefitted most from the passage of the 1945 War Brides Act and the 1946 Fiancees Act (Cheng et al. 1984: 10), which allowed them to enter as non-quota immigrants (Yung, 1986:80).

ARTIFACTUAL EVIDENCE

Census records and other documents show that Chinese women were present in the western United States, but were far fewer in number than were Chinese men. While overseas Chinese archaeological sites yield much evidence for Chinese occupation, in the form of objects imported from China (particularly ceramics, medicine bottles, coins, and opium paraphernalia), these artifacts cannot tell us the sex of their users, although it is usually assumed to be male. Written documentation for individual sites is generally scanty at best.

Because Chinese women were originally present in such small numbers in the West, it is not surprising that there is little trace of them in the archaeological record. The few relevant artifacts that are known from archaeological reports will be briefly summarized. In addition, other objects of Chinese manufacture, which originally would have been owned by Chinese women, are sometimes seen in museums and private collections. Since such objects generally have the potential for being found archaeologically, they too will be discussed. Not included here are Euroamerican artifacts with female associations which have been recovered on Chinese sites, and museum collections of Euroamerican clothing and jewelry which belonged to Chinese women.

Figure 50. Greta [Mrs. Harry] Fong in her wedding finery, 1927.
Mr. Fong was a merchant in Boise, Idaho. He returned to China to be married,
and brought his bride back to Idaho at a time when wives of merchants could
enter but wives of others could not. Photograph by Ansgar Johnson Sr.,
courtesy of Raymond Fong; print courtesy Lois Palmgren.

Several items relating to Chinese women were found during an archaeological project at Lovelock, Nevada in 1977. The site, at Ninth and Amherst, was identified as the location of Chinese homes and businesses from 1900 until the 1930s (Jensen and Rusco, 1979:61). Some of the artifacts were excavated, and others came from the loft of a standing building. Included in the assemblage are jewelry, a hairdressing stand, cosmetic packages, a medicine bottle wrapper or label, and a fan handle. While other jewelry was recovered, only two excavated pieces, an earring and a decorated heart, bear Chinese characters.

The earring is bright yellow-gold, measuring 27 mm in diameter and 7.5 mm in width. Decoration is formed by five-petalled flowers and dragonflies, in relief. The post is undecorated, as the earring was intended for a pierced ear (Callaway, 1979:302, Figure 21a). Four characters are stamped onto the inside of the piece. On the left they read *yuán jīn (yüan chin)*, meaning "natural, true, or original" gold; on the right they read *tían yuán (t'ien yüan, tin yuen* in Cantonese), "which is the store name of a goldsmith listed in the 1913 Chinese International Business Directory at 737 Jackson Street, San Francisco" (Wey, 1979:544). A similar earring, though broken, was recovered from the Chew Kee Store in Fiddletown, California (Callaway, 1979:303). It has no inscription and is not gold (Wey, 1979:544). Another such earring is in the Asian American Comparative Collection at the University of Idaho's Laboratory of Anthropology (Figure 51), and others can be seen worn by Chinese women in old photographs (Luchetti and Olwell, 1982:54).

The heart found at the Ninth and Amherst site is also gold, with a jadeite stone in the center. It measures 9 × 10 mm, with an outline and a border of twisted gold wire. A spot of solder on the back "indicates a finding was once attached;" the heart was probably "a stud of some sort" (Callaway, 1979:302, Figure 21b). Four characters, one partially obliterated, appear on the back of the piece. The two on the left read *? jīn (t'ing chin)*, or "definitely gold;" if those on the right are *tì shēng (tai sang;* Cantonese, *tie sang)*, which seems likely, then this was "the store name of another San Francisco goldsmith . . . at 1005 Grant Avenue" (Wey, 1979:544).

Photographic sources at times show Chinese women, as well as Chinese men, wearing bracelets on their wrists (Elsensohn, 1970:Plate XIV; Lee, 1981:10). These are presumed to be of jade, which, to the Chinese, represents nobility, purity, and virtue; it also is thought to help keep travellers safe from harm (Jones, Davis, and Ling, 1979:40).

Fragments of what were reported to be jade bracelets were found during excavations at Idaho City (Jones, Davis, and Ling, 1979:40-41) and at Boise's Chinatown (Jones, 1980a:47-48). Another in the Asian American Comparative Collection, was collected by the author near northern Idaho's Cabinet Landing site, 10-BR-413. While these fragments appear to be stone, an elemental composition analysis has revealed that they are mostly, but not entirely, glass. Minerals of a jadeite nature, in minute quantities, are incorporated into the material of the bracelets (Charles R. Knowles, 1989:personal communication).

(a)

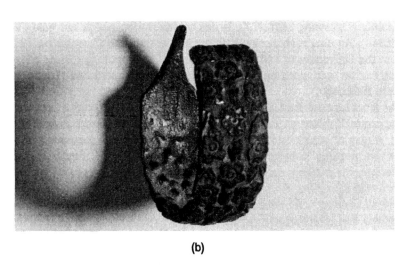

(b)

Figure 51. Chinese woman's earring, found in Idaho.
a) front, b) back. Asian American Comparative Collection, ACC-86-50.

It is possible that the fragments may instead be glass rings from the lids of sewing baskets. Decorated also with Chinese coins, beads, and tassels, these baskets came in many sizes and were popular during the 1920s, mostly among Euroamerican women. They are, however, still used in rural China as sewing baskets (Roderick Sprague, 1991:personal communication). While the baskets and their decorative elements were all imported from China, some are known to have been assembled in this country by Chinese families who attached the separate components to the tops of the baskets (John Fagan, 1983:personal communication).

The glass rings used on the sewing baskets may originally have been manufactured as bangles to be worn on the wrist. They "can be for babies, for males, and/or females. Jade is worn for protection as well as ornament so glass is not a substitute" (Ruthanne Lum McCunn, 1986:personal communication). For this reason, although the glass bangles are often similar in appearance to the jade bracelets, they are not likely to have been worn with the intent to deceive by person who could not afford the genuine article. However, a minute amount of jade added to the glass may have provided economical protection. Fragments of several glass "bracelets" found in Fiddletown, California, are now in a local private collection (Julia Costello, 1987:personal communication); excavations at Riverside, California produced fragments of one jade bracelet and pieces of three bracelets made of "Peking glass" (Noah, 1987:396-397, 402-405). The latter report cites several sources indicating that glass bracelets were worn or given away by Chinese persons.

Early photographs of Chinese in the United States often show both men and women holding fans. An ivory fan handle was found during the Lovelock, Nevada excavations. It is carved in a latticed, floral pattern, and measures 19.2 × 1.5 × .8 cm, and the plain end is split to hold the fan (Brown, 1979:575; Figure 18). Wooden remains of a fan handle, probably Chinese, were recovered from a Palus (Indian) burial at a site in eastern Washington (Sprague, 1965:8).

A rosewood hairdressing stand, complete with five of the six original glass inlaid pictorial panels, was also found at Lovelock, Nevada, in a loft. It has compartments for combs, brushes, and other items, and a drawer that may have held a mirror (Brown, 1979:572, 575; Figure 15). One picture, of a woman, is "an auspicious symbol, wishing that the beauty of the woman who uses the stand be immortal" (Wey, 1979:543).

Cosmetic packages found in the loft included two boxes of face powder, one full and one empty, as well as their wrappers; rouge packaging material; and a brown-glazed ceramic jar which once contained perfume or incense (Brown, 1979:571-572, Figures 13-14). The face powder wrappers translate "Snow Beauty Facial Powder Kum Tin Gut Manufacturer one cent silver each box," and the boxes themselves measure 5.35 × 3.80 × 2.06 cm (Brown, 1979:572, Figure 13). The rouge packaging material was accordion-folded cardboard with paper labels pasted to the ends; these translate "Kin Tin Gut Extra Concentrated Rouge" (Brown, 1979:572, Figure 14). The ceramic jar, with a brown glaze inside and out, was originally sealed with a strip of pasted red paper which held the lid onto the jar. Glued to the top of the lid was a label describing the contents as perfume or incense from Guangdong (Brown, 1979:572, Figure 14).

Also from the loft was a fragmentary wrapper or label from a medicine bottle. The medicine was for "restoring the strength and building up the blood of women who were menstruating or who had given birth to a child." A unicorn and pagoda are pictured, and the characters *wán yìng (wan ying)*, translating as "ten thousand uses," appear on the label fragment (Wey, 1979:545). Two small teardrop-shaped bottles with intact red paper labels are housed in the Asian American Comparative Collection at the Laboratory of Anthropology, University of Idaho; these once contained "eye medicine for old ladies" (Dora Mih, 1982:personal communication).

Bottles which once contained a cologne called "Florida water" are sometimes found on overseas Chinese archaeological sites. One is known from a private collection in Boise, Idaho (Verna McConnell, 1983:personal communication), and others have been found in Cumberland, British Columbia (Bressie and Bressie, 1972:[103]). Another was recovered from an overseas Chinese site in North Queensland, Australia (Jack, Holmes, and Kerr, 1984:56, 57, Figure 11).

Florida water is a lightly-scented floral cologne which has been manufactured since at least the mid-1800s (Moss, 1968:40). Its use was probably not confined to women, since the bottles have been recovered from sites at which women are not known to have been present. It is still being produced today. "Girl Brand" (Moss, 1968:42) or "Two Girls Brand" (Asian American Comparative Collection artifact CCC-84-61), made by the Kwong Sang Hong Company of Hong Kong (Moss, 1968:41, 42), is available in at least four sizes in stores selling Chinese goods. Chinese characters embossed on the bottles, from right to left reading *shuāng mèi me huā lù shuǐ*, translate as "Twin Sister (Brand) Flower Dew Water" (Wei Du, 1985:personal communication). The similarity of the Chinese words "Flower Dew" to "Florida" is remarkable, and no doubt deliberate.

As a child, Annie Soo was acquainted with an elderly Chinese woman with bound feet, whose granddaughters would "bring a wash basin and a pitcher of warm water to bathe her feet. They would sprinkle a little Florida water into the basin" (Soo, 1976:254).

Early photographs occasionally show women wearing hair ornaments (Luchetti and Olwell, 1982:55) similar to ones which are known from a private collection of artifacts from Cumberland, British Columbia (Bressie and Bressie, 1972:100), and others which are illustrated with more "women's adornments" elsewhere (Williams, 1941:98). A late 19th century source notes that some women wore "large fantastic pins" in their hair (Far, 1897:62). A fragment of a carved and decorated bone hair pick was recovered at Riverside, California (Noah, 1987:408-409); modern bone hair picks, although plain, can still be purchased in San Francisco's Chinatown. Chinese women were also present in Los Angeles' Chinatown; as "women's jewelry, shoes, [and] beads" have been recovered from recent Metro Rail excavations there (Chang, 1990:B4, quoting archaeologist Roberta Greenwood).

Two types of wooden Chinese hair combs are frequently seen in museum and private collections, and examples of both were recovered from the San Francisco Waterfront excavations. These do not appear in the published report, but are in storage at the Lowie Museum, University of California, Berkeley. Both types of combs may have been used by both men and women, and modern examples can still be purchased. Those with two rows of closely-set teeth may occasionally have been used for removing head lice (Connie Chou, 1985:personal communication) or, more likely, dandruff (Ruthanne Lum McCunn, 1986:personal communication); both statements have been confirmed by a third informant (Wei Du, 1986:personal communication). A comb from the Palus burial site has a Chinese inscription that translates as "From our house to your house with good wishes" (Roderick Sprague, 1991:personal communication).

Occasionally, one finds objects in museum collections that were made in China and that could have been used by Chinese women. Examples include inlaid boxes and trays, and what is described as a "Chinese marriage cup" (Sr. M. Catherine Manderfeld, 1988:personal communication). A headdress somewhat similar to that already depicted in Figure 50 can be seen in the Jake Jackson Museum in Weaverville, California.

Clothing is naturally not likely to be recovered archaeologically, and of the few Chinese garments that have been preserved in museums, most would have been worn by men. The Idaho State Historical Society in Boise, however, does have one example of a very interesting artifact once worn by a woman. It is a shoe for a bound foot, and is about five inches long. Such shoes are known from other museums, such as one in Cottonwood, Idaho (Sr. M. Catherine Manderfeld, 1988:personal communication), and from private collections; a tiny pair of shoes belonging to a San Francisco woman was once worn by her mother (Vyolet Chu, 1985:personal communication). The custom of footbinding, overly-sensationalized in the past, is one which today arouses revulsion in most people. A knowledge of how the practice developed might lead to a more enlightened understanding of it.

Footbinding may have originated in northwest China just over 1000 years ago (Osgood, 1975:1003), probably as an innovation by palace dancers (Levy, 1967:45). In subsequent years it came to be considered an attribute of general feminine beauty. It was never accepted by the Manchus, founders of the Qing dynasty (1644-1911), however, and although they attempted to ban it by imperial decree in 1902 (Levy, 1967:18), they were not entirely successful during their reign. Footbinding did not die out completely until perhaps as late as the middle of the 20th century, and a few women with bound feet, particularly merchants' wives, were among Chinese women who immigrated to the West in the 19th century. Men who purchased wives or concubines would generally pay a higher price for women with bound feet than for those with unbound feet (Trull, 1946:97). As recently as 1983, some two million women with bound feet still survived in China, and approximately one million pairs of tiny shoes were then being made each year (Shing, 1983:4D).

Binding the feet was an indication of a woman's social position; bound feet rendered a girl useless for physical labor, so it was only the wealthier or upwardly mobile families who could afford that luxury. Footbinding was usually begun before the age of seven, and at first was intensely painful. "After the first few years there was little or no pain involved" (Osgood, 1975:1003). The bandages stopped the foot's growth, and were seldom permanently removed; the tiny shoes were worn over them. A fact seldom mentioned, but perhaps the main reason why the custom lasted so long, was that the bound feet, called "golden lotuses" or "golden lilies," became a fetish with men (Shing, 1983:4B):

> . . . unbinding the foot and fondling it was an integral part of making love. Kissing a woman's unbound foot was considered infinitely more erotic than kissing her lips.

Such scenes are common in Chinese erotic art (Beurdeley, 1969:188). A more scholarly account describes the history of footbinding and its erotic implications; interviews with bound-foot women are a major contribution (Levy, 1967).

Ample evidence exists in old photographs for the type of clothing which was worn by Chinese women in this country, usually "a large-sleeved robe of silk or cotton, over a long garment, under which are loose trousers sometimes fastened around the ankle" (Williams, 1941:97, 99). Wishing to distinguish themselves from prostitutes, married women generally wore clothing which was darker and more subdued (Tchen, 1984:46). In some rare cases "storied rebellious women" may have dressed like men in order "to walk through the streets without drawing unwanted attention" (Tchen, 1984:93).

Once in this country, Chinese women gradually began to adopt western-style clothing for themselves and their families. About the third quarter of the 19th century, a typical family photograph would show all family members dressed in Chinese-style garments (e.g., Luchetti and Olwell, 1982:53). A later typical photograph, taken near the turn of the century, shows the adults still in Chinese dress, with only two younger daughters out of twelve children in the picture wearing Chinese-style outfits. These outfits were probably first worn and handed down by the girls' older sisters, who are now wearing western-style clothing (Luchetti and Olwell, 1982:21). In this family and other large families, the hand-me-down Chinese clothing may have been saved for special occasions or family photographs.

In some cases, early 20th century adults appear to have retained their Chinese-style clothing while dressing all their children in western clothes (e.g., Chinese Historical Society of America, 1976:xxxiii). This may indicate that most adults could use the same clothing until it wore out, while growing children needed more frequent clothing replacement. A Portland street scene, about 1900, shows children wearing both styles (Ho, 1978:16); those in Chinese clothing are perhaps more recent arrivals to this country. Using dated photographs as evidence, the transition to western clothing seems to have occurred quite rapidly around the turn of the century, and is probably best explained by increasing acculturation (Judy Yung, 1987:personal communication), or possibly by the greater availability of western-style garments, which may also have been less expensive.

At the turn of the century, some modern Chinese American women readily adopted western fashions (e.g., Lee, 1981:12). Other families wore western everyday clothing, changing to Chinese outfits for holidays and special occasions (e.g., Lee, 1981:10). By the 1920s, however, the transition to western-style clothing appears to have become virtually complete (e.g., Dicker, 1979:86, 100; Lee, 1981:12).

As more is learned about the presence of Chinese women in the West during the late 19th and early 20th centuries, there is no doubt that more artifacts associated with them and with their different occupations will either be excavated or will find their way into museum collections. Further research might also investigate those objects of Euroamerican origin which were adopted for use by Chinese women. For now, however, our knowledge remains extremely limited.

REFERENCES CITED

ABBOTT, ELIZABETH LEE
    1976   Dr. Hu King Eng, Pioneer, in "The Life, Influence, and the Role of the Chinese in the United States, 1776-1960," *Proceedings/Papers of the National Conference held at the University of San Francisco July 10, 11, 12, 1975*, Chinese Historical Society of America, San Francisco, pp. 243-249.

BEURDELEY, MICHEL
    1969   *Chinese Erotic Art*, Chartwell Books.

BLAIR, KAREN J. (ed.)
    1988   *Women in Pacific Northwest History: An Anthology*, University of Washington Press, Seattle.

BONNERS FERRY HERALD
    1910   Bonners Ferry, Idaho.

BRESSIE, WES and RUBY BRESSIE
    1972   *Ghost Town Bottle Price Guide: Average Market Price Guide for Antique Bottle Collectors, with an Expanded Section on Oriental Relics*, Caxton Printers, Caldwell, Idaho.

BROWN, BONITA
    1979   Artifacts from the Loft, in "Archaeological and Historical Studies at Ninth and Amherst, Lovelock, Nevada," E. M. Hattori, M. K. Rusco, and D. R. Tuohy (eds.), *Archaeological Services Reports*, Nevada State Museum, Carson City, pp. 549-595.

CALLAWAY, CASHION
    1979   Metal Artifacts from Ninth and Amherst, in "Archaeological and Historical Studies at Ninth and Amherst, Lovelock, Nevada," E. M. Hattori, M. K. Rusco, and D. R. Tuohy (eds.), *Archaeological Services Reports*, Nevada State Museum, Carson City, pp. 251-347.

CHAN, SUCHENG (ed.)
1991　*Entry Denied: Exclusion and the Chinese Community in America, 1882-1943,* Temple University Press, Philadelphia.
CHANG, IRENE
1990　Metro Rail Excavation Casts New Light on 'Old Chinatown,' *Los Angeles Times,* B1, B4, November 14.
CHAR, TIN-YUKE (comp. and ed.)
1975　*The Sandalwood Mountains,* University Press of Hawaii, Honolulu.
CHEN, JACK
1981　*The Chinese of America,* (paperback edition 1982), Harper and Row, San Francisco.
CHENG, LUCIE, SUELLEN CHENG, JUDY CHU, FEELIE LEE, MARJORIE LEE, SUSIE LING, ELAINE LOU, and SUCHETA MAZUMDAR
1984　*Linking Our Lives: Chinese American Women of Los Angeles,* Chinese Historical Society of Southern California, Los Angeles.
CHINESE HISTORICAL SOCIETY OF AMERICA
1976　The Life, Influence and the Role of the Chinese in the United States, 1776-1960, *Proceedings/Papers of the National Conference held at the University of San Francisco, July 10, 11, 12, 1975,* Chinese Historical Society of America, San Francisco.
CUNNINGHAM, JUDITH (comp.)
1986　Chinese/Calaveras County, California, photocopy of typescript on file in the Asian American Comparative Collection, Alfred W. Bowers Laboratory of Anthropology, University of Idaho, Moscow.
1987　Chinese Marriages in Calaveras County Records, photocopy of typescript on file in the Asian American Comparative Collection, Alfred W. Bowers Laboratory of Anthropology, University of Idaho, Moscow.
DANIELS, ROGER
1988　*Asian America: Chinese and Japanese in the United States since 1850,* University of Washington Press, Seattle.
DICKER, LAVERNE MAU
1979　*The Chinese in San Francisco: A Pictorial History,* Dover, New York.
DILLON, RICHARD H.
1962　*The Hatchet Men: The Story of the Tong Wars in San Francisco's Chinatown,* Coward McCann, New York. [Reprinted with different pagination by Ballentine Books, New York, 1972.]
ELSENSOHN, SISTER M. ALDREDA
1970　*Idaho Chinese Lore,* Idaho Corporation of Benedictine Sisters, Cottonwood, Idaho.
1979　*Idaho County's Most Romantic Character: Polly Bemis,* Idaho Corporation of Benedictine Sisters, Cottonwood, Idaho.
FAR, SUI SEEN
1897　The Chinese Woman in America, *The Land of Sunshine,* 6:2, pp. 59-64.
FISK UNIVERSITY
1946　Orientals and their Cultural Adjustment: Interviews, Life Histories, and Social Adjustment Experiences of Chinese and Japanese of Varying Backgrounds and Length of Residence in the United States, *Social*

Science Source Documents, No. 4, Fisk University, Social Science Institute, Nashville.

GAN, CAROLYN
1986   Bay Area Merry-Go-Round, *Asian Week, 8*:16, p. 16, November 28.

GATES, HILL
1989   The Commoditization of Chinese Women, *Signs, 14*:4, pp. 799-832, Summer.

HIRATA, LUCIE CHENG
1979a   Chinese Immigrant Women in Nineteenth-Century California, *Women of America: A History,* by C. R. Berkin and M. B. Norton (eds.), Houghton, Mifflin, Boston, pp. 223-244.

1979b   Free, Indentured, Enslaved: Chinese Prostitutes in Nineteenth-Century America, *Signs, 5*:1, pp. 3-29, Autumn.

HO, NELSON CHIA-CHI
1978   *Portland's Chinatown: The History of an Urban Ethnic District,* Portland Bureau of Planning, Portland Historical Landmarks, National Trust for Historic Preservation, City Council, Portland, Oregon.

HOFFPAUIR, CORINNE G. (comp.)
1986   Shasta County, California, Chinese Marriages (American Style), photocopy of typescript on file in the Asian American Comparative Collection, Alfred W. Bowers Laboratory of Anthropology, University of Idaho, Moscow.

JACK, R. IAN, KATE HOLMES, and RUTH KERR
1984   Ah Toy's Garden: A Chinese Market-Garden on the Palmer River Goldfield, North Queensland, *Australian Journal of Historical Archaeology, 2,* pp. 51-58.

JAMESON, ELIZABETH
1988   Toward a Multicultural History of Women in the Western United States, *Signs, 13*:4, pp. 761-791.

JENSEN, ANDREW and MARY K. RUSCO
1979   Excavations at Ninth and Amherst: Field and Laboratory Methods, in "Archaeological and Historical Studies at Ninth and Amherst, Lovelock, Nevada," E. M. Hattori, M. K. Rusco, and D. R. Tuohy (eds.), *Archaeological Services Reports,* Nevada State Museum, Carson City, pp. 61-71.

JONES, TIMOTHY W.
1980a   Archaeological Test Excavations in the Boise Redevelopment Project Area, Boise, Idaho, *University of Idaho Anthropological Research Manuscript Series,* No. 59, Alfred W. Bowers Laboratory of Anthropology, University of Idaho, Moscow.

JONES, TIMOTHY W., MARY ANNE DAVIS, and GEORGE LING
1979   Idaho City: An Overview and Report on Excavation, *University of Idaho Anthropological Research Manuscript Series,* No. 50, Alfred W. Bowers Laboratory of Anthropology, University of Idaho, Moscow.

LA FARGUE, THOMAS
1940   Some Early Chinese Visitors to the United States, *T'ien Hsia Monthly, 6*:2, pp. 128-138.

LAI, HIM MARK, GENNY LIM, and JUDY YUNG
1980   *Island: Poetry and History of Chinese Immigrants on Angel Island 1910-1940,* HOC DOI Project, San Francisco.

LEE, DOUGLAS W.
1981   Sojourners, Immigrants and Ethnics: The Saga of the Chinese in Seattle, *Portage: The Journal of the Historical Society of Seattle and King County,* 2:3, pp. 10-15.
1984   Willard Jue, A Chinese American for All Seasons, *The Annals of the Chinese Historical Society of the Pacific Northwest,* D. W. Lee (ed.), Chinese Historical Society of the Pacific Northwest and Center for East Asian Studies, Western Washington University, Bellingham, Washington, pp. 1-24.

LEVY, HOWARD S.
1967   *Chinese Footbinding: The History of a Curious Erotic Custom,* Bell Publishing Company, New York.

LOOMIS, REV. A. W.
1869   Chinese Women in California, *The Overland Monthly,* 2:4, pp. 344-351. (Reprinted by AMS Press, New York, 1965.)

LUCHETTI, CATHY and CAROL OLWELL
1982   *Women of the West,* Antelope Press, St. George, Utah.

LYMAN, STANFORD M.
1970   *The Asian in North America,* ABC-CLIO, Santa Barbara.
1974   *Chinese Americans,* Random House, New York.

MARK, DIANE MEI LIN and GINGER CHIH
1982   *A Place Called Chinese America,* Organization of Chinese Americans, Kendall Hunt Publishing Co., Dubuque, Iowa.

MARTIN, MILDRED CROWL
1977   *Chinatown's Angry Angel: The Story of Donaldina Cameron,* Pacific Books, Palo Alto.

McCUNN, RUTHANNE LUM
1979   *An Illustrated History of the Chinese in America,* Design Enterprises of San Francisco, San Francisco.
1981   *Thousand Pieces of Gold,* Design Enterprises of San Francisco, San Francisco.
1988   *Chinese American Portraits: Personal Histories 1828-1988,* Chronicle Books, San Francisco.

McLEOD, ALEXANDER
1948   *Pigtails and Gold Dust,* Caxton Printers, Caldwell, Idaho.

MILLER, STUART CREIGHTON
1969   *The Unwelcome Immigrant: The American Image of the Chinese, 1785-1882,* University of California Press, Berkeley.

MOSCOW MIRROR
1890   Moscow, Idaho.

MOSS, DEWEY
1968   Bottle World: Florida Waters, *Western Collector,* 6:8, pp. 39-42.

NOAH, ANNA C.
1987   Brass, Glass, Stone, and Bone: Items of Adornment from Riverside Chinatown, *Wong Ho Leun,* Vol. 2, Great Basin Foundation (eds.), Great Basin Foundation, San Diego, pp. 395-413.

NOVAK, CLARE C. (managing ed.)
1982   United States Notes, *Signs,* 8:2, p. 377.

OSGOOD, CORNELIUS
1975   *The Chinese: A Study of a Hong Kong Community,* 3 vols., University of Arizona Press, Tuscon.
PALMER, ALBERT W.
1934?   *Orientals in American Life,* Friendship Press, New York. (Reprinted by R and E Research Associates, San Francisco, 1972.)
PETRIK, PAULA
1987   *No Step Backward: Women and Family on the Rocky Mountain Mining Frontier, Helena, Montana, 1865-1900,* Montana Historical Society Press, Helena.
RANDALL, GAY
1961   The West's Most Fabulous Ghost Town, *True West, 8*:3, pp. 22-26, January-February.
SHING, LIU HEUNG
1983   Chinese Foot Binding—A Painful Tradition, *Idaho Statesman,* Boise, p. 4D, April 2.
SOO, ANNIE
1976   The Life, Influence, and Role of the Chinese Women in the United States, Specifically in the West, 1906-1966, in "The Life, Influence, and the Role of the Chinese in the United States, 1776-1960," *Proceedings/Papers of the National Conference Held at the University of San Francisco July 10, 11, 12, 1975,* Chinese Historical Society of America, San Francisco, pp. 243-289.
SOO, ANNIE (ed.)
1986   Query, Chinese Historical Society of America *Bulletin, 21*:9, p. 2, November.
SPRAGUE, RODERICK
1965   The Descriptive Archaeology of the Palus Burial Site, Lyons Ferry, Washington, *Report of Investigations,* No. 32, Washington State University, Laboratory of Anthropology, Pullman, Washington.
TAKAKI, RONALD
1989   *Strangers from a Different Shore: A History of Asian Americans,* Penguin, New York.
TCHEN, JOHN KUO WEI
1984   *Genthe's Photographs of San Francisco's Old Chinatown,* Dover, New York.
TRULL, FERN COBLE
1946   The History of the Chinese in Idaho from 1864 to 1910, Master's thesis, University of Oregon, Eugene.
TSAI, SHIH-SHAN HENRY
1986   *The Chinese Experience in America,* Indiana University Press, Bloomington.
UNITED STATES CODE
1875   *The Statutes at Large of the United States from December, 1873, to March, 1875,* . . . Vol. 18, Part 3, Government Printing Office, Washington, D.C.
WEGARS, PRISCILLA
1991   The History and Archaeology of the Chinese in Northern Idaho, 1880 through 1910, Ph.D. dissertation, University of Idaho, Moscow.
WEY, NANCY
1979   Chinese Written Material and Other Artifacts from Ninth and Amherst, in "Archaeological and Historical Studies at Ninth and Amherst, Lovelock,

Nevada," E. M. Hattori, M. K. Rusco, and D. R. Tuohy (eds.), *Archaeological Services Reports,* Nevada State Museum, Carson City, pp. 539-548.

WILLIAMS, C. A. S.
1941   *Outlines of Chinese Symbolism and Art Motives,* (3rd Revised Edition), Kelly and Walsh, Shanghai. (Reprinted by Dover, New York, 1976.)

WOLF, MARGERY
1968   *The House of Lim: A Study of a Chinese Farm Family,* Appleton-Century-Crofts, New York.

YUNG, JUDY
1986   *Chinese Women of America: A Pictorial History,* University of Washington Press, Seattle.
1990   Unbinding the Feet, Unbinding their Lives: Social Change for Chinese Women in San Francisco, 1902-1945, Ph.D. dissertation, University of California, Berkeley.

CHAPTER 10

Chinese Opium Smoking Techniques and Paraphernalia

Jerry Wylie and Richard E. Fike

Opium was a popular and even fashionable drug in American society in the late 19th century. Americans drank it in an incredible array of so-called "cure-all" patent medicines. Chinese immigrants, however, preferred the more effective smoking method, a habit some Americans adopted after 1870.

Though there is abundant historical information, researching the subject of opium smoking can be difficult for several reasons: 1) opium smoking was a complex process involving a highly specialized set of paraphernalia; 2) most archaeological collections contain only fragmentary specimens and are missing many kinds of artifacts needed for this kind of study; 3) typological comparisons are difficult due to a lack of uniformity in descriptions, illustrations, and analytical techniques; and 4) there are some contradictions in historical references, both on how opium was smoked and its effect on regular users.

This topic is also seriously tainted by negative connotations. Chinese consider it a symbol of foreign exploitation, Chinese Americans associate it with anti-Chinese racist stereotypes, and most of us consider the regular use of "serious" drugs to be destructive and anti-social. While such attitudes are real and require special consideration for the feelings of Chinese Americans, who may be offended by careless or sensational treatment of this topic, this says more about today than the period we are trying to understand. We hope serious scholarly research will overcome these problems and contribute to a better understanding of the range of opium behavior and its role in overseas Chinese culture.

Source of Information

This study began as a brief description of Idaho material (Wylie, 1980; Wylie and Geer, 1983) which was expanded (Wylie and Fike, 1985) and reported at the 1986 Society for Historical Archaeology meetings in Sacramento (Wylie and Fike, 1986). Other studies containing significant information on opium paraphernalia have been helpful, including Briggs' (1974) description of Chinese railroad camps in Texas; Kuffner's (1979) work on opium paraphernalia from Lovelock, Nevada, including a comprehensive discussion of contemporary descriptions and historical information; Etter's (1980) report on opium artifacts from Donner Summit, California and Virginia City, Nevada; excavations at *Yema-Po*, near Berkeley, California reported by Miller (1983) and Gallagher (n.d.); an investigation of the Chinese laundry in Woodland, California, including an interesting and well- researched examination of the socioeconomic role of opium (Felton, Lortie, and Schulz, 1984); a study of opium pipe mending in California (Schulz and Felton, n.d.); a comprehensive study of historical references and opium artifacts from excavations in New Zealand (Ritchie, 1986); and the analysis of the opium paraphernalia and role of opium at Riverside Chinatown, California (Wylie and Higgins, 1987).

A BRIEF HISTORICAL OVERVIEW OF OPIUM

Historical Background

The opium poppy (*Papaver somniferum*), indigenous to southern Europe and western Asia, has been under cultivation for 4000 years, primarily for medicinal use in sedatives, pain relievers, and dysentery remedies. The medicinal use of opium spread from the Middle East to China as early as A.D. 700 (Courtwright, 1982:64) and perhaps as late as A.D. 1295 (Holmes, 1884:788). At first, a raw opium was mixed with liquids and drunk, or eaten dry. After the introduction of tobacco smoking, opium was commonly mixed with small amounts of tobacco and smoked (Leslie, 1877).

Opium smoking in China may have begun in the 1600s, when Dutch sailors introduced tobacco smoking to Taiwan (White, 1985:162), or it could have been brought from Java by Chinese traders in the early 1700s (Dudgeon, quoted in Ball, 1903:448). Sometime after that, specialized smoking equipment was developed and refined opium was smoked without tobacco. However, the practice of smoking opium/tobacco mixtures in standard "dry" and "wet" pipes did not die out entirely.

Initially monopolized by British imports from India, the Chinese soon produced their own opium for domestic consumption and export. By 1870, opium poppies were being grown in ten provinces, sometimes producing two or three crops per year. The result was a somewhat inferior but significantly cheaper product which successfully competed with imported opium (*The Illustrated London News,* 1883). By 1884, 80 percent of the opium used in China was domestically grown (Holmes, 1884:791). Viewed as a degrading symbol of foreign domination, resistance to opium use grew, fueled by a growing sense of nationalism. By 1911, with the collapse of the Qing Dynasty, opium importation into China was forbidden altogether (Maveety, 1979:6), although domestic cultivation continued.

Though opium smoking was illegal in China, estimates of usage during the 1870s-1890s range from 10 percent (Ball, 1903:491) to 25-30 percent (Holmes, 1884:794). In 1886, 25 percent of Chinese adult males were thought to be "addicted" (Masters, 1896:54). Up to 60 percent of the Chinese miners in New Zealand were thought to indulge (Ritchie, 1986:365). Estimates of the number of Chinese opium smokers in the United States at the same time show an ever greater range. However, these data reveal more about the biased sources than the level of opium use. The lowest estimates (5-15%) are from pro-Chinese, pro-immigration advocates; figures from knowledgeable but disinterested sources are slightly higher (20-45%); newspapers reported a slightly higher rate (30-50%); and police sources claim nearly all Chinese were involved (Courtwright, 1982:70). For other references suggesting 35-40 percent usage in China and American Chinatowns, see Felton, Lortie, and Schulz, 1984:99.

High rates of opium usage among Chinese in this country should not be surprising. Opium use in China at this time was widespread and most overseas Chinese came from the Canton area of southern China, a region long associated with the opium market. Cantonese immigrants, therefore, were especially likely to have been exposed to opium use (Courtwright, 1982:67).

A study of Chinese labor on the West Coast about 1888 indicated that expenditures for opium equalled that of food "in the vast majority of cases." Total yearly cost of living for a broom maker, not counting "recreational" activities such as smoking/gambling, was $85, of which food expenses were $73. Opium consumed 23 percent of the subject's $315 annual income (Meriwether, 1888).

The rate of addiction is harder to determine. Figures range from 15 percent of the overseas Chinese population (Masters, 1896:55) to as high as 50 percent (Courtwright, 1982:70). A light smoker was considered to be someone who consumed 1.5 pounds a year, versus 6 pounds for a heavy smoker (Wright, quoted in Courtwright, 1982:184). One worker in New Zealand consumed a "tin" every five weeks; another smoked a "tin" every two weeks (Ritchie, 1986:366). Occasional social smoking was common and did not lead to dependency. Such recreational use without addiction is attributed to Chinese attitudes toward moderation and a feeling that opium smoking was more appropriate for holidays (Courtwright, 1982:70). Although he offered no explanation or data, Dobie (1936:250) considered opium addicts to be the exception rather than the rule in San Francisco's Chinatown. In contrast, another researcher noted that "although the authorities differed over percentages, they were virtually unanimous on one point: that

addiction to smoking opium afflicted a significant portion of the Chinese immigrant community" (Courtwright, 1982:70).

Use of Opium by Non-Chinese

Only 20 percent of the opium imported into the United States during the late
19th century was smoked by Chinese (Terry and Pellens, cited in Kuffner,
1979:602). The vast majority was consumed by non-Chinese in the form of patent
medicines laced with laudanum, a mixture of opium, alcohol, and flavoring
(Holmes, 1884:794). Adding opium to medicinal "cure-alls" during this period
was also popular; heavy consumption often led to dependency and increased sales.
In Victorian England, opium and its preparations were readily available in pubs,
drug stores, and grocery shops (Berridge, 1978).

From 1850 to 1870 opium smoking in this country was limited to Chinese. After
1870 white addicts began to appear, drawn primarily from prostitutes, pimps,
gamblers, and other underworld characters who had the most frequent contacts
with urban Chinese users "on the other side of the tracks" (Courtwright, 1982:70).
Smoking also became prestigious in upper-class society after 1875, and was
considered particularly fashionable by white females (Courtwright, 1982:78). By
1884 nearly one million persons were smoking opium in the United States
(Holmes, 1884:794), a trend that was clearly recognized by at least one contemporary weekly magazine (*Harper's Weekly*, 1880a:222):

> The consumption of opium in this country is by no means confined to the
> Chinese. It is spreading to an alarming extent among people of American
> birth.

Harper's Weekly also reported that (1882:215):

> . . . the evil of opium-smoking has been growing with alarming rapidity in
> New York City during the past few months. In the dens where it is most
> fostered no Chinamen are seen; those who keep these places and those who
> frequent them are nearly all Americans.

In Lovelock, Nevada even Indians were occasionally arrested for smoking
(Kuffner, 1979:604). Young Euroamerican men and women were seen visiting
opium dens in Riverside Chinatown in 1886, and a 1914 drug raid in that community arrested Chinese, Euroamericans, Mexicans, and Indians (Raven,
1987:239-240).

Anti-Opium Laws

Although ordinances banning opium smoking were passed in San Francisco in
1875 and Virginia City in 1876, enforcement was sporadic. A California state
statute in 1881 stipulated a fine of up to $500 and six months in jail for persons

opcrating or patronizing opium dens (Courtwright, 1982:79). A similar law enacted in Idaho that same year stipulated a penalty of $100 and six months' imprisonment (Derig, 1972:7). Federal controls on opium for non-medical use began in 1909, but there was little enforcement until the 1914 Harrison Narcotic Act took effect in 1915. Until then, opium and other narcotics could be purchased over the counter (Courtwright, 1982:83; Harney and Cross, 1973:13). By 1915, twenty-six states had passed anti-opium smoking laws (Courtwright, 1982:79).

OPIUM SMOKING TECHNIQUES

Early Accounts

In contrast to other mood-altering drugs, opium was smoked lying down, usually with other smokers, in a passive, inactive state. By all accounts, it was a very social activity, and its preparation and smoking was an elaborate, time-consuming process requiring special skill and equipment. As described by Ball (1893:336):

> It is a great waste of time, as the process of smoking is a slow one and requires long preparation, and, as the habit increases, more has to be smoked to produce an effect, and consequently longer time spent over it: from a quarter, or half an hour, at first it increases till hours are required, and a great part of the night is wasted in it instead of being asleep.

The preparation of each pipeful of opium took from five to ten minutes, and the actual smoking about thirty seconds (Sampson, quoted in Holmes, 1884:794). Careful "cooking" of the molasses-like opium prior to smoking caused moisture to be steamed off and was considered an art. Too much heat would dry it out; too little and it would stick to the needle and not smoke properly (Masters, quoted in Dobie, 1936:254; Kane, 1882:43). Some veteran smokers served as professional cooks for less experienced smokers for a fee, or in exchange for a smoke (Byrnes and Williams, in Courtwright, 1982:185). In addition to cooking, the sharp end of the needle or "dipper" could also be used to manipulate the burning opium during smoking to ensure complete combustion (Holmes, 1884:794). However, in later years opium was also available in powder and pill form at American drugstores (O'Connell, 1980); these forms did not require preparation.

The most detailed and often quoted contemporary description of the technique is by Dr. H. H. Kane, a New York physician who specialized in the treatment of white opium addicts (Kane, 1881:647):

> The smoker entering a joint usually removes his coat, collar, and shoes, hangs them upon a peg, and, stretching himself transversely across the bunk beside a tray containing the necessary apparatus, calls for a pipe and some opium. . . . Having the necessary articles and opium brought to him by the keeper of the joint, the smoker settles himself comfortably upon his side, takes

up a little of the treacle-like opium, which is brought to him in a small clam shell, upon a long steel needle . . . and holding it above the flame of the lamp, watches it bubble and swell to eight or ten times its original size. In doing so it loses its inky hue, becomes of a bright golden brown color, and gives off a creamy odor, much admired by old smokers. Poor opium does not yield so pleasant an odor, is liable to drop from the needle into the lamp, and rarely gives so handsome a color, the golden brown being streaked here and there with black. This process is known as "cooking" the opium. Having brought it to a proper consistence, the operator, with a rapid, twirling motion of the fingers, rolls the mass, still upon the *yen hauck* [needle], upon the broad surface of the bowl, submitting it occasionally to the flame, catching it now and then upon the edge of the bowl and pulling it out into strings, in order to cook it through more thoroughly. . . . Rolling it again upon the bowl until formed into a pea-shaped mass, with the needle as a centre, the needle is forced down into the small hole in the bowl, thus leveling off the bottom of the pea. . . . Then grasping the stem of the pipe near the bowl in the left hand, the bowl is held across the flame of the lamp to warm it, the bottom of the opium mass being at the same time heated, the needle is thrust into the aperture in the centre of the bowl, and withdrawn with a twisting motion, leaving the opium, with a hole in its centre, upon the surface of the bowl. Inclining the body slightly forward, the smoker tips the pipe bowl across the lamp until the opium is just above the flame. Inhaling strongly and steadily, the smoke passes into the lungs of the operator, and is returned through the mouth and nose. This smoke is heavy, white, and has a not unpleasant fruity odor. . . . Having finished this bolus, which requires but one long or a few short inhalations, the habitue cools the bowl of the pipe with a damp sponge, and repeats the operation of cooking, rolling, and smoking until the desired effects are obtained.

Other contemporary descriptions provide similar details of opium preparation and smoking, e.g., Huc (1871:53), *Harper's Weekly* (1880b:565), Sampson (quoted in Holmes, 1884:794), and Masters (1896:55; also quoted in Dobie, 1936:253-254). Minor variations are known, however. For misconceptions concerning exhaling smoke through the eyes and ears, see Kane (1881:647, 1882:32,43) and Masters (1896:55).

Alternative Smoking Methods

Other accounts describe somewhat different smoking techniques, perhaps due to the use of different forms of opium and/or variations in equipment. In 1891, as a seven-year old boy, Wallace Clay observed a Chinese railroad worker smoking opium "pills" at Blue Creek Station, Utah (Clay, 1969:6):

He quickly fishes out another opium pill from his wallet and puts it in his pipe and lites [sic] it with a Chinese match (the reader of this probably never saw one, which with 99 others glued together at their bases made a square bunch only 2 inches long by 3/4ths across and when lit smelled strongly of sulfur) and as the opium pill begins to burn and bubble the agonized expression on his face changed to a contented smile again. **An opium pill looked a**

lot like those little licorice pellets kids used to buy at about 10 for a penny and about the same color. When **the pill is in the opium pipe bowl** the flame from it keeps sputtering and boiling somewhat like a batch of homemade candy which is about to burn. Should that flame sputter out the opium smoker is quick to relight it and all the while he keeps stirring the boiling opium with a little stick so he will get the right quality of sweet smoke to inhale from the stem of his pipe (emphasis added).

Opium Grades and Reuse

Opium prepared in China was distinguished from other opium by the name *kung in* (superior opium). Pipe bowl scrapings were reboiled and mixed with fresh opium and marketed under the name of *i in* (number two opium), or as *in ski ko* (politely translated as "opium refuse mass") for one-half to one-quarter the price of fresh opium (Culin, 1891:498-499; Sando and Felton, Chapter 6 herein.) Although less potent, opium scrapings were considered to be more damaging to a smoker's health (Kane, quoted in Culin, 1891:499). They were used to manufacture anti-opium medicines (Ball, 1903:497) and were also drunk with a mixture of water, wine, or liquor as *yen shee suey* (Harney and Cross, 1979:17). We would expect this practice to have been limited to smokers who lacked the money to purchase regular opium.

Low grades of Indian opium occasionally were also mixed with sand, brown sugar, or cow dung (Fay, 1975:13). Indian opium (patna) contained less morphia and had a superior flavor, whereas Persian and Turkish opium had a higher morphia content and a bitter taste (Dobie, 1936:248). Chinese-grown opium may have been inferior in quality but was cheaper and less adulterated, and thus was a better product overall (Huc, 1871:55).

The quality of opium was judged by various criteria, including color, purity, taste, and aroma (Holmes, 1884:794). In addition to a "creamy . . . not unpleasant fruity odor" (Kane, 1881:647, 1882:42), burning opium is variously described as "sickening sweet" (Clay, 1969), "enough to turn a horse's stomach" (Masters, in Dobie, 1936:254), "burning peanuts with a sickly sweet tinge" (Dobie, 1936:255), and by a user himself simply as "stale and tepid" (Farrère, 1941:144).

Opium Cans, Prices, and Servings

Prepared smoking opium was sold in white porcelain pots in China and exported in rectangular metal containers, known as five-tael cans, each containing about six and two-thirds ounces (250 cc) (Culin, 1891:498). Canned opium was the consistency of molasses (Derig, 1972:18-19):

At least one mailman and indirectly one shopkeeper found this method of packaging a disappointment. The mailman was carrying a big sack of mail on foot from McCall to Warrens [Idaho]. After several hours out, one spot in the mailbag that seemed to house a hard corner began to irritate his back. He decided to fix to spot one night while he camped. Without opening the bag, he mashed the corner smooth, and the next morning went on without any trouble. By the time he arrived at Warrens, a sticky substance from the can had oozed out and he untied the bag to find the mail all glued together.

References to opium stored in earthenware pots are known from San Francisco (Masters, 1896:55), but these were exceptions. Crude opium processed in San Francisco was probably imported (illegally) in dry form and not in standard cans.

The price of a standard 5-tael can in San Francisco in 1871 was $9 for Number One grade Chinese opium, $6.80 for a weaker grade prepared in Victoria, British Columbia, and $2 to $5 for Number Two grade opium (Culin, 1891:498). In the early 1880s the price on the East Coast was about $8 (Kane, 1881:646), and $10 in Tucson, Arizona (Ayres, 1988:9). The price jumped to $70 by 1917, $200 by 1924, and $600-$700 by 1940, due to restrictions on importing and selling opium (Courtwright, 1982:83, 190).

Individual servings in dens sold for 25 cents, the amount varying from 32 to 181 grains depending on quality and shop policy. The average was about 60 grains (0.14 oz.) of Number One grade opium. Servings ranged from 32 to 64 grains (6-10 "fun" or *fan*) of Number One, to twice that amount for Number Two grade opium in New York (Kane, 1881:646) and 54 to 70 grains in Philadelphia (Culin, 1891:497, 500). It was customary for shops to sell blends of all grades to match their clients' tastes. Mixtures would include as much as 181 grains per 25 cent serving (Culin, 1891:500). How many smokes were in a twenty-five cent serving is not known. A novice smoked one to two pipes (*Illustrated London News,* 1858:483) and an experienced smoker ten to twenty pipes (Maveety, 1979:2) per session. An addicted white prostitute interviewed in 1884 claimed to smoke about twelve pipes per session (Morton, 1974:115).

THE SMOKING KIT

According to one contemporary description (Kane, 1881:647), a typical smoking kit contained the following opium paraphernalia (Figure 52):

- **Small containers** ("fun" or *fan*) to hold the opium (e.g., shell, buffalo horn, folded playing card, or ceramic dish).
- **Needle** (or "spoon") (*yen hauck*) for picking up, cooking and manipulating the opium.
- **Glass lamp** for preparing and smoking the opium.
- **Scissors** for trimming the lamp wick.
- **Straight and curved knives** (*yen shee gow*) for cleaning the bowl and needle.
- **Sponge** to cool the pipe between "hits."
- **Container** for the ash (*yen tshi*).
- **Tray** to hold the kit.

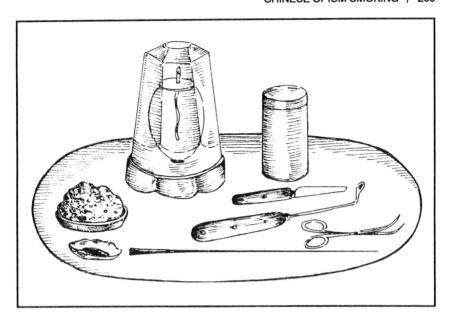

Figure 52. Opium smoker's outfit: lamp, sponge, shell with opium,
bowl cleaners, scissors, needle, horn box for opium, and tray.
(After Kane, 1882:36). Drawn by Jennifer Chance.

The term *yen* in Cantonese and Mandarin is literally "smoke," but was also a common euphemism for opium (Cohen, 1986:2).

In addition, some dippers or needles had flattened ends which could be used as scrapers (Holmes, 1884:794). Sixteen-inch-long whiskers from Steller sea lions may have been used as pipe cleaners on the West Coast (Gentry, 1987:496).

The Opium Pipe

The most important piece of equipment in the smoking kit was the pipe or opium "pistol" (*Yen Tsiang* or *Teiung*) (Figure 53). *Yen Tsiang* is probably Cantonese for the Mandarin *yen ch'iang,* meaning literally "smoke spear/rifle." With a prefix adjective syllable meaning "hand," *chi'ang* is also used for "pistol" (Cohen, 1986:2). It is described in greatest detail by Dr. H. H. Kane (1881:647):

> So far as can be learned, opium has always been smoked in the kind of pipe now in use. The large amount of ash, the necessity for holding over a flame during the smoking, and the advantage of a flat mouth-piece for long inhalation, make the one style of opium pipe the only one that can be used with any satisfaction. This pipe, the origin and antiquity of which are unknown, though supposed to have originated in Arabia, consists of two parts, a stem and a bowl. The stem is of bamboo, so cut that it includes the space between two

Figure 53. Chinese opium pipe or "pistol" (*yen tsiang*), length 56.5 cm. (22¹/₄ in.).
University of Idaho Asian American Comparative Collection artifacts
ACC-86-30a, b (pipe stem); WCC 62 (pipe bowl).
Photo by Mark LaMoreaux

joints and one-quarter of the next. The best measure twenty-four inches in length and about four inches in circumference. . . . When new they are of a straw-color, but with long smoking become black and glossy, the coloring matter of the opium having thoroughly permeated the wood. In poor pipes this color is imitated by staining with a dye.

The value of a good pipe increases with its age, it acquiring a strength and odor much prized by old smokers. . . .

There is a pipe known as "the lemon pipe," the stem and sometimes the bowl of which are made of rings of lemon-peel cemented together, layer over layer. When thoroughly dried they are smoothed off, and are much liked by some on account of the peculiar lemon flavor that is given off when opium is smoked in them. They are worth $25. An ordinary pipe costs $5, a good one from $15 to $50.

The Chinese, in preparing the best stems, coat the inside with "cooked" Chinese opium, in order to give them a rich flavor and hasten their coloring.

At the junction of the middle and lower third of the stem, and just back of the joint, which is usually marked by some oddly carved image made from the stump there protruding, a place is hollowed out of the side of the stem, and communicates with the longitudinal performation. About this hollow fits closely a metallic shield, usually of brass, sometimes of gold or silver, having a raised rim. Into this is fitted the bowl.

The stems are plain, carved, or ornamented with bands of silver, gold, or ivory. Good pipes are always ivory-tipped. That part of the stem from the bowl down is for ornament, to equalize the weight of the whole, and for convenience of holding and guiding while smoking.

The hollowed-out distal end of the pipe was not connected to the air-way and served as a storage place for bits of rag used to secure the bowl to the brass fitting (Kane, 1882:35).

Pipes shorter than Kane's "24-inch optimum" are known, and may actually be the rule rather than the exception. Rapaport (1979:144) states that opium pipes range from 40 to 50 centimeters in length, or about 16-20 inches. The average length of 47 opium pipes displayed at the Stanford University Museum of Art in 1979 was 21.5 inches (Maveety, 1979). An even smaller 17-inch specimen was collected on an island at the mouth of the Canton River by a British officer during the 1842 Opium War (Fay, 1975:8), and shorter versions are also known from Borneo and New Guinea (Rapaport, 1979:148).

The origin and antiquity of the Chinese "opium pistol" style pipe is unclear. Kane supposes it to have originated in Arabia. Others suggest it was invented sometime in the 1700s in Canton (Dudgeon, quoted in Ball, 1903:488) or Formosa (Rapaport, 1979:144). When opium smoking was first introduced into southern China, and before the invention of the "pistol," a short bamboo tube filled with opium, tobacco, and fiber from coconut husks was used (Dudgeon, quoted in Ball, 1903:488). The development of the "pistol" and prepared (distilled) smoking opium apparently allowed for opium to be smoked more efficiently and without additives.

An early reference, ca. 1840-1842, described a ceramic pipe bowl made of "fine clay handsomely chased, and resembling in shape a flattened turnip, with a puncture about the size of a pin's head on the upper side; the diameter . . . is nearly three inches" (Bingham, quoted in Fay, 1975:8). Culin (1891:499), describing pipe bowls in Philadelphia, mentions their great beauty of workmanship, graceful proportions, decorations of Chinese characters, and one ingenious type resembling a grey crab with movable projecting eyes. Masters (1896:56) noted that the "knob [bowl] is supposed to resemble a poppy head." An unusual brass bowl shaped like a flattened pear is described in Rapaport (1979:148).

Kane, in his usual scientific manner, provides considerably more detail (1881:647):

> The bowl, which is usually of a hard red clay and hollow, may be bell-shaped, ovate, or hexagonal. On its under surface is a flange, or neck, by which it is fitted into the stem. This flange is usually chipped off, and its place taken by a metal rim which is fastened to the pipe-bowl by means of burnt alum. In order to make it fit tightly, this flange is ordinarily wrapped with a narrow piece of soft cloth. This is held in place by means of a little smoking-opium which, when dry, forms an excellent glue. The upper surface of the bowl is either flat or sloping slightly downward and outward. In its centre is an opening of about sufficient size to admit an ordinary knitting-needle.

Other Pipe Types

In addition to the "opium pistol," the Chinese used two other styles of pipes: a **water** and a **dry tobacco** pipe (Rapaport, 1979:137). The water pipe was made entirely of metal and shaped somewhat like a small watering can with a long gooseneck stem (Figure 54 and Rapaport, 1979:145-146). The dry pipe, on the

Figure 54. Opium smokers in Canton, China, 1900. Part of a stereo
photo pair that illustrates the use of metal water pipes and
opium "pistols." This may have been a staged photograph
(Worswick and Spence, 1978:86).

other hand, had a long, thin stem with a small metal bowl at one end (Rapaport, 1979:140, 141, illustrated). Although designed for tobacco, it was not uncommon for both pipe types to have been used for smoking opium (Rapaport, 1979:137). A writer in the early 1880s described "a short, tiny pipe, often made of silver" which was used to smoke pea-sized opium pellets (anonymous, quoted in Kane, 1881:647). The account of young Wallace Clay quoted above, involving the smoking of an "opium pill . . . like little licorice pellets" **inside** the pipe bowl, also suggests a different type of pipe may have been used in some cases (Clay, 1969:6).

Another young boy growing up in Elko, Nevada, also befriended an aging Chinese railroad worker nicknamed "Bad Eye," the town's last Chinese resident. In the early 1930s, when Bad Eye was probably in his eighties, young James Hefferon and his friends (Hefferon, 1986):

... would watch the old fellow when he puffed and it smelled good to us. ... His pipes were made of ivory and carved like a dragon. The stem was yellow white. He gave me one. ... **It was more than a foot long and carved like a dragon** with horns and all ... and in his mouth was a small brass cup. Old Bad Eye would dip his opium in the end of it, but he never used much. **The bowl of the pipe was the brass cup and very small** compared to the pipes my dad smoked. ... It seems to me he mixed his opium some way, but I really can't tell what he did (emphasis added).

In addition to tobacco, opium, and tobacco/opium mixtures, Chinese or Japanese ("dry") metal pipes may have been used to smoke other drugs (*Harper's Weekly*, 1888:918):

They [Chinese] are most all smokers, and while many of them smoke tobacco, they are very few who do not smoke opium. **Hashish smoking, too, is somewhat common among them.** This they smoke in the leaf in pipes, or in the gum like opium, or in the nargile [water pipe] (emphasis added).

ANALYSIS OF OPIUM PIPE BOWLS

Pipe Bowl Features and Terminology

Pipe bowls, by far the most common form of opium paraphernalia, are found at virtually every overseas Chinese site. While exhibiting remarkable variation in shape, ceramic pipe bowls have certain characteristics in common (Figure 55), as described below (after Wylie and Higgins, 1987:335-336).

All bowls have a convex upper **smoking surface** on which the opium is prepared and smoked. The outer edge is almost always the maximum diameter of the bowl and is commonly circular or eight-sided, or rarely six-sided, four-sided, or elaborately scrolled. In cases where the maximum diameter is not the edge of the smoking surface, judgment is used to determine the classification. For example, one type has a circular smoking surface but is classified as eight-sided because of its predominant shape. The smoking hole is located in the center of the smoking surface and is often surrounded by wear and charring. The area around the smoking hole is thinned, and sometimes cut out for the use of a ceramic or metal insert. In rare cases, tops are removed by sawing.

Smoking holes (Figure 55a) commonly range from 1 to 3 mm in diameter. Larger holes indicate the use of inserts. Fractures of the smoking surface are also common, probably from rapid heating and cooling, and smoking holes are frequently enlarged and broken. This is the weakest part of the bowl, due to the thinning of the interior wall surfaces immediately surrounding the smoking hole during manufacture. The reason for this thinning is unclear, but one possibility is that it allows for quick pre-heating and cooling between smokes. Whatever its purpose, it was apparently important enough to risk weakening this area, resulting in many fractured bowls.

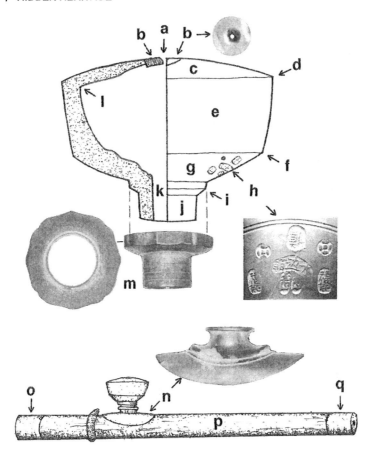

Figure 55. Opium pipe parts and terminology.
a) smoking hole; b) insert; c) top (smoking surface); d) rim; e) side;
f) shoulder; g) base; h) stamps; i) flange; j) stem; k) basal hole;
l) rim joint; m) metal connector; n) saddle; o) end piece;
p) pipe stem; q) mouth piece.

Many bowls have modified smoking holes which are enlarged and ground for **inserts,** and a few have intact inserts (Figure 55b). Some are made from glazed tableware or storage jars, ground to fit and drilled through the center from the convex side. These are inserted with the concave side toward the inside of the bowl, with the curvature of the disc matching the curve of the smoking surface. Metal inserts are usually a simple drop of metal, drilled to form the smoking hole, but can also consist of a small cup-shaped piece.

Missing inserts explain the larger than average smoking holes in some bowls. The diameters of unmodified smoking holes range from 0.5 to 5.8 mm, with an average of 2.6 mm. Smoking holes modified for ceramic inserts are much larger (8.5 to 13.5 mm). Six miscellaneous ceramic inserts examined from various private collections are slightly larger, ranging in size from 11.9 to 19.0 mm, with an average of 14.8 mm. Three ceramic and eight metal inserts were also examined from the Riverside Chinatown (Wylie and Higgins, 1987:333-334). All were circular and ranged in size from 11 to 16 mm for the ceramic types to about 2 mm for the metal ones. One of the stoneware inserts was incomplete, with a rough margin and a partially drilled hole.

In addition to round holes, square and triangular shapes are also known (Priscilla Wegars, 1986:personal communication; Schulz and Felton, n.d.). We believe the inserts were primarily functional and necessary to repair a weakened or enlarged smoking hole. Some bowls seem to have been manufactured with inserts as "original equipment." Inserts, especially metal ones, may explain the puzzling contemporary accounts of Chinese pipemenders drilling their customers' broken pipes (Culin, 1891:500). Such mending was apparently a common craft specialization in 19th century American Chinatowns (Culin, 1891:500; Schulz and Felton, n.d.). For a discussion of pipe bowl mending, see Wylie and Higgins (1987:359); for an illustration of a sidewalk mender in San Francisco, see McCunn (1979:67).

The **rim** is the edge which separates the top from the side of the bowl, and is usually sharply defined (Figure 55d). The **rim joint**, inside the pipe bowl where the sidewall connects with the top, frequently shows evidence of manufacturing techniques (Figure 55l).

The **shoulder** is the transition from the side to the base of the bowl and is commonly rounded, but may also be sharply defined where sidewalls are flat (Figure 55f).

The **base** (Figure 55g) is the side of the bowl opposite the smoking surface, containing the low flange and projecting stem encircling the large basal opening. Some bowls are made without stems, presumably to facilitate the attachment of a metal connector directly to the ceramic flange.

The **flange** is a low, circular projection of clay on the base of the bowl through which runs the 12 to 20 mm diameter aperture connecting to the pipe stem (Figure 55i). In the absence of a clay neck, it serves as the attachment for the metal connector, which attaches the bowl to the pipe stem. It frequently exhibits flaking scars, cut marks, and grinding from the removal of the clay neck. A few flanges have been completely removed, either intentionally or accidentally, during the detachment of the neck.

Although most bowls were made with clay **stems** (Figure 55j), these were frequently removed by flaking and grinding and replaced with **metal connectors** (Figure 55m). Some types were made without stems. In addition to allowing the attachment of a metal connector, such modifications may also provide easier access to the interior of the bowl for cleaning (Schulz and Felton, n.d.). Surprisingly, there is no evidence for removal by sawing, although one specimen was vertically scored down to the top of the flange with a saw before flaking. A few bowls have stems made separately and attached at a later stage, prior to firing.

The paste or **clay** color can range widely, even on the same specimen, depending on imperfections in firing, use-blackening, different surface finishes, and post-depositional weathering. In the type descriptions it is described as it appears freshly broken. **Finish** describes gross surface character, including such obvious exterior treatments as glazing, burnishing, or slips. **Earthenware** is porous (sticks to the tongue) and soft (easily scratched), whereas **stoneware** is harder and usually nonporous.

Most bowls exhibit interior features relating to manufacture. **Turning striations** are very fine, evenly spaced, parallel lines produced by manipulating the sides of pipe bowls on wheel-thrown specimens. They differ from **wiping marks**, which are usually coarser, uneven, and broken. **Swirled** and **rippled marks** are distortions produced in wheel-thrown specimens where excess clay is compressed during formation of the basal opening and flange/stem. Where tops are made separately, they can be attached to the body with a **coil weld** (a small coil of clay) or a **slip weld** (a thin wash of clay). Coil welds produce a large ring of excess clay on the inside rim joint. Slip weld joints are much cleaner and have the appearance of being "glued."

Virtually every bowl has one or more **Chinese marks** (Figure 55h) consisting of characters, symbols, or designs. These are usually stamped on the bottom of the bowl near the flange, or sometimes on the sides of bowls, and are almost always oriented with the upper end towards the top of the bowl. Stamps come in two forms, those with characters pressed into the surface (**negative stamps**) and those where the stamp itself is sunk below the surface and the characters within it are raised (**positive stamps**). Chinese characters were also incised free-hand, or made using inlays of contrasting clays or twisted wire pressed into the wet clay.

Stamps also include bats, a rooster, a brush with scroll, a brush with vase, and a flower. These are thought to represent Taoist and Buddhist emblems (Fred Mueller, 1987:personal communication). Special *shòu* marks (longevity) are reminiscent of those found on Chinese pottery and porcelain (Hobson, 1915:225, Cox, 1970:1141). Small circular stamps with four petals surrounding a central dot have been called "money marks" by translators and may represent "cash" coins or wealth (Priscilla Wegars, 1986:personal communication).

Translations are difficult, even for native speakers, because many alternative meanings are possible and many characters are missing. The order in which characters are read and their associations with surrounding characters influences their meaning, and the beginning stamp or sequence is not always obvious. For example, a string of characters may encircle the base of the bowl, or a principal character may be placed in the center of a pattern for emphasis or aesthetics. Some appear to represent place names, owners' or makers' names, and occasionally dates. Dates are somewhat ambiguous, however, because of the sixty-year cycle of the Chinese calendar; the same date is used for different years (e.g., 1838, 1898, 1958, and so on).

Similar stamps and translations are reported from Ventura, California (Benté, 1976:483) and San Francisco (Garaventa and Pastron, 1983:320). Those that can be read at Lovelock, Nevada are thought to be shop marks from the Canton area (Praetzellis and Praetzellis, 1979:157, 191). Translations of New Zealand specimens consist of "euphoric phrases" such as "Double Radiance" or "Moon over the Flowers" (Ritchie, 1986:372).

Apart from their translated meanings, these marks can be useful in classifying bowl types and perhaps determining common factory or geographic connections. For example, all bowls manufactured using Technique I (wheel-thrown in one piece) share similar stamp arrangements or characters, most of which are unique to this group.

Pipe Bowl Manufacturing Techniques

Based on examinations of interior features, at least four distinctive manufacturing techniques can be identified for opium pipe bowls (Figure 56). Techniques I and II involved a single piece of clay formed entirely on a potter's wheel; III and IV were made in molds with tops added at a later stage. Interestingly, each technique seems to have a different set of clay types, firing, exterior treatments, and stamps. This may reflect specific kilns or manufacturing areas.

Technique I: Wheel-thrown in one piece — In this method, bowls were made upside-down like small vases, with the smoking surface on the bottom and the stem end up. Each piece was started with a wide mouth, so the interior could be worked by hand. Fingernails were used to make the sharp rim joint, turning striations were produced by pulling up and thinning the sidewalls, and fingertips were used to make the rounded shoulder joint. The wide opening was then reduced to a narrow neck and the flange and stem were formed by trimming excess clay. Excess clay on the interior was twisted and rippled by this compression and turning. The final steps cleared the stem with a round tool and incised the double lines around the exterior.

Seven types of pipe bowls were manufactured using this technique, including Circular ($n = 6$) and Elaborate ($n = 1$). All are made of a distinctive grey-green earthenware and have highly polished light grey tops, very similar arrangements of stamped characters, and beveled flanges made with stems. Sidewalls are uniformly 4-5 mm thick. It seems likely that these bowls were made in a single factory.

Technique II: Wheel-thrown in a solid piece, with carved interior — These bowls were also turned on a wheel and then hollowed out with special tools. This produced a distinctively rounded interior with carving and scraping tool marks

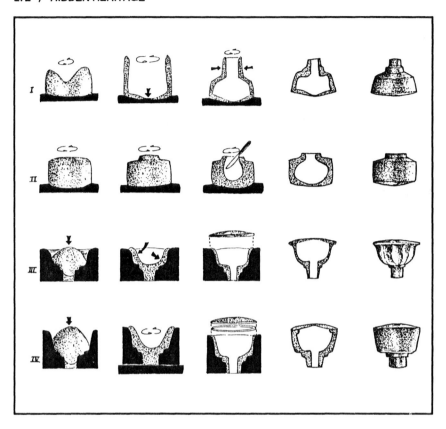

Figure 56. Clay pipe bowl manufacturing techniques.
I. wheel-thrown in one piece; II. wheel-thrown in a solid piece, with
carved interior; III. two-piece mold with slip-welded top; IV. two-piece
mold with coil-welded top. Techniques I, II, and perhaps IV were turned
on a potter's wheel. Drawn by Jennifer Chance.

and very thick walls, especially at the rim/shoulder joints and facet corners. Probably because of the need to get tools into the interior, these bowls were made without stems.

Twelve types were manufactured using this technique, including Circular ($n = 8$), Eight-sided ($n = 3$), and Six-sided ($n = 1$). All are stoneware, generally coarse, with rose-brown or mottled grey clay. Sidewalls vary between 4.5 and 7.5 mm thick. Similarities in stamps are present, crossing type boundaries, but not among specimens with different clay color. This suggests that more than one factory or area of manufacture was involved. One of these is probably the Yixing region, near Shanghai, noted for its distinctive "sandy" clays; specifically *zisha* or the "rose-brown" or "dark purplish-red" variety (Lo, 1986:12, 20). Yixing stoneware opium pipe bowls have been tentatively identified by Paul Chace (1988:personal communication) and Gallagher (n.d.:121).

Technique III: Molded in two pieces with slip-welded top — The body and tops of these bowls were hand molded separately and then joined with a thin wash of clay. The clay was hand-pressed into the molds which included stems. The body was made without the top, with the stem end down, giving complete access to the interior. Rim joints show drip marks on the inside and sometimes a faint horizontal line on the exterior. Fingerprints and wipe marks are common and usually quite obvious.

Twelve types were manufactured by this technique, including Circular ($n = 7$), Eight-sided ($n = 4$), and Six-sided ($n = 1$). While paste and exterior color vary, all are of soft earthenware and are very different from other bowls. Typical colors range from orange to brown, with minor amounts of grey probably due to incomplete oxidation. Slipped exteriors are common and are sometimes very pronounced on the bright orange specimens. Sidewalls are very thin, typically in the 2-3 mm range. This resulted in very light weight and fragile specimens which were easily broken, especially along the rim joint.

Technique IV: Molded in two pieces, usually with coil-welded top — These bowls were also made in two parts, except that the body, and perhaps the top, was wheel-thrown inside a mold, and then usually joined with a coil of wet clay. The excess clay forced out of the joint was almost always left untrimmed on the inside. A few specimens have slip-welded tops. Wipe marks and turning striations are obvious and fingerprints are rare. All exhibit thick walls, smoothly rounded interiors and turning striations, and lack any indication of being pressed into a mold.

This technique was used to manufacture the greatest number and range of types. Thirteen types include Circular ($n = 5$), Eight-sided ($n = 5$), Six-sided ($n = 1$), Four-sided ($n = 1$), and Elaborate ($n = 1$). All are of stoneware, with a generally fine texture. Most have rust-brown paste with dark grey exteriors, but dark and light grey specimens are also present. Pipes are made with and without stems; stemmed varieties have had the stem attached at a later stage. This is unique to this technique and may have been done to avoid the extra effort required to extract the bowl from the mold.

There is some similarity among stamps, but less so than with the other three manufacturing techniques. In addition to being slip-welded, two types have narrower than average sidewalls and little or no evidence of a coil-welded top. Another unusual feature is exhibited by other bowls, where some kind of pronged tool was inserted into the body cavity through the basal opening prior to firing, creating deep "needle-like" holes in the thick clay around the inside of the stem. The purpose of this is unknown but may be related to drying or hanging the bowl during firing.

Stone Bowls

Twelve stone pipe bowls were examined (Figure 57). The stone in all cases appears to be different varieties of highly polished "jade." Colors range from white and yellow, to orange, green, and brown. The stone bowls' overall similarity to ceramic bowls is striking, despite the obvious differences in material and technology. Although exact typological comparisons are not possible, they are dominated by Circular and Eight-sided types ($n = 4$). One specimen even has a circular smoking surface and ten sides. Three others have no ceramic counterparts. Two have circular smoking surfaces with scalloped bodies (eight-lobed) and one has an elaborate margin with rounded projections.

None of the stone bowls have necks, although all but one have the same low flange as ceramic bowls. This may be due to the need for wider access into the interior during manufacture. The interior cavities have been carved, much like Technique II clay bowls, but have smaller interior volumes than their ceramic counterparts.

Smoking surfaces are uniformly convex, although three have pronounced extensions or "nipples" immediately around the smoking hole. (Only one ceramic specimen has this feature.) These nipples may have assisted in holding the opium, or perhaps they help hold commercially prepared opium **pellets**. Smoking holes are generally large. Four bowls show especially large openings for circular inserts. One specimen has a deep, cup-shaped ceramic insert in place. Stone bowls are probably less likely to require repairs to smoking holes, yet they show a higher frequency of inserts than their ceramic counterparts (42% vs. 22%). Perhaps this was a way to have a thin wall at the smoking hole without weakening the entire top.

While not reported from archaeological sites, stone bowls are not uncommon. Four of the forty-seven pipe specimens exhibited at the Stanford University Museum of Art in 1979 had stone bowls (Maveety, 1979:9, 10, 12). A good illustration of four other pipes with stone bowls is published in Rapaport (1979:149).

Descriptive Classification of Ceramic Pipe Bowls

A total of fifty separate bowl types has so far been identified (Table 35). This classification is based primarily on the shape of the smoking surface as suggested by Ritchie (1986), overall form, manufacturing technique, and clay. The sources of the type specimens are fifty-seven bowls, primarily from private collections in the western United States (Wylie and Fike, 1985), and 199 classifiable specimens from Riverside, California (Wylie and Higgins, 1987). We speculate that this represents about half to three-quarters of the total number of types present at all overseas Chinese sites.

Based on shape of the smoking surface, bowls are organized into the following basic groups: A (Circular) (Figures 58-61), B (Eight-sided) (Figures 62-63),

Table 35. Summary of Opium Pipe Bowls

Construction Technique	Distinguishing Attributes	Types	Totals
I	Grey earthenware with grey-green sides and polished grey tops. Stem with grooved flange.	A2, A3, A21, A22, A23, A24, E3?	7
II	Rose-brown (Yixing?) stoneware. No stems.	A9, A18, A20, B13	12
	Grey stoneware. No stems.	A5?, A28, A29, A30?, A31, B11, B12, C3	
III	Orange to light grey earthenware. Slipped. Stemmed.	A1, A6, A8, A13?, A15, A19, A26, B1, B2?, B3, B4, C1	12
IV	Rust-brown stoneware. Polished dark grey exterior. Unstemmed (or stems made separately).	A7?, A10, A25, A27, A32, B5, B7, B8? B9? B10?, C2, D1, E1	13
Unknown		A4, A11, A14, A16, B6, E2	6
		Total Types	50

Note: Type A9 includes former Type A17, Type A18 includes former Type A12.

C (Six-sided) (Figure 64), D (Four-sided) (Figure 64), and E (Elaborate) (Figure 65). Circular bowls are by far the most common (n = 30 types), followed by eight-sided (n = 13). Bowls with elaborately scrolled tops are rare (n = 3), as are six-sided bowls (n = 3) and four-sided bowls (n = 1). Care should be taken in applying type descriptions too rigidly, as many are based on single specimens, most of which are fragmentary.

In decreasing order, pipe bowl types were classified based on examination of the following numbers of whole or reconstructible specimens: Type A2 (n = 24); A3 (n = 13); Types A1 and A8 (n = 6); Types A9, B3, and B5 (n = 3); Types A4, A10, A15, A18, C2, and D1 (n = 2). All other types are based on a single specimen.

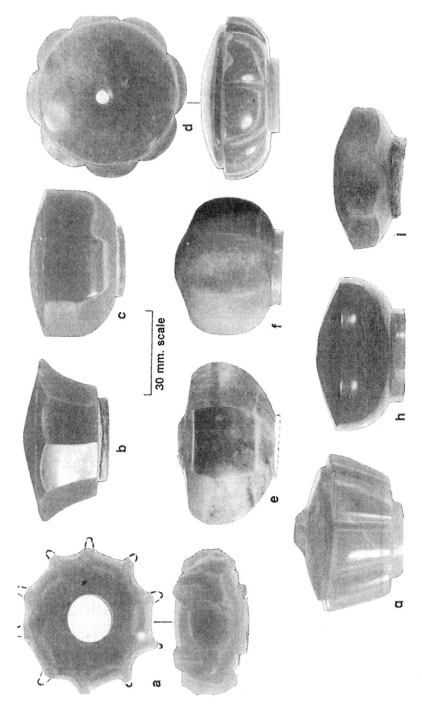

Figure 57. Stone opium pipe bowls. a) elaborate; b) ten-sidd with circular top; c) eight-sided; d) scalloped; e and f) eight-sided; g) scalloped (eight lobes); h) circular; i) eight-sided.

30 mm. scale

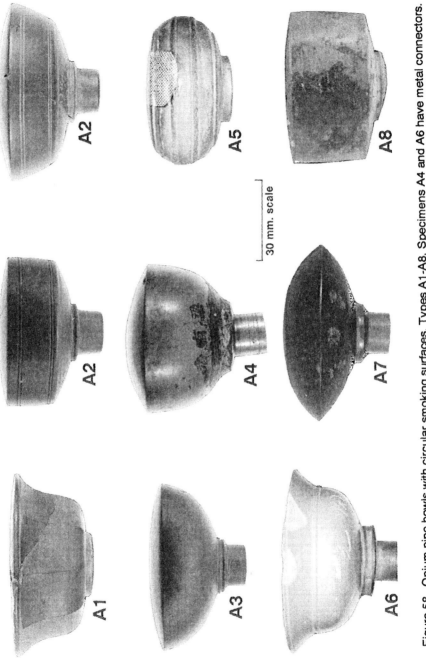

Figure 58. Opium pipe bowls with circular smoking surfaces, Types A1-A8. Specimens A4 and A6 have metal connectors. Type A5, photographed in a private collection, has been repaired (with a bandaid patch) by the owner.

277

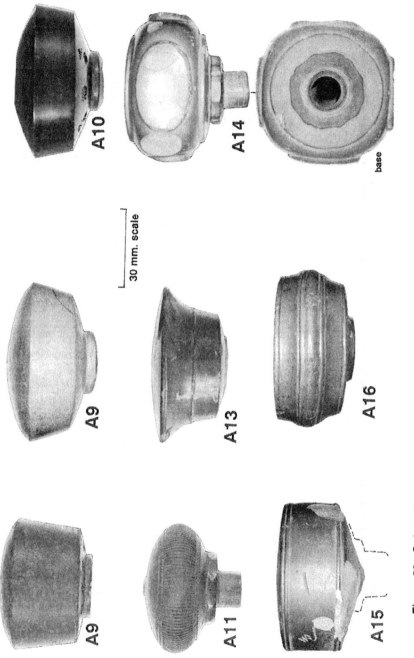

Figure 59. Opium pipe bowls with circular smoking surfaces, Types A9-A16. A12 and A17 have been absorbed by other types. Type A14 has a metal connector and a slightly squarish body but a circular smoking surface.

278

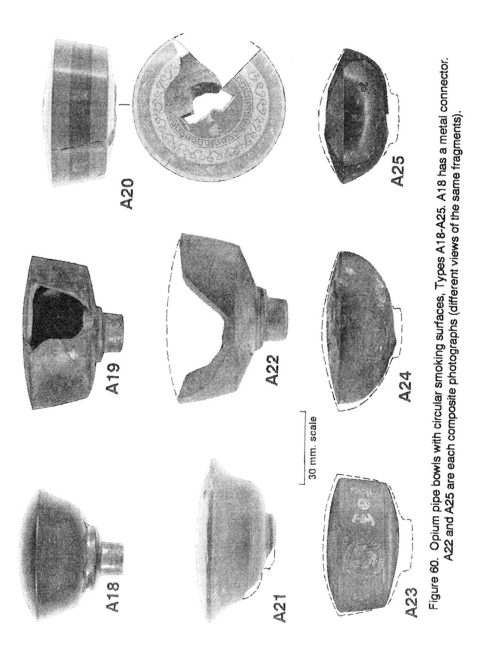

Figure 60. Opium pipe bowls with circular smoking surfaces, Types A18-A25. A18 has a metal connector. A22 and A25 are each composite photographs (different views of the same fragments).

A20

A25

A19

A22

A24

A18

A21

A23

30 mm. scale

279

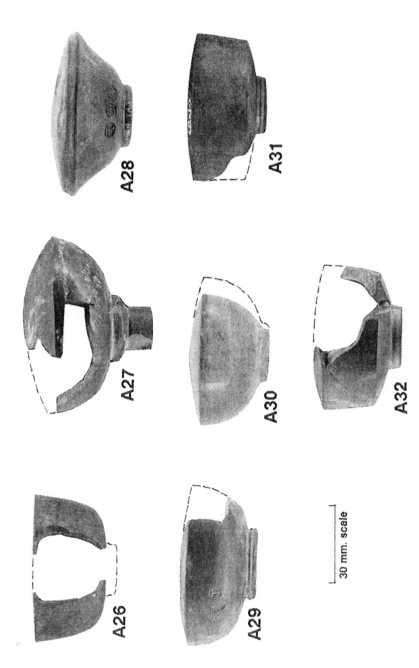

Figure 61. Opium pipe bowls with circular smoking surfaces, Types A26-A32. A26 is a composite photograph (different views of the same fragment).

30 mm. scale

280

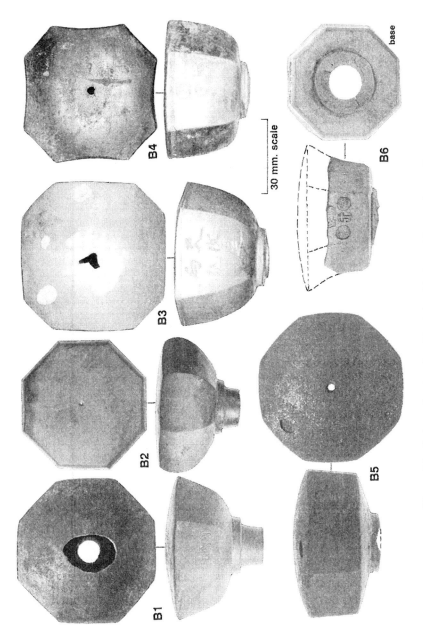

Figure 62. Opium pipe bowls with eight-sided smoking surfaces, Types B1-B6.

30 mm. scale

B1 B2 B3 B4 B5 B6 base

281

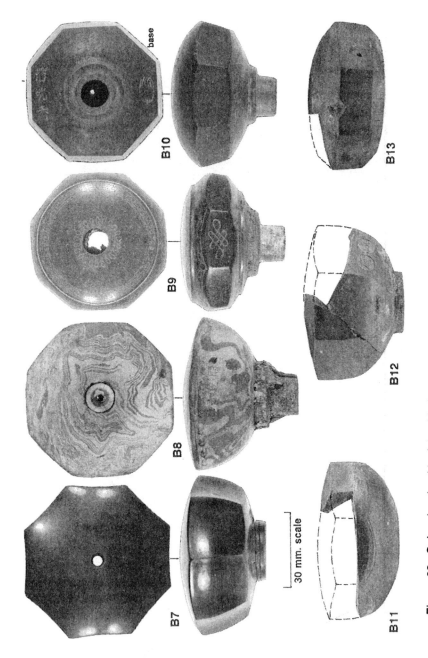

Figure 63. Opium bowls with eight-sided smoking surface, Types B7-B13. B8 and B9 have metal connectors. B8 has a ceramic insert. B7 and B9 have also been modified for inserts.

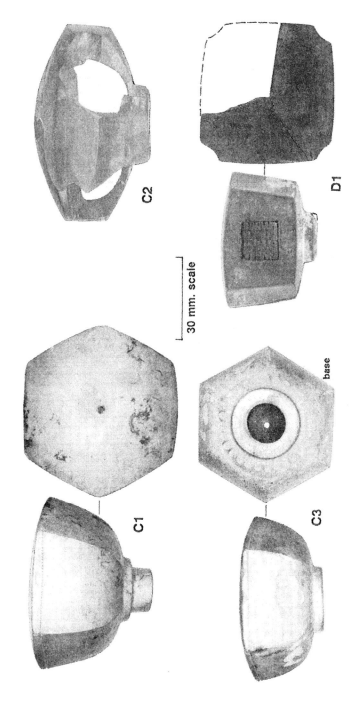

Figure 64. Opium pipe bowls with six-sided smoking surfaces, Types C1-C3, and a four-sided smoking surface, Type D1. C2 is a composite photograph (different views of the same fragment).

30 mm. scale

C2

D1

C1

C3

base

283

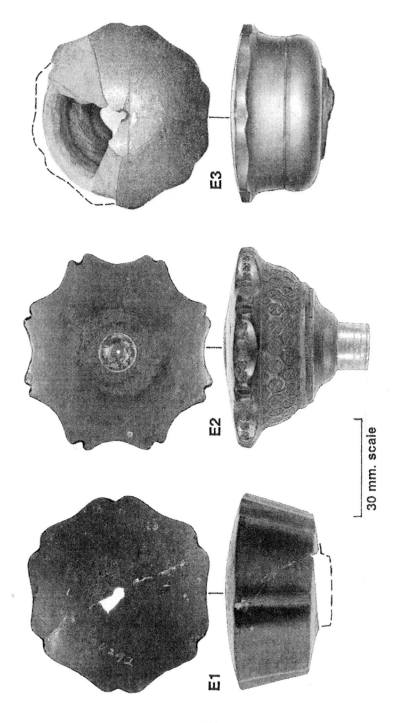

Figure 65. Opium pipe bowls with elaborate smoking surfaces, Types E1-E3. E2 has a ceramic insert and a metal connector.

E3

E2

E1

30 mm. scale

284

Full descriptions of these opium pipe bowl types (including specifics on bowl top, sides, base, diameter, marks, clay/finish, construction, examples, and comments) are on file at the Asian American Comparative Collection, Laboratory of Anthropology, University of Idaho, Moscow, ID 83843.

OTHER ITEMS ASSOCIATED WITH OPIUM SMOKING

Stone Fists

Five "jade" and soapstone "fists" were examined (Figure 66a). Carved in the shape of clenched fists, representing both right and left hands, they have two large holes connecting at a 90-degree angle. The wrist hole connects with the pipe stem and the other hole connects with the neck of the bowl (Rapaport, 1979:147, illustrated). Some fists have metal "bracelets," probably for attachment. Hole diameters range from 16.8 to 19.3 mm and average 17.5 mm. Heights range from 41.3 to 51.7 mm.

Pipes with stone fists are shorter, have bowls attached to the terminal end of the stem, and lack the usual extension beyond the bowl attachment. The reason for this is unclear, but perhaps the opium smoking bowl could be removed and the rest of the pipe used for tobacco, or at least disguised. Such a pipe minus the specialized opium pipe bowl would not be as obvious (or illegal) as the uniquely shaped "opium pistol."

Although none of the specimens we examined were attached to pipes, other sources do show them that way. The Stanford University Art Museum display contained several pipes identified for use with opium and tobacco. The one illustrated specimen has a bowl and a fist on the end (Maveety, 1979:12). A photograph of the Terry collection in North Carolina also shows a similar pipe, also with a stone bowl (Rapaport, 1979:149).

Opium Serving Dishes

We examined four items reputed to be containers for individual servings of opium. All are circular and, with one exception, quite shallow. One specimen is a shallow, dish-shaped bowl of white clay glazed on all but the base. With an inside diameter of 28 mm and 4 mm deep, it has an estimated volume of 1.5 cc. Tests show it could comfortably hold 2.5 grams of syrup, suggesting it was used for half-size servings (30 grains or 2.0 grams). Another specimen is white "jade," with a separate lid, and is 33 mm in diameter and 10 mm deep (Figure 66b). A third specimen is a shallow stone dish 52 mm in diameter and 6.5 mm high with a surface that is only slightly concave. A fourth specimen is ivory, 45 mm across and 5 mm high, and also has a surface that is only slightly concave.

Small metal trays made of metal cut from opium cans are also known to have been used as serving dishes (Figure 66c). These are presently known as **fans** (pronounced "funs"), referring to a Chinese unit of measure used in selling

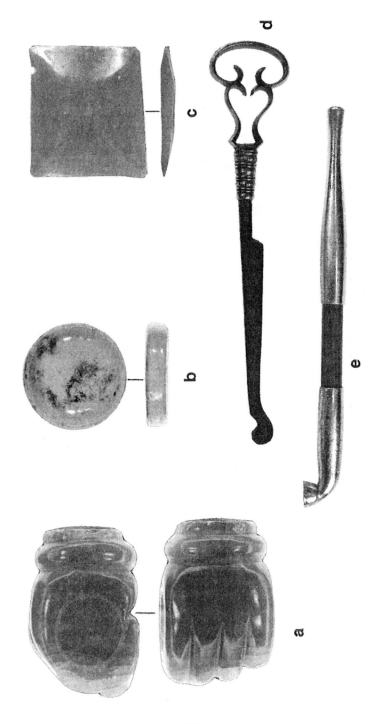

Figure 66. Miscellaneous opium smoking paraphernalia. a) jade "fist" bowl connector; b) ceramic opium serving dish; c) metal opium serving dish (fans); d) pipe cleaning tool; e) Japanese "tobacco" pipe. Items not shown to the same scale.

286

individual opium servings (Ritchie, 1986:389; Wegars, 1984:2). They are roughly square, with slightly raised sides, and measure from 2.3 to 3.4 cm on a side.

Cleaning Tool

A multi-purpose cleaning tool examined from a San Francisco opium kit measures 15 cm in length and consists of what appears to be an iron blade set in an elaborate brass handle (Figure 66d). The blade is wedge-shaped in cross section; one edge is fairly sharp and the opposite side is flat. The sharp side was apparently used to scrape opium ash from the smoking surface of the bowl; the rounded end is small enough to have been inserted into the neck of the bowl to clean the inside of the pipe, and the V-shaped notch may have been used to clean the cooking needle. It was the only cleaning tool in the kit.

Metal Pipes

We examined four Japanese pipes with small metal bowls reputedly used for smoking tobacco (Rapaport, 1979:137-144). One specimen was hammered brass; three others had separate metal mouthpieces and bowls connected by a reed or wooden stem (Figure 66e). They ranged in length from 180 mm to 445 mm, but despite their wide variation in sizes and styles, all had bowls approximately 10 mm in diameter. Similar pipes recovered from the Tucson Chinatown have tested positive for opium (James Ayres, 1988:personal communication).

Opium Cans

Although commonplace, the standard five-tael containers used to import Chinese opium to this country have, until recently, not been studied in great detail (Figure 67a). However, a study of cans initiated at the University of Idaho in 1985 has begun to systematically examine these artifacts (Wegars, 1985:2). There are apparently two types, a large rectangular one and a narrower version with rounded sides. Both held equal amounts of opium. Good descriptions of the former can be found in Callaway (1979:320) and Felton, Lortie, and Schulz (1984:67-70). The oval cans were made in China and Mexico, probably after the turn of the century (Ayres, 1988:7; Lister and Lister, 1989:80, 84).

Rectangular cans are made from five pieces of sheet metal: top and top edge strip, together forming the detachable lid; heavier gauge interior reinforcing band; side piece, folded to form the body; and bottom. The entire container measures 9.3 × 6.5 × 4.3 cm, and holds approximately 250 cc. Stamps indicating the opium brand or company are found on the lid and occasionally on the base (Figure 67b). At least twenty different lid stamps have been identified (Wegars, 1985:2). One of the most popular brands is "Source of Beauty" (lì yuán) (Sando and Felton, Chapter 8, herein). Not much is known about the narrow, round-sided variety of opium cans except that they measure 11.5 × 6.0 × 2.5 cm (Harney and Cross,

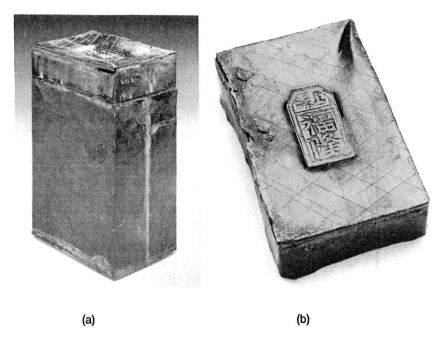

(a)   (b)

Figure 67. Metal opium can. a) complete can; b) example of lid stamp
showing cross-hatching cancellation. University of Idaho Asian American
Comparative Collection artifacts WCC-75a and b. Photo by Mark LaMoreaux

1973:49; Wegars, 1986:3). We speculate that they may have contained opium in
"pill" form.

Cross-hatched incised lines on the can lids (Figure 67b) provide a clue for
dating. If these are cancellations of federal revenue stamps, as suggested by
specimens from Lovelock (Callaway, 179:320) and others from Utah seen by the
authors, they could only have been in use during the legal importation of smoking
opium, sometime prior to 1909. The absence of incised lines would not be
significant, however, because we do not know when the practice began, or if some
were imported illegally and thus evaded taxation.

Glass Lamps

Opium lamps of glass are thought to have been made in Birmingham, England
and imported to this country from China (Kane, 1882:36). They consist of four
main parts: circular base with four air intake ports, egg-shaped oil reservoir,
circular wick cap, and a bell-shaped cover (Figure 68a-f). Some glass wick
supports also have a small metal tube for the wick. These elements are found at

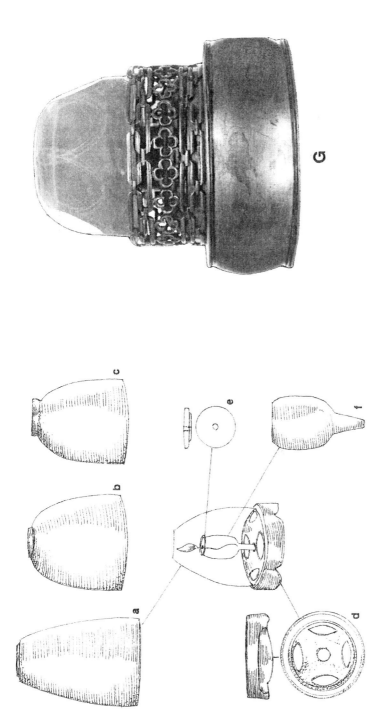

Figure 68. Glass opium lamp parts and metal lamp. a-c) glass chimney types; d) glass base; e) glass wick holder; f) glass oil reservoir; g) metal lamp with faceted glass cover. a-f drawn by Jennifer Chance.

289

many overseas Chinese sites, but never in large quantities or as complete specimens. Bottles were sometimes modified for use as covers (LaLande, 1981:163-165; Sisson and Harrison, 1983:4).

Metal Lamps

References to metal opium lamps in the archaeological or historical literature are rare. They may have been used primarily by travelers (Kane, 1882:37; Culin, 1891:499). We examined two specimens from the West Coast which are said to date from ca. 1880-1900 (Figure 68g). A rectangular lamp is 52.9 mm high and 109.2 mm long; the circular specimen (Figure 68g) is 50.5 mm high and 75.3 mm in diameter. Each has a base reservoir topped by a screw-in wick assembly, a removable air-intake collar, and a small, faceted glass chimney supported by the collar. The wick assemblies, elaborately decorated collars, and chimneys are identical and interchangeable. Only the bases differ; one is circular and the other is rectangular. The latter also houses a detachable funnel and a small cylindrical container, both with lids. The interiors of all items, including the reservoir bases, appear to be copper lined. The rectangular lamp has two basal stamps; the circular lamp has one.

DISCUSSION

Kinds of Opium Smoking Behavior and Rationale for Smoking

There were many different kinds of opium smoking, and many different reasons for smoking. Opium could be smoked during the day to endure physical labor, or at night for relaxation prior to sleeping. Undoubtedly, many Chinese smoked because it was enjoyable and a normal part of their culture; others smoked because they were addicted. Opium provided a temporary escape from feelings of alienation, loneliness, sexual abstinence, and debt (Wylie and Higgins, 1987:362). Medicinally, it was an effective treatment for pain, spasm, inflammation of mucous membranes of the nose and throat, diarrhea, local and general nervous disorders, and insomnia (Holmes, 1884:793). In the upper class, opium was offered as a token of hospitality at social gatherings and as a part of conducting business, and was a popular way of treating guests, business associates, even policemen and doctors calling on a residence (*Harper's Weekly*, 1880b:566; Ritchie, 1986:266). Opium use by the working class Chinese is likely to have centered around commercial opium "dens" or other locations where socialization occurred, such as stores and boarding houses. Such recreational smoking may have served as a "safety valve" for the stress of everyday life (Courtwright, 1982:68), while reinforcing social bonds and ethnicity. Urban opium smoking may also be associated with Chinese laundries, which were noted for their long hours and difficult working conditions (Felton, Lortie and Schulz, 1984:105).

A work-related smoking pattern dominated the nonurban work camps, which were characterized by poorer working and living conditions, strenuous labor, a lack of professional medical care, and fewer recreational outlets. In this regard, we need to more carefully examine the relationship of Chinese laborers to their work places and places of residence. Sleeping arrangements may be particularly important, because considerable smoking was done just prior to sleep. Chinese boarding houses might be incorrectly identified as opium "dens," and work areas could also serve as living/sleeping quarters.

The pattern of heavy opium use in work camps is reflected in the archaeological record. Table 36 measures intersite differences in opium use by comparing ceramic pipe bowls with tablewares. For example, excavations at Pierce, Idaho

Table 36. Urban Versus Nonurban Opium Use Levels
(Opium pipe bowls compared with Chinese tablewares)

	Sherds	Min. Specimens	References
Urban Sites			
Virginia City, NV	1% (3/503)		Evans, 1980
San Francisco, CA		2% (7/443)	Garaventa and Pastron, 1983
Weaverville, CA	3% (3/95)		Brott, 1982
Riverside, CA		3% (88/2766)	Wylie and Higgins, 1987
Lovelock, NV	11% (39/350)		Hattori, Rusco, and Tuohy, 1979
Ventura, CA		17% (21/122)	Evans, 1980
Woodland, CA	23% (55/240) and	49% (25/51)	Felton, Lortie, and Schulz, 1984
New Zealand urban sites		49% (41/84)	Ritchie, 1986
Nonurban Sites			
Donner Summit, CA	15% (154/1019)		Evans, 1980
Columbia, CA	17% (1/6)		Evans, 1980
Val Verde, TX	23% (195/857) and	50% (23/46)	Briggs, 1974
Jacksonville, OR	32% (7/22)		LaLande, 1981
New Zealand work camps		100% (86/86)	Ritchie, 1986
Pierce, ID	62% (34/55)		Stapp and Longenecker, 1984

Source: Wylie and Higgins, 1987:364-365.

yielded thirty-four opium pipe sherds compared to fifty-five tableware sherds, or a value of "62 percent." Increases or decreases in opium use can be measured against culinary behavior, which we assume to be relatively uniform. Absolute numbers could be misleading; large amounts of opium paraphernalia, from large sites or large samples, do not necessarily indicate "high" opium use.

These data show that opium use is generally higher in work camps and that a "high" incidence of opium use is anything above a 1:10 sherd ratio in urban sites and 1:4 in nonurban work camps. It also shows that breakage patterns differ between pipe bowls and tablewares, as might be expected. Pipe bowls are smaller and, in many cases, more durable, thus break less often and produce fewer sherds. Consequently, relative percentages based on minimum numbers are twice as high as sherd percentages at Woodland and Val Verde.

Variation in Effects

Not only was there considerable variation in opium behavior, the physical effects were not always the same. Historical accounts can be found which demonstrate that Chinese both benefited and suffered from regular opium use (see Felton, Lortie, and Schulz, 1984:102-106). Due to the complex properties of this drug, we speculate that different effects were possible depending on such factors as regularity of use, quantity, diet, exercise, environment, smoking equipment, smoking technique, and quality of the drug. For example, heavy users in labor-intensive jobs might show little effect, but be buffered from work-related discomforts as long as they had an uninterrupted supply and avoided the debilitating effects of withdrawal (see Masters, quoted in Dobie, 1936:251).

Smoking equipment and techniques may also have played a role in limiting adverse effects. Poisonous alkaloids were deposited inside the pipe before reaching the smoker's mouth (Holmes, 1884:784). The "opium pistol" style of pipe may have been designed to enhance this precipitation and protect the smoker's health. Use of higher grades of opium, containing a lower percentage of morphia, may also have limited the risk of addiction (Masters, 1896:56). Individuals most likely to afford the best opium would probably be the merchants and workers with steady jobs.

Related Opium Behavior and Artifacts

In addition to smoking, there was a range of activities relating to opium. These included opium production, paraphernalia manufacture, importation/marketing, operation of opium "dens," pipe bowl repair, opium recycling, and treatment of the effects of opium use (Wylie and Higgins, 1987:358-361). The first two of these were limited to China, with the exception of some processing of raw opium in San Francisco and Victoria and Vancouver, British Columbia (Culin, 1891:498; Morton, 1974:212), and a few failed attempts at growing opium in the United States (Lawton, 1987:313-315; Holmes, 1884:792).

No special artifacts are associated with the importation or marketing of opium or opium paraphernalia, other than the standard opium cans with cancelled duty stamps. Opium "dens," on the other hand, would be expected to yield the full range of paraphernalia. For example, a feature at Riverside Chinatown interpreted as a "den" yielded ninety-three pipe bowl sherds from eight different bowl types, a pill can, seventeen lamp parts, an opium cooking needle, and a pipe endpiece (Wylie and Higgins, 1987:355). Opium cans would also be expected, except where site conditions resulted in poor preservation. The presence of pipe bowl menders is indicated by various modifications of pipe bowls, primarily smoking hole inserts, as well as through their mending tools, including bow drills, saws, files, burnishers, and hammers (Schulz and Felton, n.d.). Curved scrapers for removing ash, and a small pestle and mortar for pulverizing it, could suggest that opium residues were recycled for smoking or drinking (Harney and Cross, 1973:17; Ayres, 1988:5). Treatment of opium effects might involve "antidote" pills, which may have been distributed in small metal cans with a sliding closure top (Ritchie and Bedford, n.d.:18-19, 20, 23; Ritchie, 1986:393; Wylie and Higgins, 1987:332-333). In addition, regular users were likely to use tongue scrapers for cleaning residues from their tongues, and laxatives to counteract the effects of chronic constipation (Culin, 1891:500; Holmes, 1884:793).

Socio-economic Differences in Opium Paraphernalia

Based on clay type, surface treatments, and overall appearance, we can tentatively classify opium pipe bowls into the following "expensive" and "inexpensive" classes:

Inexpensive Pipe Bowls	Expensive Pipe Bowls
Techniques I & III	Techniques II & IV
Earthenware Types:	Stoneware Types:
A1-A4, A6, A8, A13-A15,	A5, A7, A9, A10, A18, A20, A25,
A19, A21-A24, A26, B1-B4,	A27-A32, B5, B7-B13, C2, C3,
C1, E3.	D1, E1, E2.

The manufacturing technique cannot be determined for Types A11 and A16, because they are whole specimens. Types A12 and A17 have been absorbed by other types. Bowls in the "inexpensive" class are earthenware. They typically have thin walls (thus are easily broken) and exhibit few surface treatments aside from slips. Most are very plain. "Expensive" bowl types, on the other hand, are made of stoneware, and typically have thicker walls and burnished, decorated surfaces. Some, like types A20 and D1, are very elaborate.

While admittedly very subjective, the above may provide a way of examining social status among opium smokers. Intrasite comparisons may indicate laborers' preference for cheaper equipment, or opium dens frequented by better paying (white?) customers. Intersite comparisons may also be revealing. All New

Zealand types with known equivalents in our typology are "inexpensive" specimens. All are closely associated with Chinese gold camps or remote mining towns.

Other "expensive" opium paraphernalia include stone pipe bowls, stone fists, stone and ivory end pieces, and metal lamps. Unfortunately, to our knowledge none of these have been recovered from an archaeological site.

Bowl Chronology

It is unclear why opium pipe bowls are not better chronological indicators; they would seem to be excellent candidates. They are common, easily recognized, durable, and highly variable. Yet, attempts to develop a bowl chronology have had very limited success. Even with large numbers of specimens from a controlled archaeological context, such as at the Chinatown in Riverside, California, the results are inconclusive (Wylie and Higgins, 1987:357). This inability to use opium pipe bowl types as chronological indicators has also been noted in New Zealand by Ritchie (1986:400).

There are several possible reasons for this. Many specimens are from private collections which, at best, can only be loosely associated with a range of dates for the occupation of a site; and cross-dating of types is hampered by the lack of a standard typology, as well as a paucity of tightly dated archaeological specimens. In the future, manufacturing techniques may prove to be time-sensitive, even if individual pipe types are not.

Two specimens do have stamped characters which refer to dates. The characters *ping tzu* on Type B5 may be 1876 (or 1816 depending on the sixty-year cycle), and *wu hsu* on Type B8 may be 1898 (or 1838). The latter specimen is thought to be associated with post-1890 Chinatown deposits at Stockton, California. This indicates that stamps may be very useful, if the proper sixty-year cycle can be determined independently.

Improvised and Homemade Paraphernalia

Opium paraphernalia which was homemade or improvised from ordinary artifacts is not as obvious and may easily be overlooked. We examined a small soy sauce container from Idaho that had been modified for use as a pipe bowl (Figure 69). A smoking hole had been ground into the shoulder, and presumably the spout had been plugged and the large opening attached to the pipe stem. This is not uncommon. Other improvised pipe bowls were made from small ceramic pots or vases (Ritchie, 1986:396; Ayres, 1988), metal door knobs or oil cans (Lister and Lister, 1989:83), or glass medicine bottles (Ritchie, 1986:396). Kane noted that when pipe bowls were in short supply, they were manufactured from ink bottles (Kane, 1882:40). Many ink bottles of this period were made of clay, coincidentally, not unlike the shape of traditional opium pipe bowls. Lamp chimneys

30 mm. scale

Figure 69. Small soy sauce jar possibly modified for use as an opium
pipe bowl. Note the smoking hole ground on the shoulder.

were easily manufactured from cut bottles (LaLande, 1981:165; Sisson and
Harrison, 1983:4).

The presence of opium paraphernalia improvised from other artifacts or made
from scratch indicates isolation from commercial sources. This trait is much more
common in remote work camps and is also noted in urban settings after the turn of
the century, when opium smoking was prohibited. These items are not as obvious
as factory-made equipment, and greater care is needed to identify them as opium-
related artifacts.

Pipe Bowl Similarities

Features common to all pipe bowls—such as general dimensions, smoking
surface, and lack of stamped or incised decoration on the smoking surface—must
have been functional. The bowls' close similarity to door knobs was probably no
accident; both were designed to be grasped comfortably. The flat or slightly
convex smoking surface was used to roll and manipulate the opium during the
cooking process. Stamps or incised Chinese characters on the smoking surface
would have interfered with this, as well as with the cleaning of ash residues.

Consequently, inscriptions were usually located on the base, or sometimes on the side of the bowl, where they would not be obscured or in the way.

Pipe Bowl Typological Variation

There is remarkable variation in the types of opium pipe bowls and the ways in which they were manufactured. Fifty types and four manufacturing techniques have been tentatively identified, and many more are likely. This is in marked contrast to other Chinese ceramic traditions, such as tablewares, which were very standardized and resistant to change. Two possible explanations come to mind: 1) commercial competition, driven by a growing market and high profits, or 2) different ceramic traditions which were responding experimentally to a relatively new demand. While traditional Chinese tablewares were highly uniform and unchanging, largely due to a long tradition of government control, ceramic pipe bowl production may have been influenced by "the frenetic change induced by the underlying premises of industrial capitalism" (Felton, Lortie, and Schulz, 1984:89). Lacking the tradition and stability of other ceramic types and driven by a growing opium market, all during a time of great social upheaval in China, it is no wonder pipe bowl types exhibit great variation.

The Yixing Example

Yixing may illustrate the factors influencing the production of opium pipe bowls in China. Yixing County in Jiangsu Province, 100 km west of Shanghai, is famous for its artistically inscribed teapots made from distinctive local clays. Yixing pottery declined rapidly during the second half of the 19th century for several reasons. The area was devastated during the siege of Nanjing (1853-1864), as part of the Taiping Rebellion. Also, the humiliation and disillusionment suffered by China in its defeat in the Opium Wars of 1839-1842 and 1856-1860 caused great national unrest and questioning of traditional values. The result was fewer pottery commissions by the wealthier class and an increase in mass-produced items for the commercial market, including opium pipe bowls (Lo, 1986:153, 241).

Today the pottery town of Dingshuzhen (in Jiangsu Province) has over twenty factories, each producing a different ware. The presence of mica and a high iron oxide content gives Yixing ware, and especially the *zisha* variety, its sandy surface and dark purplish-red color, features which distinguish it from other Chinese wares. This special combination produced pottery with the porosity of earthenware and the stone-like durability of stoneware. Although chemical analysis of the clay is needed for positive identification, pipe bowl Types A9, A18, A20, and B13 closely match the description of Yixing wares. In addition, Type A20 exhibits elaborate inlaid inscriptions on the side and bottom, a characteristic Yixing feature, and unique to this type.

Variations in Smoking Techniques and Equipment

There were at least two methods of smoking opium, each involving different forms of the drug and different kinds of equipment. The most common involves an elaborate set of equipment centering around an "opium pistol" and intensive socializing. A much simpler method utilizing a pipe with a small metal bowl may have involved solid opium "pills" or opium/tobacco mixtures. Although it is presently unclear, these different methods may reflect personal versus social smoking, a concern with concealment, and/or a shift in the form of opium available. The use of tall metal "water pipes" is less well understood, but might also have been for smoking mixtures of tobacco and opium. The use of hashish in pipes with small metal bowls or in water pipes should also not be ruled out.

Advantages, Disadvantages, and Other Factors

Studies examining opium use have proposed many reasons for the high rates of opium use in overseas Chinese culture. But, as suggested above, the simple answer is that **opium did many things for many people**. Obviously, the reasons for smoking or selling opium were important enough to outweigh the disadvantages. Not only were the "advantages" significant, they were interrelated, involved more than just smoking, and were closely tied to opium use and marketing in China. These included financial profit, medicinal effects, enhanced work performance, psychological release, pleasure, and reinforced social bonds and ethnicity. Disadvantages included the risk of addiction, cost, time lost smoking, nausea and chronic constipation, and the possibility of fines and imprisonment. Socioeconomic factors affecting an individual's involvement included access to the opium market network, price and the user's ability to pay, and the local working conditions.

SUMMARY AND CONCLUSIONS

Despite this section's title, the following are presented more as working hypotheses and starting points for further study. In developing these statements, we have not been timid in pushing the data as far as possible in hopes of stimulating new thinking. While some are quite elementary and others are very speculative (or even contradictory), they provide an outline for a "model" of overseas Chinese opium behavior.

1. *We must look to China to understand opium behavior.* Overseas Chinese opium behavior was largely influenced by opium use and marketing in China. High levels of use in the U.S. reflected use in China, especially the Canton area.

2. *There was a link between tobacco and opium smoking.* The early practice of smoking opium and tobacco together never died out entirely. Some dry and wet "tobacco" pipes were also used for opium.

3. *Chinese opium smoking was not necessarily a "vice."* There were many positive social, physical, and psychological benefits from the regular use of opium which outweighed the disadvantages. Addiction was a calculated risk and could be avoided.

4. *Non-Chinese opium smoking was a different pattern of behavior.* Although Chinese equipment and techniques were borrowed intact, non-Chinese smokers used opium differently, more like alcohol. White smokers were dominated by certain groups and were not representative of the general population.

5. *The classic "opium pistol" pipe is a highly complex and specialized piece of equipment.* It allowed for opium to be smoked by itself and more efficiently, and may have been designed to maximize user comfort and minimize harmful effects. Prior to that, raw opium was mixed with tobacco.

6. *Pipe bowl inserts were functional.* They served to repair broken smoking holes or avoid breakage. They may also have been used to adapt bowls for smoking other drugs, including hashish and tobacco.

7. *The uniformity in pipes was related to function.* Pipe bowl dimensions, thinning of the wall around the smoking hole, and the general shape of the "opium pistol" were related to the size of the average user's hand, arm length, and the functional requirements of smoking.

8. *The diversity of bowl types is more apparent than real.* Much of the variation is due to manufacture by wheel-thrown techniques and an overemphasis by researchers on shape. Differences are exaggerated by the use of small sample sizes and fragmentary specimens.

9. *The diversity of bowl types is real and significant.* As many as 75 to 100 bowl types may exist as distinguishable entities, making them a notable exception to the uniformity and stability usually exhibited by Chinese ceramics. Different factories, diverse manufacturing techniques, commercial competition, experimentation, and lack of government control are possible explanations for this diversity.

10. *Bowl manufacturing techniques represent different factories or areas in China.* Yixing is the only specific area to be tentatively identified. Manufacturing techniques are more easily identified than individual bowl types when classifying pipe bowl fragments.

11. *Very expensive opium paraphernalia was limited to China and large overseas Chinatowns.* Stone bowls, stone fists, and other exotic items are rare and not found in archaeological sites. "Expensive" ceramic pipe bowls are expected only in urban contexts.

12. *Reasons for smoking opium varied considerably.* Relaxation, coping with emotional stress, enhancing work performance, and medication were the primary reasons for smoking opium.

13. *Urban and nonurban opium patterns differ.* Urban areas had greater access to marketing networks, more competition, and a wider range of paraphernalia. Larger populations allowed more variation in types of smoking and opium related behavior, including pipe mending, and specialized areas for smoking. Both expensive and inexpensive ceramic bowls were present. Nonurban work camps had less diversity of opium behavior and artifacts, more improvised equipment, and a higher level of use relative to culinary behavior (ceramic tablewares). Inexpensive bowl types were dominant.

14. *Opium smoking did not necessarily lead to addiction.* The effects of opium use depended on a number of cultural, technological, and physiological factors. These were recognized by smokers and used to reduce the risk of addiction while enjoying the advantages of opium use.

15. *Many opium artifacts may represent non-smoking activities.* Marketing, operating "dens," and pipe repair also involved opium paraphernalia.

16. *Opium pipes differed.* These differences may reflect private versus social smoking patterns, a shift in the form of opium, or concern for concealment.

17. *Opium use was reinforced by a unique series of physical and cultural feedback mechanisms.* Addiction, profit, employment, and "blowing off steam" interacted to sustain and increase opium use. Increases in any one sparked increases in others, resulting in even greater opium use.

REFERENCES CITED

AYRES, JAMES E.
1988 Chasing the Dragon with an Opium Pistol, paper presented at the 21st Annual Meeting of the Society for Historical Archaeology, Reno, Nevada.

BALL, J. DYER
1893 *Things Chinese,* (2nd Edition), Charles Scribner's Sons, New York.
1903 *Things Chinese,* (4th Edition), Kelly and Walsh, Hong Kong.

BENTÉ, VANCE G.
1976 Good Luck, Long Life, in *The Changing Faces of Main Street,* R. S. Greenwood (ed.), Redevelopment Agency, City of San Buenaventura, Ventura, California, pp. 457-495.

BERRIDGE, VIRGINIA
1978 East End Opium Dens and Narcotic Use in Britain, *Pharmacy in History,* *20*:3, pp. 91-100.

BRIGGS, ALTON K.
1974 The Archeology of 1882 Labor Camps on the Southern Pacific Railroad, Val Verde, Texas, Master's thesis, University of Texas, Austin.

BROTT, CLARK W.
1982 Moon Lee One: Life in Old Chinatown, Great Basin Foundation, Weaverville, California.

CALLAWAY, CASHION
1979   Metal Artifacts from Ninth and Amherst, in "Archaeological and Historical Studies at Ninth and Amherst, Lovelock, Nevada," E. M. Hattori, M. K. Rusco, and D. R. Tuohy (eds.), Nevada State Museum, *Archaeological Services Reports,* Carson City, Nevada, pp. 251-347.

CLAY, WALLACE
1969   Personal Life of a Chinese Coolie 1869-1899, ms. on file at the Asian American Comparative Collection, University of Idaho, Moscow.

COHEN, AL
1986   Letter to Priscilla Wegars, Asian American Comparative Collection, University of Idaho, Moscow, Idaho.

COURTWRIGHT, DAVID T.
1982   *Dark Paradise: Opiate Addiction in America Before 1940,* Harvard University Press, Cambridge, Massachusetts.

COX, WARREN E.
1970   *The Book of Pottery and Porcelain,* Volume 1. Crown Publishers, Inc., New York.

CULIN, STEWART
1891   Opium Smoking by the Chinese in Philadelphia, *American Journal of Pharmacy, 63*:10, pp. 497-502.

DERIG, BETTY
1972   Celestials in the Diggings, *Idaho Yesterdays, 16*:3, pp. 2-23.

DOBIE, CHARLES C.
1936   *San Francisco's Chinatown,* D. Appleton-Century Company, New York.

ETTER, PATRICIA A.
1980   The West Coast Chinese and Opium Smoking, in *Archaeological Perspectives on Ethnicity in America: Afro-American and Asian American Culture History,* R. L. Schuyler (ed.), Baywood Publishing Company, Amityville, New York, pp. 97-101.

EVANS, WILLIAM S., JR.
1980   Food and Fantasy: Material Culture of the Chinese in California and the West, Circa 1850-1900, in *Archaeological Perspectives on Ethnicity in America: Afro-American and Asian American Culture History,* R. L. Schuyler (ed.), Baywood Publishing Company, Amityville, New York, pp. 89-96.

FARRÈRE, CLAUDE
1941   *Black Opium,* Robert C. Fairberg, New York.

FAY, PETER WARD
1975   *The Opium War 1840-42: Barbarians in the Celestial Empire in the Early Part of the Nineteenth Century and the War by which They Forced Her Gates Ajar,* University of North Carolina Press, Chapel Hill.

FELTON, DAVID L., FRANK LORTIE, and PETER D. SCHULZ
1984   The Chinese Laundry on Second Street: Archeological Investigations at the Woodland Opera House Site, "The Chinese Laundry on Second Street: Papers on Archeology at the Woodland Opera House Site," D. L. Felton, F. Lortie, and P. D. Schulz (eds.), *California Archeological Reports,* No. 24, State of California Department of Parks and Recreation, Sacramento, pp. 1-120.

GALLAGHER, SHARON
n.d.   Opium Smoking and Its Paraphernalia at Yema-Po: The Overseas Chinese at Lake Chabot Dam, Oakland, California, ms. in preparation, University of California, Hayward.
GARAVENTA, DONNA M. and ALLEN G. PASTRON
1983   Chinese Ceramics from a San Francisco Dump Site, in "Forgotten Places and Things," A. E. Ward (ed.), *Contributions to Anthropological Studies*, No. 3, Center for Anthropological Studies, New Mexico, pp. 295-320.
GENTRY, ROGER L.
1987   Seals and Their Kin, *National Geographic*, April, pp. 475-501.
HARNEY, MALACHI L. and JOHN C. CROSS
1973   *The Narcotic Officer's Notebook*, (2nd Edition), Charles C. Thomas, Springfield, Illinois.
HARPER'S WEEKLY
1880a   An Opium Palace, *Harper's Weekly*, 24:1214, pp. 221-222, April 3.
1880b   Opium Smoking in China, *Harper's Weekly*, 24:1236, pp. 565-566, September 4.
1882   Waifs and Strays, *Harper's Weekly*, 26:1320, p. 215, April 8.
1888   The Chinese Boarding-House, *Harper's Weekly*, 32:1667, p. 918, December 1.
HATTORI, EUGENE M., MARY K. RUSCO, and DONALD R. TUOHY (eds.)
1979   Archaeological and Historical Studies at Ninth and Amherst, Lovelock, Nevada, *Archaeological Services Reports*, Nevada State Museum, Carson City, Nevada.
HEFFERON, JAMES WILLIAM
1986   Oral history recorded and edited by John Eldredge, manuscript in the possession of John Eldredge.
HOBSON, R. L.
1915   *Chinese Pottery and Porcelain: An Account of the Potter's Art in China from Primitive Times to the Present Day*, Cassell and Company, Ltd., New York.
HOLMES, EDWARD M.
1884   Opium, *Encyclopaedia Britannica*, (9th Edition), Charles Scribner's Sons, New York, pp. 787-795.
HUC, M.
1871   *A Journey Through the Chinese Empire*, Vol. 1, Harper and Brothers, New York.
THE ILLUSTRATED LONDON NEWS
1858   Untitled article on opium smoking from unnamed special artist and correspondent in Canton, September 27.
1883   The Chinese Opium Manufacture, December 8.
KANE, HARRY HUBBELL
1881   American Opium-Smokers, *Harper's Weekly*, September 24, pp. 645-646.
1882   *Opium-Smoking in America and China: A Study of its Prevalence, and Effects, Immediate and Remote, on the Individual and the Nation*, Putnam, New York. (Reprinted 1976, Arno Press, New York.)
KUFFNER, CARMEN S.
1979   Opium Containers and Paraphernalia from Ninth and Amherst, "Archaeological and Historical Studies at Ninth and Amherst, Lovelock, Nevada,"

E. M. Hattori, M. K. Rusco, and D. R. Tuohy (eds.), *Archaeological Services Reports,* Nevada State Museum, Carson City, Nevada, pp. 596-613.

LALANDE, JEFFREY M.

1981   Sojourners in the Oregon Siskiyous: Adaptation and Acculturation of the Chinese Miners in the Applegate Valley, ca. 1855-1900, Master's thesis, Oregon State University, Corvallis.

LAWTON, HARRY W.

1987   A Brief Note on Opium-Growing by Riverside's Founders, in *Wong Ho Leun: An American Chinatown,* Vol. Two, Great Basin Foundation, San Diego, pp. 313-315.

LESLIE, FRANK

1877   The Opium Habit, *Frank Leslie's Popular Monthly.*

LISTER, FLORENCE C. and ROBERT H. LISTER

1989   The Chinese of Early Tucson: Historic Archaeology from the Tucson Urban Renewal Project, University of Arizona, *Anthropological Papers* No. 52, Tucson.

LO, K. S.

1986   *The Stonewares of Yixing From the Ming Period to the Present Day,* Sotheby's Publications, Hong Kong University Press, Hong Kong.

MASTERS, FREDERICK J.

1896   The Opium Traffic in California, *The Chautauquan, XXIV*:1, pp. 54-61.

MAVEETY, PATRICK

1979   *Opium: Pipes, Prints, and Paraphernalia,* exhibit catalogue, May 29-August 19, 1979, Stanford University Museum of Art, Stanford, California.

McCUNN, RUTHANNE LUM

1979   *An Illustrated History of the Chinese in America,* Design Enterprises, San Francisco.

MERIWETHER, LEE

1888   The 'Labor Question' on the Pacific Coast, *Harper's Weekly,* October 13.

MILLER, GEORGE

1983   Wild Horses, Water Barons, and Chinese Sojourners: Archaeology of Yema-Po, A Chinese Construction Camp in San Francisco's East Bay Hills, *C. E. Smith Museum Bulletin, 1*:2, pp. 2-8.

MORTON, JAMES

1974   *In the Sea of Sterile Mountains: The Chinese in British Columbia,* J. J. Douglas, Ltd., Vancouver.

O'CONNELL, ANNETTE O.

1980   Chinese Opium Pipes, *Old Bottle Magazine, 13*:10, pp. 8-11.

PRAETZELLIS, ADRIAN and MARY PRAETZELLIS

1979   The Lovelock Ceramics, "Archaeological and Historical Studies at Ninth and Amherst, Lovelock, Nevada," E. M. Hattori, M. K. Rusco, and D. R. Tuohy (eds.), *Archaeological Services Reports,* Nevada State Museum, Carson City, Nevada, pp. 140-198.

RAPAPORT, BENJAMIN

1979   *A Complete Guide to Collecting Antique Pipes,* Schiffer Publishing Co., Exton, Pennsylvania.

RAVEN, SHELLY
1987   Red Paper and Varnished Ducks: Subjective Images of Riverside's Chinatown, in *Wong Ho Leun: An American Chinatown,* Volume One, Great Basin Foundation, San Diego, pp. 215-275.

RITCHIE, NEVILLE A.
1986   Archaeology and History of the Chinese in Southern New Zealand during the Nineteenth Century: A Study of Acculturation, Adaptation, and Change, Ph.D. dissertation, University of Otago, Dunedin, New Zealand.

RITCHIE, NEVILLE A. and STUART H. BEDFORD
n.d.   An Analysis of the Metal Containers from Chinese Sites in the Cromwell Area, Central Otago, New Zealand, ms. on file, Asian American Comparative Collection, Laboratory of Anthropology, University of Idaho, Moscow.

SCHULZ, PETER D. and DAVID L. FELTON
n.d.   Archaeological Perspectives on a 19th-Century Chinese Craft: Opium Pipe Bowl Mending, preliminary draft, ms. on file at California Department of Parks and Recreation, Sacramento.

SISSON, DAVID A. and RICHARD HARRISON
1983   Chinese Occupation in the Lower Salmon River Canyon of Central Idaho, paper presented at the 16th Annual Meeting of the Society for Historical Archaeology, Denver.

STAPP, DARBY, C. and JULIA G. LONGENECKER
1984   1983 Test Excavations at 10-CW-159, the Pierce Chinese Mining Site, *University of Idaho Anthropological Research Manuscript Series,* No. 80, Moscow.

WEGARS, PRISCILLA
1984   Chinese Comparative Collection *Newsletter, 1*:1, University of Idaho, Moscow.
1985   Asian Comparative Collection *Newsletter, 2*:2, University of Idaho, Moscow.
1986   Asian Comparative Collection *Newsletter, 3*:4, University of Idaho, Moscow.

WHITE, PETER T.
1985   The Poppy—For Good and Evil, *National Geographic, 167*:2, pp. 143-189.

WORSWICK, CLARK and JONATHAN SPENCE
1978   *Imperial China: Photographs 1850-1912,* Pennwick Publishing.

WYLIE, JERRY
1980   Opium Pipes and other Chinese Artifacts from Boise Basin, Idaho, USDA Forest Service, Intermountain Region, Boise National Forest, Boise.

WYLIE, JERRY and RICHARD FIKE
1985   Overseas Chinese Opium Smoking Material Culture Survey: Preliminary Results and Request for Assistance, ms. in possession of the authors.
1986   A Survey of Opium Pipes and Related Smoking Paraphernalia, paper presented at the 19th Annual Meeting of the Society for Historical Archaeology, Sacramento.

WYLIE, JERRY and WILLIAM GEER
1983   Opium Pipe Bowls and Celadon Ware from Southern Idaho, paper presented at the 16th Annual Meeting of the Society for Historical Archaeology, Denver.

WYLIE, JERRY and PAMELA HIGGINS
1987   Opium Paraphernalia and the Role of Opium in Riverside Chinatown, in *Wong Ho Leun: An American Chinatown,* Volume Two, Great Basin Foundation, San Diego, pp. 317-383.

PART FOUR
Analytical Techniques

Researchers have long wanted to be able to analyze Chinese sites and artifacts with more precision, particularly for dating purposes. Unlike objects such as Euroamerican ceramics or glass, Chinese artifacts rarely have datable marks on them. In other cases the date on the object is too early for the site on which it was found, because some objects, such as ceramics, had "heirloom" value while others, such as coins, might remain in use for several hundred years.

In recent years, Chinese artifacts, particularly ceramics, have begun to be subjected to scientific analysis in order to solve problems of dating, composition, and attribution. Harvey Steele describes how the techniques of X-ray fluorescence spectroscopy and optical emission spectroscopy can be applied to the underglaze blue component of Asian porcelains. The elements manganese and cobalt are important constituents of these glazes, and the amounts of each vary with the purity of the glaze. With spectroscopy, these amounts are expressed as ratios of manganese to cobalt, and can then be compared with known standards for various Asian porcelains. Under ideal conditions, subject to more refinement of the methods, wares made in China can be differentiated from those made in Japan, and date ranges can be assigned to them.

Research by Alison Stenger expands on the above approach to produce "element profiles" of various wares with which archaeological specimens can be compared. Again using X-ray fluorescence spectroscopy and optical emission spectroscopy, several types of ceramics were analyzed and dated on the basis of their chemical resemblance to wares of known date and composition. These analyses have generated some controversy, in that wares believed to be Chinese on stylistic grounds have been shown to have element profiles more consistent with Japanese manufacture.

CHAPTER 11

The Manganese/Cobalt Ratio in Nineteenth and Twentieth Century Asian Porcelain

Harvey Steele

Since the work of Ebelman and Salvetat (1851), a large variety of technical studies of Asian ceramics has been recorded. The studies have focused largely on pre-19th century wares and have comprised two major orientations: 1) the work of craft potters and chemists seeking to reproduce elemental combinations for replication of desired classic glaze effects (Wood, 1978), or 2) the work of chemists and museum curators seeking to understand the chronology of glaze and composition differences (Steele, 1981).

Until recently, few Asian items of 19th or 20th century origin were included in compositional analysis studies. The reasons for this lack of interest in late wares are not hard to document. Sir Harry Garner, a respected authority on Chinese porcelain, has summarized some of these reasons (1977:51-53):

> (1) The decline in standards, started in the reign of Ch'ien Lung [Qian Long] continued rapidly in the subsequent reigns of the Ch'ing [Qing] dynasty, . . . The decline is particularly noticeable in the quality of the porcelain itself and the white glaze. . . .
>
> (2) Something should be said about the Chinese blue and white of the twentieth century. Porcelain of far higher quality than anything produced in the nineteenth century, devoted entirely to copies of the earlier Ming and Ch'ing wares, has been made in China in recent years. . . . But the outlook of the craftsmen who made the pieces and conditions of manufacture are so different, in the genuine wares and the copies, that it is only a matter of time before they all appear in the right perspective.

Thus, the late wares have been regarded as technically and chronologically unimportant, and very little attention, analytic or otherwise, has been allocated to their study.

Archaeological and ethnographic work on overseas Chinese sites, particularly in the American West, has stimulated new interest in the ceramics produced in Asia in the 19th and 20th centuries. Research by Chace (1976), Garaventa and Pastron (1983), Olsen (1978), Pastron, Gross, and Garaventa (1981), and others has focused attention on ceramic types which Garner and other antiquarians would have dismissed as unimportant.

PRESENT RESEARCH

Since 1977, the author has directed technical studies of 19th and 20th century Asian wares at three technical laboratories for the U.S. Customs Service, at San Francisco, Los Angeles, and Savannah, Georgia. The studies have centered on glazes and bodies, with somewhat more emphasis on the former. The aim has been to discover significant elemental ratios in well authenticated wares to use as a guide in authentication of poorly documented wares. In general, two main instrumental methods have been employed: optical emission spectroscopy and X-ray fluorescence spectroscopy.

Optical emission spectroscopy is a well-established technique for the analysis of trace elements in artifacts. It involves the excitation, by means of an electric arc, of the elemental atoms in the sample, and the analysis of the constituent wavelengths of the light released when excitation ceases. The wavelengths, separated by a prism, are each characteristic of individual elements, and the intensity of light or particular wavelengths indicates the relative concentration of each element. Fred Davis, who has performed most of such studies at the San Francisco laboratory of the U.S. Customs Service, emphasizes that such results are only semi-quantitative at best (Steele and Davis, 1980, 1981, 1982). For a given element, e.g., cobalt, the concentration scale differentiates "much" (over 10%), "some (1-10%), "little" (0.1-1%), and by "trace" (less than 0.1%) amounts.

X-ray fluorescence spectroscopy is a physical method of analysis that determines the chemical composition of various substances, including pottery. The specimen is subjected to irradiation by primary X-rays, releasing energy in the form of fluorescent X-rays. Since each element emits these secondary X-rays at characteristic wavelengths, an identification of the elements can result through the determination of the wavelengths, separated using a diffraction crystal grating. The concentration of each element can be estimated from the intensity of the X-rays, expressed in "counts." Paul Doemeny, U.S. Customs laboratory, Los Angeles, and Carson Watts, U.S. Customs laboratory, Savannah, have employed this method on imported Asian ceramics, under the direction of the author (Steele and Doemeny, 1981; Steele and Watts, 1981; Watts, 1980).

Since 1977, nearly 300 samples of ceramics, most of them of Asian origin, and some of them of well-documented 19th or 20th century manufacture, have been tested by the three U.S. Customs laboratories under the direction of the author. More recently, similar studies, requested by Stenger (1985), have been performed at the San Francisco U.S. Customs laboratory, and at two other independent laboratories in the Portland metropolitan area. The results, not yet completely interpreted, are beyond the scope of this chapter. However, one focus of the original work, the determination of the manganese/cobalt ratio in the underglaze blue decoration of blue and white Asian ceramics, is well understood.

The term "ratio," as applied in this context, is the relationship between two similar magnitudes in respect to the number of times the first contains the second. For example, a Mn/Co ratio of 2.0 means that the proportion of manganese to cobalt in the sample is 2:1, or "two to one."

A brief summary of the research on the manganese/cobalt ratio would start with the development, in 1955, of the X-ray fluorescence method of spectroscopy, at the Oxford University Research Laboratory in Oxford, England. Following that discovery, Sir Harry Garner directed an analysis of eighty-five well-documented Chinese porcelain specimens, with the results published in 1956 (Young, 1956). Following this study, eighty-three separate well-documented specimens, selected by Margaret Medley, were tested and reported by Banks and Merrick (1967). Adrian Joseph tested sixteen more samples and his results, plus a summary of all the previous work on the manganese/cobalt ratio, were subsequently published in Joseph (1970). As established in these early studies, the Mn/Co ratio indicates and distinguishes the periods of Chinese porcelain production in which a cobalt oxide of low manganese content, presumably the cobalt imported from the Middle East, the so-called "Mohammedan Blue," was used, from those periods in which native cobalt sources, with a higher manganese content, were used (Young, 1956:43-47). Beals and Steele (1981:17) have summarized and charted the mean of high values recorded by Young (1956) and by Banks and Merrick (1967).

Yap and Tang (1984, 1985) have reported on more recent Mn/Co research, specifically directed to late 19th and 20th century samples. Twelve samples considered to have been produced between ca. 1875 (the first year of the reign of Emperor Guangxu [Kuang Hsu]) and ca. 1935 have an Mn/Co ratio ranging from 2.59 ± 0.20 to 4.93 ± 0.64, indicating a cobalt source (native Chinese?) with a high manganese impurity level. Thirty-three modern samples, ranging from ca. 1947 production to ca. 1982 production, and including two Japanese items and two Thai items of approximately the same period, had an Mn/Co ratio of well under 1.0, indicating a cobalt oxide of relative purity, probably a technical grade manufactured in Germany.

Table 37 summarizes the research on the Mn/Co ratio in studies directed by the author. Generally the results, whether X-ray fluorescence (as in the original studies) or emission spectroscopy, are consistent with those obtained in the earlier studies. They indicate that native cobalt oxides, with relatively high manganese

Table 37. Manganese/Cobalt Ratios of Porcelain Samples Tested by U.S. Customs Laboratories

Chronology[a]	Mn/Co[b]	Description	Sample	Reference
Early 19th C	Under 1.0	Blue/white, floral pattern	Bing-1	Davis, 1979
Ca. 1830	2.50	Blue/white, floral pattern	'83	Watts, 1980
19th C	Over 1.5	Polychrome, Canton ware	9	Davis, 1985
19th C	7.77[c]	Blue/white, floral pattern	25	Watts, 1980
19th C	Over 2.0	Blue/white, floral pattern	Misson	Davis, 1980
19th C	Over 2.0	Blue/white, floral pattern	Stupfel	Davis, 1980
Late 19th C	Over 2.0	Blue/white, Bamboo pattern	7	Davis, 1985
Late 19th C	Over 2.0	Blue/white, Bamboo pattern	8	Davis, 1985
Late 19th C	Under 1.0[d]	Blue/white, floral pattern	1900	Watts, 1980
1875-1908	Over 2.0	Blue/white, floral pattern	1875	Doemeny, 1981
1900	Over 2.0	Blue/white, floral pattern	OM-1	Davis, 1979
1920s	Over 1.0	Blue/white, floral pattern	PRC-1	Davis, 1979
1920s	Over 2.0	Blue/white, floral pattern	1925	Doemeny, 1981
1975	Under 1.0	Blue/white, floral pattern	1975	Doemeny, 1981
1979	Under 1.0	Blue/white, floral pattern	1979	Watts, 1980

[a] Assumed chronology based on established provenience or manufacturing records.
[b] Except in two samples, exact Mn/Co ratios were a mean of three or more numerical values.
[c] Although this was a Chinese-type vessel, with Chinese peony motifs, the crudeness of the painting style suggests that the origin may have been Southeast Asia. The high Mn/Co ratio would make that attribution more plausible, although there is also the possibility that an earlier production period in China might be indicated.
[d] This vessel was sold by Sotheby's Hong Kong and authenticated as "ca 1900," usually a reliable authentication, at least in the antiquarian trade. However, the relatively pure Mn/Co ratio indicates probably later production, after 1918, or, even more likely, after 1949.

impurity levels, were used in China well into the 20th century. In Japan, where less evidence is available, Stitt (1974:126) has commented on the use of the native *gosu* (a native Japanese cobalt of high manganese impurity levels) until about 1869. Later samples tested indicate a shift to technical grade cobalt oxides, also probably of German origin, having an impurity level well below 1.0 Mn/Co. The German source for high purity cobalt oxide in Japan was a likely result of the work of Dr. Gottfried Wagner, an influential German chemist (Stitt, 1974:121). Normalization of German-Chinese trade relations following the 1911 revolution in China probably resulted in the importation of similar high-purity German cobalt oxides, although such importation was perhaps interrupted somewhat by the 1914-1918 war in Europe.

Although reasonably well-documented samples have been tested, there are still some remaining cautionary reservations about the research on the Mn/Co ratio: 1) the selection of samples to be tested has been dependent on a few antiquarians who, however well-respected, are relying primarily on stylistic traditions; 2) the identification of cobalt sources and even the modern technical grades has not been established in systematic fashion; and 3) the historical research, necessary as a corollary to documentation of temporal shifts in cobalt sources and procurement, has been incomplete and inconclusive.

Recent research on archaeological sites in Oregon indicates a mixture of Chinese and Japanese ceramics in well-documented contexts dating from about 1880 to about 1920. Systematic testing of material from such sites, such as has been attempted by Stenger (1985) for the Rocky Point site, may be one avenue for provenience control in more precise determination of the significance of the Mn/Co ratio and other elemental ratios or relationships applicable to 19th and 20th century Asian ceramics.

The samples in Table 37 were all of well-documented Chinese origin. In comparison, six samples of documented Japanese ceramics have been tested for the Mn/Co ratio of the underglaze blue. Yap and Tang (1984:79-80) found two ca. 1980 to 1982 samples of Japanese porcelain to have an Mn/Co ratio well under 1.0, indicating a relatively more modern technical grade of cobalt. Davis (1980) determined the Mn/Co ratio of four documented Japanese samples, two of the Arita-district Imari-type polychrome wares and two ca. 1980 imported porcelains. The two ca. 1980 samples and the Imari ware identified as ca. 1920 were found to have Mn/Co ratios of approximately 1.0 or slightly lower, whereas the ca. 1840 Imari porcelain fragment had an Mn/Co ratio in excess of 2.0, indicating the probable use of the native *gosu* (Stitt, 1974:126).

SUMMARY

Although the number of documented 19th and 20th century samples of Asian porcelain tested for the Mn/Co ratio is relatively small: forty-five by Yap and Tang (1984, 1985), fifteen by three U.S. Customs Laboratories (Davis, 1979,

1980, 1985; Doemeny, 1981; Watts, 1980), and two by Banks and Merrick (1967), some fairly clear patterns emerge from the data. With few exceptions, the results support the generalization that Chinese potters were using cobalt of high manganese impurity levels (over 2.0 Mn/Co) well into the 20th century, probably until the government of the People's Republic of China resumed porcelain production in 1949, at which time technical grades of cobalt oxide (with Mn/Co levels well under 1.0) were used. The data suggested that the shift in Japan to technical grades of cobalt oxide noted by Stitt (1974:126) did occur late in the 19th century, predating the Chinese shift by thirty to forty years or more.

The utility of the Mn/Co ratio to archaeologists interpreting sites of the overseas Chinese, ca. 1850-1980, is threefold: 1) Chinese blue and white wares can be divided into roughly two Mn/Co populations (1850-1949—over 1.0, and 1949-1980—under 1.0); 2) Japanese blue and white wares of the same period can be divided into roughly two Mn/Co populations (1850-1870—over 1.0, and 1870-1980—under 1.0); 3) sherds of approximately equal Mn/Co ratios (e.g., within about 20%) are probably from the same manufacturing context.

It would be unwise to suggest implications beyond those indicated above. Unless refinements in authentication methods are accomplished, only a more precise fully quantitative approach to Mn/Co determinations, e.g., using neutron activation analysis, can yield a reliable chronology of Mn/Co ratios which field archaeologists could use with confidence.

As the study by Beals and Steele (1981) has suggested, shifts in the Mn/Co ratio in the Ming (1368-1644) and early Qing (1644-1796) periods are relatively well understood because of the greater number of samples tested. A program of testing well-authenticated 19th and 20th century Asian porcelains, such as that initiated by C. T. Yap at the Department of Physics, National University of Singapore (Yap, 1988, 1989), might expand our knowledge of the shifts, if any, in Mn/Co ratio chronology that have occurred in the modern period. Another obstacle to formulating complete and accurate Mn/Co chronologies, the problem of comparing results from one technical method with data from another method, has been addressed in recent work by Tite and Bimson (1991). With the continuation of this research, the pioneering studies of Young (1956) and Banks and Merrick (1967) may finally be updated.

REFERENCES CITED

BANKS, M. S. and J. M. MERRICK
    1967   Further Analysis of Chinese Blue and White, *Archaeometry, 10,* pp. 101-103.
BEALS, HERB and HARVEY STEELE
    1981   Chinese Porcelains from Site 35-TI-1, Netarts Sand Spit, Tillamook County, Oregon, *University of Oregon Anthropological Papers,* No. 23, Eugene.

CHACE, PAUL G.
1976   Overseas Chinese Ceramics, in *The Changing Faces of Main Street,* R. S. Greenwood (ed.), Redevelopment Agency, City of San Buenaventura, Ventura, California, pp. 509-530.

DAVIS, FRED
1979   Laboratory Report, ms. on file at the U.S. Customs Laboratory, San Francisco.
1980   Laboratory Report, ms. on file at the U.S. Customs Laboratory, San Francisco.
1985   Laboratory Report, ms. on file at the U.S. Customs Laboratory, San Francisco.

DOEMENY, PAUL
1981   Laboratory Report, ms. on file at the U.S. Customs Laboratory, Los Angeles.

EBELMAN, W. and J. SALVETAT
1851   Research on Chinese Porcelain, *Journal of the Franklin Institute, 23*:2, Philadelphia, pp. 257-261.

GARAVENTA, DONNA M. and ALLEN G. PASTRON
1983   Chinese Ceramics from a San Francisco Dump Site, "Forgotten Places and Things: Archaeological Perspectives on American History," in *Contributions to Anthropological Studies,* No. 3, A. E. Ward (comp. and ed.), Center for Anthropological Studies, Albuquerque, pp. 295-320.

GARNER, SIR HARRY
1977   *Oriental Blue and White,* Faber and Faber, London.

JOSEPH, ADRIAN M.
1970   *Ming Porcelains: Their Origins and Development,* Praeger, New York.

OLSEN, JOHN W.
1978   A Study of Chinese Ceramics Excavated in Tucson, *Kiva, 44*:1, pp. 1-50.

PASTRON, ALLEN G., ROBERT GROSS, and DONNA GARAVENTA
1981   Ceramics from Chinatown's Tables: An Historical Approach to Ethnicity, and Appendix C—Catalog of Chinese Ceramic Ware Collected at N-5, in *Behind the Seawall: Historical Archaeology along the San Francisco Waterfront,* A. G. Pastron, J. Prichett, and M. Ziebarth (eds.), San Francisco Clean Water Program, San Francisco, pp. 365-469, 653-682.

STEELE, HARVEY
1981   Technical Analysis of Chinese Porcelains: A Critical Review, ms. on file at the Ceramics Analysis Laboratory, Portland State University, Portland, Oregon.

STEELE, HARVEY AND FRED DAVIS
1980   Recent U.S. Customs Analyses of Oriental Porcelain, ms. on file at U.S. Customs, Portland, Oregon.
1981   Recent U.S. Customs Analyses of Oriental Porcelain, ms. on file at U.S. Customs, Portland, Oregon.
1982   Recent U.S. Customs Analyses of Oriental Porcelain, ms. on file at U.S. Customs, Portland, Oregon.

STEELE, HARVEY AND PAUL DOEMENY
1981   Recent U.S. Customs Analyses of Oriental Porcelain, ms. on file at U.S. Customs, Portland, Oregon.

STEELE, HARVEY and CARSON WATTS
1981   Recent U.S. Customs Analyses of Oriental Porcelain, ms. on file at U.S. Customs, Portland, Oregon.

STENGER, ALISON
1985   Rocky Point: Land of Few, Home of Many, ms. on file at the Ceramics Analysis Laboratory, Portland State University, Portland, Oregon.

STITT, IRENE
1974   *Japanese Ceramics of the Last 100 Years,* Crown, New York.

TITE, M. S. and M. BIMSON
1991   A Technological Study of English Porcelain, *Archaeometry, 33*:1, pp. 3-27.

WATTS, CARSON
1980   Laboratory Report, ms. on file at the U.S. Customs Laboratory, Savannah, Georgia.

WOOD, NIGEL
1978   *Oriental Glazes,* Watson-Guptill, New York.

YAP, C. T.
1988   A Quantitative Spectrometric Analysis of Trace Concentrations of Manganese and Cobalt in Ceramics and the Significance of As/Co and Mn/Co Ratios, *Journal of Archaeological Science, 15,* pp. 173-176.
1989   A Non-Destructive Scientific Technique of Detecting Modern Fake Reproduction Porcelains, *Oriental Art, 35,* pp. 48-51.

YAP, C. T., and S. M. TANG
1984   X-Ray Fluorescence Analysis of Modern and Recent Chinese Porcelains, *Archaeometry, 26*:1, pp. 78-81.
1985   Energy Dispersive X-Ray Fluorescence Analysis of Chinese Porcelains Using Am-241, *Archaeometry, 27*:1, pp. 61-63.

YOUNG, STUART
1956   An Analysis of Chinese Blue-and-White, *Oriental Art, 2,* pp. 43-45.

CHAPTER 12

Sourcing and Dating of Asian Porcelains by Elemental Analysis

Alison Stenger

Numerous historic sites dating from 1850 to 1910 have yielded evidence of a Chinese labor force in the western United States. The existence of this population group is most often attested to by the ceramics, through the many fragments that were left behind when these people moved out of the area.

Unlike European or American ceramics, which often have datable manufacturing marks, Asian ceramics frequently are unmarked. Others carry marks that are ambiguous, or that reflect the markings of earlier periods (Beals and Steele, 1981:7). Also problematic in the dating of these vessels is the continuation of decorative styles. Common motifs such as "Double Happiness" and "Bamboo" were produced throughout the historic period, so that both the early and later versions are frequently visually identical.[1] Therefore, in order to date these wares, a means of discriminating among them, other than through pattern or shape, is necessary.

PREVIOUS RESEARCH

Earlier work at the Ceramics Analysis Laboratory concentrated on the visual differentiation of glazes from several Chinese historic periods. Through the analysis of various glaze chemistries, it has been established that opacity is a sensitive indicator of elemental differences during different historic periods of Chinese ceramic manufacture (Kaplan, 1952; Stenger, 1980). Elemental

---

[1] "Bamboo" has also been called "Swatow Ware," "Three Circles and Dragonfly," or "Three Circles and Longevity." For an illustration of this pattern, see Sando and Felton, Chapter 6 herein.

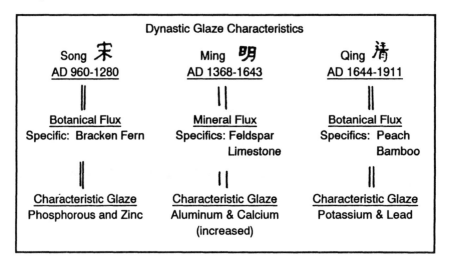

Figure 70. Basic glaze constituents for three discrete production
periods for Chinese ceramics, by dynasty.

differences, resulting from the use of different fluxes and other elemental combinations (Figure 70), are crucial to the relative transparency of ceramic glazes.

During the early period of porcelain manufacture, Song potters used an organic
ash, generally from low-growing plant species such as bracken fern, as their
fluxing agent. This glaze was approximately 70 percent silica, and had enough
phosphorous to produce opacity.

The Ming dynasty potters changed to a mineral flux, usually feldspar, which
lowered the silica percentage to approximately 50 percent. The result was a glaze
of reduced opacity and increased clarity. In the last Chinese dynasty, a change
again occurred. Qing potters reemployed ash as the fluxing agent, but used ash
sources different from those of the Song potters., Thus, it was anticipated that the
use of plant ash in both the Song and Qing glazes would result in wares that would
evidence opacity, and dynastically distinct glaze bubble patterns, under magnification. Conversely, the mineral-based glazes of the Ming dynasty were
expected to maintain their clarity, while exhibiting a bubble pattern quite different
from the Song and Qing glazes.

A 40-power binocular microscope was used to examine wares from various
time periods. Relative differences in glaze opacity and bubble distribution were
observed among Song, Ming and Qing ceramics. Specimens were then
reexamined under the lower magnification of 15x, and the initial differences were
maintained. We had therefore established that dynastic identification could be
non-destructively confirmed (Medley, 1962; Stenger, 1980). Although this technique is useful for differentiating among dynasties, most ceramics found on

overseas Chinese sites in the United States date from the Qing dynasty or later. While some differences were observed between earlier and later Qing dynasty wares examined in this way, visual identification did not prove precise enough to differentiate the 19th century ceramics from those produced in the 20th century. We therefore began to seek a more precise means of dating these wares.

Following research by Kaplan (1952), we were able to construct an initial chronology of glaze types which has since been applied in numerous analyses. To test the glaze types against information known about the composition of Chinese ceramics at various periods, data complied by other authors were studied (Paine and Young, 1953; Tregear and others, 1985). Finally, through the technological examination of the glazes of identifiable dynastic periods, we were able to verify formulas that had been suggested through historical accounts.

In this chapter we will advocate the use of two types of technical analysis as suggested ways to approach the problems inherent in the dating of the more recent Asian ceramic wares. Both methods of elemental determination have been widely used in similar studies and have yielded meaningful results. The investigative techniques are X-ray fluorescence spectroscopy and optical emission spectroscopy.

METHODS

Tite (1972) has published a definitive study of spectrographic techniques, including the two methods we have employed in the analysis of the ceramic types discussed in this chapter (Tite, 1972:260-272). Spectrographic procedures have proven to provide a highly accurate method of semi-quantitative analysis. The method depends upon the fact that light (or secondary X-rays) emitted by an element upon volatilization shows a characteristic pattern when split by a prism into its spectrum. In a compound or mixture, the elements present can be identified by the lines in the resulting spectrum. Measurement is then made of the intensity of the lines in comparison with control specimens of known composition produced under the same conditions.

It should be noted that optical emission spectroscopy requires that a small (10 mg) sample be taken from the artifact (Tite, 1972:261). In X-ray fluorescence spectroscopy, no sample removal is required, provided the artifact is small enough to fit within the chamber of the spectrometer (Tite, 1972:268). However, because of the small chamber size of the instrument used for our studies, samples of approximately one-eighth inch square were removed from the original specimens for the purpose of analysis.

PROCEDURE

The majority of the ceramics discussed in this chapter were from well-provenienced sites in Oregon, Washington, Idaho, and Nevada (Figure 71). The

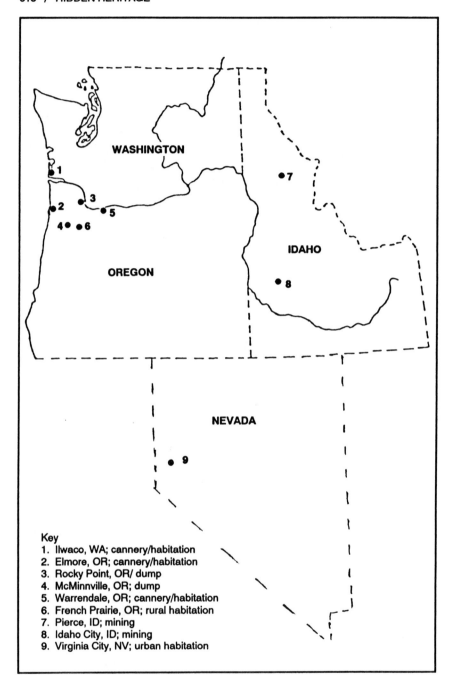

Key
1. Ilwaco, WA; cannery/habitation
2. Elmore, OR; cannery/habitation
3. Rocky Point, OR/ dump
4. McMinnville, OR; dump
5. Warrendale, OR; cannery/habitation
6. French Prairie, OR; rural habitation
7. Pierce, ID; mining
8. Idaho City, ID; mining
9. Virginia City, NV; urban habitation

Figure 71. Map showing locations of sites which supplied samples for analysis.

"overseas" ceramics were divided into two groups: 1) wares having an estimated manufacture date of 1850 through 1890, and 2) wares having a post-1890s date of manufacture. Each ceramic assemblage was dated by its association with other artifacts from the site, as well as from the historical context of the site itself. Dates obtained by this method were later compared with the dates subsequently indicated by technical analysis.

After the approximate manufacturing dates had been established, all specimens scheduled for laboratory testing were assigned new identification numbers, which then accompanied the specimens to the testing facilities. These numbers were always selected at random, and were the only identification the samples would have until the completion of the project. In this way, the results of the analysis and the interpretation of those results could not be prejudiced. Further, the actual spectrographic work was accomplished through sub-contract by the Ceramics Analysis Laboratory to independent laboratories in the private sector. Thus, the microscopists had no familiarity with the context of the ceramics until after the completion of the project report.

Blue and white wares were the first to be tested. The majority of the early samples were obtained from archaeological sites and independent researchers, while samples dating from the overseas Chinese period were obtained from both archaeological sites and the United States Customs Service. The examination of 320 samples produced the results summarized in Table 38.

For comparison with the visual examination previously described, the opacity of the Song dynasty ceramic glazes is indicated by the presence of phosphorous. With the Ming dynasty, certain changes appear in the levels of most elements, as well as an absence of phosphorous and zinc and the general disappearance of silver. The ash sources used by the Qing potters changed the levels of potassium and other elements. It is not until the 20th century that we see a reemergence, and at high levels, of numerous elements, including manganese, cobalt, zinc, copper, lead, silver, and iron. Also, a detectable amount of phosphorous recurs in the late 19th and early 20th century samples.

COMPARATIVE ANALYSIS

The results of these tests on samples from dated contexts provided a chemical pattern of constituent elements with which subsequent samples could be compared. To test the validity of the techniques, before applying them to samples of unknown date, we selected six examples of similarly decorated "Bamboo" pattern blue and white wares of known date in order to compare the wares of three recent periods of manufacture with the elemental profile already established. On visual examination, each of the ware types appeared to have the same color of decoration and body.

Two wares each, from known time periods, were chosen for testing (Table 39). Wares from archaeological contexts dating to the 19th century and to the early

Table 38. Analysis of Blue and White Porcelain Glazes on Asian Ceramics of Known Date[a]

Period	Mn	Co	K	Zn	Sb	Cu	Pb	Ag	Fe	V	P	Mg	Ca	Sr	Cr	Ni
Song	2	2	3	2	—	2	2	2	2	1	1	—	—	—	—	2
Ming I to 1450	2	1	2	—	—	1	—	—	3	1	—	3	3	2	—	1
Middle Ming to 1550	4	2	3	—	1	—	1	—	3	—	—	—	—	—	—	2
Later Ming to 1644	2	1	2	—	—	1	—	—	2	1	—	3	4	3	3	—
	2	2	2	—	—	1	1	1	—	2	—	—	—	—	—	1
	2	—	1	—	—	2	—	—	—	2	—	—	—	—	—	—
Qing, 1750 to 1820	2	1	2	—	—	2	1	—	1	1	—	2	3	2	—	2
	2	—	2	—	—	1	—	—	2	1	—	3	4	—	—	—
Qing, 1830 to 1900	—	—	1	—	—	—	—	—	1	1	—	—	2	—	—	—
	2	—	3	—	—	1	2	—	2	2	—	3	3	2	—	—
	2	—	3	—	—	1	2	—	2	1	1	3	3	2	—	—
20th century	4	4	—	4	—	4	4	4	4	4	1	1	4	—	—	4

Key: Mn = manganese; Co = cobalt; K = potassium; Zn = zinc; Sb = antimony; Cu = copper; Pb = lead; Ag = silver; Fe = iron; V = vanadium; P = phosphorous; Mg = magnesium; Ca = calcium; Sr = strontium; Cr = chromium; Ni = nickel
1 = trace; 2 = little; 3 = some; 4 = much
Note: Results, per dynastic period, utilizing X-ray fluorescence spectroscopy and emission spectroscopy. All measurements are qualitative, not quantitative, through these means of elemental analysis.
[a]Sample size: 320 (Stenger, 1980, 1985)

Table 39. Blue and White Wares of the 19th and 20th Centuries[a]

	Mn	K	Co	Ni	Zn	V	Cu	Pb
19th century	3.0	3.0	—	—	—	2.0	2.0	3.0
19th century	3.0	1.5	1.0	—	0.5	1.0	1.0	—
1900-1920	4.0	4.0	3.0	2.0	—	2.0	2.0	2.0
1900-1920	4.0	4.0	3.0	—	—	—	2.0	2.0
People's Republic of China								
(post-1949)	1.0	1.0	3.0	—	1.0	—	3.0	4.0
(post-1949)	1.0	2.0	3.0	—	2.0	2.0	3.0	3.0

Key: Mn = manganese; K = potassium; Co = cobalt; Ni = nickel; Zn = zinc; V = vanadium; Cu = copper; Pb = lead
.5 = barely observable; 1 = trace; 2 = little; 3 = some; 4 = much
Note: This chart indicates the parameters of the elements within each group, and does not reflect numeric designations.
[a]Sample size: 6 (Steele, 1984:4-6)

20th century (pre-1920) were selected, together with modern examples from the People's Republic of China (post-1949). Of the elements tested, eight seemed to be significant in the identification of the period of production. Of primary importance were manganese, potassium, nickel, copper, and lead.

Table 40 lists the major elemental differences between the two centuries, as we observed in both archaeological and U.S. Customs samples. In general, the 20th century wares are higher in all of the elements tested. The reintroduction of nickel is important, as it is present in the 20th century wares but not in the ceramics of 19th century production. Aluminum, cobalt, phosphorous, sodium, and zinc were also absent from the 19th century ceramics tested.

Recently, a somewhat controversial aspect of this work has emerged, involving evidence that some of the wares occurring on Chinese sites, previously thought to be Chinese, were of Japanese origin (Stenger, 1986). Because of their archaeological context and visually "Oriental" appearance, Asian ceramics excavated from late 19th century Chinese sites have consistently been classified as Chinese. However, in the past two years, the Ceramics Analysis Laboratory has examined, at least in part, the Asian ceramic assemblages from nine Chinese occupation areas (Figure 71) and found that a number of the wares appear to be of Japanese origin.

By working definition, the sites classified as "overseas Chinese" 1) were of a context dating between 1850 and 1910, 2) contained enough Asian wares to indicate a Chinese labor force, as opposed to casual contact between the

Table 40. Thirteen Elements Defining Glaze Characteristics of 19th and 20th Century Underglaze Blue and White Wares[a]

	Al	V	Co	Cu	Fe	Pb	Mn	Ni	P	K	Ag	Na	Zn
19th century	—	2	—	2	3	3	3	—	—	1.5-3.0	2	—	—
20th century	3	4	4	4	4	4	4	2	1	4	4	3	1-2

Key: Al = aluminum; V = vanadium; Co = cobalt; Cu = copper; Fe = iron; Pb = lead; Mn = manganese; Ni = nickel; P = phosphorous; K = potassium; Ag = silver; Na = sodium; Zn = zinc
1 = trace; 2 = little; 3 = some; 4 = much
[a]sample size: 36

Euroamericans and the Chinese, and 3) yielded types of wares which were utilitarian and not predominantly formal or ceremonial.

Sites ranged in description and purpose from riverine, with labor intensive areas on or near the shore line, to inland occupation areas. Included in this survey were mining sites, canneries, a "China House," and a riverbank area used over several decades for casual dumping.

Each site, regardless of type or specific period of occupation, contained at least two types of Japanese ceramic wares. Further, the majority of sites evidenced four varieties of non-Chinese production ceramics. The Japanese wares that were recovered included underglaze blue and white transfer printed wares, mono-chromatic green glazed wares, monochromatic green wares having overglaze enamelling, and, often, another form of ware called "Moriage" (Figure 72). This last ware is usually a beige to brown monochromatic ground that is

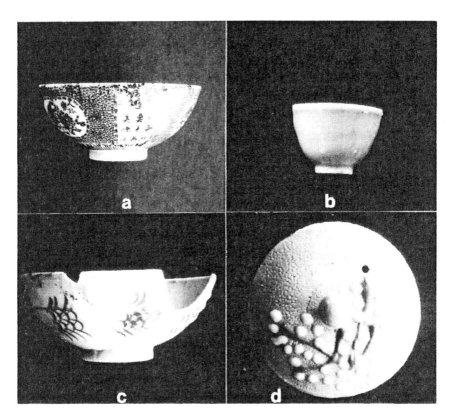

Figure 72. Examples of Japanese ceramic types found on overseas Chinese sites. a) blue and white transfer printed wares; b) monochromatic green wares (Celadon); c) green glazed wares with overglaze enamel decoration; d) "Moriage."

hand-decorated with heavily applied overglaze enamels (Stitt, 1974:126) and raised decorations.

Blue and White Wares

The Japanese blue and white wares are generally of underglaze, transferprint decoration. The blue coloring is an intense medium-dark blue, which is covered by a highly reflective glaze. This ware type is quite different from the typical Chinese blue and white handpainted ware from the same period, where the underglaze blue is less intense and generally grayer. The reason for the intensity of the Japanese underglaze blue is the purity of the cobalt ore. When analyzed after firing, the ratio of manganese to cobalt in Japanese wares is approximately 2.2. This is quite different from the manganese to cobalt ratio of the Chinese wares of the same period, which is approximately 1.0 (Fred Davis, 1985:personal communication). The high level of cobalt used by the Japanese indicates a different source for the cobalt oxide than that used by the Chinese.

The Japanese blue and white evidenced the transfer printing of designs onto thin porcellaneous bodies. This technology was adopted by the Japanese during the first part of the 19th century. By the later part of the century, this method of decoration was quite commonly used. However, although the Japanese produced examples of transfer printing techniques onto porcelains as early as 1820, the Chinese do not seem to have used this method until at least the post-Qing period, or post-1911.

The lack of evidence for the existence of transfer printed blue and white porcelains produced in China made us reevaluate the contents of sites originally identified as having had only Chinese ceramics. Specifically, if an "overseas Chinese site" was not occupied after the turn of this century, then the blue and white transfer printed wares must have been of Japanese origin. The identification of this porcelain type requires the recognition of Japanese ceramics within Chinese site contexts. Further, the regular occurrence of Japanese blue and white wares argued for the probability of other types of Japanese ceramics at these sites.

To verify the manufacturing origins of the Chinese and Japanese blue and white wares, we employed two spectrographic methods to obtain chemical profiles for the wares. As hypothesized from a preliminary assessment, the Chinese and Japanese wares differed noticeably in their content of specific elements. When comparing the mid-19th century blue and white wares, the Japanese transfer prints and underglaze handpainted Arita porcelains exceeded the Chinese "Bamboo" pattern ceramics in their content of manganese, cobalt, potassium, copper, lead, and calcium (Table 41). By 1880, however, the Chinese wares showed higher levels of manganese, potassium, and iron.

Turn-of-the-century Japanese blue and white wares are higher in their content of copper, lead, and calcium than those of the Chinese, while both countries' wares are quite high in manganese and cobalt. The Chinese wares are significantly

Table 41. Differences in Chemical Composition of Glazes on Japanese and
Chinese Blue and White Wares During Various Time Periods[a]

	Mn	Co	K	Cu	Pb	Fe	V	Ca
1850 Japanese	3.0	2.0	3.0	2.0	1.0	—	—	5.0
1850 Chinese	2.5	—	2.5	1.0	.5	1.0	.5	3.0
1880 Japanese	2.0	2.0	2.0	1.0	2.0	—	1.0	4.0
1880 Chinese	3.0	1.5	3.0	.5	.5	1.0	.5	3.0
1900 Japanese	4.0	3.0	3.0	2.5	3.0	—	2.0	4.0
1900 Chinese	4.0	3.0	4.0	2.0	2.0	4.0	3.0	3.0

Key: Mn = manganese; Co = cobalt; K = potassium; Cu = copper; Pb = lead; Fe = iron; V
= vanadium; Ca = calcium
.5 = barely observable; 1 = trace; 2 = little; 3 = some; 4 = much
Note: Not only can the Japanese and Chinese wares be differentiated from one another,
but each also varies over time.
[a]Sample size: 40

higher in iron, and higher in potassium and vanadium. Figure 73 graphically
illustrates these wares' different chemical "fingerprints."

Green Glazed Wares (Celadons)

Three types of green glazed wares are found on overseas Chinese sites in the
United States. Utilitarian wares, mainly spice and storage jars primarily for
foodstuffs, comprise a category which is not included in this discussion because
they are not "Celadon." The second category, that of the monochromatic green
glaze wares with overglaze enamelling (Figure 72), is known to be Japanese (Chu
and Chu, 1973:108). The third type of green glazed ware is undecorated,
demonstrating only a single blue-green color, devoid of the enamelling that
typifies the wares of category two.

Overseas Chinese ceramics researchers have long assumed that the monochromatic green glazed tablewares are of Chinese origin. This assumption
appears to be based mainly upon the fact that the wares are found on overseas Chinese sites and are not of European manufacture; therefore implying
that the wares must be Chinese. Olsen (1978:18) notes that the southern Chinese
name for these wares, dōng qīng ("winter-green;" see also Sando and Felton,
Chapter 6 herein), "is probably a corruption, at least in terms of its written
form, of 'eastern green' which is also pronounced dōng qīng." It is quite possible that "eastern" refers to an origin in Japan. Notably, attributions to Japan
are well-founded historically, as a number of Chinese ceramic types did evolve

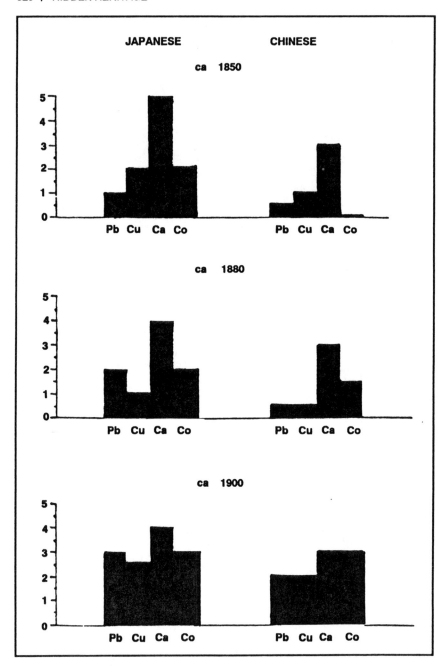

Figure 73. Proportion of significant elements in late 19th century Japanese and Chinese blue and white wares. (For key, refer to Table 41.)

from outside influences. Included in this development of a special ware type are the tea ceremony wares and the earlier Celadons produced during the Ming dynasty.

Once we realized that the identity of the country that produced the green monochromatic wares was uncertain, we decided to determine the wares' origin, if at all possible. In visually examining the greenwares, we noted that the potting of these wares appeared to be Japanese. The strict control exercised in the production of both the bodies and the glazes of the wares was typical of the wares associated with the Arita and Seto area kilns (Gorham, 1971:85-87). The monochromes were of pale blue-green color, with white interiors. The same sharp white of the interior was also evidenced inside the thin and roughly trimmed foot-ring. The wares with overglaze enamelling and heavier bodies, accepted as being Japanese, had the same white interior as the monochromes. Further, when the visual inspection was begun, samples were sent to technical advisor Jay Frierman. While preparing the specimens for elemental analysis, Frierman noted the thinness of the glazes. At that time, he suggested a Japanese origin for the wares (Jay Frierman, 1985:personal communication).

To elementally define the monochrome wares, it was necessary to examine documented Japanese ceramics, and then to compare the results of this examination to the chemical make-up of the monochromes. From this phase of the analysis, we selected several different Japanese ware types, including the enamelled greenwares described above, the blue and white transfer-decorated porcelains, and green monochrome porcelains that had been obtained in Japan by the director of Portland State University's Ceramics Analysis Laboratory. The results of our analysis (Table 42 and Figure 74) were consistent with reports by Wood (1978) of his Japanese porcelain analysis.

Chemically, the glazes of 19th century Japanese greenwares contained far more calcium and phosphorous than the Chinese wares of the same approximate date (Wood, 1978). Glazes of the 20th century Japanese greenwares contained phosphorous. Notably, that element was absent from the 20th century Chinese Celadon wares provided by U.S. Customs (see also Wood, 1978). Further, the 20th century Japanese greenwares were lower in calcium. They also contained chromium oxide, as first recognized by Frierman (Jay Frierman, 1985:personal communication). Tests by other researchers further verified the differences between the Chinese and Japanese ceramic wares (Wood, 1978:Chapter 8, on district or province attributable wares).

Once the approximate levels of element content had been established for a control group of Chinese and Japanese wares of different manufacturing periods, it was possible to identify the probable age and origin of the wares from overseas Chinese sites. Specifically, by comparing the chemical composition of the excavated wares with standards established by our control group, the overseas wares could be defined by date of manufacture and by origin.

Table 42. Differences in Chemical Composition of Glazes on 19th and 20th Century Japanese and Chinese Monochromatic Green Glazed Wares[a]

	Ca	P	K	Fe	Mn
19th century Japanese (ca. 1870-1890)	5.0	1.5	2.0	.5	—
19th century Chinese (ca. 1870-1890)	3.5	.5	3.0	1.0	—
20th century Japanese (ca. 1910-1930)	2.0	1.0	2.5	1.8	2.0
20th century Chinese (ca. 1910-1930)	3.0	—	3.0	1.0	3.0

Key: Ca = calcium; P = phosphorous; K = potassium; Fe = iron; Mn = manganese
.5 = barely observable; 1 = trace; 2 = little; 3 = some; 5 = much
Note: Not only do the Japanese and Chinese wares differ from one another, but each also varies over time.
[a]Sample size: 30

Moriage

The third type of Japanese ware common to overseas Chinese assemblages is "Moriage." Like the enamelled greenwares, these wares have a heavy body and white interior. The beige or brown ground of this type of porcelain allows for the impact of the white and green enamelling (glaze drizzling) that is applied over the glaze for decorative purposes. This style, and the execution of its decoration, is exclusively Japanese. The history of this type of overglaze enamelling dates back to the 17th century, with this specific form of decoration typifying late 19th century wares (Trubner, 1972).

SUMMARY

When considering the ceramic assemblage from an overseas Chinese site of the later 19th century, one recognizes the Chinese blue and white wares of southern Chinese production, the overglaze polychrome enamel wares reminiscent of the earlier export traditions, the myriad brown glazed utilitarian vessels, and the wares discussed above. In almost every site, in combination with the three types of Chinese wares, are these four Japanese ceramic ware types.

As of this date, we have examined only one overseas Chinese site ceramic assemblage that contained Chinese Celadons. Further, we have not been able to document 19th century attempts by the Chinese to duplicate the Japanese blue and white transfer wares, or the Moriage variety of ceramic. And, because many of the Japanese specimens were marked (Scheans, 1986:51-53), we were further able to substantiate the Japanese origin of many of the pieces.

It is not known why the Chinese would have employed these types of Japanese wares instead of wares made in their own country. The fact remains, however, that

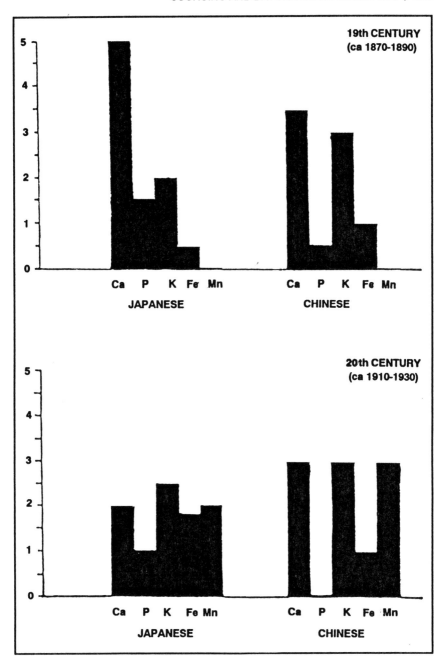

Figure 74. Proportion of significant elements in 19th and 20th century
Japanese and Chinese monochromatic green glazed wares (Celadons).
(For key, refer to Table 42.)

no identifiably Chinese transferwares, moriage, or enamelled green wares have been excavated from these sites. Further, only one site's green monochromes have been elementally characteristic of Chinese origin.

Through continued research of the overseas Chinese sites, the people, the wares and the traditions, we hope to find the answer to the occurrence of the Japanese wares in these ceramic assemblages. The fact that this large and consistent a mix of wares exists raises many questions with complex social implications, which we hope to be able to answer at some future time.

CONCLUSIONS

The purpose of this project was to attempt to establish criteria by which overseas Chinese ceramics could be dated. The visually identical appearance of many of the 19th and 20th century wares necessitated this investigation (Stenger, 1991). Due to an understanding of the components of Chinese ceramics, it was initially possible to predict the basic element profiles of the wares. By then examining the ceramics that had verifiable proveniences, these anticipated results were confirmed, and the original list of elements was expanded. An unexpected result of this research on ceramics from overseas Chinese sites was the identification, on such sites, of wares that were manufactured in Japan.

The result of this study was the development of a semi-quantitative method of discrimination that allows for the verification of identifiable differences between Chinese and Japanese ceramics, over time. Through this study we were able to establish which element combinations were reflective of both country of origin and ceramic age, with dates being narrowed to within portions of each century. Elemental analysis of Asian porcelains is thus a viable means of sourcing and dating this artifact type.

REFERENCES CITED

BEALS, HERBERT, K. and HARVEY W. STEELE
    1981   Chinese Porcelains from Site 35-TI-1, Netarts Sand Spit, Tillamook County, Oregon, University of Oregon, *Anthropological Papers*, No. 23, Eugene.
CHU, ARTHUR and GRACE CHU
    1973   *Oriental Antiques and Collectibles, a Guide*, Crown Publishers, New York.
GORHAM, HAZEL H.
    1971   *Japanese and Oriental Ceramics*, Charles E. Tuttle, Rutland, Vermont.
KAPLAN, SIDNEY M.
    1952   Toward a Classification of Chinese Glazes: A Preliminary Report, *Far Eastern Ceramics Bulletin, 4*:2, pp. 781-791.
MEDLEY, MARGARET
    1962   Regrouping 15th Century Blue and White, *Transactions of the Oriental Ceramic Society, 34*, pp. 78-85.

OLSEN, JOHN W.
1978   A Study of Chinese Ceramics Excavated in Tucson, *Kiva*, *44*:1, pp. 1-50.
PAINE, R. T. and W. J. YOUNG
1953   A Preliminary Report on the Subsurface Structure of Kuan and Kuan-Type Wares, *Far Eastern Ceramic Bulletin*, 5:3, pp. 2-20.
SCHEANS, D. J.
1986   Hanamono Japanese Export Wares to the United States 1868-1921, ms. on file at the Ceramics Analysis Laboratory, Portland State University, Portland, Oregon.
STEELE, HARVEY W.
1984   The Manganese to Cobalt Ratio in 19th and 20th Century Oriental Porcelain, ms. on file at the Ceramics Analysis Laboratory, Portland State University, Portland, Oregon.
STENGER, ALISON
1980   Dating Chinese Ceramics by Visual Glaze Analysis, ms. on file at the Ceramics Analysis Laboratory, Portland State University, Portland, Oregon.
1985   Sojourner Wares from Rocky Point: A Technical Report, paper presented at the 38th Annual Northwest Anthropological Conference, April 18-20, Ellensburg, Washington.
1986   Japanese Ceramics From Chinese Sojourner Sites, paper presented at the 19th Annual Meeting of the Society for Historical Archaeology, Sacramento, California.
1991   The Universal Overseas Site: A Predictable Ceramic Assemblage, monograph on file, Institute for Archaeological Studies, Portland, Oregon.
STITT, IRENE
1974   *Japanese Ceramics of the Last 100 Years*, Crown, New York.
TITE, MICHAEL S.
1972   *Methods of Physical Examination in Archaeology*, Seminar Books, London and New York.
TREGEAR, M., N. WOOD, H. HATCHER, and A. M. POLLARD
1985   *Ceramic Changes at Jingdezhen in the Seventeenth Century*, paper presented at the International Conference on Ancient Chinese Pottery and Porcelain (ICACPP), Beijing.
TRUBNER, HENRY
1972   *Ceramic Art of Japan*, Seattle Art Museum Publication, Seattle, Washington.
WOOD, NIGEL
1978   *Oriental Glazes*, Watson-Guptill Publications, New York.

PART FIVE
Comparative and
Theoretical Studies

Although archaeological excavations of late 19th and early 20th century Chinese sites have been conducted in several countries, the most extensive ones outside the United States have taken place in New Zealand. Neville Ritchie, the archaeologist most responsible for Chinese site recording there, discusses aspects of overseas Chinese settlement patterns and archaeology in that country. His chapter will allow New Zealand's sites, artifacts, and structures to be compared with those of the United States, and is important for the identification and understanding of both differences and similarities in the experiences of the overseas Chinese in the two countries.

The final chapter, by Roberta Greenwood, provides a theoretical summary based upon nearly two decades of research on, and excavation of, a variety of overseas Chinese sites. Greenwood brings a unique and valuable perspective to her penetrating examination and evaluation of past efforts, present conditions, and proposed future directions for overseas Chinese studies. As we approach the 21st century we can expect more sophisticated analyses, more thoughtful interpretations, more theoretical discussions, and more fruitful interaction with other disciplines in assessing the impact of the overseas Chinese experience.

CHAPTER 13

Form and Adaptation: Nineteenth Century Chinese Miners' Dwellings in Southern New Zealand

Neville A. Ritchie

The study of 19th century goldfield architecture in New Zealand is still very much in its infancy. Most published books and articles featuring "goldfield buildings" in southern New Zealand (e.g., McGill, 1980; Thornton, 1983; Angus, 1983) are limited to brief descriptions of a few, generally European, structures/ settlements, and discussion of their construction in relation to available building materials. Little energy has been expended on analyzing morphology, stylistic influences, or social aspects. Even less has been written on the humble field dwellings of the gold miners. While this chapter makes no pretense at providing all the answers, it attempts to define structural parameters, identify key influences, and examine the social role of one group of such structures, namely, the habitations of the Chinese miners on the southern goldfields of New Zealand, in more detail than hitherto.

Data incorporated in this chapter are drawn from three main sources: historical records and observations, particularly the records of the Rev. Alexander Don, a missionary assigned to the Chinese on the southern goldfields by the Presbyterian Church (see Ritchie, 1986:28 for biographical details, contemporary newspaper accounts, and photographs); archives, notably the New Zealand Census which recorded numbers and types of Chinese dwellings; and archaeological investigations and documentation of Chinese habitations in Central Otago (Ritchie, 1986), especially those in the vicinity of Cromwell (Figure 75). The discussion is centered primarily on the dwellings of the miners, both rural and urban. Specialized

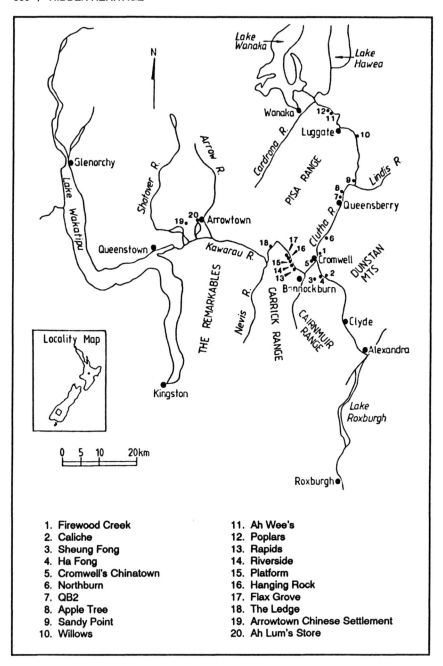

1. Firewood Creek
2. Caliche
3. Sheung Fong
4. Ha Fong
5. Cromwell's Chinatown
6. Northburn
7. QB2
8. Apple Tree
9. Sandy Point
10. Willows

11. Ah Wee's
12. Poplars
13. Rapids
14. Riverside
15. Platform
16. Hanging Rock
17. Flax Grove
18. The Ledge
19. Arrowtown Chinese Settlement
20. Ah Lum's Store

Figure 75. Map of study area.

social venues such as temples or "tong" and public halls, and businesses such as stores or shops for opium and gambling are generally beyond the scope of this chapter, even though business buildings frequently included accommodations for the proprietor and some staff.

The discussion is presented under the following subheadings: origins and traditional dwellings, the nature and distribution of Chinese settlements in New Zealand, social insights, internal layout and furnishings, architectural features, some comparisons between European and Chinese miners' dwellings, and conclusions.

ORIGINS AND TRADITIONAL DWELLINGS

Almost without exception, the approximately 15,000 Chinese who entered New Zealand in the 19th century came from the counties surrounding Guangzhou (Canton) in Guangdong Province, south China. Seventy percent originated from the northern part of Poon Yue County, with lesser numbers from the Si-yi Counties and Tsangshing and Heungshan Counties. These areas are literally studded with hundreds of villages with populations varying from 100 to 1,000 with a few exceeding 20,000 (Ritchie, 1986:7).

Unlike in the crowded cities, the size and quality of homes in the rural areas of China depended to a large extent upon individual families' resources of money and labor, rather than available space. In the south, peasants are noted for having large houses, to which additional rooms are added when a son takes a wife. Of course poorer people, now and in the past, could not afford substantial structures (Sachs, 1982:71).

Chinese houses in the nucleated villages around Guangzhou were described by the Rev. William Mawson, a New Zealand missionary who served in China with the Canton Village Mission, as low, windowless, and constructed of sun dried and fired bricks held together with a mixture of sand, lime, and clay (Mawson, 1926:12). The floors were either of clay or large tiles, while the roofs were of light tiles laid on pine rafters. According to Mawson, little wood was used in construction because of the destruction caused by ants. Two-storied buildings were relatively uncommon and were usually owned by those who had accumulated wealth overseas.

Another description of a Cantonese village was provided by Yee (1975:9-10), who was brought up in the village of Loan Gon Doan. The village consisted of fifty families all descended from one ancestor who established the community many hundreds of years ago. All the houses in the village were symmetrical and exactly alike in design and materials. All had brick walls, concrete floors, red tile roofs, and mahogany doors "half a foot" thick. The central part of each house, the living room, was two stories high. The two side sections were divided into two rooms on each side, the front half of each side serving as a kitchen, while the rear rooms were bedrooms (the second kitchen was used for catering during festive occasions). There were no windows on the ground floor. The upstairs section consisted of four bedrooms and storage areas.

Smith (1899) also provides some insights into the nature of Chinese villages in the late 19th century. He commented on what he perceived as their apparent lack of planning; they "just growed like Topsy." Paths of varying widths and alleys traditionally used for access between the structures and the outside world constituted the "streets." Smith also noted the windowless nature of the walls facing the public thoroughfares (1899:21). He considered that "By far the most common material of which the Chinese build their houses is that which happens to be nearest at hand. Bricks are everywhere made in great quantities [for house construction] but the vast majority of country dwellings are made simply of the soil, moulded into adobe bricks, dried till they cease to shrink" (Smith, 1899:22). The cost of making uncompacted adobe bricks was never more than a *cash* apiece, whereas rammed earth bricks were "three to four times as much." The foundations (wall footings) of all houses were built of brick (Smith, 1899:23). Poorly levelled earth constituted the floor of most common dwellings (Smith, 1899:28). The excavation of vast quantities of earth for building purposes over the centuries often resulted in the formation of extensive pits around each village. These filled with water and became useful ponds (Smith, 1899:24).

These and other accounts (e.g., Knapp, 1986) suggest that there was a high degree of uniformity within the vernacular architecture of the Guangzhou area, that sun dried and baked earth constituted the main construction materials in the rural areas (the better-off could afford bricks), and that most Chinese knew the basics of house construction using these materials.

THE NATURE AND DISTRIBUTION OF CHINESE SETTLEMENTS IN NEW ZEALAND

The first real influx of Chinese miners into New Zealand did not occur until late 1866. They came initially from Victoria, Australia, in response to an invitation from the Otago Chamber of Commerce (prompted by depressed trading conditions) enjoining them to come and work on the Otago goldfield. The invitation included a written statement conferring a "right of protection " guaranteed by the Otago Provincial Council.

By 1867, there were 1185 Chinese distributed throughout the Otago goldfields (Forrest, 1961:92). Generally, the miners among them only stopped long enough in the port of entry, Dunedin, to buy supplies and basic mining equipment before heading inland. Although the first year's immigration saw the Chinese widely distributed throughout Otago, the main concentrations were centered on the Waipori-Tuapeka and Dunstan fields and around Naseby (Forrest, 1961:92). By the year's end, the Chinese formed 5 percent of the province's population (Butler, 1977:7).

Seven years later, there were 3500 Chinese in Otago and 1320 in Westland and Nelson (Butler, 1977:31). During the boom years (1870-1885) the main Chinese settlements in Otago-Southland were established, centered on Round Hill (population ca. 400). Lawrence (400), Alexandra (150), Naseby (150), Switzers (100), Cromwell (100), and Queenstown (100). However, the populations of the Chinese settlements were not static. They waxed and waned in response to mining fortunes, the annual winter/summer migrations caused by either too much or too little water, and a desire for a change of scene occasionally.

Contemporary newspaper reports indicate the large Chinese camp at Lawrence was well established within three years of the first Chinese arriving in the area (*Otago Daily Times*, October 1, 1869:7):

> The Tuapeka . . . is the only place in Otago that can boast of a Chinese camp. . . . In outward appearance it presents nothing that would be called imposing. Its architectural dignity is supported by sheets of galvanized iron and flitches of weatherboarding, and its brand is essentially that of a digging township in the early stage of existence. The buildings are wedged a trifle too closely together to suit modern ideas of good ventilation and sanitary improvement. Still the want of such scientific aids to domestic comfort is not unprecedented in the history of goldfield settlement. . . . A closer inspection brings out the foreign element in its broadest aspect-the hieroglyphical tracings on the sign boards. . . . The habitations are devoted to a variety of pursuits more or less intimately associated with the social and domestic instincts of the race. . . . They include one or two general stores, with stocks as large and well-assorted as any establishment of the kind under European supervision. . . . Among the other curiosities of the camp, the eating houses are, perhaps, the most inviting. . . . Native artisans are few in number, still there are one or two ingenious tradesmen amongst them. There is a working jeweler, a carpenter, a baker and a hairdresser, all apparently doing a fair stroke of business. One building devoted to benevolent purposes is used as a refuge for new comers in destitute circumstances. Here lodgings and rations are provided, until such time as the inmate gets work, when he is expected to refund the cost. . . . There is only one female resident, a good stout South of Ireland wench, who is reported to have espoused one of these sons of Shem some years ago while residing in Victoria. . . .

The *Tuapeka Times* described the Lawrence camp in 1883 as an area of less than an acre in extent, where there were from sixty to seventy habitations, "narrow, dark and dingy, constructed of boards, kerosene tins and sugar bags. Scattered around with fine disregard for sanitation there were ash-pits, cesspools, pigsties, fowl houses and wells." (Mayhew, 1949:90). The Chinese stores and "gambling dens" were also in this area. Nearby was the "Chinese Empire Hotel," originally of wooden construction, but replaced in the 1890s with a brick building. The latter was built by Sam Chew Lain, a giant Chinese man who was held in high regard by both the Chinese and European communities (Mayhew, 1949:90). Part of his hotel, which has been used as a dwelling, still stands. It is the only structural remnant of the Lawrence "Chinese camp" remaining on site.

The rest of the Lawrence Chinese camp site is now occupied by a small European-owned market garden and featureless grassed paddocks, a far cry from its heyday, as depicted in an 1882 survey map when the settlement had two main thoroughfares bordered by surveyed sections. To the author's knowledge, this was the only Chinese settlement with officially surveyed land-titles in New Zealand.

The similar-sized settlement (in terms of population) at Round Hill in Southland was much more haphazardly arranged because of the broken terrain. Don described it thus (1894:2):

> The Chinese settlement of a hundred and twenty huts covers about five square miles of spur and gully, but like a sort of nucleus near the centre, is a collection of 38 houses, by Europeans called 'Canton'-by the Chinese called 'The Street of Chinese Men' . . . of the 38 places, five are business houses, 24 are for gambling and opium smoking, whilst the use of most of the remainder is too easily guessed [presumably they were brothels].

Although the Round Hill settlement was much more spread out (Don divided it into "districts" in his notes) than the urban settlements in Central Otago, the "nucleus" at Round Hill played a similar role, supplying everyday needs and recreational services, and providing a sense of community for the Chinese miners in the area (in this case up to 400). Among the all-wooden structures at Round Hill, there was a double-storied building which was a tea shop owned by a Riverton firm, two hotels ("The Peaceful Tower" and the "Universal Peace"), and two restaurants. The Round Hill settlement also differed in that it was virtually a "Chinese town" (Orepuki being the European settlement, although a few Chinese lived there too), whereas most of the other urban Chinese settlements were established within or adjacent to pre-existing European mining centers.

Besides the large settlements with their wide choice of supplies and recreational services, numerous smaller Chinese settlements or camps were established on the periphery of established goldfield towns (e.g., those at Roxburgh, Clyde, Cromwell, and Arrowtown). These smaller settlements offered a correspondingly lesser range of services; but like the larger centers, in addition to the resident Chinese, they serviced large numbers who lived and worked in the surrounding hinterland, often in remote gullies. For example, Cromwell was the main center for the 300 Chinese miners in the upper Clutha district (*Otago Daily Times*, October 1, 1869:7). In fact, at least as many Chinese lived in remote situations, mining in groups of one to eight, as lived in the "urban" centers. Their distribution reflected the discontinuous spread of the alluvial gold they sought, as is illustrated by this quote from Don's records (1893:8):

> This is the disposition of the 14 on the Cardrona: Near the head, 2 men, $^1/_2$ mile lower, 1 man, three miles lower, 2; four miles still lower, 3; $^1/_2$ mile

further, 2; two miles further, 1; two miles yet, 2; one mile off, 1. . . . Nearly as
scattered are the 22 men in the Kirtleburn [the Roaring Meg].

Although the Chinese were seldom the first on the scene, occasionally large
numbers moved into an area within a short space of time, creating the impression
of a "Chinese rush," for example, seventy established in the Motatapu Valley in
such circumstances in 1873 (*Arrow Observer*, March 21, 1873). Once they felt
outnumbered, the European miners in an area often sold out or left, leaving the
Chinese with large areas to themselves, e.g., Don (1895:11) described the upper
Nokomai "as practically a Chinese River, there being forty Chinese to zero
Europeans."

Like their European counterparts, many of the Chinese "rush" settlements were
established "overnight," but the more usual pattern was a gradual build-up of
population and dwellings, as word of good prospects got back to clansmen in other
locations. The all-too-brief heyday of most settlements or mining districts was
followed by their decline and gradual abandonment. This pattern is well illustrated
in the six or so known and dated photographs of the Cromwell Chinese camp.
They show that the central cluster of huts was established and abandoned over a
period of two to four decades, perhaps as kin arrived or departed.

But the Chinese settlements grew out of more than just a desire to live together.
From the outset, the Chinese miners were exposed to cool, if not hostile, attitudes
from European miners and government officials. They were also frequently reviled
in the newspapers (Ritchie, 1986:69). It is not hard to understand why they
clustered together for protection and comradeship. Furthermore, in the absence of a
Chinese language newspaper on the southern goldfield the settlements played a vital
role in disseminating information. Most settlements had at least one person who could
translate the local newspaper, interpret mining regulations, and relay news.

The inland Chinese settlements (e.g., Figures 76 and 77) initially obtained their
supplies from Chinese storekeepers in Dunedin, the main source of supply
(Ritchie, 1986:33). As the Chinese became more established in the hinterland, a
network of supply and "recreation" stores developed. Each community was served
by as many stores as the market could bear. By the 1880s there were at least forty
Chinese supply stores servicing the southern goldfields (Ritchie, 1986:703). The
majority were established in settlements, as opposed to being isolated trading
posts. In addition to their provisioning function, many also provided gambling and
opium smoking facilities. The population of the settlements usually swelled in
winter when those who could afford not to work over the coldest months would
"come in" and stay until the spring thaw.

Construction Materials and Techniques

Understandably, since few, if any, of the Chinese miners were accompanied by
other family members, there was little need or social pressure to recreate replicas

Figure 76. A panoramic view, taken in 1887, of the Arrowtown Chinese settlement and gardens beside Bush Creek, Arrowtown, Central Otago (Arrowtown Museum).

342

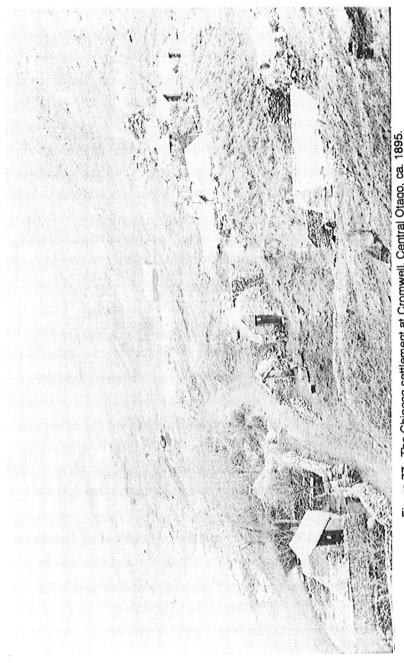

Figure 77. The Chinese settlement at Cromwell, Central Otago, ca. 1895. Print courtesy of Otago Early Settlers Museum, Dunedin, Album 31, p. 16.

of contemporary Chinese villages or houses in New Zealand. However, from the outset, the Chinese exhibited a remarkable adaptability and versatility with regard to dwelling construction. According to Don (1906:2), they had a definite preference for huts rather than tents, although his assertion is contradicted to some extent by data recorded in the census returns.

> He liked a home of finer stuff than calico. He built a hut of turf on the grassy plots, of slabs in the bush, of cobblestones on the shingle, of adobe where stones were scarce, of whatever stuff came handiest. And for roofing what better stuff than the bags that held his rice, or thatch of the great tussock of those days?

Field surveys, excavations, census data, contemporary accounts, and photographs indicate that the range of construction techniques and materials, the latter largely drawn from the local environment, was even wider and more varied than that outlined by Don. Potter provided this description of dwellings in the 'Canton' at Round Hill which he visited in 1888 (1890:13):

> The huts, hovels or houses are stuck up anyhow regardless of either line or order; the chimneys-huge piles of timber, sod and zinc cases-being placed in several instances where Europeans would put their front door. . . . The [single] street is only seven feet wide and is thickly built upon the both sides, if buildings they can be called-canvas, fern-tree and slabs entering largely into their construction. . . .

The forested environment of the Round Hill area and the habitations the Chinese built there were more akin to those their countrymen constructed on the West Coast of the South Island, which also has a wet climate and is forested. In the dry, virtually treeless environment of Central Otago, the Chinese resorted to many different methods of construction, including in one instance living in abandoned mine drives (Don, 1911:14).

Laborers employed by Chinese mining companies usually lived in large dormitory-style huts such as those on the Shotover River described below (*Otago Witness*, October 9, 1875):

> Messers. Am Kimm and Co. form quite a little colony [23 men] by themselves, and are encamped in a small camp close to their claim. . . . There is a large cookhouse and dining room. . . . Ranged alongside is the Celestial abode or dwelling place. It is a very extensive building, and similarly constructed of sod walls with a thatched roof, the whole presenting a comfortable and warm appearance. The Celestial abode is 120 feet long and divided into four cottage-like compartments with their doorways facing toward the cookhouse. Each compartment is then subdivided again into sleeping places, some with only a narrow passage between the bunks or beds, while in others there is room for a table and a few seats, so that the inmates might enjoy the luxury of

gambling or amuse themselves with a little music on their native fiddle, flute or guitar. . . .

According to McArthur (1945:11):

> I should say there were about 200 [Chinese]. They seemed to work like one family, work, eat and sleep in the same hut. . . . They had two big huts. . . . Each was about 60 or 70 feet long, built with what we call wattle and dab [daub]. This consisted of stakes driven in the ground with saplings and tussocks in between, finished up with puddled mud. The roofs were thatched with tussocks tied on with flax. . . .

Many Chinese, especially those mining in the river gorges, lived, full-time or temporarily, in the natural caves which abound within the schist massifs of Central Otago. They formed shelters by selecting rock overhangs or open spaces under boulders and erecting walls of packed earth or rock, thus forming "homes" four to twenty meters in area, the size being dependent on the space available under the overhang. In some locations, particularly in the main river gorges, suitable rocks for shelters were very numerous and the Chinese put them to good use, as evidenced by this quote from Don (1901:25):

> On January 9th 1901 we were a day among caves. We counted twenty—only six occupied-in 3 miles of the Molyneux River [the old name for the Clutha River below Cromwell] above Roxburgh [the Roxburgh Gorge]. In winter, when the great stream is low, the empty caves will have their occupants. Some of these caves are very roomy and comfortable—cool in summer and warm in winter. But there is absolutely no ventilation and when the door, usually a thick rice bag, is shut, it is almost pitch dark.

There are seventy-seven rockshelters in the Roxburgh Gorge (Harrison, 1982:24). Although this is the most dense concentration in Central Otago, it is suspected that as many again were flooded when the bottom of the gorge was inundated by the formation of Lake Roxburgh in 1956.

In addition to the various types of goldfield dwellings, some of the urban Chinese lived in "lodging houses" and "hotels" run by one or more of their countrymen. There were two Chinese lodging houses at Alexandra (Don, March 1, 1887:167), one at Invercargill (Don, 1901, 21), another at Queenstown (Don, 1901:32), and at least two in Dunedin. The latter were reported to be "insanitary" in 1900 (Clark, 1961:86). By the early 1870s, two (and probably more) Chinese hotels were in business at Round Hill (Ritchie, 1986:705), and a few years later the "Chinese Empire Hotel" was established at Lawrence.

The 1874 census records indicate that by that date, 918 Chinese were living in semi-permanent houses built of brick, stone, wood, or lath and plaster (New Zealand Census, 1874). What constitutes a "house" is not defined in the census; most are likely to have been small one to two room dwellings. Another 2288

Chinese lived in huts, and 1156 were living in tents or dwellings with canvas roofs. Later censuses (e.g., New Zealand Census, 1878) record a steady decline in the numbers living in tents or canvas-topped structures.

Social Aspects of the Miners' Living Spaces

The type of tenure is not recorded in early records. It appears "ownership" on unoccupied Crown land depended to some extent on who built or paid for the materials in a hut. For example, during the course of a court case in Cromwell, Ah Kew, a gardener who lived and worked on the Cromwell Flat, stated that he owned three huts in the Chinese camp at Cromwell (*Cromwell Argus,* September 24, 1889). Presumably, he leased or loaned the huts. In the Maniototo, only the fifty Chinese who "owned" huts were listed on the ratepayers (property tax) roll (Angus, 1977:33). The Arrowtown Borough Council levied a rate only on Chinese commercial buildings up until 1883. After that date, hut owners or lessees in the Arrowtown Chinese camp on unsold Crown land were rated too (Arrowtown Borough, 1870s-1900).

According to Don, "The Chinese at Round Hill usually lived three or four in one small house, but there is an exception in the case of the partners in a claim, who work together and eat together, but sleep each in separate houses, any one of which is large enough (by ordinary Chinese reckoning) for all three" (August 1, 1883:24). But Don's records indicate that the normal occupancy of Chinese huts on the Central Otago goldfields varied between one and eight persons depending on factors such as the date of occupation, in terms of the discovery or exhaustion of particular diggings; the size of the structures; the amicability of the men; and the nature of the claims. By the late 1880s, it appears that two was about the average number of occupants per hut. For instance, there were twenty-one men in twelve huts at Bendigo (Don, March 1, 1887:164), twenty-nine in eighteen huts in Lawrence-Tuapeka area (Don, October 1, 1887:63), seventeen in ten huts at Waikaia (Don, December 1, 1888:106), thirty in twenty-eight huts at Cromwell (Don, March 1, 1887:164), seventy-six in fifty-one huts at Naseby (Don, 1893:16) and 229 in the 110 inhabited huts at Round Hill (Don, August 1, 1885:26).

The "average one to three man, one-room Chinese hut" in Central Otago varies from 2.5 to 4.5 meters in length and two to three meters in width (internal dimensions), but from a study of contemporary photographs it appears that in some areas the huts were considerably bigger (notably at Waikaia; see "architectural features" discussion, p. 350). Don recorded a few exceptionally large Chinese huts. He considered the "finest Chinese hut on the goldfield" was a then-abandoned cob dwelling at Blacks (Ophir) which measured 12 x 45 feet (Don, April 2, 1888:185). He also referred to a "six man hut at Round Hill" of which he did not state the dimensions, but the possibility was discussed of reducing it in length by 8 feet, indicating it must have been a substantial structure. The seven men who shared a hut dubbed "The Harmony Producing Hall" in the upper Nevis (Don, 1901:22), and the eight living in a hut at Waikaia (Don, March 1, 1887:164) probably lived in larger than average dwellings. In 1908, Don commented that the "Loyal Harmony Hall" (a hut) at Orepuki, "once the busy home of eight men" was now down to a sole occupant (Don, 1908:3).

In the situations where houses were occupied by two or more men, the occupants usually had clan or locality of origin as a common factor. Their mutual accommodation arrangements would endure so long as personality conflicts did not arise. Disputes resulted in one or more "hut mates" finding alternative accommodation. In the case of real or imagined "serious offenses" or disease threats, individuals were ostracized and obliged to live alone. Houses and their contents (utensils, furniture, books and papers) were invariably abandoned after a death or suicide had occurred (Don, August 1, 1884:25; 1893:5), and this practice was sometimes extended to the huts near one in which someone had died (Don, January 1, 1885:126). Others left huts "because of demons", rats in this instance (Don, June 1, 1887:225). Don was at a loss to explain why "the contents of abandoned huts were frequently strewn about." The Chinese attributed it to "the ghost of the deceased" (Don, December 1, 1889:106).

Houses were also deliberately burned down to make way for mining and to avoid the risk of potentially fatal landslips induced by mining (Don, February 1, 1883:146, 148). These and other reasons, such as declining fortunes or a personal desire for a change of scene, meant that there were times of considerable mobility and change in individuals' housing arrangements, even within short spaces of time (Don, 1897:9). A busy gully one year could be deserted the next. Houses were often pulled down and the materials stockpiled for relocation elsewhere (Don, 1895:52).

While crude huts could be built quite cheaply in some areas from natural resources such as mud or stone, the construction of more substantial dwellings usually represented a considerable monetary outlay. Sometimes, virtually new huts were abandoned if mining expectations were not realized. An indication of the amount of money the Chinese spent on houses was provided by Don when he recorded the following new house or hut costs after the Chinese at Alexandra reestablished their settlement. They decided to abandon the old site following continual physical harassment from a group of Europeans "who wanted them out of the town proper. . . . Seven new places were built at outlays of from 26 to 210 pounds, the total being 563 pounds" (Don, 1895:21).

The length of time individual miners stayed in one place varied considerably. Some reasons for relocating were outlined earlier. Don's "Roll of Chinese [Miners] in New Zealand" (1883-1913) provides some insights. Commencing in 1883 and continuing through to 1913, Don kept a record of the movements of the Chinese miners around the goldfield and beyond. Given the proviso that the peak of the mining boom had passed, a random sample selected from his data indicates that during this period about 90 percent of the miners were making substantial moves every five years (as opposed to annual winter/summer migrations), usually to and from the more remote areas and the Chinese enclaves in the established European mining towns. The majority of the more sedentary miners lived in or near the urban settlements or European farms where they could find occasional work. This pattern is understandable in view of their advancing ages and the increasing difficulty of ekeing out a living by mining.

The longevity (serviceable life) and period(s) of tenure of an individual dwelling was also highly variable. In the author's estimation, few of the stone and adobe Chinese goldfield dwellings in Central Otago would have been inhabited for more than twenty to thirty years, during which they might have been occupied from one to six times (although reoccupations are rarely defined archaeologically). The serviceable life of goldfield dwellings largely depended on the standard of their roofing. For example, thatched roofs on mud huts had to be replaced at least every second year to prevent the walls from becoming waterlogged and collapsing. The longevity of all-wooden dwellings in high rainfall areas such as at Round Hill was probably no more than twenty years without substantial refurbishment. But in terms of a dwelling's tenure, its structural soundness was only a minor factor because dwellings generally remained serviceable for longer than the time it took to win the easily-recoverable gold in most areas. Consequently, as fortunes declined, many perfectly serviceable dwellings were abandoned. Other factors, such as lack of company or a desire for a change of scene, also influenced individuals to abandon or sell their "home" and move on.

Internal Layout and Fittings

The Chinese usually built their own dwellings and furnishings (cf. Sachs, 1982:73-76). Houses or huts on the southern goldfield were sparsely furnished, usually having only a chimney-fireplace, a sleeping platform about forty inches wide (Don, 1894:10; 1895:60), recesses or box-cupboards for food storage, a meat safe, a wash basin or bucket, and water containers (commonly made out of old kerosene cans). According to Don they almost invariably had some form of "chest" for storing bulk rice (Don, January 1, 1883:128). Wooden boxes were often used for seating. Don (1911:34, 52) mentioned that candle, tobacco, kerosene, and peanut oil boxes were used in this fashion. Elsewhere (1897:46) he noted, "The thousands of home-made articles in Chinese huts everywhere are so many witnesses to their handiness." He also noted another distinctive feature of the Chinese miner's dwellings (Don, February 1, 1883:147):

> One can always tell a house in which Chinese have lived, by the sure presence of the "chop-block," on which meat and vegetables are cut small for eating with chopsticks. Some of the unoccupied houses here [at the Round Hill workings] are very old, and the existence of the chop block proves that the Chinese have been living years ago on ground which others are now working again.

Sachs (1982:73-74) documents some traditional Chinese household furniture among the artifacts in the Chinese structures in the historic Barkerville township in British Columbia, Canada. They include "the standard southern Chinese bed . . . with thinly crafted plain [wooden] legs in the corners, and . . . a wood deck on which a thin mattress can be laid," and tables and stools "on traditional Chinese lines." No historical or archaeological evidence of the importation of traditional Chinese house furniture into New Zealand, or detailed descriptions of the layout of Chinese miners' huts in southern New Zealand, are known to this author. Despite the lack of evidence, it is fairly certain that some traditional house furniture was imported (particularly by the more well-to-do merchants), but such acquisitions appear to have been beyond the financial scope or interest of the miners. Sleeping platforms made of sawn timber and planking (and in some instances, shelves) were probably the only regularly built-in furniture in the modestly furnished huts. Limited field and documentary evidence suggests that single sleeping platforms were built across the end wall of the miners' dwellings, farthermost from the entrance. Additional sleeping platforms were sited along the sidewalls, again at the rear of the huts.

The wooden platforms described above differ from the traditional Chinese sleeping platforms (*kang*) described by Smith (1899:26). These were made of "arrangements of adobe bricks" on which bed quilts were laid. The latter style is more akin to the inferred "elevated sleeping platforms" found in many of the Chinese rockshelters in Central Otago. The rockshelter platforms were formed by building a riser/low retaining wall (twenty to forty centimeters high) of stone slabs (usually schist) and backfilling the area behind it with soil or gravel. This created an elevated sleeping space at the rear of a rockshelter (refer later discussion on "flooring"). In the Platform shelter, the elevated area was covered with bracken fern (*Pteridium esculentum*) bedding.

Frequently, houses were "decorated" inside and outside with auspicious inscriptions, usually on red paper or written in red. Some of these marked the occasion of building a new house, e.g., "Let prosperity come in the new house." An apparently almost universal door inscription stated "May (the people at) this door become wealthy" (Don, January 1, 1883:126). In some instances houses were given names. For example, Don noted that one of the miners at Round Hill had "christened" his house "The Mansion of the Followers of Equity" (Don, December 1, 1882:103). The term "Hall" was commonly incorporated into house names, for example, the three largest Chinese houses in Orepuki were called "Peace Harmony Hall," "Vast Harmony Hall," and "Sincere Harmony Hall" (Don, 1901:17). These structures, and many others described by Don, "were gay with red paper inscriptions" placed on the doors, and in this case on the house shrine, the rice bin and the meat safe (Don, 1901:17). "Vigorous as the Dragon-Horse," possibly a reference to virility, was a common inscription over the bed or sleeping platform (Don, 1901:56). House names were sometimes changed in the hope that it would bring a change of fortunes (Don, August 1, 1883:25). Some inscriptions were more pragmatic, like this one which was pinned to the sack door of a cave-house beside the Molyneux River: "Outsiders require not enter in; Things missing many suspicions begin" (Don, 1892:12).

Keeping vegetable gardens was much more common among Chinese than European miners. Many of the Chinese established a small garden near their dwelling and often planted fruit trees such as apple and plum. Vegetable gardens were usually enclosed with light fences made of saplings or brush. Some of the miners raised a few chickens and occasionally a pig (Ritchie, 1986:587-646). Cats and dogs were sometimes kept in the homes as pets (Don, 1901:15; 1910:8).

Another purported characteristic of Chinese miners' dwellings on the Central Otago goldfield was "the number of chicken bones which could be seen around their huts." According to Burton (1982:23) the "Otago diggers said" the volume of chicken bones gave a fair indication of a Chinese miner's fortunes.

ARCHITECTURAL FEATURES

This section presents an archaeological perspective on Chinese living spaces based on field remains. It should be noted that the architectural evidence assembled here is from the Clutha study sites; it may not reflect "Chinese housing" further afield, especially beyond Central Otago, although there are certainly common threads. As noted previously, the Chinese exhibited considerable versatility in house construction, generally utilizing whatever was at hand. As a consequence, Chinese dwellings often varied in appearance from one mining district to another. For example, the majority of the Chinese huts on the Waipori goldfield were built of mud brick or cob (puddled mud), whereas at Round Hill, wooden shingles, *punga* logs (tree fern trunks), and rough timber (possibly mill offcuts) were used extensively. Many of the Chinese houses at Waikaia were made of sawn timber weatherboards. In the Clutha-Wakatipu basins, relatively little timber was readily available, so stone (cobbles and/or schist slabs), and puddled mud, or a combination of mud and stone, were the principal materials used. Temporary structures or the huts of poor men were often built of rice sacking (Don, 1894:28). Rockshelters were used extensively in the river gorges and rocky side gullies.

Rockshelters

A typical Chinese rockshelter in the Cromwell area consists of a one room chamber formed by erecting a wall along the front of a natural overhang or the cavity beneath one or more large boulders (Figure 78). In some instances, e.g., the Hanging Rock site, the height of the overhang (four meters) is such that it was not practical to "wall up" the whole height, so a light roof was constructed, in effect creating a hut under an overhang. In those shelters where it can be determined, the doorways measure between thirty-five and sixty centimeters in width and vary

Figure 78. One of forty-four Chinese rockshelters in the Cromwell Gorge, Central Otago.

from 1.3 to 1.6 meters high. Construction features of the excavated rockshelters are summarized in Table 43 and discussed below.

The table clearly shows the predominant usage of mud mortared schist slabs for walling. Of about 100 Chinese rockshelter dwellings observed in Central Otago by the writer, some 70 percent incorporate schist slab walls, while schist and cobbles were utilized in about another 10 percent. This pattern is not hard to understand. Schist is ubiquitous in Central Otago. Detrital pieces, suitable for building, are liberally scattered around the numerous outcrops. The stone has natural flat surfaces which can be interlocked. Used in conjunction with mud mortar, cheap, durable, and weatherproof walls and structures can be built rapidly. Chinese miners' dwellings (rockshelters and huts) of similar construction have been observed by the writer on the Salmon River (Sisson, 1983 and Chapter 2 herein).

Although materials such as packed earth, vegetation, or canvas are less likely to have survived as well as stone walls, field observations indicate that if the Chinese built a shelter with any degree of permanence in the Cromwell area they utilized stone; either schist slabs if they were readily available, or cobbles recovered from the tailings in mining claims. The use of caliche (a naturally occurring calcium carbonate precipitate) in the Caliche shelter is an interesting exception, but understandable since there was a convenient source of the material at hand. Packed mud was used occasionally for walling-in rockshelters, if there was no ready source of stone nearby. About 20 percent (nine) of the Chinese shelters in the Cromwell Gorge had no apparent solid walling. Careful examination of the front of the overhangs often reveals nails (or nail holes) suggesting that canvas, calico, or sacking had been hung over the entrance. In the absence of timber to build a door or door frame, the Chinese sometimes made a "wire netting mattress" the same size as the doorway. The netting mattress was stuffed with tussock and other vegetation and pulled into the entrance as a door and draft-stopper (Roebuck, 1981-1983:personal communications).

Initially, rockshelter habitations were widely used by the Chinese in the Cromwell area because the river gorges, where the main strikes were made, abounded with suitable overhangs and caves for constructing shelters. As the gold in the river gorges was worked out, rockshelter usage declined, although they continued to be used in some areas such as the Molyneux (Roxburgh) Gorge and Conroy's Gully (Don, 1906:28) long after they had been generally abandoned in other areas. Don described them as "cozy in winter and cool in summer" (Don, 1906:28). Many of the former "cave-dwellers" built huts in the settlements or on claims that they had started working elsewhere, but some maintained rockshelter dwellings which they returned to at specific times of the year, in order to work the beaches when the rivers were low.

As can be seen from a perusal of the internal dimensions of the shelters listed in Table 43, they varied considerably in size, but it is difficult to quantify their relative degree of "creature comfort." Those at the bottom end of the scale are

Table 43. Rockshelter Construction Features

Site Name	Wall Type	Door Position	Fire Position	Floor Type	Other Features	Av. Internal Dimensions
Firewood Creek	a	—	none	o	—	3.0 × 2.0 m
Caliche	b	i	k	n,p	t,u	4.0 × 2.5 m
Sheung Fong	c	g	k	o,p,n	q	4.0 × 2.0 m
Ha Fong	c	i	j	n,o,q	r	5.5 × 2.5 m
Rockfall 1	a,c	—	—	o	u	7.0 × 3.0 m
Northburn	c	i	k	p	—	3.0 × 1.5 m
Kawarau	e	g	j	o	—	2.5 × 2.5 m
Hanging Rock	c	h	k	o,p	v	4.5 × 2.0 m
Riverside	c	g	k	o,p	—	4.0 × 1.5 m
ACS/16	f	—	—	o	w	2.0 × 1.5 m
Flax Grove	c	g	—	o,p	—	6.0 × 2.0 m
Platform	c	g	j	o,p	x	2.5 × 2.0 m

[a]Canvas or sacking wall indicated by nails in rock above entrance
[b]Wall formed of large pieces of caliche, gaps plugged with mud
[c]Wall made of mud-mortared schist slabs
[d]Wall made of mud-mortared river cobbles
[e]Wall made of cobbles and slabs
[f]Wall has timber framing
[g]Door in center of wall
[h]Door in left hand side of end wall
[i]Door in right hand side of end wall
[j]Fireplace built into wall beside doorway
[k]Fireplace built into one end of shelter (by the door)
[l]Outside fireplace
[m]Floor deepened by excavation to increase head height
[n]Floor "split level," i.e., elevated sleeping area
[o]Floor material: natural gravel
[p]Floor material: natural clay or silt
[q]Floor partially covered with schist slabs
[r]Vent in wall (usually a bottomless tin box)
[s]Fireplace built of schist slabs
[t]Fireplace built of earth-filled kerosene cans
[u]Evidence of earlier prehistoric occupation
[v]Essentially a hut built under an overhang
[w]Uncertain as to whether it was a dwelling
[x]Bracken covered sleeping platform
Note: The internal dimensions presented in this table are of necessity averaged. The square meterage of each shelter is to some extent based on an assessment of its usable area.

characterized by the following features: low head room (sometimes improved by digging out the floor); dampness and seepage; uneven, rocky floor surfaces, rock surfaces which are prone to spalling; difficult access; poor ventilation; and generally cramped conditions. In addition, some had poor access to water and firewood, and little ground suitable for gardening in the vicinity.

At the other end of the scale there are those shelters which appear to be well sheltered, dry, and spacious both inside and out. These dwellings were probably at least as comfortable as huts of similar dimensions. Field observations, and the volumes of occupation refuse recovered from the smallest and least comfortable shelters, suggest that they were usually only occupied for short periods. However, the inverse is not true of the larger and seemingly more comfortable structures. Field evidence indicates the longevity of their occupation varied considerably, probably being dependent to a large extent on the availability of water and accessibility of gold in the vicinity.

Excavated Chinese Structures: Construction Features

As noted previously, the majority of the Chinese miners' huts in Central Otago were made of stone or mud (both mud brick and cob). Most are simple, rectangular, ridge-beam constructions, characterized by a door and chimney at one end. Frequently one or more of the walls was built into an adjacent bank or slope. There appear to be few structural differences between the rural and urban huts, although, as elaborated in the following discussion, there are several interesting differences between the construction of the huts in the Cromwell and Arrowtown settlements.

Structural features of the study sites are summarized in Table 44. The possibility that the construction of some of the described structures has changed over the years, particularly with regard to roofing materials, cannot be totally ruled out. However, the use of the materials cited below was confirmed by archaeological investigations, or in the case of the structures in the urban settlements, through study of contemporary photographs. Following the discussion on materials and related aspects, the dimensions and orientation of the structures are examined, and some distinctive differences between Chinese and European dwellings in the study area are documented.

Discussion

Wall construction — The immediately discernible features of Table 44 are the differences between the huts in the Cromwell and Arrowtown settlements. Whereas the majority of the huts at Cromwell were built of cobbles, those at Arrowtown are predominantly of mud construction or a mud/stone combination. The use of cobbles for house construction at Cromwell is readily understandable. The settlement there was established in an area which had already been mined by Europeans. Consequently, there was an abundant supply of cobbles available for construction purposes among the tailings. Elsewhere in the study area, field evidence suggests that the Chinese generally preferred to use detrital slabs of the ubiquitous schist rock for construction if they were readily available, presumably because schist slabs had more inherent stability and were easier to stack than cobbles. The possibility that the miners helped one another to construct their huts is suggested by the lack of consistency in the stacking of the cobbles within and between individual huts in Chinatown. They are often stacked horizontally, vertically, or diagonally within a short section of wall.

The procedure for creating the mud walls of many of the Arrowtown huts was observed firsthand by a recently deceased Arrowtown resident (Austin Dudley, 1983: personal communication). The first step involved deciding on the size of the proposed hut. The "interior" was then dug over and puddled by the addition of water. This material was then dug out (up to thirty centimeters below the ground level) and packed to form the walls. If there was a shortage of mud (or for some other reason) some sections were built up with stone (e.g., ACS/3 and ACS/4).

As can be seen in Table 44, other construction techniques were also used at Arrowtown. ACS/1 was a pre-built corrugated iron structure brought on to the site after 1900 (Austin Dudley, 1983:personal communication), but the use of pre-built huts was uncommon. Generally, construction materials, such as earth, clay, stone, and tussock, were obtained from the local environment. The main cost would have been in terms of one's labor input. Insights into the construction of two of the other former hut sites in the Arrowtown settlement are now available only from contemporary photographs, because all trace of both sites has been completely obliterated. ACS/7 was a combination mud and wood construction, while ACS/14 had vertical wooden cladding. Ah Lum's store is included in the table because it also served as a habitation. From title and ratebook research, it appears the stone and timber building was originally erected for Wong Hop ca. 1883 (Mark Hangar, 1984:personal communication). Its size, shaped schist masonry, and relative grandeur would have been beyond the means of the average miner.

The construction of most of the rural hut sites listed in Table 44 is typical of those in the upper Clutha area. However, the Rapids and 12 Mile Creek sites are interesting exceptions. The wall outline in the Rapids site is evidenced by a rectangle of schist slabs, seldom more than two stones deep, which may have secured a canvas structure. The 12 Mile Creek site was not excavated. It is included in the table because it is believed to be typical of Chinese hut construction in the few forested areas of Central Otago. The hut, one of several adjacent to 12 Mile Creek, is in an area of beech forest. All that now remains of the sites are stone chimney bases and cultural debris scatters. It is likely that the Chinese used the timber at hand for construction, but as anyone familiar with beech (*Nothofaqus menziesii*) knows, it deteriorates very rapidly when exposed to damp conditions. A common feature of perhaps 70 percent of the Chinese huts around Cromwell is that one or more walls is built into an adjacent bank or slope. As indicated in Table 44, a similar percentage of huts in the Cromwell settlement have two walls built into an adjacent bank, the other huts being freestanding or built back to back.

Table 44. Chinese Structures: Summary of Construction Features

Structure Name or Number	Wall Construction	Chimney/door Construction	Roofing Material	Free-standing or Otherwise
Ch/1	*b*	*m?*	*s*	*w*
Ch/2	*b*	—	*s*	*w*
Ch/4	*a, b*	*k*	*s*	*v*
Ch/6	*b*	*j*	*o?*	*x*
Ch/7	*b*	—	*o?*	*v*
Ch/12	*b*	*j*	*o*	*w, x*
Ch/14	*b*	*j?*	*o*	*w, x*
Ch/16	*b*	*j*	*o*	*w, x*
Ch/18	*b*	*j*	*o*	*w, x*
Ch/19	*b*	—	*o*	*w, x*
Ch/21	*b*	*j*	*o*	*w, x*
Ch/23	*b*	*j*	*o*	*w*
Ch/24	*b*	*j*	*o*	*w*
Ch/26	*b, z*	*j*	*o*	*w*
Ch/27	*b*	*j*	*o, q?*	*w*
Ch/33	*b*	*j*	*s*	*w*
Ch/34	*b*	*j*	*s*	*v*
QB2	*a, z*	*j*	*s*	*w*
Apple Tree	*a*	*y*	*s*	*w*
Sandy Point	*a, z*	*k*	*s*	*w*
Ah Wee's	*d*	*?*	*s*	*v*
Poplars	*a*	*j*	*s*	*w*
ACS/1	*g*	*k?*	*o*	*v*
ACS/2	*a*	*k*	*p*	*v*
ACS/3	*e*	*j*	*p*	*w*
ACS/4	*e*	*k*	*p*	*v*
ACS/5	*a*	*l*	*s*	*w*
ACS/6	*a*	*k?*	*p*	*w*
ACS/7	*d*	*?*	*p*	*v*
ACS/8	*d*	*k?*	*p*	*v*
ACS/11	*d*	*?*	*p*	*v*
ACS/14	*f*	*?*	*s*	*v*
Long House	*f*	*t*	*o*	*v*
Ah Lum's	*a, z*	*u*	*o*	*v*
The Rapids	*h?*	*?*	*v*	*v*
Willows	*a*	*k*	*w*	*w*
12 Mile Creek	*i?*	*?*	*v*	*v*

Table 44. (Cont'd.)

Notes: The prefix 'Ch' denotes a structure in Cromwell's Chinatown. The prefix 'ACS' denotes a structure in the Arrowtown Chinese settlement.

Key
[a]Walls made of mud-mortared schist slabs
[b]Walls made of mud-mortared cobbles from tailings or rivers
[c]Walls made of a combination of schist slabs and cobbles
[d]Walls made of cob (i.e., puddled mud)
[e]Walls made of a combination of mud and stone
[f]Walls made of timber
[g]Walls made of corrugated iron
[h]Walls possibly made of canvas
[i]Walls possibly made of beech trees
[j]Chimney to right of doorway at one end of the structure
[k]Chimney to left of doorway at one end of the structure
[l]Doorway in side wall, chimney at one end
[m]Doorway in side wall, chimney also in side wall
[n]No evidence of chimney
[o]Roof made of corrugated iron
[p]Roof made of tussock thatch
[q]Roof believed to have been partially covered with flattened cans
[r]Roof believed to have been partially covered with canvas
[s]Roofing material not known
[t]Door in one end, chimney at opposite end
[u]Sole fireplace in kitchen
[v]Structure free-standing
[w]Structure built into bank or slope
[x]Structure built onto adjacent structure
[y]Door in end wall, chimney in side wall
[z]Cupboards or shelves set into walls

Similarly, the QB2, Apple Tree, Sandy Point, Poplars, ACS/5 and Willows huts are built into adjacent slopes. The common denominator seems to be that the walls of these structures are made of stone which is occasionally plastered on the interior walls. The rationale for constructing huts in this semi-subterranean fashion is uncertain; it was not a feature of traditional houses in Guangdong. While they may have been more sheltered and warmer, and probably required less technique to build, this type of construction must have increased the likelihood of problems with ground water seepage. There was no real saving in construction materials either since the walls built into the banks had to be of stout construction because they served as retaining walls. Mud huts, such as Ah Wee's and the majority of those at Arrowtown, are invariably freestanding.

U.S. archaeologists (e.g., Hardesty, 1988) have documented several instances of Chinese miners living in excavated subterranean "dugouts." This author is unaware of any truly subterranean Chinese habitations in New Zealand. While the possibility that "dugouts" were used here cannot be discounted, they were certainly uncommon.

The other major structural difference between the Cromwell and Arrowtown settlements is the central mass of huts built back-to-back at Cromwell (see Ritchie, 1986:85-138 for plans and photographs of the sites). Although this form of construction has historical precedents in China for defensive and social reasons, there seems no definite reason for resorting to it at Cromwell. It might reflect a social grouping (perhaps members of the same clan), but it certainly does not reflect the building-on of accommodation to house wives or family in the all-male community. There was no saving in construction materials either, because where the walls abut, they are of double thickness.

While walled courtyards are a common component of houses in China, stone or adobe-walled enclosed yards are an infrequent feature of Chinese miners' dwellings on the southern New Zealand goldfields. Contemporary photographs indicate that the Chinese erected wooden fences along the boundaries between houses in the larger settlements at Lawrence and Round Hill, but elsewhere light saplings and brush were used, principally to demarcate and protect garden plots.

About 10 percent of the Chinese stone huts in the study area had wooden boxes and/or stone-lined recesses built into the walls to serve as shelves. The most common location for such features is in the sidewall adjacent to the fireplace. Archaeological evidence indicates that shelves in this position were commonly used to store items such a food bowls and tins of wax vesta matches.

Local legend holds that the Chinese miners installed glass bottles (with their bases removed and necks sloping towards the exterior) through the walls of their huts, specifically for the purpose of urinating at night without leaving the hut. While this would seem an ingenious response to an oft pressing problem, I am unaware of any archaeological, documentary, or pictorial evidence of it, and conclude that it was a relatively rare practice.

Chimney construction — Both field observations and study of contemporary photographs indicate that most Chinese huts in Central Otago had mud-mortared stone chimneys, the main exception being "mud huts" where the chimneys were built of the same medium. The solid chimney bases, many complete with hearth stones or bricks and firebars, are now the only visible remnant of many mud huts. During their heyday, the chimneys were often surmounted by a "chimney pot" (e.g., a kerosene can with its end cut out), or a short piece of mining pipe. These fittings presumably improved the chimney draft and avoided smoke problems. On the Round Hill field, many of the wooden huts also had wooden chimneys, so fire was a constant threat. Huts were frequently destroyed by fire (Don, January 1, 1883:126; March 1, 1883:183), and in 1883, a fire threatened to destroy the business part of the Round Hill settlement (Don, April 2, 1883:183).

The second column of Table 44 records the position of the chimney in the various structures. While it is difficult to precisely ascertain the sociological or physical significance of chimney placement, some points can be made:

1. The juxtaposition of the door and chimney in an end wall. In effect, this allowed one to tend the fire and keep an eye on what was happening in the area immediately outside the door. This positioning may have been influenced in part by deeply entrenched Chinese superstitions, which motivated one to "be ready" or "not be taken by surprise" by either physical "disturbances" or evil spirits.
2. In all the positively Chinese structures in the Cromwell Chinatown, the chimneys are located on the right side of the doorway as you enter, whereas at Arrowtown and in the rural hut sites, the chimneys are located either right or left of the doorway in fairly equal ratios. Why there should be such consistency in the positioning of hut chimneys in the Chinatown settlement is difficult to explain, because it does not seem to be a response to a physical factor such as the direction of the prevailing wind. It seems beyond the bounds of chance that every hut builder at Cromwell would elect to build the chimney on the right hand side of the doorway, unless there was some factor governing this construction behavior. Possibly new hut builders were advised by existing members of the community to build in such a fashion.
3. In only two instances, ACS/5 at Arrowtown and in the Apple Tree site in the upper Clutha, are chimneys located other than in an end wall adjacent to the door. In ACS/5 the doorway is built into the side of the house, but still within clear view of the fireplace which is built into the end wall. In the Apple Tree hut, the doorway is in the right hand side of one end wall, but the fireplace is built into the opposite side wall. As such it is rather unusual, and may not have been built by a Chinese person.

Windows and doors — The recovery of European-style door hinges, padlocks, slide bolts, and handles, together with the study of contemporary photographs, indicates that most Chinese huts had a door made of wooden planking. Often the top of the door was angled in line with the slope of the roof, to increase the clearance. Doors were hinged within a wooden frame, or in some instances, pivoted at the top and bottom. For example, in ACS/4, a cart stub axle was set into the ground on one side of the doorway, and the door pivoted by using the concavity in the end of the axles. In the Poplars and Horseshoe Bend hut sites, the "kick-ups" of upturned bottles were used in a similar fashion. At the latter site, another bottle base was used to pivot the gate leading from a small paved enclosure in front of the doorway.

Contemporary photographs (e.g., Butler, 1977:63) show that some Chinese huts (both stone and mud brick) had small square to rectangular vents or windows above the door. They appear to have been formed by setting wooden or metal boxes, with their bases and lids removed, into the wall. The role of these features is not clear, but they probably served as vents and allowed some natural light and fresh air into the often windowless structures. The Ha Fong shelter has a similar feature set into the wall.

Although Don (1883:17) recorded that "Scores of time the men here (i.e., the Chinese miners) have spoken with admiration of the way they can leave doors unlocked . . . which we dare not do in China," in Cromwell's Chinatown there was obviously some concern about security. European-style padlocks and lock fittings were found in over half (ca. 12) of the hut sites. Security artifacts are rarely found in rural sites. Perhaps the absence of traditional Chinese padlocks is attributable to the fact that they can be opened easily. According to Smith (1899:28), "Chinese padlocks can generally be picked with a wire, a chopstick, or even a dry weed, and afford no real protection."

In the absence of glass fragments, it is often difficult to ascertain whether a structure in a ruinous state had glazed windows. The study of contemporary photographs and the absence of window glass fragments in archeological contexts indicate that many rural Chinese huts did not have windows or had very small ones. Window glass was found in only one of the rural sites, the Flax Grove shelter. It was present in six of the huts in the Arrowtown settlement, but in only two at Chinatown. This is probably attributable, in part, to the high incidence of European larrikinism and vandalism which was directed towards the Cromwell settlement and its inhabitants.The Chinese may have foregone windows, rather than put up with the expense and hassle of replacing broken panes, and the risk of injury from breaking glass and stones.

Roofing materials — Again, study of Table 44 shows there is an immediately discernible difference between the types of roofing utilized at Cromwell and Arrowtown. At the former, most of the huts were roofed with corrugated iron, whereas at Arrowtown, tussock thatch was the main roofing material. The thatch was replaced annually (Austin Dudley, 1983:personal communication). Many of the Chinese huts photographed by Don on his travels around the goldfields had tussock thatch overlaid with rice bags and canvas. In Don's opinion (October 1, 1887:63), "huts with sod walls, clay floors and a thatch roof had an air of mustiness." This factor, together with iron's greater durability, may partly explain the preference for corrugated iron at Cromwell, despite the capital outlay it involved. Other materials used by the Chinese for roofing included wooden shingles, used extensively at Round Hill (Figure 79), sacking, canvas, turf (supported on saplings), and flattened kerosene cans.

Flooring — Whether free-standing or built into a slope, the Chinese miners' huts in the study area were generally built directly on the ground surface, that is, they did not have elevated wooden floorboards on some form of foundation. Field observations and archaeological evidence indicate that the floors were formed, in roughly equal ratios, by either laying a paving of schist slabs or by compaction of the underlying gravels by trampling in the course of use. In many instances, the paving is restricted to the front half of the structures, or there are just a few hearthstones. Rockshelters were paved in a similar manner, except that the natural basal rock often forms part of the floor. ACS/1, a prefabricated corrugated iron hut

Figure 79. A Chinese miner beside his shingle-roofed hut, Round Hill goldfield, southern New Zealand. The European is Rev. George H. McNeur. Courtesy McNeur Collection, Alexander Turnbull Library, Wellington, New Zealand, No. F19167 1/2.

in the Arrowtown Chinese settlement, is the only structure among those studied which appears to have had an above-ground wooden floor.

The rockshelters inhabited by the Chinese in Central Otago often have split-level floors: lowest at the entrance (usually at or slightly below the outside ground level), and separated by a stone-lined riser/retaining wall (20 to 40 centimeters high) from an area of higher elevation at the rear. By backfilling the area behind the riser with gravel, the usable area within a shelter was extended by creating a more level surface at the expense of decreasing the headroom. The elevated platforms served as the sleeping areas. Split-level construction has only been found in one hut site (QB2) in the upper Clutha valley. This structure also differs from the others in that it has a stone-lined pit in the left rear corner of the elevated rear area. The pit was probably originally used as a cool place to store provisions, but when it was exposed during the excavation it was found to be backfilled with loose rock rubble.

Although observers often described the structures and sanitary conditions around the urban Chinese settlements in disparaging terms, there were no major disease outbreaks (unlike in some European settlements), suggesting that the hygiene standards of the Chinese belied the often crude appearance of their dwellings. Don, one of the few Europeans who ever regularly ventured into and stayed in the Chinese miners' dwellings, occasionally commented on the interiors of individual huts which were particularly messy, but overall, one gains the impression that they were kept reasonably clean and tidy considering their all-male occupation and frontier circumstances. Don did note however (February 1, 1884:147), that the Chinese on the Round Hill field, unlike those in China, rarely swept the floors of their huts.

Hut Sizes and Dimensions

Table 45 shows the floor areas of the excavated Chinese huts and their internal dimensions. The average floor area of the twenty-six huts listed in Table 45 is 8.3 square meters.

The immediately obvious feature is that the huts at Arrowtown are generally smaller than those at Cromwell. At Cromwell, the average floor area of the surviving structures is 8.3 square meters, whereas at Arrowtown it is 7.3 square meters, but only 6.25 square meters if the larger socializing hut, ACS/2 is omitted from the calculation. However, the size of two of the largest huts, 7 and 14, cannot be determined from the ground evidence. Consequently, one can only say that the majority of the Arrowtown huts are smaller than those excavated elsewhere in the Clutha catchment. Whatever the reason for the construction of generally smaller houses in the Arrowtown settlement, it is unlikely to be income-related. The Arrow was, and still is, one of the most productive gold-bearing rivers in the study area.

As stated previously, Chinese miners seldom lived alone before the turn of the century; usually between two and eight shared a hut together. Three was a

Table 45. Floor Areas of Chinese Miners' Huts
(in descending order of size)

Structure Name	Floor Area (sq. meters)	Structure Name	Floor Area (sq. meters)
ACS/2	12.5	ACS/5	7.5
Poplars	12.0	Apple Tree	7.0
Ah Wee's	12.0	Ch/16	7.0
Ch/1	11.5	ACS/8	6.75
Ch/12	11.25	Ch/14	6.65
Ch/26	10.8	Ch/18	6.60
Rapids	10.5	Willows	6.25
Ch/34	10.4	Ch/24	6.20
Ch/33	9.5	ACS/3	6.0
Ch/23	9.25	ACS/6	6.0
QB2	8.2	Ch/19	5.7
Ch/21	7.9	Ch/27	5.25
Sandy Point	7.5	ACS/4	5.0

common number judging from Don's numerous comments. Hut sizes varied accordingly. Study of contemporary photographs, dimensions of huts measured during the course of field recording, and Don's comments indicate that the 'standard' two to four man huts varied from three to five meters in length and were two to three meters wide. The width component, usually between two and three meters has considerably less variability than the length component, which ranges from about two to five meters. The length variability probably reflects notions such as:

1) ease or familiarity in building elongated structures;
2) an elongated structure provides better separation of sleeping and cooking areas, and generally better use of space;
3) a square/elongated structure enables better use of some materials, e.g., corrugated iron;
4) a square/elongated structure is easier to extend.

Hut Orientation and Door Positions

While a number of consistencies in the materials and layout of the Chinese structures have been documented thus far, there are also some interesting patterns evident in the orientation of the structures. These possibly reflect, to some extent, the maintenance of traditional Chinese concepts based on the cosmological principles of *feng shui* geomancy and demon spiritology, discussed below.

Table 46. Hut Door Orientation (to nearest major cardinal point)

Chinatown	Orientation	Arrowtown	Orientation	Rural Sites	Orientation
Ch/1	NW	ACS/1	W?	QB2	E (tr)
Ch/4	E (tr)	ASC/2	NW (tr)	Apple Tree	SE
Ch/6	SE (tr)	ACS/3	NW (tr)	Sandy Point	NE
Ch/12	NE	ACS/4	NW (tr)	Ah Wee's	?
Ch/14	NE	ACS/5	NW (tr)	Poplars	NE (tr)
Ch/16	E (tr)	ACS/6	W?	Hanging Rock	E
Ch/18	E (tr)	ACS/7	NW (tr)	Willows	W (tr)
Ch/19	NW	ACS/8	NW (tr)		
Ch/21	E (tr)	ACS/11	S?		
Ch/23	NE	ACS/14	NW?		
Ch/24	E (tr)	Ah Lum's	E		
Ch/26	SE (tr)	Long House	NW (tr)		
Ch/27	NE				
Ch/33	W				
Ch/34	W				

Note: If the hut door faces towards the adjacent creek or river it is indicated by (tr).

Table 46 reveals a trend for hut doors at Chinatown, and in most of the rural sites, to be orientated in the easterly quarter, even though few huts face in exactly the same direction on the ground. At Arrowtown, the dominant orientation is towards the northwest, and there is considerably more consistency between huts; most have a fairly similar door orientation. It is difficult to isolate a dominant motive for the varying orientation of the huts. Clearly, particularly at Chinatown, it is partly dependent on topographic restraints. There also seems to have been an inclination towards facing out onto open or lower land rather than towards a slope. While "a desire to obtain a view" is an understandable reason for orientating a structure or positioning a door in a particular place, there may have been a more practical reason, such as a defensive reaction to prevent European louts from throwing stones or other missiles through the open doorways from a higher vantage point.

At Arrowtown, a notable feature of the hut door orientation is that the majority of doors face out to the northwest, overlooking what would have been open creek bed. At Cromwell, approximately half of the hut doors face east or southeast toward the river, while a similar pattern holds for the rural sites. Orientation toward water is understandable both in terms of "obtaining a good view" and "keeping an eye on the river." The latter reason might have been particularly influential because mining returns were affected both favorably and adversely by the level of the rivers. The majority of the doorways in the gorge rockshelters face toward the rivers too, but their positions are often governed by the shape and orientation of the space under suitable overhanging rocks.

The easterly orientation of most of the Chinatown huts may have been partly influenced by a desire "to maximize the morning sun," although this does not seem to have been an important consideration at Arrowtown. Placement so as to maximize privacy when the door was open, and to avoid the prevailing wind by orientating the door away from it does not seem to have been an overriding consideration either; again, at Arrowtown most of the hut doors are directly exposed to the northwesterlies.

A possible major but less tangible factor influencing the orientation of structures lies in Chinese notions such as *feng shui*; see also Sisson (Chapter 2 herein). *Feng shui*, literally "wind" and "water," is a long established philosophical concept or art concerned with the orientation and placement of objects and structures so as to maximize good fortune by selecting places with good *ch'i* (the life essence), and conversely minimizing the deleterious effects of evil spirits (Rossbach, 1985). *Feng shui* is a complex language of symbols, many of which are derived from the environment, such as the imagery (e.g., dragons) conjured by the shape of hills (Rossbach, 1985:31). Locations with "good *feng shui*" tend to have or offer:

1) shelter (from the north wind in China);
2) surrounding hills or slopes which provide a "protective armchair" formation (Rossbach, 1985:40);
3) fertile ground which is not excessively flood-prone or swampy (Rossbach, 1985:37);
4) watercourses which are "balanced," (i.e., not flowing too fast or too slowly), and are not straight, "which threatens money, life and prosperity" (Rossbach, 1985:38);
5) trees, which improve a *"feng shui* landscape" by protecting against malign winds (or killing *ch'i*) and fostering good growing *ch'i* (Rossbach, 1985:39);
6) a view out onto water or open ground.

There is also complex *feng shui* lore concerned with the positioning and shape of structures and their internal fittings in order to maximize *ch'i* (Rossbach, 1985:71-140).

The difficulty, in more prosaic archaeological terms, is to evaluate whether the varying orientation of structures was influenced primarily by *feng shui* considerations or other factors. The problem is compounded because successful application of the concept involves consideration of many factors which someone not aware or concerned about *feng shui* would also consider when establishing a new home, such as its orientation and position in relation to shelter from the wind, obtaining a view, having sufficient elevation to avoid flooding, and positioning so as to maximize the hours of sunlight.

The Chinese are unlikely to have neglected the deeply-entrenched notions of *feng shui* when they established their settlements and homes on the goldfields of southern New Zealand. But for the reasons noted above, it is virtually impossible to ascertain just how much effect adherence to *feng shui* principles had. Rossbach (1985) documented some considerations which seem to be pertinent. First. there seems to have been fairly conscious avoidance of having hut doorways directly facing each other (Rossbach, 1985:111). Secondly, the Chinese generally avoided settling on flat, waterless areas (traditionally recognized as being devoid of *ch'i*). Obviously there are very practical reasons for avoiding such areas too. Thirdly, the Chinese appear to have preferred to settle in locations which backed onto terrace risers or sloping ground, and overlooked rivers or streams. These places are traditionally associated with "good *feng shui*." Fourth, many Chinese miners established their huts at the confluence of rivers and streams. These locations are also renowned for their good *feng shui* (Rossbach, 1985:38). Fifth, as documented, most of the Chinese miners' huts were rectangular, a shape reputed to have good *feng shui* (Rossbach, 1985:71, 77). Finally, with regard to the settlements at Cromwell and Arrowtown, there seems to have been a conscious avoidance of erecting structures in straight lines (which would facilitate the passage of evil spirits).

Don, who was familiar with Chinese superstitions, alluded to such a consideration when he described the Cromwell Chinatown settlement in 1908 (1908:11):

> I had two hours in the wonderful collection of huts called 'Chinatown'. . . .
> The 21 dwellings are nearly all set at different angles, built of different materials, and are of different sizes. Long straight lines are "unlucky," since the demons can thus easily travel. . . .

While the placement factors outlined above may have been influenced by *feng shui* notions to some extent, some important *feng shui* considerations appear to have been neglected by the Chinese miners at Cromwell's Chinatown, if not elsewhere. Several of the huts at Chinatown had doors with slanting tops, evident in contemporary photographs, and presumably also had angled roof beams. Such doors and angled timbers "can destroy good *feng shui* . . . and can bring on an unusual horrible, unimaginable occurrence." (Rossbach, 1985:112). Mirrors are the aspirin of *feng shui*. The mystic appeal of mirrors runs deep in Chinese history. Whether a problem was weak or bad *ch'i*, or a badly shaped or positioned structure, the cure was more often than not to hang mirrors or other shiny objects inside and outside a house to keep evil spirits at bay (Rossbach, 1985:68-69). If the Chinese miners in Central Otago maintained this defensive practice, they either did not break and discard many mirrors, or they took them with them when they left. However, they may have used other shiny objects to divert evil spirits.

SOME COMPARISONS BETWEEN CHINESE AND EUROPEAN DWELLINGS

From site recording, excavations, and study of early photographs, a number of differences are apparent between Chinese and European dwellings in the upper Clutha valley:

1) The Chinese made much more extensive and prolonged use of natural shelters such as rock overhangs and caves formed under rockfalls than did the Europeans.
2) The majority of the Chinese huts in the Cromwell-Arrowtown area, regardless of their construction materials, follow a simple model characterized by the following features: rectangular shape (almost square in the case of small huts), ridge-beam construction, no windows, and the chimney and door built adjacent to each other in one end wall (neither in the central position). Placement of the door in one of the long side walls is uncommon. European huts exhibit considerably more architectural variety. Some Chinese huts have a small window-vent built into the wall above the door.
3) Stone huts constructed by the Chinese are frequently built into adjacent banks or slopes.
4) Chinese huts are generally smaller than those of Europeans. Their construction also tends to be lighter, but they are at least the equal of European huts in terms of structural soundness.
5) The Chinese huts in the study area also have a lower roof angle and ridge height than their European counterparts.
6) There is less concept of "street" in the Chinese settlements. The huts tend to be built in relatively haphazard patterns in line with the topography.

There are relatively few detailed descriptions available of nonurban 19th century Chinese settlements in other countries for comparative purposes. However, the Chinese settlement at Atherton in North Queensland, Australia, reveals some interesting similarities and differences between the structures there and those in Central Otago (Grimwade and Reynolds, 1986:23):

> Chinatown in 1897 was an orderly little town of about a dozen single- or double-roomed huts arranged on either side of a short main street. Each hut was constructed from sawn wood, roofed with corrugated iron and fronted by a verandah. The style of the huts was similar but not identical to the architecture of the slab huts of the European pioneers. The most pronounced differences were the smaller dimensions and the considerably lower roof angle.

The "Chinese features" mentioned above are also typical of the Chinese miners' dwellings in Central Otago, the notable difference being a general absence of verandas on both European and Chinese miners' dwellings in New Zealand. Compared with the Chinese miners' huts in southern New Zealand, Australian similarities include the use of corrugated iron for roofs, the use of sawn timber, the low roof angles of the huts, and the huts' generally smaller dimensions than their European counterparts. The most notable difference is the general absence of verandas on both European and Chinese huts in southern New Zealand.

CONCLUDING DISCUSSION

The habitations of the Chinese miners in southern New Zealand were markedly different from those of their homeland, but this is not surprising when the much colder climate of southern New Zealand (particularly the winters), the frontier nature of the goldfields, and the less rigid social structure of New Zealand society are taken into consideration. Since few of the Chinese miners were accompanied by family members, there was little need or compulsion to recreate traditional patterns of settlement, or to be tightly bound by the strict social mores of their homeland. Given the virtually all-male nature of the New Zealand Chinese mining fraternity and the economies of working claims in small groups, the emergence of a pattern whereby one to eight partners (usually clansmen) shared crude but relatively comfortable huts (or 2 room houses consisting of living and sleeping areas) is readily understandable.

The imprint of many centuries of rigid social organization in China, did, however, have some carryover effect on the development of Chinese settlements and the nature of Chinese dwellings in New Zealand. From the outset the Chinese exhibited a remarkable adaptability and versatility with regard to house construction, based on inherited skills associated with family home building, and maximizing the use of local resources. Archival, photographic, and archaeological evidence indicate the owner-builders used a wide range of natural and manmade resources, despite an initial unfamiliarity with many of them. The construction materials included turf, mud bricks and puddled mud, *pungas* (tree fern trunks), forest trees (notably beech), weatherboards, mill offcuts, canvas, cobblestones, schist slabs, corrugated iron, and various combinations of the above, depending on local circumstances. In addition, in the river gorges and gullies of Central Otago where suitable sites abounded, the Chinese formed comfortable homes by walling up the front of natural overhangs or caves using mud-mortared schist slabs and cobbles, or, more rarely, adobe. Their building strategies, weighted towards low investment, expediency, use of abundant free materials, and low technology, were pragmatic responses to their situations.

In the earlier discussions, several characteristic features of the Chinese miners' dwellings in Central Otago were identified but, because of a lack of detailed data on the construction and layout of houses in southern China, it is difficult to ascertain the carryover of particular traits, although some are apparent. For example, many of the miners' huts in Central Otago are windowless, a common security feature of the houses in contemporary Guangdong (Mawson, 1926; Smith, 1899:26). Traditional features such as hut shrines and inscriptions on doors and walls were also common, and the huts commonly had a chopping block outside, which according to Don (February 1, 1883:147), who spent some time in China as a missionary, is a positive indication of Chinese occupancy.

Despite these similarities, overall it is obvious that the Chinese dwellings on the goldfields of southern New Zealand were considerably different from those of Guangdong. While most of the changes appear to have been forced on the Chinese by circumstances rather than choice, reflecting the undeveloped frontier nature of the New Zealand goldfields, some other architectural aspects can be identified.

The first observation is that the architecture of Chinese structures (including huts, houses, stores, lodging houses, and other urban building) on the goldfields and associated service towns exhibited relatively few traditional Asian architectural features such as upturned eaves, decorative eave brackets, tile roofing, and fretwork patterns on fascia boards (see Kerr, 1979:10-11 for a detailed list and discussion of Chinese architecture features). In their basic form, Chinese buildings in Dunedin and on the goldfields of southern New Zealand did not differ significantly from contemporaneous timber and stone European structures. Architectural character was defined by function rather than style or strong vernacular influences. In design and layout, Chinese dwellings and business buildings on the southern New Zealand goldfields were adaptive rather than imbued with symbolic content. This was probably because the majority of the Chinese were from the peasant classes and had never had the resources to build in the high styles of Chinese architecture, and also because most came as sojourners, never intending to settle permanently. Similar conclusions were reached by Kerr and Bugslag (1978:8) who studied Chinese architecture in British Columbia, Canada. Even if the better-off Chinese merchants in New Zealand hoped to see the development of "grand" Chinese structures, their aspirations were probably thwarted by the lack of skilled craftsmen who were familiar with building in such styles. For the poorer Chinese miners and laborers, money spent on elaborate accommodations would have been counterproductive, merely prolonging their sojourn in New Zealand.

Generally the architecture of the majority of 19th century Chinese buildings and settlements in New Zealand was similar to established western models, although contemporary accounts indicate that their structures were often more densely grouped than those of Europeans. In locations ranging from the most ephemeral mining camps on the goldfields to the more established urban enclave in Dunedin, European buildings were adopted for Chinese use. Chinese ownership and role was signified by bold but superficial ornamentation such as painted signs and inscriptions employing Chinese characters. Probably because the majority of the

Chinese in New Zealand returned to China, and subsequent Chinese immigrants have tended not to settle in enclaves, a distinctive Chinese architectural expression has never developed in New Zealand. To Europeans, the most overtly "Chinese buildings" on the goldfields were the so-called "joss houses" (combination temples and public halls) at Lawrence and Round Hill. Only the elongated inscription panels attached to the veranda posts and front walls, large Chinese characters painted or carved into the doors, and other minor external ornamentation (see *Otago Witness*, April 6, 1904:38; Butler, 1977:74) mark these buildings as being distinctively different from contemporary European halls of similar size.

To conclude, although few Chinese commercial buildings have survived in New Zealand, they are, almost without exception, of European-style construction and merely adapted for Chinese usage. Physical remains and documentary evidence of the humble but vastly more numerous stone and adobe Chinese miners' dwellings abound on the Central Otago goldfield. From these, it is possible to define differences and similarities as well as European and Chinese influences. However, it must be remembered that for every Chinese structure that survives, dozens have disappeared or are evidenced now by only the scantiest archaeological remains. Because the Chinese tended to use the materials at hand, there is a very marked pattern of differential survival, in no small part influenced by regional microclimates. Where they built of stone, such as around Cromwell, there is still substantial highly visible ground evidence. In contrast, in wet areas such as Round Hill and the West Coast, where timber, shingles, and *punga* logs were used extensively, the sites are much more elusive. The European-style weatherboard dwellings of the Chinese miners in Lawrence, Waikaia, and other established towns are undoubtedly the most devastated category; the majority of these buildings have been demolished, modified beyond recognition, or replaced by European buildings.

REFERENCES CITED

ANGUS, JANET C.
  1977   *Maniototo Milestones: A Centennial History of the Maniototo County Council*, Maniototo County Council, Ranfurly, New Zealand.
ANGUS, JOHN H.
  1983   Goldmining Towns, in *Historic Buildings of New Zealand: South Island*, New Zealand Historic Places Trust, Wellington, pp. 222-229.
ARROW OBSERVER
  1873   Arrowtown, New Zealand.
ARROWTOWN BOROUGH
  1870s- Arrowtown Borough rate books, Arrowtown, New Zealand.
  1900
BURTON, DAVID
  1982   *Two Hundred Years of New Zealand Food and Cookery*, A. H. and A. W. Reed, Wellington, New Zealand.

BUTLER, PETER
1977   *Opium and Gold: A History of the Chinese Miners in New Zealand*, Alister Taylor, Martinborough, New Zealand.

CLARK, W. A. V.
1961   The Slums of Dunedin 1900-1910, *New Zealand Geographical Society, Proceedings of the Third Geography Conference*, Palmerston North, New Zealand.

CROMWELL ARGUS
1889   Cromwell, New Zealand.

DON, REV. ALEXANDER
1891-   *Annual Inland Tour* [Quotations from these reports are cited thus (Don,
1911   1896:13)], Hocken Library, Dunedin, New Zealand.
1882-   Our Chinese Mission, *New Zealand Presbyterian* [Quotations from this
1889   source are cited thus (Don, December 1, 1884:145)], Hocken Library, Dunedin, New Zealand.
1883-   Roll of Chinese in New Zealand, 1883-1913, unpublished record of the
1913   movements of 1080 Chinese miners with whom Don had contact between 1883-1913 [Data from this source are cited thus (Don, 1883-1913)], Ng collection, Alexander Turnbull Library, Wellington, New Zealand.

DUDLEY, AUSTIN
1983   Personal observations on the Arrowtown Chinese, ca. 1915-25, Arrowtown, New Zealand.

FORREST, JAMES
1961   Population and Settlement on the Otago Goldfields, 1861-1870, *New Zealand Geographer*, 17:1, pp. 64-78.

GRIMWADE, GORDON P. N. and BARRIE REYNOLDS
1986   *Report on Atherton Chinatown, North Queensland I: Site Survey,* Material Culture Unit, James Cook University of North Queensland, Townsville, Australia.

HANGAR, MARK
1984   Personal communication re tenancy (title-holders) of Ah Lum's store, Arrowtown, New Zealand.

HARDESTY, DONALD L.
1988   The Archaeology of Mining and Miners: A View from the Silver State, Society for Historical Archaeology, *Special Publication Series*, No. 6, Society for Historical Archaeology, Ann Arbor, Michigan.

HARRISON, ANN P.
1982   *Lake Roxburgh Archaeological Survey*, New Zealand Historic Places Trust, Cromwell, New Zealand.

KERR, ALISTAIR W.
1979   The Architecture of Victoria's Chinatown, *Datum*, 4:1, pp. 8-11.

KERR, A[LISTAIR W.] and J. BUGSLAG
1978   Some Basic Observations Concerning the Architecture of the Chinese in B. C., [Canada], *Datum*, 3:2, pp. 8-11.

KNAPP, RONALD C.
1986   *China's Traditional Rural Architecture: A Cultural Geography of the Common House*, University of Hawaii, Honolulu.

MAWSON, THE REV. WILLIAM

1926   *The Story of the Canton Villages Mission of the Presbyterian Church of New Zealand*, Dunedin, New Zealand.

MAYHEW, W. R.

1949   *Tuapeka, The Land and the People: A Social History of Lawrence and Surrounding Districts*, Otago Centennial Historical Publications, New Zealand.

McARTHUR, JOHN

1945   The Narrative of John McArthur, written by McArthur in March, 1945 (recalling the 1870s-1880s), copy in possession of P. Chandler, Ettrick, New Zealand.

McGILL, DAVID

1980   *Ghost Towns of New Zealand*, A. H. & A. W. Reed, Wellington, New Zealand.

NEW ZEALAND CENSUS

1874   Department of Statistics, Christchurch, New Zealand.

1878   Department of Statistics, Christchurch, New Zealand.

OTAGO DAILY TIMES

1869   Dunedin, New Zealand.

OTAGO WITNESS

1875   Dunedin, New Zealand.

1904   Dunedin, New Zealand.

POTTER, H. W.

1890   *Westward Ho!: A Trip through The Western District of Southland, its Goldfields, Coal Measures and Agricultural Resources*, Phoenix Printing Co., Invercargill, New Zealand.

RITCHIE, NEVILLE A.

1986   Archaeology and History of the Chinese in Southern New Zealand during the Nineteenth Century: A Study of Acculturation, Adaptation, and Change, Ph.D. dissertation, University of Otago, Dunedin, New Zealand.

ROEBUCK, LOU

1981-   Former resident of Clyde who lived with some of the Chinese in
1983-   Dunedin
        ca. 1920, tape recorded discussions about the Chinese.

ROSSBACH, SARAH

1985   *Feng Shui: Ancient Wisdom for the Most Beneficial Way to Place Furniture, Rooms, and Buildings*, Rider imprint of the Hutchison Publishing Group, London, (first published by Dutton, New York, 1983).

SACHS, MARK

1982   Aspects of Chinese Living and Working Spaces in Historical Barkerville, unpublished report submitted to Barkerville Historic Park, Barkerville, British Columbia, Canada.

SISSON, DAVID

1983   *Lower Salmon River Cultural Resource Management Plan*, U.S. Department of the Interior, Bureau of Land Management, Coeur d'Alene District, Cottonwood Resource Area, Cottonwood, Idaho.

SMITH, ARTHUR H.
  1899   *Village Life in China: A Study of Sociology*, Fleming H. Revell Co., New York.
THORNTON, GEOFFREY
  1983   Earth and Stone Buildings of Central Otago, in *Historic Buildings of the New Zealand: South Island*, New Zealand Historic Places Trust, Wellington, New Zealand, pp. 204-213.
YEE, RHODA
  1975   *Chinese Village Cookbook: A Practical Guide to Cantonese Country Cooking*, Yerba Buena Press, San Francisco.

CHAPTER 14

Old Approaches and New Directions: Implications for Future Research

Roberta S. Greenwood

It has been a decade since a volume with the theme of archaeological perspectives on ethnicity (Schuyler, 1980) devoted roughly one-third of its pages to the Asian American (read:Chinese) cultural experience. Since then, many sites have been investigated and many pages of documents have been turned, the body of literature has expanded greatly, and it is appropriate to pause, reflect, evaluate, and either ratify or reorient the research directions which have evolved. There is an urgency in focusing research designs, improving field and laboratory methods, and defining curatorial and reporting standards since the remaining sites—in both urban and rural contexts—are dwindling in numbers and integrity.

As illustration of the expansion of studies in the archaeology of Chinese sites, the bibliography published in 1980 cited only a small number of systematic excavation reports. The major studies included, but were not limited to, investigations at Ventura (Greenwood, 1976a) and the Harmony Borax Works in California (Teague and Shenk, 1977); Lovelock, Nevada (Hattori, Rusco, and Tuohy, 1979); Idaho City (Jones, Davis, and Ling, 1979) and Boise, in Idaho (Jones, 1980a, 1980b); and Olsen's thesis on the ceramics from Tucson, Arizona (1978). Non-archaeological data were contained in such articles as Spier's on the Chinese diet (1958a) and Chinese tool use (1958b). Few authors were drawing upon comparative material about China itself, such as Chang's volume on the homeland diet and role of food within the traditional culture (1977), or Hommel's study of the peasant industries (1937), and the body of literature already compiled in other disciplines such as sociology, history, geography, or even early childhood education.

Within the decade, encouraged by both research interests and environmental regulations, the number of excavations proliferated. The following is not intended as a comprehensive list of all the investigations, merely a suggestion of their number and geographic dispersion. The collections reported include those from El Paso, Texas (Staski, 1985); Woodland (Felton, Lortie, and Schulz, 1984), Sacramento (Praetzellis and Praetzellis, 1982, 1990), San Francisco (Pastron, Gross, and Garaventa, 1981), and Weaverville, in California (Brott, 1982); mining camps of California's Sonoran Mother Lode (Greenwood and Shoup, 1983); Igo in northern California (Ritter, 1986); Riverside, California (Great Basin Foundation, 1987); and Tucson, Arizona (Lister and Lister, 1989). Field methods, level of analysis, and integration of historical data vary greatly; some are the results of two-day, *ad hoc* monitoring (Brock, Sawyer, and Wormser, 1988), and other excavations have never been reported at all. Academic contributions include LaLande's thesis (1981) and Ritchie's dissertation (1986). There are contributions which have never been formalized beyond oral presentations at meetings (e.g., Schulz and Lortie, 1981; Mui and Mui, 1981), and unstudied collections in both private and institutional hands. There are unpublished manuscripts in public agency files. Materials from some excavations have not been reported, e.g., San Jose (Roop, 1988), San Luis Obispo, El Pueblo de Los Angeles (Norman Wilson, 1989:personal communication), and Santa Barbara (David Stone, 1991:personal communication).

It is fair to observe that most of these studies have arisen from the requirements of the environmental or planning processes. While the excavations may have been followed by partial or total site destruction, most have at least culminated in an analysis and report of findings. Prior to such enactments as the National Environmental Policy Act, 36 CFR 60.4 (criteria for eligibility to the National Register of Historic Places) and the National Historic Preservation Act, or California's Environmental Quality Act, many Chinese sites were simply destroyed without so much as recordation, as in Los Angeles, Sonora, other Mother Lode towns, and a long list of western cities where urban property values were changing rapidly.

The growth of environmental concern is well illustrated in Los Angeles. The earliest Chinese deposits and structures in and around El Pueblo were lost during State Park acquisition and improvements dating back to the 1950s (Norman Wilson 1989:personal communication), and subsequently during municipal administration and highway construction. Chinese tunnels under the Plaza were simply cleaned out in years past without regard for the historicity and associations of the artifacts, and some excavations in the area have not culminated in written reports. In contrast, the current construction of Metro Rail is proceeding under a Memorandum of Agreement, and scientific excavation is taking place. Some agencies, unfortunately, fulfill the letter of the law by funding field work, but fail to support collections analysis and publication. A notable example was the excavation of deposits in San Jose, California; a summary narrative listed the physical attributes of twenty-five features, but the 17,986 catalogued artifacts including ceramics "that have not been previously reported in California or, in some cases, in North America" have not been reported (Roop, 1988:45, 50). No provisions were made for the analysis and reporting of Chinese assemblages in Phoenix or Santa Barbara.

EARLY APPROACHES

From the inception of Chinese sites archaeology, certain truisms had been accepted: that the national origin of things Chinese could be readily recognized even when the function of an item was not identified; that settlement patterns were most often spatially limited and populations unmixed; that the quantity of cultural materials was often very high; that dating of artifacts which were conservative in form, pattern, and technology was difficult; that women were very few or absent. Theoretical constructs were rare, as the early efforts were focused on recognition, identification, and description. The primary assumption was that Chinese sojourners maintained the traditional way of life, manifest most obviously in the remains associated with the preparation and consumption of food, various forms of recreation, and the healing arts. For the early sites, this was interpreted partly as a matter of choice, since the Argonauts did not expect or wish to remain permanently and thus lacked incentives to acculturate, and partly as an adaptive response to the prejudice and persecution amply documented in historical sources. When even the Indians were able to impose taxes on the Chinese miners (Greenwood and Shoup, 1983:284), their status within California society was very evident.

In later, industrial sites, such as the Harmony Borax Works which began operations in 1883 or 1884, Teague and Shenk demonstrated that instead of living in rural isolation, the Chinese employees were supplied with goods from San Francisco by an extremely reliable and efficient commercial network. While they concluded that acculturation had progressed because of the use of American tools and clothing, no doubt incident to the necessities of the employment, the fact remained that more than 99 percent of the ceramics were Chinese (1977:213-217). In the urban context of Ventura's Chinatown at the turn of the century, trait lists of Chinese features were compared to Euroamerican features, and patterns for typical Chinese and non-Chinese ceramic assemblages were suggested. In this context, the low level of acculturation was attributed to both aggregative forces from within the compact and socially isolated settlement and external sociocultural barriers to expansion on the part of the host community (Greenwood, 1980:119).

THE DECADE OF THE EIGHTIES

In California, particularly, the number of Chinese sites studied in the 1980s reflected the newly enacted environmental regulations; rapid development of cities, highways, and water projects; and the increased militancy on the part of

Native Americans toward the excavation of prehistoric sites which prompted a new interest in historical sites. As a result, not all of those who approached Chinese sites were necessarily qualified in historical archaeology, versed in Chinese cultural traditions, or dedicated to the kind of research needed to identify artifacts or behaviors outside of the Euroamerican experience.

Such ethnocentrism has occasionally affected efforts to explain the proportions of artifacts within a deposit. For example, Blanford compared the glass container assemblages from a number of sites to discriminate a "Chinese ethnic bottle pattern" and interpreted the apparent clustering to geographical location or relative acculturation as a function of chronology (1986). Unless the deposits used as a data base can be confidently dated and assessed as unmixed, inferences about acculturation and change may reflect a Euroamerican perspective and not the Chinese way of life. Another possible consequence of ethnocentrism is that some of the artifact identifications which tend to get perpetuated in the literature were erroneous. A carved toothbrush handle has been illustrated as a hairpin (Noah, 1987:408), and the hasp of a box lock as jewelry although the key to the lock was recognized (Hattori, Rusco, and Tuohy, 1979:297a, 261d). The small perforated objects of bone or ivory which were, and still are, used to fasten boxes or documents have been called bookmarks.

The selection of illustrations was not always the most judicious; for example, while soy sauce jars and liquor bottles were photographed or drawn ad nauseam, the carved toothbrushes and double-sided combs, for which illustrations might have helped subsequent investigators, were only mentioned in such reports as Felton, Lortie, and Schulz, 1984. Reporting tended to be selective, emphasizing the whole, glamorous, or recognized artifacts. The sites tended to be those facing imminent destruction, and the field work might thus be both hasty and limited to an area of immediate impact. Laboratory methods were not routinely described, e.g., whether all ceramic fragments were washed and examined, and it was not always clear how the quantification of artifact types was computed— whether from whole items or minimum numbers figured from bases, necks, weights, or other measures. Artifacts from discrete features or deposits were sometimes lumped and described as a single assemblage, obscuring any functional or chronological distinctions, or separate inventories were presented for each feature without relating the separate deposits to each other or to the site as a whole.

Function of the features and dating of the artifacts continued to pose problems. The persistence of traditional forms, technology, and decorative motifs (Figure 80) made dating difficult without a secure context, although the place of origin was readily recognized. This presents a contrast to historical Euroamerican ceramics where forms, technology, and methods of decoration evolved fairly rapidly; unless there were base marks, the analyst who could estimate the date could not safely distinguish between European and American products. Progress was made during the decade in standardizing nomenclature of forms and patterns.

Figure 80. Persistence of Double Happiness design. a) rice bowl from mining site, Shasta County, California, ca. 1860; b) small jar, ca. 1820, diameter 7.8 cm, China; c) brand name on cigarettes, matches, hard candy, China, 1983.

Ceramic typologies multiplied, perhaps because investigators did not have access to perfectly adequate schemata already developed by others.

The same explanation may account for the various claims of "first," "biggest," or "only," and so on, which embellished some of the reports. There was very little which was actually "new" in identification or innovative in approach. While most of the reports included separate, and sometimes very comprehensive, sections on local Chinese history, such chapters usually stood alone and unrelated to the archaeological assemblage. The documentary sources cited might not coincide with the period of deposition being described. Synthesis and context were often not developed.

NEW DIRECTIONS

The present chapters reflect the current status of studies of the overseas Chinese—some purely historical, some purely archaeological or technical, and a few which attempt to synthesize the physical remains of a culture with the written history, within the framework of prevailing anthropological theory. The inconsistencies between some of these chapters suggest the measure of the gap between objectives and performance. It is a recurring theme in published reports and in attempts to justify further excavation that there is no history relevant to the American experience of the overseas Chinese. Yet, the kinds of documentation provided by Fagan (Chapter 9 herein), Sando and Felton (Chapter 6 herein), and Stapp (Chapter 1 herein) suggest the wealth and variety of information which is available and its relevance to the understanding of physical remains.

It is often written that women were few in number, either absolutely or as a proportion of the total Chinese population. The statement is valid, but is an outstanding example of the need to put such truisms into context. There is no question that early immigration was predominantly male and that the labor force in the mines, railroad camps, or agricultural fields would be male, no matter what the national origin of the workers. There are discrepancies in various accounts; one writer reports 1769 Chinese women over the age of fifteen in San Francisco in 1870 (Wegars, Chapter 9 herein), while another listed only 627 females in the same year (Stephens, 1976:73). Even by the latter, smaller figure, 22 percent of the Chinese population in San Francisco in 1870 was female. For the country as a whole in the same year, 8.5 percent of the Chinese population was female (Novotny, 1985:10), emphasizing the difference between settlement in a city which was one of the major ports of entry and the demography of more remote or undeveloped areas.

However disproportionate the sex ratio certainly was, this must be considered against the state and national averages for all nationalities and races. In 1850, prior to the greatest influx of Chinese, there were twelve men to every woman in California, with a greater disparity in the remote mining areas. The scarcity of Euroamerican female labor in San Francisco was, in fact, one of the reasons why

Chinese men were at first welcomed so heartily to work in laundries, restaurants, and domestic service. In 1870, the sex ratio was 165.8 (males per 100 females) for the state as a whole, but reached 235.9 in nonmetropolitan areas. In the same year, the national male/female ratio for Chinese was 13 to 1, but it was consistently more equitable on the West Coast, signifying greater family formation nearer the ports of entry. At the turn of the century, there was still a disproportionate number of both Chinese and white males in California, reflecting the immigration of both native- and foreign-born at a time when newcomers accounted for 87 percent of the state's population increase (Thompson, 1955:47-49).

Repercussions of the imbalance were more pronounced in the smaller cites, such as San Diego, where the population was not large enough to sustain losses from the aging of the early immigrants or their return to China; in San Francisco and Los Angeles, the community was large enough to perpetuate itself until augmented by later immigrations (Liu, 1987:11). Historical accounts do document Chinese family formation in the urban areas (Wong, 1954:11). Church mission schools were established by the 1880s in San Francisco, Ventura, and Los Angeles, and probably elsewhere. As part of the 19th century enthusiasm for early childhood education, kindergartens for Chinese children were established in Los Angeles and San Francisco by women's service clubs (Lothrop, 1986). Archaeologically, the presence of children is demonstrated by the marbles, dolls, and other toys regularly found in excavations; the adult female member of the household is represented by jewelry, cosmetic containers, clothing parts, and perhaps the more elaborate types of ceramic and glass tableware. The greater exposure of the children to the outside world is demonstrated by the occidental nature of their toys and recreation, whereas the women's jewelry and cosmetics were typically Chinese imports.

While some of the earlier studies approached the overseas Chinese culture as rigid, unchanging, and monolithic, Stapp (Chapter 1 herein) points out that the society was complex. There were distinctions between the more and less prosperous, the rural and urban areas, large and small communities, and most particularly, through time. Census data reveal the different waves of immigration (Figure 81) prompted by events in both the United States and China, the aging of the Argonaut population, and their replacement around the turn of the century by a differently motivated group of immigrants who intended to remain, and thus had greater incentives to adapt American ways. After the Exclusion Act of 1882, professionals and others of higher rank than the early immigrants were still permitted to enter. In Los Angeles, as elsewhere, while the Chinese population grew, the number of those born in China gradually decreased. In 1890, of the 1871 Chinese in Los Angeles, only 2 percent, mostly children, were natives of the United States. In 1900, approximately half of the Chinese mothers in Los Angeles were born in the United States (CHSSC, 1984:34). In the same year, 10 percent of the 2111 Chinese in the city were native-born, and in 1910, 24 percent (Mason, 1967:16).

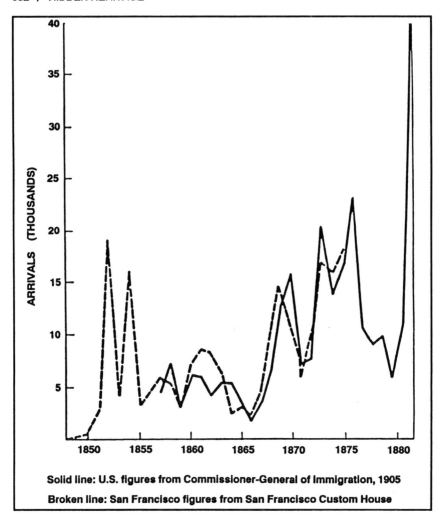

Figure 81. Chinese immigration to the United States,
1848-1882 (Mei, 1984:225).

The nature of urban occupations also changed; for example, as the vegetable peddlers who grew and vended most of the fresh produce consumed in 19th century Los Angeles were replaced by large scale corporate agriculture in the San Joaquin Valley, many of the Chinese growers turned to wholesale brokering and prospered (Mason, 1967). The Chinese in San Diego similarly monopolized truck gardening in the 1890s, raising crops outside of the population center and delivering them door to door. As sojourners, the San Diego Chinese were economically motivated and dependent upon filling economic niches. Beginning as fishermen, they were displaced, in turn, into heavy construction, market gardening, and service occupations, but when the city's economy as a whole stagnated after 1890, the Chinese lost their employment and left the area (Liu, 1987:11-12).

The Chinese population that arrived in the 20th century brought a different kind of immigrant, both in economic status and place of origin. During the first quarter of the century, capitalist enterprises were developing in China, and a capitalist middle class grew in wealth, influence, and awareness of western opportunities for trade and education. Many came from Shanghai, the most cosmopolitan of China's new cities, or the industrial and commercial districts of Tianjin. Many were speakers of Mandarin, rather than Cantonese, and together with the second- or third-generation residents who had achieved some measure of advancement, they formed a new elite and added to the stratification of Chinese Americans (Chen, 1980:202-227).

Sites of this later period might be expected to evince greater, rather than less, assimilation because of the differing expectations, greater anticipation of permanence, participation in commercial and educational networks, and the higher social and economic status of the new arrivals. The extent to which the more prosperous families moved away from Chinatown and the speed of their dispersion into the greater community is one variable often not factored into the acculturation equations. Archaeological sites and deposits cannot be treated or compared as representative of homogeneous occupations, and explanations must be sought when a late assemblage seems to demonstrate less, rather than greater, use of American market commodities. Such interpretations might relate to the size and survivability of the local Chinese community, the status of the unit which deposited the discards, the degree of mixing within the deposit, or the replacement of the more successful families by newly arrived immigrants.

The data provided by Sando and Felton contribute to studies of the availability and values of goods, and implicitly demonstrate the social and economic diversity of the immigrants. Merchants were among the first to arrive in California and were engaged in trade in San Francisco at least by 1849. They brought capital with them, and had previously established trade networks in China and Hong Kong. The more prosperous had affiliates in Canada and Yokohama, and expanded to offer luxury goods such as silks and lacquerwares to Chinese and whites alike. They constituted approximately 2 percent of the Chinese population in 1877 (Mei, 1984:232-233). Their prominence within the communities is illustrated by the centripetal force exerted by the Chinese Chamber of Commerce in Los Angeles (McDannold, 1973:47) and the Merchants' Exchange in San Francisco (Sandmeyer, 1939:22). Within Los Angeles Chinatown, non-Chinese businessmen were never able to penetrate the concentration of 184 stores and shops (McDannold, 1973:45).

City and county directories in Los Angeles document that Chinese merchants offered both Chinese and Japanese goods. Such information helps to resolve questions about the Japanese ceramics which are recovered in Chinese sites.

Clearly, they were available by 1877 (Sando and Felton, Chapter 6 herein) and in places where there was little, if any, Japanese population. They were sold not only by Chinese merchants, presumably to Chinese, but in gift or "curio" shops and by national catalogues at least by 1895 (e.g., Montgomery Ward, 1895:533). One of the patterns of Japanese bowls which has been recovered at San Jose (Hampson, n.d.), Napa (Hampson and Greenwood, 1989:74), Los Angeles, Santa Barbara, and other sites (Costello and Maniery, 1988:52-57) was offered in the Butler Brothers catalogue of 1907 (Butler Brothers, 1907:180e, f). Thus, the presence of Japanese ceramics no more confirms the presence of Japanese on a site than the recovery of Chinese export porcelain on an early mission or shipwreck site testifies to the presence of Chinese. Again, it is essential to establish the chronology of a specific deposit or differentiate between successive settlements on the same property. At Redlands, where historical maps confirm a Chinese occupation in 1888, the Japanese ceramics can be dated and associated confidently to Japanese residents on the same block by and after 1919 (Brock, Sawyer, and Wormser, 1988). The presence of porcelain on historical sites, in the past sometimes interpreted as evidence of high status, needs evidence of economic scaling—as reflected in store inventories, shipping records, and merchandise catalogues, national origin, and availability. The Japanese were exporting substantial quantities of ceramics to the United States by 1876, had equalled the British as the leading shippers of ceramics to the United States by 1917, and became the major supplier by 1920, surpassing all other exporters (Greenwood et al., 1980:207-209, Tables 7-8). The lessons are that their wares were available very early, from Chinese merchants for Chinese use, and in the later years at least, were among the less costly table and decorative wares available to all customers.

The search for regularities in architecture reaches antic proportions when rectangular structures are considered as evidence of good *feng shui*. Ritchie (Chapter 13 herein) found no convincing considerations of *feng shui* in his study, and points out that then, as today, there are practitioners who offer talismans or rituals to overcome fears among the believers. Sisson summarizes (Chapter 2 herein) some of the conditions for ideal *feng shui*: The structure should face south, calm water in front is good, the confluence of streams is desirable (but a location at "branching streams" is bad), town plans and dwellings are square, towns are aligned on a north-south axis when possible. He, too, found great variability in the exposure and construction of buildings, or the location of chimneys and entrances within buildings. Both authors emphasize the resourcefulness of the Chinese in using whatever materials were locally common, and their practicality in reusing existing habitations. Both traits would tend to obscure the measure of *feng shui* influence.

Context and chronology are equally essential to discussions of Chinese architecture and the influence of *feng shui*. Lack of historical context has led to overlooking some of the obvious variables in the location of either individual structures or entire Chinese communities. The Chinese, as a factor of their own economic and social condition, often reoccupied existing structures as land values and social patterns within California's towns and cities changed. In Ventura, they simply moved into the adobes along the east-west Main Street abandoned by the pioneer Hispanic settlers; earlier structures built either by or for the Chinese were aligned along both sides of the existing north-south Figueroa Street and faced either east or west. In Los Angeles as well, the first settlement was a reoccupation of the adobes, streets, and alleys adjacent to the Plaza (McDannold, 1973), while the structures built in the 1880s were aligned east-west on previously vacant property where any other orientation would have been possible. In the Mother Lode mining districts, reoccupation has been demonstrated by archaeological stratigraphy, and the siting of the structures was originally conditioned by topography, access to the ore bodies, and the nature of the mining technology being utilized (Greenwood and Shoup, 1983). In Santa Barbara, the second generation of Chinese shops and dwellings which replaced those damaged by the earthquake of 1925 was built by a non-Chinese (Quon, 1982:1-2).

It is difficult to search for regularities which can be attributed to national background or *feng shui*, when the attributes of low-cost vernacular architecture are so greatly conditioned by expediency, rather than by symbolic content which reflects social differentiation, anticipation of permanence, and higher investment. There are, of course, regularities in the location of Chinatowns within the cities. They typically developed in proximity to the ports and docks, as in San Diego or San Francisco; near the railroad station (Boston, Pittsburgh, or St. Louis); or on lands subject to flooding or of low value (Ventura and Los Angeles)—all on properties considered undesirable by others. The Los Angeles Chinatown was near the smoky, odoriferous gas plant, adjacent to the noisy and sooty railroad yards, with only two of the thirteen existing streets and twenty-two passage ways paved as late as 1922 (Sterry, 1922:70-71). In Ventura, municipal utilities and sewer hook-ups were not extended into Chinatown until 1925, although service was provided to the adjacent blocks on Main Street in 1903 (Greenwood, 1976a:453). Factors which influenced settlement in both cities persisted until the enclaves were eventually driven out by pressures for urban growth or redevelopment.

As for regularities, there appear to be some differences between New Zealand and America. Ritchie observed that the Chinese huts he studied were characterized by a lower ridge height and lesser roof angle than others, while historical photographs of wood frame Chinese houses in California almost invariably show steeply pitched roofs. Ritchie's huts at Cromwell which averaged 8.3 square meters of living space (89.3 square feet) were said to be smaller than those of the Europeans. However, in California's Mother Lode, the measurements of Euroamerican tents and cabins recorded in diaries which also give the number of miners who occupied the shelters, suggest a range from 2.03 square meters of space per miner in a tent to 5.75 square meters per person in a cabin (Greenwood and Shoup, 1983:210-212). Comparisons are difficult unless it is known how many individuals occupied the space, or who built the structure.

In the cities where historical maps and photographs are available, it is easier to adduce Chinese traits. Contrary to the principles of *feng shui*, Sanborn maps in city after city show that Chinese buildings were in fact contiguous, arranged in straight lines, were not square, were frequently in low-lying areas subject to floods (Napa, Ventura), and opened in other directions as often as south. The "joss house" (Chinese temple) at Riverside was at the north end of Mongol Street, where it was "supposed" to be, but the one in San Bernardino was at the east end of Chinatown (Mueller, 1987:12, 15) and the one in Ventura (Figure 82) was actually at the extreme south of the community, facing east. In Los Angeles, the first joss house was south of the Plaza occupation area facing the east, while by 1889, another was at the northeast corner of Chinatown, opening to the west. We cannot know whether mirrors, trees, or other talismans were employed to offset the adverse effects of untraditional location and orientation, or whether the principles were not being observed.

The regularities which are apparent from the historical sources include high-pitched gable roofs and the maximum utilization of space within the restricted environment through the creation of narrow alleys and passageways to subdivide the blocks. The balconies on the two-story dwellings were also a device to expand the living area, as historically and currently practiced in China. Dwellings tended to be long and narrow, of single wall construction. The longer dimension was perpendicular to the street to maximize exposure to the frontage, with the entrance under the gable. In Los Angeles, where lumber was scarce, brick buildings replaced the early adobes; elsewhere, wood frame construction was predominant, commonly with vertical board and batten siding and shingle roofs. Houses tended to be flush with the street and contiguous in the row with no apparent division between properties (Figures 82, 83). In the urban setting, the intermingling of dwellings and shops, and the presence of a joss house and theater were common.

Sterry's (1922:71-73) description of the Los Angeles Chinatown in 1922 offers the following details:

> There is no yard in front of any house. . . . A few houses have a bit of unoccupied land in the rear . . . but these spaces are invariably used for chicken coops or rubbish dumps . . . almost every house possesses certain inside rooms for sleeping quarters, rooms which have no other light nor ventilation than that afforded through the narrow entrance from the unlighted hall. In a survey made by the State Commission of Immigration in 1916, of 1572 rooms visited 878 were found totally dark and windowless.
>
> The ground plan . . . consists ordinarily of several rather narrow rooms in a straight line, connected by a narrow dark hall. There are windows in the front and the rear rooms only. . . . There is no provision for heating these houses and only a few of them have either gas or electricity . . . none of the property is owned by the Chinese.

Figure 82. Chinatown on Figueroa Street, Ventura, ca. 1890. ("Joss house" at far left (south) of view, with false front) (courtesy of Ventura County Museum of History and Art).

Figure 83. Apablaza Street, Los Angeles Chinatown, ca. 1890.
(Courtesy of Seaver Center for Western History Research,
Natural History Museum of Los Angeles County.)

The writer quoted is describing structures built in the 1880s and 1890s (Figure 83), but the conditions regarding utilities and sanitation were those still prevailing in 1922. The population density and living conditions in San Francisco's Chinatown right up to World War II is suggested by the fact that an average of 20.4 persons shared each bathroom and 12.3 persons each kitchen (Palmer and Walls, 1960:20). Sterry reported that one typical lodging house had thirty-two rooms on one side and thirty-four on the other; the first floor alternated between store and sleeping rooms, while all the rooms on the second floor were rented to lodgers. One community kitchen would be shared by tenants in several buildings. Most of the 184 shops in Los Angeles Chinatown had living quarters in the rear. The same State Commission report of 1916 found seven privy vaults in the corrals at the east end of the buildings, five of them nothing more than a hole in the ground with a board frame. "Hundreds of men" slept in the corrals at night, sharing the space with the horses and the produce to be peddled the next day (Sterry, 1922:73-74).

The abundance of trash pits at Chinese sites is partly a result of the disposal practices described by Sterry as late as 1922, and these may in turn be derived from the absence of municipal services provided to other neighborhoods. The presence of eggshells in many such deposits cannot be interpreted as consumption of commercially marketed foods, since almost every historical or ethnohistoric account includes the mention of raising chickens, as well as pigs and vegetables wherever space permitted. Studies of foodways relying on bone alone understate the role of vegetables in the Chinese diet, both in the homeland and in their access to produce. Prior to the growth of heavily capitalized and industrialized agribusiness, Chinese practically monopolized truck gardening in California from the days when they supplied the Gold Rush miners. In addition to backyard and suburban plots, possible terraced gardens have been recorded in California's gold mining context in Tuolumne (Greenwood, 1976b) and Shasta Counties (Johnson and Theodoratus, 1984:70-71), and probably many other locations in reports not widely accessible. In 1880, Chinese comprised 48 percent of California's gardeners and 14.2 percent of the (wage) laborers in agriculture (Chiu, 1967:65). To their own plots, they brought traditional homeland methods such as the foot pump, channeled irrigation, draining of wetlands, and terracing.

In the cities, they raised produce for sale on vacant lands outside of Chinatown. In Los Angeles, fifty of the sixty vegetable peddlers were Chinese in 1880, and by 1894, there were 103 registered Chinese wagons. The congestion of wagons, horses, and stables around Chinatown ultimately led to the formation of a more remote wholesale produce market, where the Chinese continued to dominate both the production and distribution of market crops (Yee and Yee, 1986:5-7).

Some faunal studies have suffered from sampling and lack of clear cultural or chronological associations. One must consider whether the market cuts such as steaks, chops, and roasts found at Woodland, Tucson, or Sacramento represented consumption by populations other than Chinese. Documentation that commercial butchers in Hong Kong, a mixed and polyglot population by the period cited, were knowledgeable of western butchering is not evidence that residents of American Chinatowns knew, preferred, or purchased such cuts. In view of the abundant historical evidence that overseas Chinese raised and killed their own chickens, even in twentieth century Los Angeles (Chung, 1979), for example, it would not be safe to date their remains in archaeological sites to the introduction of industrial incubators. The samples analyzed by faunal consultants were only samples, with not enough description of provenience or proportion within the total assemblage, or the field and laboratory methods which produced them. It is likely that fish remains are underrepresented; turtles were present at Ventura although not caught in Gust's sample. Chronological control is also essential; the samples from Sacramento ascribed to 1850-1860 and Lovelock for 1920-1930 are paired for contrast to deposits from Ventura and Tucson, both dated to 1890-1910. Distinctions between urban and rural networks and identification of those responsible for the deposits are needed before measures of self-sufficiency or acculturation can be addressed. Within the total subsistence pattern, non-bony animal consumables such as tendons, grains, and vegetables will not appear in the faunal studies, although reliance on imported foods can be evaluated to some degree by quantitative studies of their containers.

The chapters by Wylie and Fike (10), Steele (11), and Stenger (12) illustrate contemporary efforts to refine analytical approaches to the archaeological record. Statements based on either typology or advanced technology are no less in need of context. If the relevance of these procedures is to establish patterns that can be applied to sites or assemblages that lack other essential data, then the results must be securely based on dated, unmixed deposits and statistically valid samples. The latter criterion is particularly relevant in categorizing hand-made artifacts. It is fair to ask how closely the conclusions, from either typology or technical studies, conform to all other lines of evidence from the same sites. The effects of sample selection, subsampling, potentially mixed deposits, or data without provenience are variables to be evaluated.

The contributions by Stenger and Steele offer valuable technical approaches to the continuing problems of dating and determining the place of manufacture of the very conservative Asian porcelains. Given more samples from tightly dated contexts in China, Japan, and the overseas sites, the manganese/cobalt ratios and elemental analyses will replace the purely subjective identifications and supplement the growing body of historical data about imports and marketing. Together with closer observations, e.g, everted and wiped rims on the green-glazed wares, foot rings, white interiors, height-width ratios of bowls, and so on, such analytical studies will ultimately lead to more confident distinctions between Chinese and Japanese products and to datable topologies.

The chapters herein, as a group, are more concerned with method and description than theory. Staski (Chapter 5), particularly, has offered useful and testable definitions of assimilation and acculturation and has addressed the concept of self-sufficiency which seems to have increased in El Paso through time, rather than conforming to the conventional assumption that there would be greater interaction within the metropolitan setting as the frontier was developed. His evidence suggests that a disparity of power is not the critical factor in maintaining ethnic boundaries, but rather such boundaries are maintained by avoiding structural assimilation. Acculturation is defined as one of the processes which leads to assimilation.

A third concept may be useful: adaptation. As Lyman has written, the Chinese sojourners did not come to America to colonize or spread the culture of China; the limited objective of their immigration did, however, require them to adapt some of America's ways to their own purposes (1976:133). Examples might include the miner's use of appropriate tools and heavy boots, the laundryman's understanding of local currency, a few words of English for the peddler, and the substitution of local goods or commodities when preferred imports were not available. These were temporary accommodations, rather than cultural or behavioral transformations. Even for the isolated individual outside of Chinatown—the construction camp cook, domestic servant, solitary laundryman in a white neighborhood, or even the student—race contacts remained rigid and formal, and cultural distance was maintained (Lyman, 1976:134-135). As often as possible, the Chinese returned to join members of their own community in Chinatown for shopping, conversation, companionship, and recreation, often in the gambling halls (Minnick, 1988:225).

It has often been assumed that acculturation can be measured by the proportion of Chinese-associated ceramics or food remains within an archaeological assemblage, and that a gradual progression toward social integration will be reflected by fewer imported goods in more recent years. In El Paso, however, if the dating of discrete features is accurate and the deposits are unmixed, the pattern is reversed, and the earlier deposits actually contained fewer Chinese goods. Staski raised two questions: whether imported goods were available in the early years, and whether the population chose not to depend upon them, possibly as a result of assimilation. Availability might not be the only answer since merchants were present and the trend toward a higher proportion of Chinese to Euroamerican goods through time was not the experience in contemporary Ventura or Los Angeles, where both imported and American supplies were readily available. All of the El Paso features contributing to the analysis were deposited between 1890 and 1915, all but two of the seven after 1900. This population was not the original sojourner group. Although some of the residents may have been native-born and families may have formed, the ethnic boundaries were still apparently drawn more tightly. It may well be, as suggested in Staski's longer report, that El Paso's Chinatown was simply not large enough to be viable (1985:30), or even that the discards were those of a newly arrived population. Another alternative is that the greater cohesion in the 20th century represented the last attempt at survival by reinvigorating traditional behaviors as a response to external hostility, and reaction to at least partial internal assimilation.

As Stapp has pointed out (Chapter 1 herein), comparisons of assemblages which span decades or generations should be prefaced by sets of assumptions concerning population, household composition, and distribution of wealth, both within the Chinese occupation and the host community. Length of residence is another variable. Evolution and change must be considered diachronically against events occurring on the broader horizon. At Pierce City, the historical propositions, e.g., that membership in the local mining community overshadowed ethnic categorization during the 1870s and 1880s, can be tested archaeologically. Stapp is pessimistic that archaeology can contribute to questions of economic organization or change in the Chinese trade networks, but the problems he has defined may well be addressed successfully as knowledge expands and methods are refined to identify dates, places of manufacture, and the comparative values of the artifacts.

FUTURE DIRECTIONS

The questions which have been raised in this volume and the methods described for approaching some of them suggest certain avenues for future research in the field, the archives, and the laboratory. This is a closed loop (or Chinese endless knot?), as excavations result in new questions, historical data suggest new theories to test, and laboratory finesse provides greater security in the identification of cultural remains. While the advantage of this feedback and interaction is recognized, if not always observed, an even broader interaction is possible and fruitful. The literature of geography and sociology abounds with the kinds of documented studies which archaeologists rarely have the opportunity to pursue. University Departments of Asian Studies are also doing research and compiling oral histories which focus on many of the same questions from an eyewitness perspective within the culture. Chinese historical societies in many communities are eager to assist with translations, old photographs, documents, personal memorabilia, oral histories, or identifications of artifacts outside of the archaeologist's experience. Private collections, however obtained, can often be examined to augment the inventories of disturbed sites. It should not need to be said that there is a reciprocal obligation to share the results of archaeological investigations.

Census and other kinds of historical records can reveal far more than population numbers; for example, the transition to giving Chinese children Euroamerican first names may be one partial symbol of assimilation, if not a mere adaptation to pressures from the public schools. Alternative explanations must always be sought. Another application of historical information relates to settlement pattern and the replacement of one ethnic or national group by another, which can be traced in many cities. This, in turn, is a reflection of broader economic events. In Los Angeles, Santa Barbara, San Diego, and San Bernardino, the religious, cultural, and economic traditions which originally fostered unity among the Mexican rancheros were attenuated after secularization in 1834, and ultimately displaced by the values of Euroamerican settlers. The Chinese for a time filled the labor market needs of Euroamerican employers that the Indians could no longer supply, and in each of these California cities, Chinese occupied the vacated central historic districts. Ultimately, the restrictions on Chinese immigration after 1882 and the growing impoverishment of Chicano laborers made the latter group effective competitors in the low-end labor market in the 1880s and thereafter (Camarillo, 1979:passim).

Ironically, in Ventura the adobes of the old historic district near the mission, which had been reoccupied by the Chinese, were to become once again the homes of Mexicans, but this time as the barrio. The working class Chicanos around the turn of the century also inherited the hostilities and prejudice which had been expressed against the Chinese in the 1880s. Many useful comparisons can be drawn in the continuing use of native languages and the importance of traditional customs in the cohesiveness of each society, as well as the successive replacement of one group by another in the cities, the fields, the mines, and other locations of both work and residence. The Chinese experience needs this broader context.

The place of manufacture of the Chinese ceramics—as opposed to the shipping port—is another subject for study. How goods transshipped or smuggled through Mexico (Staski, 1985) were different from the ceramics distributed in the northwest by the Hudson's Bay Company or consigned to San Francisco, or those sold by the emerging enterprises in central and northern China, warrants investigation. Whether the place of origin of the immigrants themselves was expressed in a preference for one type of ware or pattern or another also needs correlation.

Better context is also needed for archaeological collections which have not been internally dated but only subjectively associated with a Sanborn map or flimsy background information. Despite the masses of sherds which have been recovered from the surface, behind the backhoes, or in mixed deposits, controlled excavation of intact or sealed, identifiable, datable features is still the exception. The emphasis in many reports upon whole vessels negates the data potential of laboriously washing, examining, and reconstructing sherds for marks or other attributes of form and technology.

During current studies at the Union Passenger Terminal site in Los Angeles, this kind of effort is yielding an unprecedented number and variety of painted, recuse, and embossed marks on Chinese stoneware and glass fragments, as well as on porcelain (Greenwood et al., 1992). Although the green-glazed, Celadon-type porcelain is usually associated mainly with cups and bowls, this project has recovered plates, spoons, and handles of this ware as well. Certain teapots and bowls recognized as Japanese, at a time when no Japanese were present in the community, have been associated with Chinese shops which advertised Japanese goods. Meticulous laboratory analysis also prevented the inadvertent discard of fragments which at first glance appeared to be clay sewer pipe, but which have been reconstructed as an old clay cooker with its grate (Figure 84). In connection with the lack of iron stove parts from the excavation and documentation about the absence of gas or electricity in the residences, this item is important and could have easily been overlooked. Once identified, others in several sizes were recognized. Other sherds have been reconstructed to reveal the presence of at least five large porcelain spittoons, a form elsewhere identified as a fine heirloom antique vase (Pastron, Gross, and Garaventa, 1981 [2]:Figure 9.01). From either historical photographs or a visit to modern China, this is an item which can be anticipated and may have been present at other sites. The point is that while many soy sauce or spirits containers have been measured and illustrated, controlled excavation and comprehensive study of sherds are still needed to inventory the full variability of Chinese cultural materials and faunal and floral remains, and to provide the context for their interpretation within the historical and cultural framework.

Comparative analysis of ceramics by X-ray fluorescence, neutron activation analysis, and other advanced techniques is a valuable adjunct to other approaches,

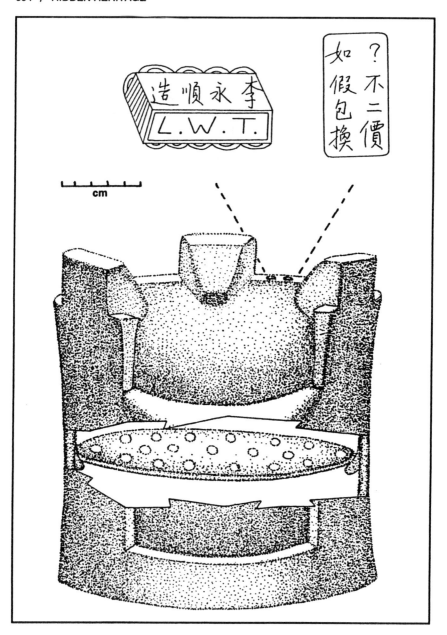

Figure 84. Clay stove from Los Angeles Chinatown. Translation:
vertical characters: If false (forgery), guarantee for exchange;
One price, no bargaining; horizontal characters: For export (made by)
Lee Wing Tsun (or Li Young Shun) (drawing by Helle Girey).

and its validity, too, depends upon dated contexts in both Asia and America. As the opportunity permits, studies in China will support descriptions of the technology of manufacture and decoration. Many of the publications which discuss Chinese and Japanese kilns (e.g., Rhodes, 1968) have focused on the manufacture of porcelain, but small enterprises turning out the stoneware containers by traditional hand methods still exist.

In 1983, one just outside the town of Shibao Block on the north bank of the Yangtze River in Szechuan Province occupied an area of about 2500 square yards, producing pottery for an outlet at the village and for transport down river. The inventory at the local outlet appeared to include several hundred vessels of eight to ten varieties. All operations beyond clay gathering took place on the spot. Four individuals in the main workshop area were making wide-mouthed jars about 2 feet high. The lower two-thirds of the height was formed in a mold attached to a diesel-driven wheel with the insertion of a cylindrical wood core attached to a long, heavy wooden bar which could be raised or lowered (Figure 85a). The bases seemed to be made of preformed hard clay. The bases were placed into wet cloth bags which were then inserted into the mold. After the lower portion of the vessel was shaped, it was taken out of the bag and the mold and placed on the floor, at first upside down, and then right side up, for partial drying. The tops and outer surfaces of the jar were finished by hand on a foot-propelled wheel, with the addition of water to the still pliable surface. The pottery was fired and glazed in a climbing kiln with seven chambers (Figure 85b). Other than the diesel wheel, the same sequence and methods are relevant to the archaeological specimens joined at the midpoint or shoulder. Another example of direct research is Sprague's description of glass beadmaking in China (1986).

Considerations of architecture have not often been integrated into cultural resource reports. Many of the regularities which can be identified appear related to factors other than *feng shui*. It is suggested that they were largely responses to high density within the constraints of low cost, vernacular western building practices rather than any attempt to create or recreate a Chinese architectural style. Overly facile conclusions must take into account who originally built the structures, whether existing streets or streams were preconditions of placement and orientation, density of the population, communal or family unit occupation, presence of business enterprises in the same structure, and—not least—the age of the buildings. Other variables must be considered before citing *feng shui* as the explanation for settlement pattern or structural orientation. In China, although geomancy has enjoyed an enduring credibility, these principles were applied primarily to imperial capitals, graves, and walled cities. Documentation of the influence of these traditions in the building of common or rural houses in the past is extremely limited; where such elements are most apt to survive today is in Taiwan, Singapore, and Hong Kong (Knapp, 1986:108-121). As with dietary customs in certain religions, the principles embodied in *feng shui* may represent institutionalization by a very practical group of people of the constraints imposed

a

b

Figure 85. Stonewares manufacture in Szechuan Province, 1983.
a) shaping the jars; b) stoneware kilns.

by topographic conditions (i.e., exposure to sunlight, protection from wind or flooding).

The embellishments such as upturned corners, decorative roof tiles, and elaborate millwork which are recognized as distinctively Chinese are apt to be late in time or designed by non-Chinese (Kerr and Bugslag, 1978:n.p.). In the 19th century, San Francisco's Chinatown was a slowly decaying slum, mostly owned by absentee landlords (Chen, 1980:185). The "oriental flavor" of the current San Francisco Chinatown was created only after the earthquake and fire of 1906 destroyed the original settlement, and was further enhanced in 1925 (Palmer and Walls, 1960:30). In Los Angeles, the population displaced by the construction of Union Station in 1933 resettled in two more attractive locations: New Chinatown, built by a Chinese corporation with an emphasis on the tourist trade, and China City, a commercial venture by non-Chinese with all the trappings of bazaars, rickshaw stations, a Great Wall, and other donations from the movie industry (McDannold, 1973:66-69). The more traditional regularities which can be sought in the urban setting through historical and archaeological research include maximum use of limited space with wood or brick buildings flush against each other, and city blocks subdivided by alleys and passageways. Structures had no setback from the street frontage; as a result of party wall arrangements between adjacent landowners, buildings were apt to straddle property lines (Minnick, 1988:199). Internally, activity areas within dark and overcrowded dwellings were maximized by use of balconies and roofs. Any open space remaining behind the dwelling was apt to be used for refuse disposal and raising plant or animal foods.

As collections and reports accrue, it becomes harder to justify data recovery to management agencies who raise the question of redundancy. It may well be that few "new" artifact types will be found, but there is little question that additional identifications of function, date, value, and place of origin are needed and can be achieved. Efforts are still needed to locate and excavate unmixed deposits with identifiable cultural and chronological context, and to apply all available information to their interpretation. There are enough data at hand to frame and test specific research questions. More than enough propositions have been offered just in the preceding chapters to warrant continued field work: that the use of market meat cuts was greater among larger and more prosperous Chinese populations; whether the ratio of Chinese to Euroamerican ceramics increased or decreased through the years; the degree to which such ratios reflect economic status, acculturation, or other influences; whether the use of imported goods was increased in the last years of a dwindling Chinatown as an integrating influence; that Japanese imports were available to the Chinese prior to substantial Japanese immigration; that *feng shui* influenced the location and arrangement of Chinese buildings and town plans; that the goods transshipped into Texas from Mexico differed from those imported directly into California; and many more.

As such investigations continue, the issue of curation will become more acute, i.e., what is to be saved. It should be immediately apparent that if all sherds were discarded, there would be no expendable material for the new testing procedures. Many of the analyses, such as faunal studies, were conducted long after the excavations because of new methods for identification and quantification, new questions being posed, and because the basic technical reports were not always funded adequately to support consultant research. Understanding of Chinese ceramic basemarks later than those of the great dynasties has progressed very little, and examples must be preserved until reference data from China become available. Many collections need to be reexamined in the light of the new information about Japanese manufactures and the rapidly expanding knowledge of ceramic forms and functions. Even small sherds have value when washed and examined; more marks may be present than inventoried in the past, and quantification is possible from diagnostic spouts or rims. As the inventory of pristine sites is finite and disappearing rapidly, the value of excavated collections is growing as each new research approach needs to be tested against cultural materials. It is not enough to retain only specimens with display value, or even one sample sherd of each type. There must be enough for statistical validation of the research objectives, and enough more to spare for emerging processes of technical analysis.

Reports which are only filed with sponsoring clients or agencies, to say nothing of those which are unwritten, must be made available through some central clearinghouse. The Asian American Comparative Collection at the University of Idaho has taken on some of this function, collecting manuscripts, photographs, inscriptions, artifacts, and data, but the success of this endeavor will depend on the cooperation of those in the field to provide the material. There should be greater awareness and better dissemination of new theses and dissertations (e.g., Stapp, 1990; Wegars, 1991). It will be more difficult to gather research conducted in other disciplines, but at the minimum, bibliographies would be of great benefit.

That archaeology is necessary because there is "no history" confuses the unique contribution that controlled excavation and comprehensive collection analysis can make to the solution of anthropological questions. It may be restated that more excavation is needed because the historical context of many of the reported sites is essentially poor, and the chronological context, social associations, and integrity of depositions still need to be established. The historical records are, in fact, richly detailed and abundant within their own objectives, such as census, assessment, fire insurance, burial, merchandise, or school records, but they will not necessarily satisfy the anthropological objectives without physical evidence of all that is unwritten. Archaeologists still need their tools, in the field and the laboratory, if synthesis is to be achieved.

REFERENCES CITED

BLANFORD, JOHN M.
1986   *The Chinese Ethnic Bottle Pattern,* paper presented at the 19th Annual Meeting of the Society for Historical Archaeology, Sacramento.

BROCK, JAMES, WILLIAM A. SAWYER, and PAUL W. WORMSER
1988   Artifacts from the LaFarge Site, Redlands, California, Archaeological Advisory Group, Newport Beach, California.
BROTT, CLARK W.
1982   Moon Lee One: Life in Old Chinatown Weaverville, California, Great Basin Foundation, San Diego.
BUTLER BROTHERS
1907   Our Drummer, Catalogue Number 633, Minneapolis.
CAMARILLO, ALBERT
1979   Chicanos in a Changing Society, Harvard University, Cambridge and London.
CHANG, K. C.
1977   Food in Chinese Culture, Yale University Press, New Haven.
CHEN, JACK
1980   The Chinese of America, Harper and Row, San Francisco.
CHINESE HISTORICAL SOCIETY OF SOUTHERN CALIFORNIA (CHSSC)
1984   Linking Our Lives, joint project with the Asian American Studies Center, University of California, Los Angeles.
CHIU, PING
1967   Chinese Labor in California, 1850-1880, State Historical Society of Wisconsin and Department of History, University of Wisconsin, Madison.
CHUNG, NELLIE
1979   Transcript of interview, eight tapes, Southern California Chinese American Oral History Project, jointly sponsored by the Chinese Historical Society of Southern California and the Asian American Studies Center, University of California, Los Angeles.
COSTELLO, JULIA G. and MARY L. MANIERY
1988   Rice Bowls in the Delta: Artifacts Recovered from the 1915 Asian Community of Walnut Grove, California, Institute of Archaeology Occasional Paper, 16, University of California, Los Angeles.
FELTON, DAVID L., FRANK LORTIE, and PETER D. SCHULZ
1984   The Chinese Laundry on Second Street: Papers on Archeology at the Woodland Opera House Site, California Archeological Reports No. 24, Department of Parks and Recreation, Sacramento.
GREAT BASIN FOUNDATION
1987   Wong Ho Leun, An American Chinatown, 2 vols., Great Basin Foundation, San Diego.
GREENWOOD, ROBERTA S.
1976a   The Changing Faces of Main Street, Ventura Mission Plaza Archaeological Project, Redevelopment Agency, City of San Buenaventura, California.
1976b   Evaluation of Historic Resources, New Melones Reservoir Project Area, submitted to the U.S. Army Corps of Engineers, Sacramento District.
1980   The Chinese on Main Street, Archaeological Perspectives on Ethnicity in America: Afro-American and Asian American Culture History, R. L. Schuyler (ed.), Baywood Publishing Co., Amityville, New York, pp. 113-123.

GREENWOOD, ROBERTA S., JAY D. FRIERMAN, MARYELLEN RYAN, and
LEO R. BARKER
1980   *Warm Springs Cultural Resources Study: Historic Archaeological Sites
        Investigation, Phase II,* Sonoma State University, Rohnert Park; submitted to
        the U.S. Army Corps of Engineers, San Francisco District.
GREENWOOD, ROBERTA S. and LAURENCE H. SHOUP
1983   *New Melones Archeological Project, California: Review and Synthesis of
        Research at Historical Sites,* Final Report of the New Melones Archeological
        Project, Volume 7, Infotec Development Co. and Greenwood and Asso-
        ciates, submitted to National Park Service, Washington, D.C. [Reprinted by
        Coyote Press, Salinas, California, 1987.]
GREENWOOD, ROBERTA S., with contributions by others
1992   Archaeological and Historical Studies of Los Angeles Chinatown, Union
        Station Site, Greenwood and Associates, submitted to Los Angeles County
        Transportation Commission. [In preparation.]
HAMPSON, R. PAUL
n.d.   Archaeological Mitigation of a Portion of the Ten Almaden Block, San Jose,
        Archaeological Consulting, Salinas. [Draft report, in preparation.]
HAMPSON, R. PAUL and ROBERTA S. GREENWOOD
1989   *Cultural Resource Investigation at China Point Park, Napa,* Greenwood and
        Associates, Pacific Palisades, California, submitted to Public Works Depart-
        ment, City of Napa, California.
HATTORI, EUGENE M., MARY K. RUSCO, and DONALD R. TUOHY (eds.)
1979   Archaeological and Historical Studies at Ninth and Amherst, Lovelock, Nevada,
        Archaeological Services Reports, Nevada State Museum, Carson City.
HOMMEL, RUDOLF P.
1937   *China at Work,* John Day, New York. [Reprinted by M.I.T. Press, Cambridge
        and London, 1969.]
JOHNSON, JERALD J. and DOROTHEA J. THEODORATUS
1984   *Cottonwood Creek Project, Shasta and Tehama Counties California: Dutch
        Gulch Lake Intensive Cultural Resources Survey,* the Foundation of Cali-
        fornia State University, Sacramento, and Theodoratus Cultural Research, Fair
        Oaks, California.
JONES, TIMOTHY W.
1980a   Archaeological Test Excavations in the Boise Redevelopment Project Area,
        Boise, Idaho, *University of Idaho Anthropological Research Manuscript
        Series,* No. 59, Moscow.
1980b   Continued Archaeological Test Excavations of Operation One Boise
        Redevelopment Project Area, Boise, Idaho, University of Idaho *Anthropologi-
        cal Research Manuscript Series,* No. 61, Moscow.
JONES, TIMOTHY W., MARY ANNE DAVIS, and GEORGE LING
1979   Idaho City: An Overview and Report on Excavation, *University of Idaho
        Anthropological Research Manuscript Series,* No. 50, Moscow.
KERR, A. and J. BUGSLAG
1978   Some Basic Observations Concerning the Architecture of the Chinese in B.C.,
        Datum, 3:2, Ministry of Recreation and Conservation, British Columbia,
        Canada, pp. 8-11.

OLD APPROACHES AND NEW DIRECTIONS / 401

KNAPP, RONALD G.
1986   *China's Traditional Rural Architecture: A Cultural Geography of the Common House*, University of Hawaii Press, Honolulu.

LALANDE, JEFFREY M.
1981   *Sojourners in the Oregon Siskiyous: Adaptation and Acculturation of the Chinese Miners in the Applegate Valley, ca. 1855-1900*, Master's thesis, Oregon State University, Corvallis.

LISTER, FLORENCE C. and ROBERT H. LISTER
1989   The Chinese of Early Tucson: Historic Archaeology from the Tucson Urban Renewal Project, *Anthropological Papers of the University of Arizona*, Number 52, University of Arizona, Tucson.

LIU, JUDITH
1987   Birds of Passage: Chinese Occupations in San Diego, 1870-1900, *Gum Saan Journal, 10*:1, Chinese Historical Society of Southern California, pp. 1-15.

LOTHROP, GLORIA RICCI
1986   Nurturing Society's Children, *California History, 65*:4, pp. 274-283.

LYMAN, STANFORD M.
1976   The Chinese Diaspora in America, 1850-1943, *The Life, Influence and the Role of the Chinese in the United States, 1776-1960, Proceedings/ Papers* of the National Conference held at the University of San Francisco, July 10, 11, 12, 1975, Chinese Historical Society of America, San Francisco, pp. 128-146.

MASON, WILLIAM
1967   The Chinese in Los Angeles, *Museum Alliance Quarterly 6*:2, Natural History Museum of Los Angeles County, pp. 15-20.

McDANNOLD, THOMAS ALLEN
1973   *Development of the Los Angeles Chinatown: 1850-1970*, Master's thesis, California State University, Northridge.

MEI, JUNE
1984   Socioeconomic Origins of Emigration: Guangdong to California, 1850 to 1882, *Labor Immigration Under Capitalism: Asian Workers in the United States before World War II*, L. Cheng and E. Bonacich (eds.), University of California Press, Berkeley, pp. 219-247.

MINNICK, SYLVIA SUN
1988   *Samfow: The San Joaquin Chinese Legacy*, Panorama, Fresno.

MONTGOMERY WARD AND CO.
1895   *Catalogue and Buyers' Guide No. 57*, Spring and Summer. [Reprinted by Dover, New York, 1969.]

MUELLER, FRED W., JR.
1987   Feng Shui: Archaeological Evidence for Geomancy in Overseas Chinese Settlements, *Wong Ho Leun*, Vol. 1, Great Basin Foundation, (eds.) San Diego, pp. 1-24.

MUI, HOH-CHEUNG and LORNA MUI
1981   *The Trade of the English East India Company at Canton During the Late Eighteenth Century*, paper presented at the 96th Annual Meeting of the American Historical Association, Los Angeles.

NOAH, ANNA C.
1987   Brass, Glass, Stone and Bone: Items of Adornment from Riverside Chinatown, *Wong Ho Leun*, Great Basin Foundation (eds.), San Diego, pp. 395-413.

NOVOTNY, ADRIAN S.
1985   *The Early History of the Chinese in California with a Focus on Orange County*, submitted to The Chinese American Council of Orange County, California.

OLSEN, JOHN W.
1978   A Study of Chinese Ceramics Excavated in Tucson, *Kiva, 44*:2, pp. 1-50.

PALMER, PHIL and JIM WALLS
1960   *Chinatown, San Francisco*, Howell-North, Berkeley.

PASTRON, ALLEN, ROBERT GROSS, and DONNA GARAVENTA
1981   Ceramics from Chinatown's Tables: An Historical Archaeological Approach to Ethnicity, *Behind the Seawall: Historical Archaeology Along the San Francisco Waterfront*, Vol. 2, A. G. Pastron, J . Prichett, and M. Ziebarth (eds.), San Francisco Clean Water Program, San Francisco, pp. 365-469.

PRAETZELLIS, MARY and ADRIAN PRAETZELLIS
1982   *Archaeological and Historical Studies of the IJ56 Block, Sacramento, California: An Early Chinese Community*, Anthropological Studies Center, Sonoma State University, Rohnert Park, California.

1990   *Archaeological and Historical Studies at the Sam Fong Chong Laundry, 814 I Street, Sacramento, California*, Anthropological Studies Center, Sonoma State University, Rohnert Park, California.

QUON, ELLA YEE
1982   Santa Barbara Chinatown: The Early Years, *Gum Saan Journal, 5*:2, Chinese Historical Society of Southern California, pp. 1-5.

RHODES, DANIEL
1968   *Kilns: Design, Construction, and Operation*, Chilton, Radnor, Pennsylvania.

RITCHIE, NEVILLE A.
1986   Archaeology and History of the Chinese in Southern New Zealand during the Nineteenth Century: A Study of Acculturation, Adaptation, and Change, Ph.D. dissertation, University of Otago, Dunedin, New Zealand.

RITTER, ERIC W.
1986   *The Historic Archaeology of a Chinese Mining Venture near Igo in Northern California*, Bureau of Land Management Cultural Resources Report, Archaeology, Ukiah District, Redding, California.

ROOP, WILLIAM
1988   *Monitoring and Recovery of Archaeological Features within the Silicon Valley Financial Center Parcel*, Archaeological Resource Service [Novato, California], submitted to the Redevelopment Agency, City of San Jose, California.

SANDMEYER, ELMER CLARENCE
1939   *The Anti-Chinese Movement in California*, University of Illinois Press, Urbana.

SCHUYLER, ROBERT L. (ed.)
1980   *Archaeological Perspectives on Ethnicity in America: Afro-American and Asian American Culture History*, Baywood Publishing Co., Amityville, New York.

SCHULZ, PETER D. and FRANK LORTIE
1981 *Archaeological and Historical Investigations at Nineteenth Century Chinese Shrimp Camps in Marin County,* paper presented at the Annual Meeting of the Society for California Archaeology, Bakersfield.

SPIER, ROBERT F. G.
1958a Food Habits of Nineteenth-Century California Chinese, *California Historical Society Quarterly, 37,* pp. 79-84, 129-136.

1958b Tool Acculturation among 19th Century California Chinese, *Ethnohistory,* 5:2, pp. 97-117.

SPRAGUE, RODERICK
1986 *Chinese Glass Trade Bead Research,* paper presented at the 19th Annual Meeting of the Society for Historical Archaeology, Sacramento.

STAPP, DARBY C.
1990 The Historic Ethnography of a Chinese Mining Community in Idaho, Ph.D. dissertation, University of Pennsylvania, Philadelphia.

STASKI, EDWARD
1985 Beneath the Border City, Volume 2: The Overseas Chinese in El Paso, *University Museum Occasional Papers,* No. 13, New Mexico State University, Las Cruces.

STEPHENS, JOHN W.
1976 A Quantitative History of Chinatown, San Francisco, 1870 and 1880, *The Life, Influence and the Role of the Chinese in the United States, 1776-1960:* Proceedings/Papers of the National Conference held at the University of San Frnacisco, July 10, 11, 12, 1975, Chinese Historical Society of America, San Francisco, pp. 71-88.

STERRY, NORA
1922 Housing Conditions in Chinatown Los Angeles, *Journal of Applied Sociology, 7:2,* pp. 70-75.

TEAGUE, GEORGE A. and LYNETTE O. SHENK
1977 Excavations at Harmony Borax Works, *Western Archeological Center Publications in Anthropology,* No. 6, National Park Service, Washington, D.C.

THOMPSON, WARREN S.
1955 *Growth and Changes in California's Population,* The Haynes Foundation, Los Angeles.

WEGARS, PRISCILLA
1991 The History and Archaeology of the Chinese in Northern Idaho, 1880 through 1910, Ph.D. dissertation, University of Idaho, Moscow.

WONG, EVERETT
1954 *The Exclusion Movement and the Chinese Community in San Francisco,* Master's thesis, University of California, Berkeley.

YEE, GEORGE and ELSIE YEE
1986 The Chinese and the Los Angeles Produce Market, *Gum Saan Journal, 9:2,* Chinese Historical Society of Southern California, pp. 4-17.

Contributors

JOHN L. FAGAN received a Ph.D. in anthropology from the University of Oregon in 1973. The research at the Warrendale Cannery began in the early 1980s while Dr. Fagan was District Archaeologist for the U.S. Army Corps of Engineers. Warrendale provided an opportunity to archaeologically examine ethnicity and culture change through artifacts and historical records which are not available to the prehistorian. Currently, Dr. Fagan is a general partner of Archaeological Investigations Northwest, an archaeological consulting firm in Portland, Oregon that specializes in both prehistoric and historical archaeology and cultural resource management.

JEFFREY M. FEE received his Bachelor of Science degree with a minor in anthropology from Weber State College, Ogden, Utah, and his Master of Arts in anthropology from the University of Idaho, Moscow, Idaho. His early archaeological career began with three years in the Southwest's San Juan River drainage. As an archaeological technician, he worked in cultural resource management for twelve years on the Payette National Forest in north central Idaho, and is currently the Forest Archaeologist on the Clearwater National Forest in northern Idaho.

DAVID L. FELTON is a historical archaeologist who analyzed the Kwong Tai Wo inventory data translated by Dr. Sando to identify archaeological correlates and implications of the materials listed. He attended college in Montana and Idaho, and received a B.A. in anthropology from La Universidad de Las Americas, Cholula, Puebla, Mexico in 1975. Since that time, he has been employed by the California Department of Parks and Recreation, specializing in archaeological and preservation components of historic building restoration projects.

RICHARD E. FIKE currently resides in Ridgway, Colorado and is employed by the Bureau of Land Management as the Montrose District Archaeologist. His graduate studies at the University of Arizona provide the background for his years of experience not only in cultural resource management but historical and prehistorical archaeology of the American West. Fike is a noted authority on historic artifacts and particularly glass and ceramics. His most recent work is on historic medicine bottles. Fike has purchased and is restoring much of the old business district of Ridgway, Colorado.

ROBERTA S. GREENWOOD is Research Associate in Archaeology at the Natural History Museum of Los Angeles County, and Principal Investigator of Greenwood and Associates, consultants in cultural resource management. She has either directed or advised studies of Chinese sites in Ventura, Napa, El Paso, Sierran gold mining camps, San Jose, and since 1987, Los Angeles.

SHERRI M. GUST began her career as a faunal analyst, after graduating from the University of California at Davis, by working on the bones from Old Sacramento, California. Since that time she has worked on numerous faunas from historical archaeological sites. Her specialty is detailed analysis of butchering patterns and integration of documentary information. She is currently finishing her Ph.D. in evolutionary morphology at the University of Southern California with a dissertation on the change through time of large mammals from Rancho La Brea.

JULIA G. LONGENECKER began her archaeological career on the High Plains, where she participated in Paleoindian excavations with the University of Wyoming. After receiving her degree from Wyoming, she moved on to the University of Idaho, where she developed her interest in faunal remains from historic sites. Julia received her Masters from Idaho in 1985. She is currently combining her archaeological knowledge with museum work to develop programs for educating the public about archaeology.

NEVILLE A. RITCHIE is a graduate of the University of Otago, Dunedin, New Zealand. He has been involved in archaeology since 1968. In 1977 he was appointed Project Archaeologist on the Clutha Power Project, a position he held for ten years. During this time he developed a special interest in the archaeology of historic sites and completed his Ph.D. on the archaeology and history of the Chinese miners in southern New Zealand. Dr. Ritchie now lives in Hamilton where he is employed as Regional Archaeologist (Waikato) by the Department of Conservation.

RUTH ANN SANDO is a cultural anthropologist who translated historical Chinese records as a consultant for the California Department of Parks and Recreation. She received a Ph.D. in cultural anthropology from the University of Hawaii in 1981 with a dissertation on rural economic change and depopulation in Taiwan. Since that time, she has worked in the financial industry as a senior analyst, industrial engineer, and manager. She is now manager of the Investment Lending Policy and Procedure Department at First Nationwide Bank in San Francisco. Sando is a fellow of the Society for Applied Anthropology and recently presented a paper on the material symbols of power and status in the workplace at that organization's 1990 annual conference.

DAVID A. SISSON is District Archaeologist for the Bureau of Land Management, Coeur d'Alene District, Idaho. He received his B.S. in anthropology and his M.A.I.S. from Oregon State University. His interests include cultural resource management and project planning, site stabilization and protection, cultural resource public awareness education, and historical archaeology.

DARBY C. STAPP completed his B.A. in anthropology at the University of Denver, then went on to Idaho to pursue graduate work. His M.A. thesis focused on copper trade goods recovered from protohistoric Native American burials. Darby began working in the Pierce locality in 1979, culminating his research with the completion of a dissertation on the historic ethnography of a Chinese mining community in Idaho.

EDWARD STASKI is Associate Professor in the Department of Sociology and Anthropology, New Mexico State University, Las Cruces. He received a Ph.D. in anthropology from the University of Arizona in 1983. His major research interests include human evolution, historical archaeology, ethnic studies, and the U.S. southwest frontier. He is conducting fieldwork at Fort Fillmore and Fort Cummings, two frontier military outposts in southern New Mexico.

HARVEY STEELE is an Import Specialist for the U.S. Customs Service in Portland, Oregon, specializing in the authentication of imported art objects and antiques. He has been editor and publications director for the Oregon Archaeological Society since 1975.

ALISON STENGER has been working with the material culture from historic sites since 1978. Although her initial area of expertise was confined primarily to the wares of the 16th through the mid-19th centuries, she began including the overseas Asian materials in her research in 1980. After the completion of field work in Southeast Asia in early 1991, she has returned to the Ceramics Analysis Laboratory to continue contract analysis for other archaeologists.

PRISCILLA WEGARS is a Research Associate in the Alfred W. Bowers Laboratory of Anthropology, University of Idaho, Moscow. There she established the Asian American Comparative Collection of objects and bibliographical materials relevant to the study of overseas Asian archaeological sites and artifacts. She received a Ph.D. in history/historical archaeology from the University of Idaho in 1991.

JERRY WYLIE is employed by the Intermountain Region of the U.S. Forest Service as the program leader for heritage resources. His undergraduate work was at San Diego State University and he obtained his Masters degree in anthropology-archaeology at the University of Utah. He has been interested in the Chinese experience in the western United States since the late 1970s and has contributed to several noteworthy Chinese historic archaeology projects, including the organization of the Overseas Chinese Research Group (with Paul Chace), three SHA symposia (with Paul Chace), a Forest Service conference (with Will Reed and Priscilla Wegars), and an SHA workshop (with Jim Ayres). Jerry currently resides in Ogden, Utah.

Index

Acculturation, 19, 128-129, 137, 140, 142, 144-145, 208, 222, 227, 248, 377-378, 383, 389-391, 397

Actresses, 238, 240

Addiction
to alcohol, 19
to opium, 19, 257-258, 292, 297-299 (*see also* Opium)

Addicts, opium, 257-259 (*see also* Opium)

Adobe, 54, 162, 338, 344, 348-349, 358, 368, 370 (*see also* Mud brick)

Adobe structures, 54, 58, 385-386, 392

African Americans, 71

Agriculture, 69, 71, 76, 91-93, 178, 207, 380, 382, 389

Ah Can, 35

Ah Choi [*see* Ah Toy (prostitute)]

Ah Cow, 9

Ah Kew, 346

Ah Lee (*see* Lee Dick)

Ah Sam, 74-75

Ah Sing, 77

Ah Toy (gardener, Australia), 55

Ah Toy (gardener, Idaho) (*see* China Toy)

Ah Toy (prostitute), 231

Ah Toy Gardens (*see* China Toy Gardens)

Alcohol, 135, 141-144, 227, 258, 298
consumption of, 141-142, 144

Alcoholic beverages, 141-142, 226-227
brand names, 135 (*see also* Liquor and names of individual types of alcoholic beverage)

Alexandra, New Zealand, 339, 345, 347

Alfred W. Bowers Laboratory of Anthropology, xxv, 243, 246, 285

Am Kimm, 344

American West, 130, 308

Americans, 3, 13, 65, 71, 75-77, 81, 93-94, 98, 102, 105, 108, 117, 134-135, 137-138, 140-143, 153, 162-163, 167, 169, 189-191, 206-208, 221-222, 226-227, 230, 238-241, 243, 246, 255, 257-259, 269, 285, 315, 375, 377-378, 380-381, 383, 389, 391, 398 (*see also* Chinese Americans, Euroamericans)

American Indians (*see* Native Americans)

Angel Island, California, 235, 239

Animals, 69, 76, 83, 85, 93, 97, 100, 102, 105, 107-110, 115, 118-119, 177, 180, 182, 189, 191, 201, 206, 390, 397 (*see also* names of individual animals)

Anti-Chinese movements, xxiii, 11, 132, 167, 169, 173, 233, 240, 255 (*see also* Discrimination, Prejudice)

Apothecaries (*see* Doctors, Physicians)

Apples, 76, 90, 350, 357, 359

Apprentices, 237

Archaeological
considerations, xxiii, 3, 5, 27-28, 58-60, 89, 93-94, 97, 108, 110, 116, 123, 125-129, 131-133, 138, 142, 144-146, 153, 157, 159-163, 165, 171, 173, 214, 219-222, 226, 241, 243, 246, 255, 274, 290-291, 298,

[Houses]
385-386, 388, 395 (*see also*
Dugouts, Dwellings, Habitations,
Homes, Huts, Rockshelters,
Structures)
Hu King Eng, 239
Hudson's Bay Company, 393
Hume, George, 215
Hume, Robert, 215
Hume, William, 215
Hung, Josie, 237
Hung, W. Q., 237
Hung Wo Company, 75
Hunting, 182
Huts, 37, 53, 55-56, 340-341, 344-350,
352, 354-355, 357-360, 362-369, 385
occupancy of, 346
orientation of, 363
sizes of, 362-363
(*see also* Dugouts, Dwellings,
Habitations, Homes, Rockshelters,
Structures)

Idaho, 1-29, 33-60, 65-94, 97-120, 229,
234, 236, 243, 246-247, 256, 259,
285, 287, 291, 294, 317, 375, 398
Idaho City, Idaho, 243, 318, 375
Idaho State Historical Society, Boise,
Idaho, 247
Igo, California, 376
Ilwaco, Washington, 318
Imari, 311
Immigration, xxiii, 12, 123, 130, 189,
191, 230, 233, 235, 238-240, 257,
338, 380-382, 386, 390, 392, 397
Immigration Act (1924), 240-241
Immigration Law (1875), 328
Improvisation, 294-295, 299
India, 169, 256, 261
Ink, 222, 294
container for, 223
Intermountain Antiquities Computer
System, 93
Inventories, 19, 25, 33, 39, 71, 90, 98,
123, 151-153, 157, 159-163, 165,
167, 169-171, 173, 378, 384,
392-393, 395, 398
Invercargill, New Zealand, 345

Irish, 28, 100, 142
Iron, 37-38, 152, 287, 296, 319, 324-325,
339, 393
corrugated, 55, 355, 360, 363, 367-368
water tank, 55
Ironing, 239
Irrigation, 76, 78, 81, 84, 86, 88, 91, 94, 389
water pipe, 265
water rights, 7, 20
water tank, 55
watering can, 86-87
(*see also* Ditches)
Italians, xxiii, 54

Jackrabbits, 183, 206
Jacksonville, Oregon, 291
Jade, 243, 245, 274, 285
Jake Jackson Museum, Weaverville,
California, 247
James, Chuck, 90
Jan, Arthur, 207
Jan, Howard, 207
Japan, 306, 311-312, 325, 327, 330, 383,
390
Japanese, 130, 397
artifacts, 286
ceramics, 153, 159, 162-163, 226, 306,
311-312, 321, 323-330, 383-384,
390, 393, 398
illustrated, 323
kilns, 395
pipes, 267, 287
Jars, 117, 219, 222, 245, 268, 295, 379,
395-396
food storage, 139
soy sauce, 378
spice, 325
Java, 256
Jewelry, 233, 241, 243, 246, 378, 381
Jiangsu Province, China, 296
Jones, W. A., 218
Joseph, Adrian, 309
"Joss houses" (*see* Temples)
Juarez, Mexico, 132
Jue Wong-yuen, 231

Kan, Sleepy, 69-70
Kane, Dr. H. H., 259, 263

Manufacturing, 42, 130, 134, 138, 140,
226, 241, 261, 267, 269-274,
292-294, 296, 298, 306-307, 309,
312, 315-316, 319, 324-325, 327,
390-391, 393, 395
Manufacture-deposition lag time, 133
Manufacturers' marks (see Marks)
Manure, 92-93
Marbles, 381
Market, 67, 84, 91-94, 107, 137, 165,
169, 171, 182, 189, 257, 296-297,
340-341, 383, 389, 392, 397
Market gardening, 93, 383
Marketing, 2, 75, 292-293, 297, 299, 390
Marks, 306, 315, 378, 398
butchering, 182, 193, 195-196,
199-200, 206, 208
manufacturers', 123, 171, 306, 315,
393
on opium pipe bowls, 269-271, 273,
285
Marriages, 67, 144, 231, 235-237, 241,
247
Marysville, California, 152
Massachusetts, 385
Massacres, 35, 73
Matches, 85, 191, 358
Mawson, Rev. William, 337
McCall, Idaho, 85, 94, 261
McCunn, Ruthanne Lum, 86, 93, 245, 247
McMinnville, Oregon, 318
McNeur, George H., 361
Meals, 102, 177
Meat, 23, 100, 104, 107-110, 116, 123,
188-191, 197, 200-201, 206-208,
348-349
consumption, 97, 103-104, 119
cuts of, 105, 108, 115, 118, 185, 193,
208, 397
kinds of, 2
most often utilized (MMOU), 185
preservation, 120
processing, 2
procurement, 108, 110, 119
quality, 115
supply networks, 98, 101
systems, 2, 97-98, 102, 108, 116,
118-120

[Meat]
weight (MTWT), 180-182, 185
Medicine bottles (see Bottles, medicine)
Medicines, 81, 167, 222, 241, 243,
245-246, 255-256, 258, 261, 294, 297
Medley, Margaret, 309
Melons, 190
Merchandise, value of, 21
Merchants, 5, 14, 19, 21, 23, 25, 28, 75,
98, 102, 104, 152, 165, 169-170, 178,
190, 219, 237-239, 241, 247, 292,
349, 370, 383-384, 391
Merchants' Exchange, 383
Metal, 226, 261, 265-269, 285, 288, 293,
297, 359 (see also Iron, Opium
smoking paraphernalia)
Metro Rail, Los Angeles, California, 246,
376
Mexican Revolution, 132
Mexicans, 125, 132, 145, 226, 258, 392
(see also Chicanos, Hispanics)
Mexico, xxiv, 123, 125, 132, 287, 393,
397
Mice, 189
Middle East, 256, 309
Middle Fork of the Salmon River, Idaho,
73
Midwinter Fair, 233
Milk, 191 (see also Dairy products)
Mineral flux, 316
Minerals, 7, 25, 35, 48, 71
Miners, 1, 3-27, 35-36, 52, 54, 56, 65, 67,
71, 73, 75, 77-78, 94, 97-98,
103-104, 108, 116-117, 178, 237,
257, 335, 337-338, 340-341,
346-350, 352, 354-355, 357-358,
360, 362, 366, 368-370, 377, 385,
389-390
Ming dynasty, 307, 312, 316, 319-320,
327
Mining, xxiv, 5-11, 19, 21, 36, 53, 58, 60,
65, 67, 69, 71, 73, 75-78, 81, 84,
91-94, 98, 103, 108, 120, 130, 213,
294, 338-341, 344-345, 347-348,
350, 352, 358, 364, 368, 380, 385,
389, 391
camps, 1-3, 9, 10, 25, 27-29, 97, 190,
234, 370, 376

Social class, 25, 103, 129, 160, 199, 233, 258, 290, 293, 296, 383, 392
Social groupings, 29, 128
Social status (*see* Status, social)
Society for Historical Archaeology, xxiv-xxv, 256
Socio-economic differences, 293
Sodium, 321
Sojourners, xxiii, 226, 370, 377, 382, 390-391
Song dynasty, 316, 319-320
Sonora, California, 376 (*see also* Mother Lode)
Soo, Annie, 246
Sotheby's, Hong Kong, 310
South Fork of the Salmon River, Idaho, 2, 36, 65, 71, 73, 76-78, 83-85, 89, 91, 93-94
South Fork Canyon, Idaho, 69, 81, 88
Southeast Asia, xxiv, 160-161, 310
Southern Pacific Railroad, 130-131, 179
Southland, New Zealand, 339-340
Soy sauce, 117, 393
  containers, 139, 294-295, 378
Spareribs, 115
Spectroscopy (*see* Optical emission spectroscopy)
Spices, 152, 325
Spokane, Washington, 33
Spoons, 153, 222, 262, 393
Squatters, 83
Squirrels, 182-183, 189, 206
St. Louis, Missouri, 385
Stanford University Museum of Art, 265, 274
Status, social, 18, 129, 169, 173, 185, 208, 236, 239, 293, 377, 380, 383-384, 397
Steamships, 235
Steelhead, 69, 94
Stereotypes, xxiii, 67, 213, 255
Stone, as building material, 1, 36-37, 42, 54-55, 57, 90, 243, 344-345, 347-350, 352, 354-355, 357-360, 362, 364, 367, 369-370, 376 (*see also* Rock)
Stone fists (*see* Opium smoking paraphernalia)

Stonewares, 117, 139, 161-162, 222, 224, 269-270, 272-273, 293, 295-296, 393, 395
  manufacture of, 395-396
Storekeepers, 237
Stores, xxiv, 10, 25, 54, 67, 75, 91, 100, 102, 123, 131, 138, 151-174, 180, 239, 243, 246, 258, 290, 337, 339, 341, 355, 358, 362, 369, 383-384, 388
  inventories, 123, 151-174, 384
Stoves, 37-38, 45, 52, 75, 81, 393-394
Strawberries, 76, 78, 81, 85, 93
Structural assimilation, 128, 145-146, 390
Structures, 1-2, 33-60, 78-79, 81-83, 94, 133, 180, 220, 332, 335-370, 376, 384-385, 388, 395, 397
  area of, 50, 55, 58, 362-363
  dimensions, 90-91, 295, 298, 346, 352, 354, 362-363, 367-368
  iron, 55
  masonry, 54
  orientation of, 47-48, 145, 354, 363-365, 385-386, 395
  prefabricated, 58, 360
  rammed earth, 54
  thatched grass, 54
  wood, 83
  wood and bark, 54
  wood and canvas, 55
Students, 104, 130, 207, 237-238, 391
Subsistence, 390 (*see also* Diet)
Sugar, 85, 152, 261, 339
Supply network, 98
Supreme Court of Idaho, 77
Swatow ware, 160, 315 (*see also* "Bamboo" pattern ceramics)
Sweet, Willis, 11
Sweetmeats, 104
Switzers, New Zealand, 339
Szechuan Province, China, 395-396

Tablewares (*see* Ceramic tablewares and utilitarian wares)
Tailoress, 237
Taiping Rebellion, 131, 296
Taiwan, 256, 395
Tassels, 244